MW01489926

THE CLIMB
STAY FOCUSED

SCOTT WADE

A PRACTICAL JOURNEY
THROUGH SCRIPTURE, BOOK 2

The Climb: Stay Focused

Copyright © 2020, Scott Wade

ISBN 978-1-938264-20-7

Unless otherwise noted, Scripture quotations are from The Holy Bible, English Standard Version® , copyright© 2001, by Crossway Bibles, a publishing ministry of Good News Publishers. Used by permission. All rights reserved.

Scripture quotation taken from The Holy Bible, New International Version®, NIV®. Copyright© 1973, 1978, 1984, 2011 Biblica, Inc.®
Used by permission. All rights reserved worldwide.

Published by:
One Stop Publications
6621 Britton Ave., Cincinnati, OH   45227
513-503-8965
www.OneStopPrintSolutions.com

This book is dedicated to all the folks who have subscribed to my daily email devotional for the past nine years, especially those young couples at Bethel Church of the Nazarene who were the first ones to receive them. Your spiritual growth and encouraging words have helped me to "stay focused"! God bless you all!

What people are saying about *The Climb...*

I must admit that I couldn't do it ... What you ask ? I just couldn't resist the urge to read more than one devotional a day from Pastor Wade's devotional book. In just a few sentences Pastor Wade gives the reader a very simple illustration or personal observation to draw you into the truth of the daily Scriptural passage in a way that says: "WOW ! Now I see what this passage means and how its truth helps me face today." As we face the challenges of these days it is encouraging for the truth of God's Word to jump off the page into our hearts and minds. I know you will be blessed and challenged by this daily devotional. Thank you, Pastor Scott Wade, for helping God's Word speak into our day.

   - Michael B. Blankenship, Pastor
Summerville Church of the Nazarene

There is always something that God wants to share with us through his Word. In The Climb: Stay Focused, Scott Wade provides a daily method for us to hear what God is sharing. This devotional book will give you perspective, encourage your heart, and help you not feel alone... because God is there with you. These divinely inspired and timely thoughts, the prayers, and scripture will lead you into a deeper conversation with God, and you will be overwhelmed by his love.

   - Samuel Flores, SC District Superintendent
Church of the Nazarene

Pastor Scott is a gifted devotional writer. He reminds us that Jesus is there to greet you every morning and when Jesus shows up – no matter what time it is – the long night ends and a new day begins. Each devotional includes a daily chapter reading, scripture focus, devotional thought, prayer, and a Psalm of the Day. With each devotional, you will look forward to starting your day with Jesus.

   - LaNora Jensen, President
South Carolina District Nazarene Missions International

"In his latest book, *The Climb: Stay Focused*, Scott Wade and company enrich the reader with insightful wisdom from the Bible. His ability to mine an entire scriptural lesson from a single word or phrase is truly a gift that is beyond most of us. From lessons that highlight the nuances of word meanings between the original Greek and our English, to personal anecdotal stories, the book is filled with blessing after blessing to help in our journey to walk in the footsteps of the Carpenter. The daily devotions are concise yet filled with subtle truths that can easily be missed with the hectic pace of daily living. This is an absolutely great way to start the morning and set the tone for the entire day.

   - Allen Montero, President
MEI

What better way to start your day than delving into the Word of God coupled with an exceptional devotional book such as *The Climb: Stay Focused*. Through these devotionals, Pastor Scott encourages the reader to stay focused on God by spending time in His Word. The devotionals are used as a tool to provide a better understanding of the Bible by applying God's Word to everyday life experiences. Pastor Scott has allowed God to use him in writing devotionals that encourage us to STAY FOCUSED on God's Word and will for our lives.

   - Angela Sandifer, Visual Arts Instructor; ESL teacher

Foreword

Isn't it exciting to receive a special invitation from a friend and then the invitation turns out to be a surprise? Here's a terrific surprise! Pastor Scott Wade has completed Book Two of his devotional series, "The Climb!" In the series, Pastor Scott issues a special invitation for all of us to encounter Christ each day through an enticing daily title, a Scripture Focus, the Devotional Thought, a Prayer and a Psalm for the Day. Pastor Scott also invited others to share their thoughts about specific Scriptures, with his oldest daughter, Jenny Wade, sharing about one devotional each week.

This practical journey through Scripture is one of the best invitations you will receive; however, in this life, the best invitation ever is when Jesus calls you to know Him personally. If you don't know Jesus, the "best" invitation is included throughout Pastor Scott's book! If you do know Jesus, there are invitations to know Christ better within "The Climb."

The late Rev. Billy Graham discusses three invitations in the Bible. The first is "to rest," the second is "discipleship" (have a relationship with Christ) and the third is "to live in the realm of God." In "The Climb," Pastor Scott Wade requests that all of us do each of those things. Pastor Scott's first devotional title for January 2020, is "Immediately." I hope we accept Scott Wade's invitation immediately by choosing the hard-copy book or the online version. Please invite others to join you. Let's all take this opportunity to "live in the realm of God."

Dr. Patty Hambrick
Super Life/Super Bus Neighborhood Mentoring
Charleston Southern University Faculty Emerita
Former Professor, PLNU, MVNU

"A journey of a thousand miles begins with a single step."

Introduction to **The Climb** *series...*

I'm going to read the entire Bible this year!" Have you ever said that? How did you do? If you are like me - and countless others! - the pleasant hill you began climbing on January 1, became an insurmountable mountain by mid-February when you were reading "Cleansing from Infectious Skin Diseases." You lost your momentum and just gave up. "Next year!" you promised yourself.

Next year never came.

Well, next year has finally arrived! *The Climb* will help you read the Bible on a consistent basis without getting bogged down. Reading "A-Chapter-A-Day" as outlined in this plan, you will read through the New Testament and Psalms each year and will complete the Old Testament over the course of five years.

Reading through the entire Bible is like a journey of a thousand miles - *up a mountain*! It begins with a single chapter. You can go that thousand miles... You can climb that steep mountain... If you stay focused!

How **The Climb** *began...*

Many years ago, I was asked by a new Christian, "What should I read in the Bible?" I prepared a thirty day schedule of one chapter per day. Soon, I began publishing a reading schedule for the entire year. Then I began sending out daily email reminders. It wasn't long before I added a few comments each day that I thought would help the reader understand and apply a verse or two from the chapter.

After several years, a dear friend suggested, "Hey, you ought to put these in a book!" After prayer and reflection, that's exactly what I did. The devotions found in *The Climb* are taken from over 8 years of daily emails.

How The Climb *works...*

Each day you will be given one chapter (sometimes two for shorter chapters) from the Bible to read.

Along with the daily chapter, there is a practical devotional article and a suggested prayer that will help you internalize what you have read and establish spiritual momentum for *The Climb.*

You also will read a short selection from the book of Psalms. The longer Psalms are divided into smaller sections. You can choose to read a section each day, or you can read the Psalm in its entirety on the day it first appears. (This may help you maintain continuity and context.)

Not starting in January? Want to move at a slower (or faster) pace? This method is adaptable for day-by-day use. Each reading has both a date and a day number on the page. If you are reading by date, just go to the date. If you choose instead to read by the day, you can follow "Day 1," "Day 2," and so on.

The most important things to read are the Bible passages (daily chapter and Psalm). Then, as time permits, read the devotional article and say the prayer that follows.

This is Book 2 of *The Climb* series, and it is called *Stay Focused.* This year the New Testament will come alive to you, and you will also continue your journey through the Old Testament, reading Deuteronomy through 1 Kings.

Let's get started on **The Climb!**

Afraid you will lose focus? Remember what the ancient pilgrims said every year as they made *The Climb* to Jerusalem for the festivals:

To you I lift up my eyes, O you who are enthroned in the heavens!
Behold, as the eyes of servants look to the hand of their master,
As the eyes of a maidservant to the hand of her mistress,
So our eyes look to the Lord our God, till he has mercy upon us.
Have mercy upon us, O Lord, have mercy upon us.
Psalm 123.1-3

Stay focused, dear friend. There is great reward for those who persevere.

— SW

THE CLIMB

STAY FOCUSED

A PRACTICAL JOURNEY
THROUGH SCRIPTURE, BOOK 2

Immediately

Daily Reading: Mark 1

And immediately... (Mark1.18)

Devotional Thought: Happy New Year! As you begin a new year by reading the gospel of Mark, you may notice the word *immediately*. We often think of immediate as being "instantaneous" but the Greek word is actually used to indicate "soon" as well. The point is that there is no delay in beginning to act. That's how Jesus' ministry is described in the opening verse of Mark: "The beginning of the gospel of Jesus Christ..."

Nine times in this one chapter the Holy Spirit directed the gospel writer to stress the immediacy of what was happening:

- The Spirit descending
- The Savior facing temptation
- The disciples leaving their jobs and families
- The disciples following Jesus
- Jesus going to "church" on the Sabbath and teaching
- A possessed and pitiful man calling out to Jesus for deliverance
- Jesus going home with some disciples
- Family members telling Jesus about their sick loved one (praying)
- Leprosy leaving a stricken man

Consider these things in your own life. And, as you begin the New Year, ask yourself, "What are the things that need my immediate attention? What are the things I should begin acting upon?"

"Whatever you can do or dream you can, begin it. Boldness has genius, power, and magic in it." - Johann Wolfgang von Goethe

Prayer: Jesus, thank you for giving me the gift of another year. Help me to hear your call and to respond with a bias for action. Amen.

Psalm of the Day: Psalm 1.1-6

Jesus Sees

Daily Reading: Mark 2

And as he passed by, he saw Levi... (Mark 2.14)

Devotional Thought: Levi was a tax collector. Because of that, he was considered an enemy of the people, a traitor, a Roman sympathizer. He didn't have a lot of friends. Most people tried hard not to see him. And, those who did see him didn't like him.

So, Jesus seeing Levi was significant. And, I believe, it was intentional.

How many times have you tried to avoid eye contact with somebody? "Oh, no! There's Sarah. She's a talker. I better go the other way or I'll never get out of here." "Uh oh! There's Sam. He always wants to talk about politics, and we don't agree! I hope he doesn't see me!"

But Jesus was different. Instead of avoiding Levi, he went toward him and looked right at him. As a matter of fact, looking past the rest of the crowd, Jesus singled him out: "Hey, Buddy, it looks like you could use a friend. Come with me!"

Yes, Levi was different. Yes, he was a "sinner." And yes, he became a true friend of Jesus.

Aren't you glad that Jesus sees us where we are? When nobody else takes notice of us, Jesus does. And, he wants us to do the same. Today, instead of looking to what's next on your schedule, take time to notice the people around you. You will find friends in the most unexpected of places!

Prayer: Thank you, Jesus, that you went out of your way to see me and to become my Friend. Help me to see others around me and love them sincerely. Help me to be a friend to the friendless. Amen.

Psalm of the Day: Psalm 2.1-6

Unforgivable?

Daily Reading: Mark 3

Whoever blasphemes against the Holy Spirit never has forgiveness, but is guilty of an eternal sin. (Mark 3.29)

Devotional Thought: Have you ever been in the situation where you despaired, "He or she will never forgive me!"? That's a terrible feeling isn't it? And, if you feel that way about God, how much worse! I remember as a young Christian wondering, "Have I committed the 'unpardonable sin'?" That was indeed a terrible prospect to consider.

To blaspheme means "to speak lightly or profanely of sacred things." When Jesus said, "Whoever blasphemes against the Holy Spirit never has forgiveness..." Does that mean a slip of the tongue? Is it shaking your fist in God's face and saying, "No!"? Is it an unknowable mistake? No. No. And, no.

I think it is helpful to notice the tense that Jesus uses when he speaks about blasphemy against the Holy Spirit. The present tense indicates something that a person is doing now and continues to do. A person in such a condition is (notice again the present tense) guilty of an eternal sin because he or she is living in a present state of rebellion against and rejection of the Holy Spirit. Such a person cannot be forgiven - not because of God's anger - but because of refusing the only source of life that is available.

So, even feeling guilt or shame or fear concerning this matter is an indication that you are not committing the unpardonable sin! It is the Holy Spirit who is convicting you, so turn to him and receive forgiveness. It is available in Jesus Christ to any who turn to him.

Prayer: Father, thank you for your indescribable mercy! Help me always to be sensitive and responsive to the wooing of your Spirit and to never give up hope that you love me and receive me. May others, who labor under a heavy load of despair, not fall prey to Satan's schemes and lies, but may they find forgiveness and freedom in Christ. Amen!

Psalm of the Day: Psalms 2:7-12

Seeds and Sowing

Daily Reading: Mark 4

> He also said, "This is what the kingdom of God is like. A man scatters seed on the ground. Night and day, whether he sleeps or gets up, the seed sprouts and grows, though he does not know how. All by itself the soil produces grain—first the stalk, then the head, then the full kernel in the head. As soon as the grain is ripe, he puts the sickle to it, because the harvest has come." (Mark 4.26-29)

Devotional Thought: I don't always fully understand Jesus' parables. I often need help internalizing them. So, I appreciate when I hear how others interpret them.

This is what I take from today's verses:

- *God's seed is good.* Regardless of what we do, planted seeds in God's Kingdom are going to grow. God is going to see to that. We aren't necessarily going to know how it happens. But, we know God is the one who makes it happen. Something else we know. God is going to harvest the seed that has ripened.

- *My sowing matters.* It may seem like we don't have much to do in this process, but that would be wrong. In verse 26, we are given much to do. We are to plant the seeds. Planting takes effort. Planting takes planning. Planting takes time. From other scripture we know there are other things we can do. We can water. We can fertilize. We can help expose the growing plant to the Son. We can try to keep weeds out from our plantings. Let us plant ourselves firmly and confidently into the process.

Scatter some seeds today!

John Wade

Prayer: Lord, thank you for all you do. Thank you for including us in your plan of salvation, both as being part of the harvested grain, and for making us sowers of your seed. Amen.

Psalm of the Day: 3.1-8

Unexpected
Daily Reading: Mark 5

And he did not permit him but said to him, "Go home to your friends and tell them how much the Lord has done for you, and how he has had mercy on you." (Mark 5:19)

Devotional Thought: Just when we feel like we've got Jesus figured out, he goes and does something unexpected!

That's what happened to the man who was delivered from demon possession in the tombs. As Jesus was preparing to depart from his region, the man begs him for permission to board the boat with Jesus, "that he might be with him." Jesus did not permit him, but instead told him, "Go home to your friends and tell them how much the Lord has done for you, and how he has had mercy on you." The man obeyed and began to tell everyone in the Decapolis, and everyone marveled.

Jesus had many followers, including his twelve closest followers who went everywhere with him. These are men who had dropped everything in their lives to follow Jesus when he called. So why not this man? Jesus had other plans for him! Although the man wanted to be physically near Jesus, he was content to stay and be used of the Lord in unexpected ways.

Are we as malleable to the will of God? There are times in every believer's life when God's plan does not line up with ours. Do we react with the same obedience as the healed man in this account, or do we stubbornly try to go about things in our own way? The healed man was effective in his testimony because it was what Jesus had called him to do. And we will be effective for the Kingdom only if we are obedient to the call of Jesus in our lives, even if it's not what we would have chosen for ourselves.

Jenny

Prayer: Lord, we ask you for the wisdom to discern your will for our lives. We acknowledge that without you, we can never be effective for your Kingdom. Please help us to be accepting when you are calling us to a task or a ministry that we would not have chosen, and empower us through your Spirit to accomplish your purposes. Amen.

Psalm of the Day: 4.1-8

You Give Them Something to Eat

Daily Reading: Mark 6

You give them something to eat. (Mark 6.37)

Devotional Thought: "Here is a boy with five loaves of barley bread and two little fish. But that is not enough for so many people." (John 6.9)

I teach a Sunday School class that is made up of 3rd grade through 5th grade children. One of the things I have learned from them is that they want to be a part of the activity or lesson of the day. They volunteer to write the memory verses on the white board or to read the next paragraph in the lesson, and they do so with enthusiasm.

In today's scripture, Jesus had 5000 people following him. He points out to the disciples that these people are hungry, and you need to find some bread to feed them. It seems the disciples had no answers for the situation, but a small boy had an answer. I can imagine that small boy overhearing Jesus say to the disciples that food was needed and becoming excited because he could share his food with others. I see him waving his arms and jumping up and down and saying, "I will share what I have!" The disciples could only see 5000 people, but the boy could see the need and had a desire to help meet the need.

What do you see? Do you see the need in your church or community? Do you have a desire to be a part of the solution? Remember you can make a difference - you can give them something to eat, for Christ "is able to do immeasurably more than all we ask or imagine, according to his power that is at work within us..." (Ephesians 3:20).

Steve Hamilton

Prayer: Father, may we see the needs that are around us today and act to do our part to help meet those needs. Let your power work through and in us today. Amen.

Psalm of the Day: 5.1-6

Clean Pots and Dirty Hearts
Daily Reading: Mark 7

You have a fine way of rejecting the commandment of God in order to establish your tradition! (Mark 7.9)

Devotional Thought: Tonight, I attended a traditional dance, an opera-style retelling of Hindu myths. It is very attractive to tourists, even if they are being unwittingly "discipled" in Hindu beliefs.

At the beginning and end (and during the especially tense fire-walking portion), a Hindu priest came out and anointed the actors with "holy" water and smoke to "bless" their performance. I was struck at how similar this ritual was to some Christian rituals. This is not the first time I have noticed these similar rituals, having attended religious events for two other world religions.

Some are disturbed by these similarities and attribute them to an idea that "all religions are the same" or human-made. I attribute them to the fact that we are all humans. As humans, we have the tendency to prefer ritual and tradition that we believe brings us closer to God (which we can control), over a heartfelt, genuine relationship with God that we cannot control.

The Pharisees were this way. They had turned the commands of God, designed to define and maintain a healthy relationship with God, into a system of traditions that kept God at bay and them in control (and "super-spiritual," too). Jesus reminded them how far their hearts had drifted from God.

It is easy to become "super-spiritual." Our relationship with God can become a series of boxes to check. It is certainly more comfortable to embrace ritual and habit than to face God. But, coming face-to-face with him is what God wants. He wants us to come vulnerably before him, putting our trust in nothing but his approval alone. To fellowship with God. To sit. To listen. To respond. To obey. Your pots may be clean, but is your heart?

Joe Young

Prayer: Lord, help us to put nothing before you. Help us to forsake our tendency to control through religiosity and embrace a vibrant, authentic relationship with you. Help us to live in and enjoy your presence, the presence of our loving, Heavenly Father. Amen.

Psalm of the Day: 5.7-12

7

Spiritual Amnesia

Daily Reading: Mark 8

> *Why are you discussing the fact that you have no bread? Do you not yet perceive or understand? Are your hearts hardened? Having eyes do you not see, and having ears do you not hear? And do you not remember?*
> (Mark 8.17-18)

Devotional Thought: Jesus just fed four thousand people with 7 loaves of bread and a few small fish. Everything had gone well, and there was food left over. If you had seen that miracle like the disciples did, would you ever worry about food again? But just a short time later, Jesus challenged his disciples to go deeper spiritually. Having just had an argument with the Pharisees, he wanted to make sure the disciples did not buy into their false gospel. It was bad yeast that could ruin a whole batch of dough.

Did the disciples get it? Nope. They had spiritual amnesia. They were thinking about lunch!

Talk about being on the wrong track. The disciples worried more about their temporal and physical needs instead of their eternal and spiritual needs. Not only did they have amnesia about the feeding of the five thousand and the four thousand but they were worried about having snacks for a boat ride!

God has already provided for our temporal needs. We do not need to worry about those needs being met. He's got it all covered. We don't need to worry about what we will eat and what we will wear. When we are worrying about temporal things, we can miss the eternal truths and spiritual warnings that God is trying to show us. My dad always told me, "We need to keep the main thing the main thing."

Let's not worry about bread, and where to get more, when we have the Bread of Life in the boat with us.

Cheryl Young

Prayer: Lord Jesus, help us to remember that you are the Bread of Life and that you take care of all of our needs; spiritual, physical, and emotional. We praise you today. Amen

Psalm of the Day: 6.1-5

Everything Is Possible
Daily Reading: Mark 9

"But if you can do anything, have compassion on us and help us." And Jesus said to him, "If you can'! All things are possible for one who believes." Immediately the father of the child cried out and said, "I believe; help my unbelief!" (Mark 9.22-24)

Devotional Thought: We live in a "show me" world. Trust seems to be at an all-time low as basic respect and community deteriorates. In this case, it hits much closer to home as the father of the possessed boy cautiously asks Jesus for a miracle, clearly struggling with his faith. Jesus strongly reminds him, and us, that of course it can be done! Once assured, he grew strong in his faith and asks for even more help to overcome.

It is important for us to recognize that even without a whole-hearted belief, Jesus is there for us, interceding on our behalf. Whether it's something as small as a stressful work day or as serious as a critical illness, we can trust the plan of Jesus and his wisdom. Even though doubts creep in when we don't understand the "why," we can come to him with the ultimate assurance that he will help us.

The final point is the power of prayer. Once he's in a quiet place with his disciples, they question why they were not able to perform the miracle. His response that "This kind can come out only by prayer" is a glorious reminder that even now, even without Jesus physically walking upon the earth, the capability is still here for physical and spiritual miracles - if we believe and when we pray.

Amy and Evan Berry

Prayer: Thank you, Jesus, for your acts of healing and helping us with our unbelief. As we remember you are limitless in your abilities, may we also be assured of your wisdom and love. Please let us stay sensitive to your plan and recognize the miracles - big and small! Amen.

Psalm of the Day: 6.6-10

Always Time for Us
Daily Reading: Mark 10

> Let the little children come to me, and do not hinder them, for the kingdom of God belongs to such as these. Truly I tell you, anyone who will not receive the kingdom of God like a little child will never enter it. (Mark 10.14-15)

Devotional Thought: Have you ever waited in a long line with your children to see Santa Claus? A couple of weeks ago, my husband and I waited in line at a local shopping center with our almost one-year-old daughter just for our turn to see St. Nick. We were fortunate - we only waited about 45 minutes! I have heard of people standing in line for 2 hours waiting their turn! Ellis screamed and hated every second of the visit with the man in red, but that's a different story.

When reading about people bringing their children to Jesus, I can't help but picture lines of parents and squirming kids, just like the Santa Claus lines today. The wait for them, however, had much higher stakes - Jesus blessing their children.

I can picture the disciples rolling their eyes - didn't Jesus and everyone understand that there were more important people to see? People to heal... people to teach... people who needed Jesus. Jesus, however, took the children in his arms and blessed them. He had all the time in the world for these children! Jesus used this as an opportunity for teaching. Children do not require an intellectual understanding to believe in something. They are trusting and feel secure when they are loved. Adults have a much harder time admitting their need for a sovereign God... especially those of us who are seemingly self-sufficient, independent, and skeptical.

May we have hearts more like children, and rest in the embrace of our loving Savior. May we receive his Kingdom, fully trusting that God is who he says he is. May we crawl into the lap of Jesus and let him love and bless us. He always has time for us!

Emily Beasley

Prayer: Jesus, thank you for loving me, your child. Help me to crawl right into your lap and receive your blessings today. Amen.

Psalm of the Day: 7.1-5

Unexpected - II
Daily Reading: Mark 11

> As they passed by in the morning, they saw the fig tree withered away
> to its roots. And Peter remembered and said to him, "Rabbi, look! The
> fig tree that you cursed has withered." (Mark 11.20-21)

Devotional Thought: Well, I didn't see that coming! I wonder if the disciples said that when they came upon that withered fig tree. A few days ago we read (Mark 5) about a demon possessed man who heard something unexpected from Jesus and was able to give an unexpected testimony and see unexpected results. In Mark 11, Jesus again does something unexpected - cursing a fig tree - and gets unexpected results - the tree withering away to its roots. While the unexpected results from Mark 5 were of a positive nature, these unexpected results serve as a warning.

What can we learn from this unexpected withering?

- *Appearance is not enough.* The Lord was not satisfied by looking at the beautiful leaves . He wanted fruit. We can dress up our lives in many ways, but Jesus wants us to bear the fruit of the Spirit.

- *Facades exact a heavy toll.* The effort required to keep up false appearances cannot be sustained for long. In the presence of the holiness of Christ, a facade will wither. We must be drawing life from the root, or we will fade quickly away.

- *Hypocrisy goes to the root of our character.* In dealing with false appearances and claims, Jesus has no choice but to go to the root of the problem. In order to be made new, we must die to self - or in the words of Jesus, take up our crosses.

The disciples did not expect such a radical reaction from Jesus, and I'm afraid that we too often do not expect Jesus to deal harshly with us. But Jesus' way is the way of the cross. Is it really that unexpected?

Prayer: Lord, you have said that we must leave all to follow you. It is a radical departure from comfortable Christianity. Work a change in my character - from the roots outward - so that I can follow you in the way of the cross. Amen.

Psalm of the Day: 7.6-13

Beware

Daily Reading: Mark 12

Beware of the scribes, who like to walk around in long robes and like greetings in the marketplaces and have the best seats in the synagogues and the places of honor at feasts, who devour widows' houses and for a pretense make long prayers. They will receive the greater condemnation. (Mark 12:38-40)

Devotional Thought: The "common" people in Jesus' day were sick of the religious elite - powerful, corrupt, and greedy. Throwing them out of the temple (Mark 11) was not enough. Jesus needed to explicitly warn the people to "Beware." "The great throng heard [Jesus] gladly," (v. 37), for their spiritual leaders - who were supposed to act as shepherds to lead and care for the sheep - were taking advantage of them. Jesus told them not to be taken in by their long robes, best seats, and long prayers.

We most likely know "religious" people like this – those who claim to be shepherds but are really wolves waiting to devour their flocks. Those who claim to have the answer but are really wanting their congregation to pay for salvation, in order to line their own pockets. Those who are skilled with words and pray beautifully, but do not really know the Lord. Jesus says to beware of them, and we should. We should also beware that we are not like these scribes – merely going through the motions of religion, appearing to have it all together but never getting to the point of the gospel - a saving relationship with Jesus Christ. Those who claim to know him but practice lawlessness will not enter the Kingdom of heaven. Jesus will declare to them, "I never knew you; depart from me" (Matt. 7:23).

Jenny

Prayer: Lord, help us. Help us to see through the deceptiveness of man, and help us to see into our own hearts when we try to be our own gods. Lead us in the way everlasting, and convict us through your Spirit. Amen.

Psalm of the Day: 7.14-17

All We Need to Know

Daily Reading: Mark 13

And then they will see the Son of Man coming in clouds with great power and glory. (Mark 13.26)

Devotional Thought: My daughters are like all other children - they want to know more. I can't blame them. I often find myself in situations where I would love to have a few more details about what is coming.

Jesus' disciples were like that, too. Jesus had told them about the future desecration and destruction of the temple that was to come. What? The temple? For centuries the tabernacle and then the temple had been the center of Jewish worship, the place where God met his people. It had incalculable value to his Jewish disciples and followers. Inconceivably, "There will not be left here one stone upon another that will not be thrown down" (v. 2).

Jesus disciples wanted to know more! But what they really needed to know was boiled down to one statement: "They will see the Son of Man coming in clouds with great power and glory."

Many believers have studied end times, the second coming of Jesus, and the events and circumstances surrounding this time period. There has been much speculation over literal versus figurative translations of end times, and it is easy to feel alarmed or frightened over what may happen. We can and should "be on guard," as Jesus instructs, but he also says, "I have told you all things beforehand," (v. 23). This does not mean that we will know all of the details in advance, but it does mean that we will know all we need to know. He wants us to trust him for provision and grace even through those frightening times.

And most importantly? Remember that we "will see the Son of Man coming in clouds with great power and glory!"

Jenny

Prayer: O Lord, "I want to be ready, I want to be ready, I want to be ready to walk in Jerusalem just like John!" Even so, come quickly, Lord Jesus. Amen.

Psalm of the Day: 8.1-9

Offended

Daily Reading: Mark 14

All ye shall be offended because of me this night: for it is written, I will smite the shepherd, and the sheep shall be scattered. (Mark 14.27, KJV)

Devotional Thought: After Jesus said to his disciples, "Ye shall be offended because of me this night" (Mark 14:27), "Peter said unto him, although all shall be offended, yet will not I." I love Peter's passion. Peter meant what he was saying. He was a committed follower of Jesus. Jesus goes on to say to him, that before the cock would crow twice, Peter would deny him three times. Oh, Peter! You meant what you were saying to Jesus!

The Greek word, skandalidzo translates offended. It means to put a stumbling block or impediment in the way, upon which another may trip and fall; to cause a person to begin to distrust and desert one whom he ought to trust and obey; to cause to fall away.

The word offended stings. Jesus says, "All of you shall be offended because of me this night." Peter with a heart devoted to Jesus, chose to deny and desert the One he should have trusted. Three times? Yes, three times! And although Peter gets the bad rap, just as Jesus foretold, all of the disciples scattered. They all were offended. And the truth is that I have offended Jesus! I have fallen asleep when Jesus asked me to be alert and in prayer. I have denied Jesus in my actions and in words I have spoken. Today, my heart's desire and my prayer is that I would neither be offended by, nor offend, my Savior and Lord!

Tutti Beasley

Prayer: Father God, thank for the gift of your Son, Jesus Christ. I know right now that you will place opportunities in my path this new year to praise you and to give testimony of your love and grace and goodness and faithfulness. Keep me strong through your Holy Spirit. in Jesus' precious name. Amen.

Psalm of the Day: 9.1-6

What Do *You* Say?

Daily Reading: Mark 15

You have said so... (Mark 15.2)

Devotional Thought: So, did he say it or not? President Trump had been reported as referring to certain countries in Africa and the Caribbean with quite unflattering, even vulgar, terms. "_____." He denied that he said it in a racist way. He even said that he might have to start recording meetings in the Oval Office. When I read that, I thought to myself, "Yeah, right! *Every* conversation in the Oval Office is recorded, just not made known. If the president wanted to, he could produce the recording."

Jesus had a meeting with Pilate, a high official in the provincial government, who asked Jesus a question, "Are you the King of the Jews?" Jesus replied, "You have said so..." When did he say so? In his question? Perhaps, but I also believe he said it in his actions. By agreeing to hear the case about Jesus, Pilate had implicitly stated that here was a man who claimed to be King of the Jews. He may have feigned ignorance, but his actions revealed what he really thought.

Each one of us reveal what we think about Jesus by our actions. Is he a man who gives good advice? Then we will take his advice under consideration and act accordingly when it suits our needs. Is he a worker of good deeds? Then we will try to get close to him to get our piece of the action. Is he the Son of God? If we believe that, then our lives will say so as well. We will live in obedience and reverence to him.

"Whom do you say the Son of Man is?" (Matthew 16.13)

Prayer: Lord Jesus, every day my life is saying something about you. Help me to live in such a way that people will believe that you are the Son of God and Savior of the world. Amen.

Psalm of the Day: 9.7-12

Obedience and Sacrifice
Daily Reading: Mark 16

When the Sabbath was past, Mary Magdalene, Mary the mother of James, and Salome bought spices, so that they might go and anoint him. (Mark 16.1)

Devotional Thought: Mary, Mary, and Salome worshiped Jesus with obedience and sacrifice. They so desperately wanted to pay homage to Jesus, but they waited until "the Sabbath was past." They obeyed. They personally bought the spices and arose early in the morning "that they might go and anoint him." They sacrificed.

The worship of God requires obedience and sacrifice on our part.

When Cain offered his grain to the Lord, he completely missed the concept of sacrifice. He made an offering, but not a sacrifice. His brother Abel sacrificed the sheep from his flock, and his worship was acceptable. God instructed Cain that he required obedience and sacrifice.

When the Israelites were awaiting Moses to come down from Mount Sinai, they discovered that sacrifice was not enough. They had fashioned a golden calf in order to make sacrifices to the God who brought them out of Egypt. But, they were disobedient to God who instructed them to have no idols - no man-made forms of God - to worship. Obedience and sacrifice.

When King David was preparing for the construction of an altar in Jerusalem, he offered to purchase the threshing floor of Araunah the Jebusite, as instructed by God. Araunah offered to give it to the king, but David said, "I will not offer burnt offerings to the Lord my God that cost me nothing." Obedience and sacrifice.

What about your worship? Does it include both obedience and sacrifice?

Prayer: Jesus, as the crucified and risen Son of God, you are worthy of my worship. Help me to worship you with obedience and sacrifice. Amen.

Psalm of the Day: 9.13-20

Eleven Days' Journey

Daily Reading: Deuteronomy 1

> *It is eleven days' journey from Horeb by the way of Mount Seir to Kadesh-barnea.* (Deuteronomy 1.2)

Devotional Thought: In my job, I travel frequently - sometimes flying, but often driving. There are times when my travel time is extended due to unforeseen conditions on the road. If there is construction or an accident, what should be a five hour drive can become an eight hour ordeal.

The journey of life is like that:
- The people of the Exodus took 40 years to go on an 11 day journey to enter the Promised Land. They blew it and never reached their destination. Even Moses wasn't allowed to cross over!
- Adam and Eve were created in direct relationship with God. They blew it and were cast out of the garden.
- Peter walked with Jesus. He blew it and denied Jesus three times.

What about us? Are we blowing it? Yes, but God redeems our failures.

Even though Adam and Eve failed, God gave them the privilege of directing their children into a relationship with him. Sure, they had the heartache of living through the consequence of their sin. They had "good" children, and they had "not-so good" children. But, they knew what it was like to have a perfect relationship with God, and they were privileged to be a part of God's plans for offering salvation to all who would come after them. And Peter's failure? God redeemed it so that Peter grew to be a rock in the Kingdom.

What about those Israelites that participated in the journey to the Promised Land, but never quite attained the goal? Did they quit? No. Were they influential in their children's lives and their nation's success? Yes. They pushed onward to the goal. God redeemed their failure by showing them his faithfulness and allowing them to prepare the next generation for life in the Promised Land.

John Wade

Prayer: Lord, I know that life is not a smooth and even trail, but a journey of starts and stops - of calm and chaos. In it all, may you redeem my failures and lead me on to the Promised Land. Amen.

Psalm of the Day: 10.1-11

Unexpected Blessings
Deuteronomy 2

> For the Lord your God has blessed you in all the work of your hands. He knows your going through this great wilderness. These forty years the Lord your God has been with you. You have lacked nothing. (Deuteronomy 2.7)

Devotional Thought: As we saw in Deuteronomy 1, the Lord is able to redeem our failures. He is even able to use us in his work after we have "blown it." In Deuteronomy 2, we see that while failure may bring hardship and pain, God is with us.

The people of Israel had failed to enter the land, and through their unbelief, they lost forty years in the Promised Land. In their wanderings, however, they had not forfeited other blessings from God. Moses reminded them:

- *God has blessed you.* Though they wandered, God had kept the Israelites together. They had faced enemies far greater than them. God helped them to defeat them. They had experienced sickness and disease. God healed them. They sinned. God forgave them.
- *God knows where you are and where you need to go.* Their wandering was not without direction. God was leading them through unfamiliar territory.
- *God has been with you.* After their failure to enter, God did not leave them. He stayed with them as seen in the pillar of cloud and fire. He met them at the mercy seat in the Holy of Holies.
- *You have lacked nothing.* When they were hungry, God gave them manna and quail. When they were thirsty, God gave them water from the rock. Even their shoes did not wear out!

Even though our wilderness wanderings seem long and lonely, even though we may have forfeited blessings that we can never reclaim, we have the assurance that God is with us to bless us, to guide us, and provide for us. Remember, God is in the business of unexpected blessings.

Prayer: Thank you, Heavenly Father, for your presence in my life and for how you have blessed me. Help me, in the abundance of what you have given me, to be a blessing to others. Amen.

Psalm of the Day: 10.12-15

Lift Up Your Eyes
Daily Reading: Deuteronomy 3

> *Go up to the top of Pisgah and lift up your eyes westward and northward and southward and eastward, and look at it with your eyes.* (Deuteronomy 3.27)

Devotional Thought: When Moses came to the end of his life, he was told to climb Mount Pisgah and to look over into the Promised Land. Though he would not enter it, God showed it to him, telling him to look to the west, north, south and east. Don't miss anything!

Just as Moses lifted up his eyes to look, let us look...
- *Westward.* To the west of Moses lay the Promised Land. What was before him was seen only from a distance. Westward indicated what lay ahead - the future. Let us always have a forward-looking mindset. As we live our lives, may we be pulled into the glorious promise of God. He has prepared a place for us, an eternal dwelling!
- *Northward.* To Moses' north lay the region of Galilee. This was to become the region where Jesus would focus his ministry. It represents the gospel of the Kingdom where lives are changed, souls saved, sins forgiven, and miracles wrought. As we look northward, may we do so with faith that God will do wonderful things.
- *Southward.* Moses looked toward Sinai and Egypt. There, God was seen in the burning bush, deliverance had come to Israel, the law was given, and the long journey of life had transpired. Looking to the south reminds us of great spiritual victories and God's great faithfulness.
- *Eastward.* That was the direction from which Moses had come. All the battles fought, the victories won, and the work completed lay behind him. There was nothing to be done with them except leave them in God's hands.

Lift up your eyes today. Don't miss anything! Celebrate the goodness and faithfulness of God.

Prayer: Lord, you have been so good to me! Help me to lift up my eyes and see all your blessings and accept with quiet confidence your will for my life. Amen.

Psalm of the Day: 10.16-18

Listen and Live

Daily Reading: Deuteronomy 4

And now, O Israel, listen to the statutes and the rules that I am teaching you, and do them, that you may live. (Deuteronomy 4.1a)

Devotional Thought: "You're not listening to me." "Yes I am, Daddy. I heard everything you just said." If you're a parent, that is a familiar conversation to you.

Parents and children interpret "Listen to me" differently. Children think in terms of "hearing." When parents say listen, however, they mean "do what I say."

In Deuteronomy 4, the Lord clears up any confusion. He tells Israel to listen and do. As you read the chapter, there are some pretty exciting verses that merit reflection:

v. 2:   You shall not add to the word that I command you, nor take from it.

v. 7:   For what great nation is there that has a god so near to it as the LORD our God is to us, whenever we call upon him?

v. 9:   Keep your soul diligently.

v. 9:   Make them [God's words] known to your children and your children's children.

v. 24: For the LORD your God is a consuming fire, a jealous God.

v. 29: You will seek the LORD your God and you will find him, if you search after him with all your heart and with all your soul.

v. 35: To you it was shown, that you might know that the LORD is God; there is no other besides him.

Reflect on these words. "Listen... and do them, that you may live."

Prayer: Lord, at times I neglect the Old Testament. Forgive me, I pray. And help me, Lord, to glean great and eternal truth from all of your Word that I may live. Amen.

Psalm of the Day: 11.1-7

The Answer to Fear
Daily Reading: Deuteronomy 5

Oh that they had such a heart as this always, to fear me and to keep all my commandments, that it might go well with them and with their descendants forever! (Deuteronomy 5:29)

Devotional Thought: While God gave Moses the Ten Commandments on Mount Sinai, the rest of the Israelites waited at the bottom of the mountain for Moses to return. Their experience terrified them. They couldn't believe that Moses had spoken with God and lived to tell about it. After hearing his voice from a distance - out of the midst of the fire that descended upon the mountain - they could no longer bear it. "For this great fire will consume us. If we hear the voice of the Lord our God any more, we shall die" (v. 25).

The Lord responded to the plea and the terror of the people through Moses, telling the people that they are right in what they have spoken – they are right to be fearful of their God! Then he told them that he wanted it to stay that way! "Oh that they had such a heart as this always, to fear me and to keep all my commandments, that it might go well with them and with their descendants forever!" The Lord loved them despite their unworthiness, despite knowing that they would stray from his covenant.

When we are walking with the Lord in obedience, do we hear the same longing from our Father? In our walk with Christ, we will go through periods of growth as well as periods of stagnation. Do you hear the Father's cry? Oh that we would have such hearts as this always! He wants to spiritually bless and prosper us, but it requires a heart of faith and obedience.

Lord, help us to walk ever closer to you!

Jenny

Prayer: Lord, we know that, like the children of Israel, we stray from your will and your presence. Help us to desire, above all other things, communion with you. Amen.

Psalm of the Day: 12.1-8

21

For What?

Daily Reading: Deuteronomy 6

He brought us out from there, that he might bring us in and give us the land. (Deuteronomy 6.23)

Devotional Thought: Have you ever stopped to think, "Why did God save me?" We know the motive was his great love. Moses, in Deuteronomy 6 however, provides insight to the purpose of God in saving us...

- *To bring us out.* The children of Israel were 'God's family.' God had 'adopted' Abraham generations before the Exodus. Over the course of time, however, the Israelites became slaves in Egypt. God saw their misery and was moved with compassion. He stretched out his hand to deliver them from that miserable existence. We see Jesus delivering people from miserable lives in the New Testament: sin, disease, exclusion, hardheartedness, selfishness and pride. Jesus saves us because his heart is moved with compassion at our plight.
- *To bring us in.* Deliverance from misery is not enough for the great love of God! He desired to bring them into abiding fellowship with him and with the other members of the family. God put the temple worship in place and he created a national identity around that worship. He even 'scheduled' regular 'family reunions'! Jesus says of us, "Whoever does the will of God is my brother and sister and mother" (Mark 3.35). In 70's parlance, Jesus saves us to make us part of the 'in crowd'!
- *To give us new life.* Centuries before God delivered the Israelites out of the old life, he prepared a new land - a land that Abraham had purchased and possessed, a land flowing with milk and honey, a land full of promise. The Israelites often grumbled about going back to Egypt, but God wouldn't allow that. He had a new life in a new land for them. Jesus saves us so we can live a new life of victory, joy, peace, hope, and love!

Prayer: Father, thank you for the wonderful gift of friendship. For any broken relationships in my life, help me, like you, to extend the olive branch of peace. Heal and restore those relationships I pray. Amen.

Psalm of the Day: 13.1-6

Holy, Chosen, Treasured
Daily Reading: Deuteronomy 7

> *For you are a people holy to the Lord your God. The Lord your God has chosen you to be a people for his treasured possession.*
> (Deuteronomy 7.6)

Devotional Thought: Yesterday, we saw how God brought out the children of Israel in order to bring them in. When he gave them their new land, he told them not to make alliances with the people and patterns of Canaan. Why? They were a people...

- *Holy.* To be holy means to be set apart, consecrated for God's purpose. Just as Israel was set apart to be the nation through whom blessing would come to the world, we are designed for the eternal purposes of God. Jesus died on the cross, the Bible says, to save people from sin. We are to be holy people in the sense that we are fulfilling Jesus' purpose in the world. Jesus was cursed on the cross to 'become sin,' even though he was without sin, pure and spotless. We are to be holy people like him, a glorious church, without spot or wrinkle, washed in the blood of the Lamb!
- *Chosen.* God said that Jesus was his chosen one, his beloved one with whom he was well-pleased. When God looks at Jesus, he sees perfection. He is pleased. When God looks at us, he does so through the prism of Jesus. He is pleased. Let us consecrate ourselves to be worthy of the calling we have received!
- *Treasured.* The Father, Son, and Holy Spirit have lived in unbroken fellowship since the dawn of eternity. It is a perfect union of love. God created us in his image that we might enter into the divine dance! He treasures us so much that he paid the ultimate price to redeem us - the life of his Son!

We are a people holy, chosen and treasured!

Prayer: Thank you, Lord, for making me holy. Thank you for choosing to save me through the blood of Jesus. Thank you for treasuring me as your special possession. I love you, Lord! Amen.

Psalm of the Day: 14.1-3

Spiritual Pride

Daily Reading: Deuteronomy 8-9

> *Know, therefore, that the Lord your God is not giving you this good land to possess because of your righteousness, for you are a stubborn people.* (Deuteronomy 9.6)

Devotional Thought: When people receive blessings and honor, it tends to 'go to their heads.' God knew that Israel would be subject to that temptation, so he warned them ahead of time, "Remember, you are here because of my love, not because of your greatness!" They were slaves. They had nothing to offer God. They didn't even know how to worship him.

The same applies to us as Christ-followers. God gives us salvation, not because we are righteous, but in spite of the fact that we are not righteous. We need to remember that for many reasons, but three stand out:

- If we think that we have gotten where we are because of our own righteousness, then we could come to believe that we are above sin, that we cannot sin. Spiritual pride is dangerous because it leads to dead legalism and smug presumption.
- We think that we, of all people, are worthy of God's love and that others have no hope! Instead of fulfilling Christ's commission to make disciples, we build walls around Jesus and refuse to let others in unless they think like us, talk like us and act like us.
- Or, just as damning, spiritual pride can cause us to think that sin is OK, so we might as well give into it. "Well, if God saved me when I was a sinner, then it must be OK to sin." Or, as Paul put it in Romans 6, "What shall we say then? Are we to continue in sin that grace may abound?" Paul would have none of that. "By no means!" he quickly rejoined. God didn't save us from sin to make us bold sinners!

Prayer: Help me, Lord, to remember that it is not because of my righteousness that you saved me. Help me to humbly and continually seek your grace in order to live a life pleasing to you. Amen.

Psalm of the Day: 14.4-7

Do You Want Sprinkles on That?

Daily Reading: Deuteronomy 10-11

And now, Israel, what does the Lord your God require of you, but to fear the Lord your God, to walk in all his ways, to love him, to serve the Lord your God with all your heart and with all your soul, and to keep the commandments and statutes of the Lord, which I am commanding you today for your good? (Deuteronomy 10.12-13)

Devotional Thought: "Do you want sprinkles on that?" I ask Lana that every time I get her ice cream. I know she wants sprinkles, but I say it just to aggravate her! We've been together long enough that we pretty much know what each other likes, so we don't really need to ask. It's good that way. But, there was a time, when we didn't know each other that well, and those questions really were legit!

In Deuteronomy 10, the nation of Israel was like that in their relationship with God. They really needed to be told what God wanted. So, God did just that, using Moses as a mouthpiece.

These things apply to us today, too. God says, "Here's what I require..."
- *Fear me.* We must realize that God is God and we are his creatures. He loves us, yes, but he is God.
- *Walk in my ways.* The way of the Lord is merciful. He walks on paths of love. Are we walking in mercy and love?
- *Love me.* Though we recognize he is God, we also realize that he loves us enough to give his one and only Son to die for us. We can love God with abandon, without fear of being disappointed.
- *Serve me with all your heart and soul.* A heart of love naturally wants to serve. "What can I do for you, Jesus?"
- *Keep my commandments.* The way of his commandments is a way of peace and significance. To walk in any other way is to miss our purpose.

Let's walk so close to God that we will know the answer to, "Do you want sprinkles on that?"

Prayer: Lord, help me to please you, to live in your way. Help me to live in freedom, love, and service and so find fulfillment. Amen.

Psalm of the Day: 15.1-5

Redefining and Rediscovering

Daily Reading: Deuteronomy 12-13

For every abominable thing that the Lord hates they have done for their gods, for they even burn their sons and their daughters in the fire to their gods. (Deuteronomy 12.31b)

Devotional Thought: How quickly morality has been redefined! We live in a culture where "anything goes!" The only boundaries, it seems, are boundaries that prevent decent people from having boundaries, from living out their moral and religious convictions. Nowhere is this seen more than it is seen in the current confusion surrounding sexuality and gender identity.

We have a new god in America. We serve him or her or cis or whatever at the altar of political correctness. When we unleashed the sexual revolution back in the 60's, we had no idea where it was headed. It has become clear. Every decent thing, every accepted truth, every Christian notion of morality is to be rejected with vehemence and retribution. We have replaced decency, modesty, and chasteness with "every abominable thing." And the god of this age will not be satisfied until all bend the knee.

But, there is trouble in paradise. The sexual revolution has come back upon the heads of those who fomented the confusion. The free 'pass' once given to abusive men has now demanded payment. Feminists, who once cried out for reproductive freedom, are now finding it necessary to join #MeToo. The pendulum has swept so far that many mothers' innocent sons (and husbands) will be crushed as collateral damage. "That's OK," says the new god. It is the necessary cost of controlling the demon released in worship of sexual freedom and gender fluidity.

Truth is at stake. Real truth, not relative truth. May God help us in the Church to rediscover the ancient paths.

Prayer: Lord God, who has given us your Word to guide us, forgive us for rejecting, ridiculing and persecuting your ways. Help us to live holy, loving, and good lives so that the name of our God will not be impugned. Amen.

Psalm of the Day: 16.1-6

The Poor

Daily Reading: Deuteronomy 14-15

> For there will never cease to be poor in the land. Therefore I command you, "You shall open wide your hand to your brother, to the needy and to the poor, in your land." (Deuteronomy 15.11)

Devotional Thought: In the Old Testament, God established ways to care for the poor. There were laws concerning levirate marriage to ensure that widows were taken care of. There were customs established to make sure that the orphans could glean. There were provisions for indentured servanthood - and its conclusion - that enabled people to work off their debt. There were laws protecting the poor in court. And finally, there was a culture of compassion fostered by the worship of God.

Why was that necessary? For two reasons...

- "There will never cease to be poor in the land." Some people are poor because life has been tough on them. Disease and death in the family, drought and famine, poor choices and addiction, debt and systemic oppression... these and many other reasons cause poverty. There is also, sadly but truthfully, a whole segment of society who have no desire to work, and we have fostered a culture of expectation that someone else will take care of me. As Jesus said, "The poor you will always have with you."
- "Therefore I command you..." People need reminded and encouraged to be compassionate. We get busy with our own lives, our own struggles, our own desires. It is so easy to walk right past a needy person and not even see them. It is also easy to look down upon and blame a poor person for their poverty. Rightly or wrongly, we assume that a poor person is somehow responsible for the mess they are in. Sometimes we need to hear the command of God in order to wake us up.

Prayer: Jesus, thank you that though you were rich, for my sake you became poor. Help me to respond with generosity and compassion to the needs around me, realizing that in so doing I am serving you. Amen.

Psalm of the Day: 16.7-11

The Foundation of Godly Leadership
Daily Reading: Deuteronomy 16-17

> *And it shall be with him, and he shall read in it all the days of his life, that he may learn to fear the Lord his God by keeping all the words of this law and these statutes, and doing them, that his heart may not be lifted up above his brothers, and that he may not turn aside from the commandment, either to the right hand or to the left, so that he may continue long in his kingdom, he and his children.* (Deuteronomy 17.19-20)

Devotional Thought: The law that God gave the Israelites on Mount Sinai has proven to be some of the most enduring and influential teachings upon which western civilization has been built. And, it was not just "a private matter" as some wish to relegate faith today. No, God instructed Israel's future leaders (kings) to know and follow "all the words of this law." Several important results would come when the leaders did this...

- *Humility.* God knew that the tendency of leaders - even godly leaders - is to begin to feel privileged and entitled. They begin to do things to protect their power and preserve their position. Wouldn't it be nice if Washington politicians lived with the same laws that are given us? By knowing the Law of God and knowing where success comes from, leaders can avoid lifting themselves up above those they lead.
- *Reliability.* I find it amazing how the positions of politicians change with the wind. What was once considered a bedrock principle, is quickly discarded when it seems politically expedient. Having the Word of God as our foundation, we can establish human laws that transcend passing cultural fads.
- *Stability.* Another advantage of leaders following the Word of God is that an environment is created in which principles can be handed down from generation to generation. How greatly policies change when executive orders are issued based on the whims and wishes of the chief executive. It is hard to build a stable society when the foundations keep shifting.

May God give us leaders who know and follow the Word of the Lord!

Prayer: Thank you, Lord God, for giving us your Word. Help us to know and follow your Word that it may go well with us and that we may live long in the land the Lord our God has given us. Amen.

Psalm of the Day: 17.1-5

I Know People

Daily Reading: Colossians 1

We heard of your faith in Christ Jesus and of the love that you have for all the saints. (Colossians 1.4)

Devotional Thought: As Jesus neared the end of his ministry, his disciples began to understand just who he was: the Son of God. They were ready to follow him into his glorious and victorious kingdom. But, he upset their apple cart when he gathered them together and washed their feet: "Never!" Peter responded. But, Jesus told him and them that the very essence of the Kingdom was not power and privilege, but was instead love and service: "By this all people will know that you are my disciples, if you have love for one another" (John 13.35).

The Apostle Paul said the same thing in a slightly different way. He linked the faith of the Colossians with the love that they had for the people of God. Faith in Christ and love for the saints go together:

- I know people who say they have faith in Jesus, but who do not enter into his family. Is this real faith?
- I know people who love the idea of ministry more than they love the people to whom they are called to minister. Is this real ministry?
- I know people who love to worship God and experience his presence, but who do not like The Church. Is this real worship?
- I know people who think that the church ought to meet all their needs, but who do nothing to meet the needs of others in the church. Is this real church?

May it be said of us that our faith in Christ Jesus has led us to love the saints!

Prayer: Lord, you died for the church, to make her holy, to present her to yourself in glory. Help us to remember that though we are imperfect, you love us anyway. And, help us to love one another. Amen.

Psalm of the Day: 17.6-12

Before and After

Daily Reading: Colossians 2

And you, who were dead in your trespasses and the uncircumcision of your flesh, God made alive together with him, having forgiven us all our trespasses. (Colossians 2.13)

Devotional Thought: Paul wrote to the Colossians that there is a sharp contrast before and after someone comes to know Christ.

Prior to knowing Christ, we are...

Dead in our sins: Our death is the result of our sin: "The wages of sin is death" (Romans 6.23). God had told Adam, "In the day that you eat of it [the forbidden fruit] you shall surely die" (Genesis 2.17). The Old Testament prophet affirmed this when he said, "The soul who sins shall die" (Ezekiel 18.4).

Sinful in actions: While not a popular concept, the truth is that there are certain things we do that are sinful. These are 'trespasses' against God's law.

Sinful in nature: We have all inherited a 'nature' from our original parents, Adam and Eve. This is what Paul means by the uncircumcision of our flesh. That nature is bent toward self-will and this leads us to sinful actions and ultimately to death.

But that is not the end of the story! After we come to know Christ, God makes us...

Alive: While the wages of sin is death, God cancels that out and gives us eternal life in Jesus! God breathes that new life into us through the Holy Spirit, the very breath of God!

Forgiven: The Son of God shed his own blood for our forgiveness. We need only accept what has been paid for on the cross of Calvary. 'All trespasses' (sinful actions) are forgiven in his name.

Holy in Christ: But, he goes beyond that. In a process and a crisis of sanctification, God makes us like Christ. 'Together with him' we are holy! We cannot be holy ourselves, but with him we can be!

Thanks be to God for his wonderful work of salvation!

Prayer: Thank you, Lord, for forgiveness of sins, for new life in Christ, and for making me holy in union with Christ. Help me today to live out the reality of what you have made me. Amen.

Psalm of the Day: 17.13-15

What's Going On?

Daily Reading: Colossians 3

For you have died, and your life is hidden with Christ in God.
(Colossians 3.3)

Devotional Thought: In Colossians 2, we saw how we who were once dead have been made alive with Christ. In Colossians 3 - just a few verses later - we read that we have died once again!

What's going on?

Let me give you an analogy from marriage. Thirty-nine years ago, I stood at the altar of the Church of the Nazarene in Fairmont, WV and married my sweetheart. The moment I said I do, I died. In marriage, God makes of two people one flesh, so I ceased being just myself and took on the identity of a new entity. I was we; me was us. The Lana/Scott thing! (Poor girl!)

Though I did not lose my personhood, I became swallowed up in a whole new reality. I still had (and have) the freedom to make my own choices, but no longer were decisions mine alone. No longer could I do whatever I wanted, whenever I wanted, with whomever I wanted. I had to consider the woman beside me, the other to whom I had pledged my life and my love.

A funny thing happened, too. More and more, when someone saw me, they saw Lana. When someone saw Lana, they saw me. I was 'hidden' inside us. She was 'hidden' inside us.

The Bible says we are hidden with Christ in God. Whenever someone sees us, they should see Christ. We are new creatures. "For me to live is Christ."

Is your life hidden with Christ in God?

Prayer: Thank you, Jesus, for taking on our nature that we may take on the very nature of God. Hide us in your love, O Lord. "Let the beauty of Jesus be seen in me!" Amen.

Psalm of the Day: 18.1-6

See To It
Daily Reading: Colossians 4

> *Say to Archippus, "See that you fulfill the ministry that you have received in the Lord."* (Colossians 4.17)

Devotional Thought: In Colossians 4, Paul reminded a minister named Archippus: "Fulfill the ministry that you have received." But, it isn't just to Archippus. God wrote the Bible for all of us, and I believe God needs to remind many, many people, "Please do what I called you to do."

What does it mean to see to our ministry?
- *Get started.* Sometimes the hardest part of a job is getting it started. I have a "workshop" in my basement that I have been meaning to clean up and clear out for literally years. I just kept putting it off. Finally, I asked a friend to come over on a particular day and help me. With her standing there staring at me, what else could I do? I had to get started! And so we cleaned out the room. (We made a mess in the garage, but that's another story!) When God calls us to do something, we need to get started!
- *Remove impediments.* Is there something preventing you from effectively serving the Lord? I know of a man who felt called to serve on his local church board, but couldn't give up smoking which disqualified him from serving. One day, he just quit, reasoning, that if his smoking was preventing him from serving, and God was calling him to serve, then the only logical thing to do was stop smoking! Are there habits that harm your testimony? Situations that stifle your witness? Prior commitments that press claims upon your time and energy? Remove them!
- *Constantly improve.* As we fulfill our ministry, God desires to give us greater and greater responsibilities. We can only handle that greater responsibility if we "study to show ourselves approved unto the Lord, a workman who needs not be ashamed."

Prayer: Lord, thank you for including me on your 'team.' Help me to take seriously the assignments you have given me and to fulfill my ministry. Amen.

Psalm of the Day: 18.7-12

Without Excuse, but Not Without Hope!
Daily Reading: Romans 1

> For his invisible attributes, namely, his eternal power and divine nature, have been clearly perceived, ever since the creation of the world, in the things that have been made. So they are without excuse. (Romans 1.20)

Devotional Thought: There is no excuse for disbelief in God. Even those who have not heard the name of Jesus have seen his invisible attributes. Paul says, "What can be known about God is plain to them, because God has shown it to them," (v. 19). In Psalm 19 we read, "The heavens declare the glory of God; the skies proclaim the work of his hands."

For those who have been exposed to God's eternal power and divine nature (a.k.a. every human being), but choose to "not honor him as God or give thanks to him" (v. 21), the outlook is grim. "Claiming to be wise, they became fools, and exchanged the glory of the immortal God for images resembling mortal man... therefore God gave them up... because they exchanged the truth about God for a lie and worshiped and served the creature rather than the Creator" (vv. 22-25). What a sad and small view of the world those people had!

And, doesn't it sound all too familiar to us? Our human-centered culture stands in extreme opposition to the truth of a God-centered anything. We honor and commend the individual human above all else, and therefore worship the creature rather than the Creator. We have no moral absolutes, but instead adopt a "whatever works for you" attitude. Therefore, we have no hope, so we spend our 80 years of life grabbing as much pleasure for ourselves as possible before we cease to exist.

But praise God: there is a Living Hope! We are no longer bound by our sinful natures, by death's finality, by hopelessness. There is a Creator who has made himself evident to all of humanity, and he loves us and has given his only Son to redeem us and make us righteous in his sight.

Jenny

Prayer: Lord, thank you for the indescribable gift of salvation through your Son! Help us to proclaim the good news to the world around us. Open the eyes and ears of those we love to the truth of your eternal power and divine nature. Amen.

Psalm of the Day: 18.13-18

Self-Evident Truth
Daily Reading: Romans 2

> *For when Gentiles, who do not have the law, by nature do what the law requires, they are a law to themselves, even though they do not have the law. They show that the work of the law is written on their hearts, while their conscience also bears witness, and their conflicting thoughts accuse or even excuse them.* (Romans 2.14-15)

Devotional Thought: "We hold these truths to be self-evident..." What makes a truth self-evident? Is it the fact that it is accepted by a majority of the population? Not necessarily. Sometimes a lot of people can be wrong! Is it because you can't imagine life without it? I wouldn't say so. History is a long line of indispensible things now discarded for other things.

A truth is self-evident when it is "written on the heart" by the Spirit of God.

Paul, a staunch Jew as a young man, was steeped in the Law of Moses. He knew the righteous requirements of the Law. He also 'knew' that the Gentiles - who did not have the Law - were hopeless. But, something happened to Paul. Jesus appeared to him and showed him that God did indeed love the Gentiles, and there were a good many who fulfilled the Law without knowing the Law. How did they know what to do? The only answer was that God had written it on their hearts.

I love the story of the Ten Commandments - how God, with his own finger, inscribed the Law on the tablets of stone. The truth of the matter is that God is still doing that today! He writes on the hearts of people so that their "conscience bears witness" and their "conflicting thoughts accuse" them. Of course, that truth can be stifled and ignored, it can be buried beneath hatred and prejudice and greed. But, it is still there. Why? Because it is truth, and truth never changes.

Pray that God would reveal his Truth to more and more people and that there would be a revival in the land!

Prayer: Father, thank you for the convicting presence of the Holy Spirit, who writes the Truth on our hearts. Help us to follow and obey you. May others know the truth that would set them free in Jesus as well! Amen.

Psalm of the Day: 18.19-24

God Is the God of You

Daily Reading: Romans 3

> *Is God the God of Jews only? Is he not the God of Gentiles also? Yes, of Gentiles also.* (Romans 3.29)

Devotional Thought: God reaches out to all people - whether they be Jews or Gentiles, Christians or non-Christians, believers or atheists. He is God of everybody!

God is our Father by virtue of creating us. On the sixth day of creation, God looked at what he had made and it was very good. The other days ended with good. The sixth and final day ended with very good. God's creative purpose reached its apex in humanity. He breathed his life into us and stamped his image upon us. God sees us all as his children because we are made in his image.

God is our Father by virtue of adopting us. Not only are we the culmination of his creative hand, humanity is also the object of his redeeming love. When our sins separated us from God, he was not content to leave us there. Through the sacrifice of his Son on the cross, he made a way for us to come back into his family. Such love, such wondrous love!

God is our Father by virtue of sustaining us. Perhaps you have heard the expression, "Any man can be a father, but it takes someone special to be a dad." Fatherhood involves more than reproducing or adopting. It is an ongoing relationship of love and provision. God has not forgotten us. He walks with us and talks with us. He wants to spend time with us - quality and quantity time.

And, yes, God is the God of you, too! Will you choose him?

Prayer: Thank you, Father, that you love me and are my God. You created me. You chose me. You sustain me. I love you, Lord, my God and my Father! Amen.

Psalm of the Day: 18.25-30

Blessed Indeed!
Daily Reading: Romans 4

> *Blessed are those whose lawless deeds are forgiven, and whose sins are covered; blessed is the man against whom the Lord will not count his sin.* (Romans 4.7-8)

Devotional Thought: Last night we had a wonderful service at our church. The presence of the Lord was there as we prayed for healing and deliverance, comfort and strength. As we prayed in Bethel, 20 miles away - in Anderson Township - a dear friend of ours, a saint of God was traveling the last mile of her journey. Diane went to be with the Lord. Her husband described her journey beautifully: "The angels just came and took Diane away to heaven... so peacefully." How is it that we, as her daughter said to me, "do not sorrow as those who have no hope"? What makes us so blessed that even in times of grief we have hope?

In Romans 4, Paul gave us three reasons for counting ourselves blessed. We are...

- *Forgiven.* No one is righteous before a holy God. All have sinned and fall short of God's perfection. But with the shedding of Christ's blood on the cross, our sins are forgiven. The debt has been paid! How blessed to know we can stand before God with a clear conscience!
- *Covered.* Not only are sins forgiven, they are covered. God has cast our sins into the depths of the sea. They are never to be remembered against us. God himself does not see them anymore. Gone is the guilt. Gone is the shame. Gone is the fear. How blessed to know that our sins are covered by the God who is our Judge.
- *Released.* Not only are our sins forgiven and covered, the debt we had accrued because of them has been canceled! How could we ever hope to pay the cost for our sins? But, as the song goes, "He paid a debt he did not owe. I owed a debt I could not pay..." How blessed that the slate is wiped clean and there is no longer any debt!

We are blessed indeed!

Prayer: Thank you, Father, for the blessedness of sins forgiven, of life eternal, of joy unceasing. We praise you and worship you today, for you are our hope. Amen.

Psalm of the Day: 18.31-34

From Suffering to Hope
Daily Reading: Romans 5

> *We rejoice in our sufferings, knowing that suffering produces endurance, and endurance produces character, and character produces hope.* (Romans 5.3-4)

Devotional Thought: Why do good people suffer? I get that question all the time. And, I still feel so inadequate when trying to answer it. As I spoke with my friend Gerry a few days ago, we struggled with that very issue. I expressed my thought that when we suffer 'unjustly' it is an opportunity for us to be like Jesus, who himself suffered through no fault of his own.

Paul wrote about Christian suffering in Romans 5. Let's look at the progression...

- *Suffering.* Paul almost seemed to take it for granted we would suffer, and for good reason. Suffering is part and parcel of living, isn't it? We should not be surprised, for Jesus came for that very purpose - to suffer. But suffering is not the end, for suffering produces...
- *Endurance.* The Scripture commends Jesus for enduring the cross and entering before the throne of God. When we endure, we are like Jesus. And not only so, we also will be able to enter into the joy of the Lord!
- *Character.* It's strange to think about Jesus' character being developed. How can a perfect character be developed? Because he became a perfect sacrifice. In the Garden of Gethsemane, Jesus' character was developed when he prayed "Not my will, but yours." As we go through the fiery trials, endurance perfects our character, just as it did for Jesus. We become "fit for the Master's use."
- *Hope.* Jesus had hope in the Father. His hope was so certain, that in the midst of his suffering, he entrusted himself to God. As our characters grow, our hope grows. We have "the assurance of things hoped for, the conviction of things not seen."

Prayer: Lord, we do not pray for suffering, but we do pray that in our sufferings we would be like Jesus. Help us to embrace our sufferings as you did and so to endure, to grow our souls and to inherit our hope. Amen.

Psalm of the Day: 18.35-45

Newness of Life
Daily Reading: Romans 6

> *We were buried therefore with him by baptism into death, in order that, just as Christ was raised from the dead by the glory of the Father, we too might walk in newness of life.* (Romans 6.4)

Devotional Thought: I remember the day when I came to know the Lord, when I was saved. I was 14 years old and found myself kneeling at the altar in the Pioneer, OH, Church of the Nazarene. How wonderful it was to have my sins forgiven, the guilt gone! What I could not begin to comprehend at that moment, was how much my life had just changed. I began walking, as Paul wrote, "in newness of life."

I had a whole new set of friends. My language began to change (for even 14 year old boys know how to curse!). I had new values. I had love in my heart. These things and many others began to show and grow in my life. Soon, I was baptized to confess to all the world that I was a follower of Jesus Christ.

Paul wrote that for us to have "newness of life" two things are required...

- Jesus Christ had to die and rise again. Without the shedding of blood there is no remission of sins, and hence no new life. But, the only way that death can lead to new life is for there to be a resurrection. Christ was the firstfruits of the resurrection, and we who believe in him enter into that life with him.
- But also, we have to die. In order to have a new identity, the old one has to go away. I was adopted when I was 9 years old. Scott Wortman died. Scott Wade came to life. I had a new identity. Baptism symbolizes the spiritual change that comes to us. Going under the water, we are dead. Rising again, we live a new life.

Are you walking in that new identity today?

Prayer: Thank you, Lord Jesus, for dying for my sins and for rising again for my life. Help me, O Lord, to honor you as I walk in newness of life. Amen.

Psalm of the Day: 18.46-50

The Age of Accountability
Daily Reading: Romans 7

> *I was once alive apart from the law, but when the commandment came, sin came alive and I died.* (Romans 7.9)

Devotional Thought: As a young lad of 14, I entered "newness of life" when I was adopted. Today, I want to go back a few more years in my childhood to discover another important spiritual reality. It's reflected in Paul's claim: "I was once alive apart from the law..." What does that mean? Paul remembered that he, as a young lad, had lived in a state of innocence. The Psalmist had written centuries before, "You [God] made me trust you at my mother's breasts. On you I was cast from my birth" (Psalm 22.9-10).

Paul and the Psalmist both allude to the fact that young children - before "the age of accountability" - are covered by the grace of God and stand guiltless before the Lord, "alive apart from the law." Children who die in this state - even though they have not been saved and baptized - are still "redeemed by the blood of the Lamb."

How do the innocent become guilty? The blameless become culpable? Paul said, "When the commandment came, sin came alive and I died." That is the age of accountability. This does not mean a child does not sin before that time. Anyone who has had a two year old knows that! God does not hold a child accountable for things they do not understand to be sinful. When a person realizes, however, that he or she stands responsible before God - when the commandment comes - at that moment, sin becomes a reality in their life, and spiritual death comes.

But, thanks be to God, a child, a teenager or an adult can confess their sins, and God is faithful and just to forgive their sins!

Prayer: Thank you, Lord, for the grace of God that covers our sins! Thank you, that even as small children, your grace covers us. Help us, O Lord, when we come to realize sin in our lives, to confess it and to receive forgiveness through Jesus Christ the Righteous One. Amen.

Psalm of the Day: 19.1-6

No Condemnation
Daily Reading: Romans 8

> There is therefore now no condemnation for those who are in Christ Jesus. (Romans 8.1)

Devotional Thought: How wonderful to have the privilege of writing on my favorite chapter of the Bible! It starts strong: "There is therefore now no condemnation for those who are in Christ Jesus." Hallelujah!

Paul wrote, "When I want to do right, evil lies close at hand. For I delight in the law of God, in my inner being, but I see in my members another law waging war against the law of my mind and making me captive to the law of sin that dwells in my members" (Rom. 7:21-23). You can sense his agony as he says, "Wretched man that I am! Who will deliver me from this body of death?" He then answers his question with the only possible answer: Jesus can! And, Jesus did.

We strive to obey, we try to do right, we want with our minds and souls to serve Jesus to the best of our ability. But on this earth, we will never escape our bodies of death. We, along with all creation, groan inwardly as we wait eagerly for adoption as sons, the redemption of our bodies (v. 23). Yet, because we have been set free from the law of sin and death, we must walk not according to the flesh, but according to the Spirit, setting our minds on the things of the Spirit (v. 5). We can rest assured that we do not have to do this in our own strength. "In all these things we are more than conquerors through him who loved us" (v. 37). And what a love it is! Nothing in all of creation "will be able to separate us from the love of God in Christ Jesus our Lord" (v. 39).

Now you understand why Romans 8 is my favorite chapter of the Bible!

Jenny

Prayer: Lord, you are worthy of the highest praise and honor! There is no power on earth, including sin and death itself, that can separate us from your incredible love. Thank you for pursuing us, for cleansing us, for justifying us, and for sanctifying us through your Spirit. Amen!

Psalm of the Day: 19.7-14

Jesus Thirsts. Do You?

Daily Reading: Romans 9

> *I have great sorrow and unceasing anguish in my heart. For I could wish that I myself were accursed and cut off from Christ for the sake of my brothers.* (Romans 9.2-3)

Devotional Thought: "I wish I could take your pain for you - even if just for an hour." That was written in a friend's 'Get Well Card' I recently read. I was moved by the sentiment, for I knew the person meant it. I knew how much she loved the friend to whom she was writing.

The Apostle Paul went even farther in his sympathy: "I could wish that I myself were accursed for the sake of my brothers." Paul was called by God to serve the Gentiles and preach the gospel to them. His heart was moved with love and affection for that class of people. But, there was a visceral yearning for the salvation of his kinspeople, the Jewish race. He identified with them. He longed for their souls to know the freedom and joy that he had in Jesus. So great was his love for them, he was willing to spend eternity cut off from Christ if only they would be saved.

Mother Theresa made the observation that when Jesus was on the cross and said, "I thirst," it was not water for which he longed. It was for the souls of those he was in that moment redeeming from the curse of sin. Jesus literally became accursed and cut off from God for the sake of those he loved, for your sake and mine.

I once read something that moved me deeply: "My soul longs for the souls for whom Christ died." Is there someone for whom you long with godly desire?

Prayer: Jesus, thank you for loving me so much that you laid down your life for me. Help me to love others in this manner. Amen

Psalm of the Day: 20.1-5

Universalist
Daily Reading: Romans 10

> For the Scripture says, "Everyone who believes in him will not be put to shame." For there is no distinction between Jew and Greek; for the same Lord is Lord of all, bestowing his riches on all who call on him. For "everyone who calls on the name of the Lord will be saved."
> (Romans 10.11-13)

Devotional Thought: "There is no distinction..." Recently, all my kids and grandkids were in. While all thirteen of us were together, the flu decided to pay us a visit as well. While not all of us got sick, I did note that there was no distinction between generations, genders, or genetics. Flu is an equal opportunity sickness!

Sin, too, is an equal opportunity sickness. The Bible says all have sinned. That's the bad news. The good news is this: "Everyone who calls on the name of the Lord will be saved!" All generations, genders and genetics (races) are eligible for God's forgiving grace.

Paul's concern with the Romans was that there were those who thought that Greeks/Gentiles had to become Jews in order to follow Christ. "Nope," Paul said, "you just need to call on the name of Jesus; you just need to believe in him..." That's good news, isn't it? I don't have to be of a particular social class, political party, income amount, education level or ethnic group to believe in and to call upon the name of the Lord. He is Lord and Savior of all the world. He will bestow the riches of his salvation on me if I call on him. While the offer is universal, however, salvation itself isn't. I must call upon him, trust in him and receive him. If I do that, I am assured that I will be saved.

Prayer: Lord, thank you that I am within 'saving distance' of you. Your arm is not short that it cannot save. And, all my loved ones and friends are also able to be saved. May the Holy Spirit speak to them, convict them of sin, and give them grace and faith to call upon you. Amen.

Psalm of the Day: 20.6-9

Stumble, but Don't Crumble
Daily Reading: Romans 11

So I ask, did they stumble in order that they might fall? By no means! Rather, through their trespass salvation has come to the Gentiles, so as to make Israel jealous. (Romans 11.11)

Devotional Thought: Recently, we spent some time in South Carolina with our one year old granddaughter, Ellis. She was learning to walk, and she loved to grab Nana's finger and lead her around the condo. We were hoping to see her walk on her own while there, but we didn't get to. We did see her stumble and fall several times, though! In a few short days after the trip, we were able to watch videos of our little girl walking on her own - and still stumbling! We weren't concerned about the stumbling, though, because we know that she got right back up!

Paul wrote that the Jews had stumbled in their faith, meaning that they did not fully understand the nature of God's salvation and had rejected Jesus as the Messiah. But, Paul said, their stumbling was not final! They stumbled in order to lead the Gentiles into salvation and then to come to faith themselves.

Often times we stumble in life, don't we? Though we don't want to, we know it is to be expected. We want to see ourselves and others walk 'on our own,' but it is a struggle and requires effort and concentration. It also requires that when we do stumble we get back up and try again! We cannot give up!

How is your walk with Christ right now? Have you stumbled? Get back up! As we read yesterday, "Call upon the name of the Lord!" Are you walking upright? Then rejoice and reach your hand of love and patience to another and help them get back on their feet!

Prayer: Thank you, Lord, that you are a God of great mercy and grace. Forgive me when I stumble and help me to get back on my feet. Also, Lord, help me to be patient and show grace to my fellow-traveler who himself/herself has stumbled. Help me to extend a hand of help and encouragement. Amen.

Psalm of the Day: Psalm 21.1-7

What Do I Owe You?
Daily Reading: Romans 12-13

> *Owe no one anything, except to love each other, for the one who loves another has fulfilled the law.* (Romans 13.8)

Devotional Thought: Romans 12-13, are very practical chapters. If you want "something to work on" in your spiritual life, concentrate on these two chapters for a week or two - or 52! One of the pressing questions answered in these chapters is, "Just what do I owe my neighbor?"

In today's entitlement society, some would have us believe that we owe them money. In today's tolerant society, some would say that we owe them acceptance of their chosen lifestyle. In today's pluralistic society, some would insist that all cultures are equal. But, what does the Bible say in Romans 13? What do I owe you? What do you owe me?

Love.

Love covers over a multitude of debts, doesn't it?
- If you love me, you will be generous and helpful in your approach to me. That doesn't mean you will give me money, for that may be the worst thing you could do.
- If you love me, you will be understanding and forgiving of my shortcomings. It doesn't mean that you want me to continue to believe the lies of Satan, but that you will love me and shine the light of God's truth on a better way, the way of life.
- If you love me, you will seek to help me find Jesus within my culture, but you will not let my culture keep me from hearing the truth about sin and salvation.

There is a perfect law, the law of liberty. It is the law of love.

Prayer: Father, help me to love you with all of my heart and soul and to love my neighbor as myself. Amen.

Psalm of the Day: 21.8-13

A Matter of...

Daily Reading: Romans 14

> *For the kingdom of God is not a matter of eating and drinking but of righteousness and peace and joy in the Holy Spirit.* (Romans 14.17)

Devotional Thought: Are we Christians because of what we do or what we believe? Yes!

In Romans 14, Paul found himself answering that question again, in a fresh way. There were some Christians who thought that others should have the same scruples as them. They insisted that all Christians maintain strict adherence to dietary regulations and eat only vegetables. Their reasoning was that meat may have been offered to idols before being purchased. There were other Christians who ate whatever they wanted, giving no thought to whether the meat had been used in idolatrous worship. Then there were the new and vulnerable Christians who didn't know what to do. Both sides spoke passionately about what they believed. Who was right?

Paul insisted that salvation does not come by adherence to dietary rules. Nor is it 'maintained' by dietary rules. Instead, we should base our confidence on "righteousness and peace and joy in the Holy Spirit." Paul was confident that the Holy Spirit is a better arbiter of our spiritual vitality than is our diet, or any other code.

So, are we Christians because of what we do or what we believe? Both - in the sense that our faith informs our actions and our actions indicate our faith. When we are following a new Reality, living a new life, the Holy Spirit gives us the righteousness of Christ, the peace that passes understanding, and the joy of the Lord as our strength.

Prayer: Lord, help me to know that it is not by my own performance that I am saved. Help me to trust in the work of Christ and then to live holy because of what he has done. Amen.

Psalm of the Day: 22.1-5

How to Be a Good Neighbor
Daily Reading: Romans 15

> *Let each of us please his neighbor for his good, to build him up. For Christ did not please himself.* (Romans 15.2-3a)

Devotional Thought: I once heard someone interpret the Golden Rule as "Do unto others as they would have you do unto them." not as you would have them do unto you. In other words, don't assume that someone else wants what you want!

Instead...
- Let us please them. While we are not 'people-pleasers', in the sense that we have to constantly worry about what others think of us, we should be concerned with what makes people happy. We all know people who aggravate others just for the sake of meanness. Paul said, "That's no way to live. Why not try to please them instead?" It makes life more pleasant - and better! - for everyone around.
- Let us do them good. We must realize, of course, that what makes someone happy may actually do them harm. It would make my grandson Grayson happy if his Mommy gave him candy for supper every night. But, would that do him good? Of course not. Sometimes by giving a person what they want, you are actually doing them more harm than good. Doing good, then, is a higher order than pleasing them.
- Let us build them up. Lest we adopt a superior attitude, however, we must temper even the good that we do with a sense of building others up. Sometimes good can be done in such a way as to destroy the hope and faith of another. Condescension and criticism bring a person down. Let's build them up!

Are you treating others with respect, with concern and with dignity?

Prayer: Lord, help me to build others up around me. I want my life to bring good to others, to bring joy and peace and hope to them. Help me to live for others as Christ lived and died for me. Amen.

Psalm of the Day: 22.6-11

Warmth and Warning
Daily Reading: Romans 16

> *...by smooth talk and flattery they deceive the hearts of the naive. For your obedience is known to all, so that I rejoice over you, but I want you to be wise as to what is good and innocent as to what is evil.*
> (Romans 16.18b, 19)

Devotional Thought: Paul wrapped up his letter to the Romans with warm, personal greetings. In the midst of these encouraging expressions of affection, he issued a stark warning against those who "cause divisions and create obstacles contrary to the doctrine that you have been taught" (v. 17).

Paul's advice is extremely helpful to all believers, both then and today. He warns to watch out for those who deceive the hearts of the naïve by smooth talk and flattery. Who are the naïve? Those who show a lack of wisdom or judgment. Paul goes on to state that he wants them to be wise as to what is good and innocent as to what is evil (v. 19). As believers, we want to be innocent and pure, but also on our guard against those who would deceive us and lead us into heresy.

What does this look like practically for us? Without the Spirit at work in our heart and lives, we do not possess spiritual discernment or wisdom. Left to our own devices and opinions, we will not be able to guard our hearts from deception. By the grace of God, he has promised wisdom to those who seek it. When we are adopted into the family of God, we receive the Holy Spirit into our hearts. Through prayer and communication with him, we can know and discern the will of God, and be "wise as to what is good."

To the only wise God be glory forevermore through Jesus Christ!

Jenny

Prayer: Thank you for not leaving us helpless! Without you, we can accomplish nothing and are sheep, easily led astray. With your Spirit, we can know you, love you, praise you, and obey you. Lord, give us the strength to reject evil and be wise as to what is good. Amen.

Psalm of the Day: 22.12-19

Property Rights

Daily Reading: Deuteronomy 18-19

> You shall not move your neighbor's landmark, which the men of old have set... in the land that the Lord your God is giving you to possess. (Deuteronomy 19.14)

Devotional Thought: I'm sorry, but I had to laugh several weeks ago when I read the following headline: "Dreamers Threaten to Leave the U.S. if DACA Is Not Preserved." Um... Isn't that what they would do anyway?

The conversation around this issue is a shame, actually. But, what is right when it comes to immigration, to refugees, to undocumented aliens? There are no easy answers.

As Christians, we must respond with compassion to the alien and exile, but we also recognize the need to protect the safety and property of U.S citizens. God showed that he was a proponent of immigration when he delivered the children of Israel out of Egypt and placed them in the Promised Land. But, he also showed the importance of having boundaries and borders. God was very careful about preserving property rights: "You shall not move your neighbor's landmark..."

God defined the borders of Israel. God carefully outlined how property was to be preserved in families and 'states' (tribes). Borders were to be recognized and preserved. In the New Testament, people kept property ownership and sold their lands as they saw fit to voluntarily help their brothers and sisters in the church. That doesn't sound like a borderless society to me.

But, God also instructs us to receive and protect the alien among us, giving them opportunity to become a part of the culture of freedom and safety. These vulnerable souls are not political pawns, but people made in the image of God. How can you use your property to give them opportunity?

Prayer: Lord, thank you for giving us a free and prosperous nation. Help us to preserve and protect it while opening its blessings up to others. Amen.

Psalm of the Day: 22.20-24

What Sins Are You Talking About?
Daily Reading: Deuteronomy 20-21

And if a man has committed a crime punishable by death and he is put to death, and you hang him on a tree, his body shall not remain all night on the tree, but you shall bury him the same day, for a hanged man is cursed by God. You shall not defile your land that the Lord your God is giving you for an inheritance. (Deuteronomy 21.22-23)

Devotional Thought: Have you ever had someone hold a grudge against you? Or, have you ever had someone who professes to forgive you but who keeps bringing up the offense? That's not fun, is it? God is not like that. When it comes to our offenses, his desire is to remove them completely from his memory. We are reminded of that in today's scripture which is quoted in the New Testament: "Christ redeemed us from the curse of the law by becoming a curse for us—for it is written, 'Cursed is everyone who is hanged on a tree'" (Galatians 3.13).

The focus of the law in Deuteronomy was to prevent the land from becoming cursed by leaving a hanged man on a tree overnight. The memory of that sin was to be wiped away from sight. The focus of the New Testament is that Jesus, who became a curse for us, wipes away even the memory of sin. God remembers our sins no more (Hebrews 8.12).

There may be people who will not forgive you. You may feel that you can't even forgive yourself. But, aren't you glad that Jesus became a curse for you, taking away your sin to bury it in "the depths of the sea", to remove it from you "as far as the east is from the west"? I love the words of that old gospel chorus: "What sins are you talking about? I don't remember them anymore."

Amen!

Prayer: Thank you, Jesus, that you became a curse for me and in so doing you have removed my sins and cleansed me from all unrighteousness. Now, O Lord, help me to live a life worthy of your sacrifice. Amen.

Psalm of the Day: 22.25-31

How Did the Obvious Become Ambiguous?
Daily Reading: Deuteronomy 22

A woman shall not wear a man's garment, nor shall a man put on a woman's cloak, for whoever does these things is an abomination to the Lord your God. (Deuteronomy 22.5)

Devotional Thought: In recent years, Purdue University in Lafayette, Indiana, issued a writing guide which instructed students to avoid using words with 'man' in them. These words, according to the university guide, are potentially sexist and biased. I had to laugh that it was actually suggested that instead of using 'man-made', the word 'manufactured' should be used. And, 'humanity' should be substituted for 'mankind.' Umm, am I missing something here?

And then there are women's groups who are beginning to resent the inclusion of transgendered women in their 'cause' because they do not have the same physical makeup and have not experienced the same limitations.

Makes you wonder how many worms are in that can we've opened up, doesn't it?

So, what does that have to do with today's scripture? God's Word says that "a woman shall not wear a man's garment, nor shall a man put on a woman's cloak." Seems straightforward enough, until you begin to realize that male and female garments are culturally, not biblically, defined. So, there must be a principle behind this prohibition. What is it?

It's not about women wearing pants or men wearing skirts (kilts or robes), but rather it is about trying to appear as the opposite sex in order to enter into forbidden sexual relationships. Today's culture has focused on gender identity in ways that are both healthy (equality and compassion), and unhealthy (fluidity and confusion). God's Word simply identifies male and female by their sexual characteristics. How did the obvious become so ambiguous?

Prayer: Lord, in this world of confusion, half-truths, and propaganda, help us to turn to your Word for our guiding principles. In all things, may we act in love. Amen.

Psalm of the Day: 23.1-6

Take a Risk. They're Worth It!

Daily Reading: Deuteronomy 23-24

> *You shall not give up to his master a slave who has escaped from his master to you. He shall dwell with you, in your midst, in the place that he shall choose within one of your towns, wherever it suits him. You shall not wrong him.* (Deuteronomy 23.15-16)

Devotional Thought: I love the story of the Apostle Paul's conversion in Acts 9. Having been a persecutor of the church - and an accomplice to murder! - Paul naturally brought terror to the hearts of early Christians who did not trust him. When he tried to join them in Jerusalem, they turned him away in fear. All but one man, that is. Barnabas became a sponsor for Paul and took him to the brothers, introducing him and reassuring them. Barnabas gave him a place in the church.

When I was saved as a teenager, the Nazarene Church in Pioneer, Ohio did the same for me. They took me in. I was a risk - not like Paul of course - but a risk in the sense that I might not stick with it, that all their efforts would be in vain, that my background would overcome my newly found spiritual life. Still, the folks at that little church opened their hearts and received me.

In today's scripture, God speaks of doing that for "a slave who has escaped from his master." Give him a place. Treat him right. Accept him as one of you. That is not only a social principle; it is a spiritual principle. When people get saved, when they escape their old master of sin and are freed from the grip of the devil, we are to take them in and give them a place with us! Just like Barnabas did for Paul. Just like Pioneer Nazarenes did for me.

Is it a risk? You bet. But, God says, "Take the risk. They're worth it!"

Prayer: Jesus, thank you that you took a risk on me. Help me to take a risk on others who are escaping their old master of sin and the devil. As you gave me a place, help me to give them a place in my heart, my life, and my church. Amen.

Psalm of the Day: 24.1-6

Don't Buy It!

Daily Reading: Deuteronomy 25-26

Remember what Amalek did to you on the way as you came out of Egypt. (Deuteronomy 25.17)

Devotional Thought: Have you ever been the target of a vindictive attack on your character? Have you ever been hurt deeply by another's cruelty or abuse? Have you ever fallen prey to a financial scam? Have you ever had your heart broken? If so, then you know the wisdom of what the Lord said to the Israelites through Moses: "Remember what Amalek did."

The story is told in Exodus 17. Unprovoked and with cruel intent, "Amalek came and fought with Israel" (Exodus 17.8). God had told them that he would "blot out the memory of Amalek from under heaven" (Exodus 17.14). Now, God told the Israelites to remember the abuse Amalek had inflicted upon them, in essence telling them to wipe out the evil regime. Why? Why not forgive and forget?

Implicit in the story of Amalek and Israel is the understanding that the evil regime had not changed, that their intention was still to do harm even after Israel initially defeated them. "The Lord will have war with Amalek from generation to generation" (Exodus 17.16).

Two things stand out:
* In our spiritual battles, we must not allow the enemy to co-exist in our lives. We must be done with the kingdom of darkness and with its control and power in our lives.
* Just as importantly, in our earthly relationships, we must recognize that some hurts go so deep, some intentions are so cruel (though hidden), some attitudes are so unchanged, that we *must not* forget them. To do so would endanger ourselves and others around us. Forgive? Of course! Forget? Of course not.

Amalek may have said, "But, we've changed." God, however, said, "Don't buy it. Do not let them threaten to undo you."

Prayer: Lord Jesus, thank you that you have forgiven my sins. Thank you that you also know how far you can trust me. Help me to be forgiving like you but not to open up myself and others to harm by trusting one that I should not trust. Amen.

Psalm of the Day: 24.7-10

And All the People Shall Say, "Amen!"
Daily Reading: Deuteronomy 27

> 'Cursed be anyone who does not confirm the words of this law by doing them.' And all the people shall say, 'Amen.' (Deuteronomy 27.26)

Devotional Thought: When the Children of Israel reached the Promised Land, they had a serious ritual to perform. The Levites led them in declaring behaviors they were to eschew in order to avoid living under the wrath of God.

Every verse in this second section starts with "Cursed be anyone who..." and concludes with what it was that the Israelites should avoid. It covers everything from sexual deviancy to murder to bribery. It then ends with the general "blanket" declaration, "Cursed be anyone who does not confirm the words of this law by doing them" (v. 26). The Israelites were to affirm their agreement with each statement with an "Amen." History shows that the Israelites didn't take these instructions too seriously.

We don't like to be told what to do any more than the Israelites did. Knowledge of sin has, historically, increased our sinning. Not just because our trespasses are made known through the Law, but also because we are rebellious and controlling in our flesh nature. In other words, we don't want anyone bossing us around, not even our Creator. This is our view of the commandments when we are not in Christ. But, when we come to know Christ, our eyes are opened to what was spiritually indiscernible to us before. The commandments that were death to us become life. Although we will always have to struggle with our flesh, may our attitudes be like that of the Apostle Paul in Romans 7.22, "I delight in the law of God, in my inner being."

And all the people shall say, "Amen!"

Jenny

Prayer: Lord, help us to remember to whom we belong. We are no longer slaves of sin. Sin is not our master. We are slaves to righteousness! You are our Master. Help us to love your commands and to find joy in obedience. Amen.

Psalm of the Day: 25.1-7

But Wait! There's More!

Daily Reading: Deuteronomy 28

And the Lord will make you abound in prosperity... (Deuteronomy 28.11)

Devotional Thought: Have you seen those commercials on TV that give an unbelievable offer if you order now? Many times, when you think the commercial is over, the narrator returns and says, "But wait! There's more!"

God had a "But wait! There's more!" in Deuteronomy 28. He had promised his people blessings for obedience: political leadership, civil prosperity, and military might could all be theirs if only they would make the Lord their God. But, there was more than prosperity for them. There was abundance: I "will make you abound in prosperity!" Abound means to have more than you need, to have something left over at the end. When the people of God come to the end, there is yet more!

When the end comes for the people of God, when houses and lands, power and prestige, fame and fortune fade away, there is still something remaining for those who obey God. Life may bring us blessings and enjoyment. But, there comes a time when "desire fails, because man is going to his eternal home, and the mourners go about the streets—[when] the silver cord is snapped, or the golden bowl is broken, or the pitcher is shattered at the fountain, or the wheel broken at the cistern, and the dust returns to the earth as it was, and the spirit returns to God who gave it" (Ecclesiastes 12.5-7). Then, child of God, we will hear our Savior say, "But wait! There's more!"

Prayer: Lord, thank you for the blessings of this life: health and home, family and friends, and so much more! But, Lord, we hold on to those things loosely. There is something more. Thank you for the promise of abundance forever and ever! Amen.

Psalm of the Day: 25.8-13

Knowns and Unknowns

Daily Reading: Deuteronomy 29-30

The secret things belong to the Lord our God, but the things that are revealed belong to us and to our children forever, that we may do all the words of this law. (Deuteronomy 29.29)

Devotional Thought: Donald Rumsfeld, United States Secretary of Defense, once famously said, "There are known knowns. These are things we know that we know. There are known unknowns. That is to say, there are things that we know we don't know. But there are also unknown unknowns. There are things we don't know we don't know."

The question the Bible poses is a lot simpler: "What are we *doing* with the things that are revealed, the things that we know?"

The secret things belong to God. There are some things that we simply don't know. We can't do anything about these things, except seek to learn what they are. The quest for knowledge is a noble thing. The quest for wisdom, nobler still.

The things that are revealed belong to us. All truth is God's. As such, if we are to know the truth, it is in a sense *revealed* to us - in God's character and creation. And, when we know it, we own it. I can't be held accountable for things I don't know, but responsibility for the things I do know belongs to me. In the Garden of Eden, God made his truth known - "You may eat..." and "You may not eat..." The important thing was what Adam and Eve *did* with this revealed truth.

That we may do all the words of this law. God reveals his Word to us so that we can do it. And, his Word is not burdensome, but rather a delight and blessing for us, that we may overcome the burdens of life (1 John 5.3-4).

Prayer: Thank you, Father, that you have given us your Word, revealing your will and your way to us. Help us to walk in accordance with your truth and thereby live a blessed and overcoming life. Amen.

Psalm of the Day: 25.14-22

Leadership Changes
Daily Reading: Deuteronomy 31

The Lord your God himself will go over before you. (Deuteronomy 31.3a)

Devotional Thought: In America, every four years we have an election to determine who will be the leader of our nation. At the most, we have a leader for 8 years. Leadership changes. I just met with the nominating committee of our church last night. We nominated new leaders for the coming business year - to be elected by the congregation in several weeks. Leadership changes. In the story of God's people, the time approached for Moses to go to his eternal reward. Joshua was named as his successor. Leadership changes.

In the midst of changing leadership, there is a constant for the people of God. "The Lord your God himself will go over before you." Israel needed that assurance. That entire generation had known no other leader but Moses. Now, as they were ready to cross over into the Promised Land, they were about to lose that beloved (and beleaguered!) leader. Another man - Joshua - would lead them. The same giants that were in the land 38 years prior were still there. The same challenges. The same unknowns. But leadership changes. The good news? "The Lord your God himself will go over before you."

What reassuring words for the people of God! Whether in our nation, our churches, or our families, we know that with the passing of one era to another, there remains one constant - the Lord God himself! So, when you face the inevitable changes in leadership, remember the words of Jesus, "Fear not, little flock, for it is your Father's good pleasure to give you the kingdom" (Luke 12.32).

Prayer: Thank you, Father, for your unchanging leadership in my life. Others will come and go, but you remain constant forever. Help me to rest in your faithfulness. Amen.

Psalm of the Day: 26.1-8

God's Portion and Heritage
Daily Reading: Deuteronomy 32

> *But the Lord's portion is his people, Jacob his allotted heritage. He found him in a desert land, and in the howling waste of the wilderness; he encircled him, he cared for him, he kept him as the apple of his eye.* (Deuteronomy 32.9-10)

Devotional Thought: As Moses said goodbye to his flock, he reminded them of how God had taken care of his people. God - who owns everything and needs nothing - has been given a portion, an allotted heritage... his people. That is amazing!

What does it mean that we are God's portion and heritage?

- *God finds us.* God found Israel in the wasteland of Egypt. He went searching for them. We are in the wasteland of sin. It wasn't that way in the beginning. God made humanity for himself - to enter into a unique bond of friendship with us. But, mankind wandered away. We have been separated from God. He sent Jesus to reestablish that original relationship. And, he sends the Holy Spirit to us, seeking his lost sheep.
- *God surrounds us.* When God found Israel, he encircled them with his protection. He stood as a wall of fire and a column of smoke between Israel and her enemies. In the same way, God shelters us today. "Underneath are the everlasting arms" (Deuteronomy 33.27).
- *God cares for us.* In the wilderness, Israel needed food and water. God provided it. Their shoes did not wear out and they had a leader to guide them in uncertain times. God provides our needs today: "And my God will supply every need of yours according to his riches in glory in Christ Jesus" (Philippians 4.19).
- *God keeps us.* When Israel lost their way, God called them back. He continually sent them prophets and leaders to remind them, to challenge them to be faithful. He gave them assurances of his love. He keeps us today. If we fix our eyes on Jesus, we will find that he is faithful to us. Nothing can separate us from his love!

Prayer: Thank you, Lord, that I am your treasured portion, that you consider me as your allotted inheritance. I humbly and gladly run into your arms and receive your love and grace. Amen.

Psalm of the Day: 26.9-12

Where Do You Stay?
Daily Reading: Deuteronomy 33-34

The eternal God is your dwelling place, and underneath are the everlasting arms. (Deuteronomy 33.27a)

Devotional Thought: Thirty-five years ago, when I moved to North Carolina, I had to undergo language therapy! I struggled with the heavy accent (and I'm sure they struggled with mine!), but I also did not get the local colloquialisms. One such phrase was the question, "Where do you stay?" I didn't know that the questioner was asking me, "Where do you live?"

I like the question, though. Where do you stay?

God considers us as his special heritage (Deuteronomy 32.9). We are the apple of his eye! Also, God is our dwelling place. The Bible says that "In him we live and move and have our being" (Acts 17.28). I like that. Living in him is not a static condition, but in him we live and move. No matter where we go, we find that we are living in Christ. Jesus said that he is with us to the very end of the age. The Psalmist marveled, "Where shall I flee from your presence? If I ascend to heaven, you are there! If I make my bed in Sheol, you are there! If I take the wings of the morning and dwell in the uttermost parts of the sea, even there your hand shall lead me, and your right hand shall hold me" (Psalm 139.7-10).

So, where do you stay? As you go through this day, remember that you stay with Jesus for "underneath are the everlasting arms!"

"Fear not, I am with thee, O be not dismayed, For I am thy God, and will still give thee aid; I'll strengthen thee, help thee, and cause thee to stand, Upheld by My righteous, omnipotent hand." (John Rippon)

Prayer: Lord, thank you that I live and move and have my being in you. Help me, to stay right there, upheld by your everlasting arms. Amen.

Psalm of the Day: 27.1-6

Note: If this is not a leap year, read tomorrow's scripture, devotion, prayer and Psalm along with today's...

How to Proclaim Jesus
Daily Reading: 1 Thessalonians 1-2

Our gospel came to you not only in word, but also in power and in the Holy Spirit and with full conviction. You know what kind of men we proved to be among you for your sake. (1 Thessalonians 1.5)

Devotional Thought: I am so thankful that my spiritually formative years were shaped by Rev. Nelson Perdue, a powerful, spirit-filled, and passionate preacher. His example has formed my conception of ministry from that day until this. He proclaimed the gospel in the manner of the Apostle Paul:

- *Not only in word.* It is purported that St. Francis of Assisi said, "Preach the gospel, and if necessary, use words." I understand the sentiment of that, but it really is not biblical. When St. Paul of the Bible said, "It pleased God through the folly of what we preach to save those who believe," he was speaking of preaching the Word. Paul preached the Word. We must speak and bear witness to Jesus.
- *But also in power.* But, Paul didn't depend on his words alone. He knew that he needed power. He preached in power. I need power to preach, also. And, you need power to be his witness.
- *In the Holy Spirit.* Where does that power come from? Jesus said, "You will receive power when the Holy Spirit comes on you" (Acts 1.8). Jesus urged his disciples to receive the Spirit (John 20.22). We are to ask for the Spirit (Luke 11.13). We have not, because we ask not (James 4.2)!
- *With full conviction.* Paul preached with conviction because he was convinced! He had met Jesus on the road to Damascus. He really met him. Jesus changed his life. Like the disciples before him, he was so convinced of the truth of Jesus' resurrection, that he staked his life on it. That's how you and I need to testify, too. We do that when we are with him, really with him.

Prayer: Father, help me to discern the difference between engaging the world versus embracing the world. Help me to surround myself with Christian influence and values, and from that foundation to be salt and light. Amen.

Psalm of the Day: 27.7-10

*Note: If this is not a leap year, read today's entry
along with yesterday's or tomorrow's*

Back-Handed Compliment
Daily Reading: 1 Thessalonians 3-4

> *Now concerning brotherly love you have no need for anyone to write to
> you, for you yourselves have been taught by God to love one another,
> for that indeed is what you are doing to all the brothers throughout
> Macedonia. But we urge you, brothers, to do this more and more.*
> (1 Thessalonians 4.9-10)

Devotional Thought: Have you ever been commended for doing something
well and then heard something like, "Now, go out and do even better!" I
call those types of things "back-handed compliments." They feel good, but
maybe there's a little sting in them, too.

Paul's letter to the Thessalonians had a "back-handed compliment." After
commending them for loving one another, he urges them to "do this more
and more." It is nice to be encouraged by other believers, especially those
"spiritual giants" in your life whom you deeply admire and respect. But, rarely
does it stop with a compliment, allowing you to pat yourself on the back in
self-pride. These words of encouragement are meant to help us grow, and
who has ever grown after feeling as though they have perfected something
in their own strength? There will always be areas for growth in our Christian
lives, and it is our true friends who will lovingly point out both the strengths
and the weaknesses.

When confronted with the conviction that we should address the splinter in
our brother or sister's eye, let us first remember to pray over the plank in our
own eye. Then, after repenting of our own sin, we can follow Paul's lead. He
did not simply tell the young Christians of the early church what they should
not be doing, he also encouraged them in love. Like Paul, we should stand
firm for the truth in love, and be receptive when our brothers and sisters do
the same.

Jenny

Prayer: Help us, Lord, because we are creatures who are quick to think
the best of ourselves and the worst of others. Give us the grace to accept
admonition, and the love to give encouragement to others - to spur them on
to good works. Amen.

Psalm of the Day: 27.11-14

What Can I Do?
Daily Reading: 1 Thessalonians 5

> And we urge you, brothers, admonish the idle, encourage the fainthearted, help the weak, be patient with them all. See that no one repays anyone evil for evil, but always seek to do good to one another and to everyone. (1 Thessalonians 5.14-15)

Devotional Thought: We often wonder, "What can I do for my brother or sister? I'm not smart enough. I don't know the Bible. I'm not a very strong Christian myself. How can I help them?" We feel inadequate. Paul told the Thessalonians some things they could do. We can do these things, too, no matter where we are on our spiritual journey:

- *Admonish the idle.* Are you busy in the work of the Lord? We admonish by example: There's nothing more admonishing than to see someone else doing what you ought to be doing! We admonish by extension: Ask someone to help you with what you are doing! No one should be idle in the Lord's house!
- *Encourage the fainthearted.* Times of discouragement come to all of us. When you see somebody feeling faint, it's not the time to say, buck up! We need to let them know that they are not abnormal and that we have been there, too. Kindness will go a long way toward encouraging the fainthearted.
- *Help the weak.* When somebody is doing a work for the Lord, their 'arms' may grow weary as did Moses' arms when he stood above the battle. Aaron and Hur had to hold up his arms. We can help those who are weak due to sickness or overwork or taking on more than they can handle alone.
- *Be patient with all.* We are not to judge, but to love. We do not know the story behind everyone's life. Patience is a fruit of the Spirit. Let the Lord do his work!
- *Seek to do good and not evil.* Jesus said it this way: "Do unto others as you would have them do unto you." Are you working for the good of - laboring in prayer for - your brothers and sisters?

Prayer: Lord, help me to take the time to see my brother and sister in need. And then, give me the grace to show them grace as you have shown me. Amen.

Psalm of the Day: 28.1-5

What God Does

Daily Reading: 2 Thessalonians 1-2

> *God chose you as the firstfruits to be saved, through sanctification by the Spirit and belief in the truth. To this he called you through our gospel.* (2 Thessalonians 2.13b-14a)

Devotional Thought: Recently, I went on a shopping expedition with my son-in-law, Evan. He has an eBay business in which he buys and resells top of the line men's clothing. It was fun watching him choose what to buy. He knew what he wanted, and before long our cart was filled to overflowing - to the point that we even had to get another cart!

God knows what he wants, too, and we have been purchased by God - not for resale, but for inclusion in the family of God. In our verses in 2 Thessalonians, Paul writes how God...

- *Selects.* The firstfruits are considered as the best that there is, and they are precious to God. We are firstfruits in God's eyes. It doesn't take him long to see and to say, "That's the one I want..." And, he does that to each one of us. We are chosen by God.
- *Saves.* Having been chosen, God then delivers us from sin. He redeems the souls of men and women with a price. Our salvation cost the blood of God's Son. Aren't you glad that Jesus shed his own blood in order to save us?
- *Sanctifies.* God has a purpose for each one of you. While my son-in-law's purchases provide a living for his family, God's purchase provides a family for us to live in. We are set apart to be his chosen possession and his instrument of salvation in a world of darkness and despair.
- *Sends.* Through his Spirit and the invitation of his family, God is calling people with the good news. God is proactive! Let us be the voice of God to call the lost to him!

Prayer: Thank you, Lord, that you have selected me in your love, saved me through the blood, and sanctified me for your purpose. Now, O Lord, send me to do your will and proclaim your name among the lost! Amen.

Psalm of the Day: 28.6-9

How to Pray for Leaders
Daily Reading: 2 Thessalonians 3

> *Pray for us, that the word of the Lord may speed ahead and be honored, as happened among you, and that we may be delivered from wicked and evil men. For not all have faith.* (2 Thessalonians 3.1-2)

Devotional Thought: Sometimes, I forget to ask for help. Paul didn't forget to ask for help. And he asked not only God, but also asked others. He asked churches to help him complete his mission. He asked the Corinthians to help him through their prayers. That's what he asked the Thessalonians, too: "Pray for us!"

We, too, can help our pastor and leaders by praying that...
- the word of the Lord may be hastened. Paul realized he was operating within a limited time. He anticipated the soon-coming return of the Lord. Even if Christ delayed his coming, Paul knew that his personal time to work was limited. He wanted to get the word out to as many as possible as quickly as possible.
- the word of the Lord may be honored. It's one thing to get the word out. It's something else for it to accomplish its purpose. For that to happen, individuals must hear it and respond to it. It will not be heard if it is held in disrepute. We should live our lives to bring honor to the Word of God!
- the word of the Lord may be heeded. Paul reminded the Thessalonians that they heeded the word of God and he encouraged them to pray that others would too.
- the people of the Lord may be helped. Paul was acquainted with persecution, imprisonment, and other drastic measures intended to silence him. Paul wanted to have freedom to proclaim the gospel. He needed to be delivered from wicked and evil people.

Pray for your pastor and spiritual leaders!

Prayer: Lord, I pray for my pastor and other preachers and teachers of the gospel. May your Word get out quickly, be accepted mentally, and be obeyed faithfully. May you keep these messengers safe and free to proclaim your Word. Amen.

Psalm of the Day: 29.1-6

Just As I Was, So Will I Be

Daily Reading: Joshua 1-2

Just as I was with Moses, so I will be with you. (Joshua 1.5)

Devotional Thought: The people of Israel had followed Moses for 40 years. At times they followed gladly. At other times they followed reluctantly. Moses had brought them out of slavery and delivered them to the very threshold of the Promised Land. But now, Moses was dead. No matter what they had thought of him before, each one had to admit that his leadership would be missed, bringing fear and anxiety into their hearts. They needed a word of assurance from God: "Just as I was with Moses, so I will be with you."

Joshua needed to hear it. It's hard to follow an iconic leader. I've had to do it a few times myself. The shadow of a great man stretches long into the future. There are times when you wonder if you could ever measure up. And, there are times when the people let you know that you don't! The assurance of God's presence and blessing is critical to new leadership.

The people needed to hear it, too. Not only did they need to know that God was leading Joshua as he had led Moses, they needed to know that God was with *them*! I remember the despair felt by many in a particular congregation. The founding and much-loved pastor had died. Some of them didn't know if they could make it without him. They needed to know that God was with them, not just their leader.

Subsequent generations need to hear it. Joshua wouldn't be there forever, either. God is the only constant we can count on. Leaders come and leaders go, but the Lord remains forever. Let us fix our eyes on Jesus, the author and finisher of our faith!

Prayer: Thank you, Lord, for the leaders that you have given your church across the centuries. Help us to know that just as you were with them, so you are with us. You will never leave us or forsake us. Amen!

Psalm of the Day: 29.7-11

Set Out
Daily Reading: Joshua 3-4

> *As soon as you see the ark of the covenant of the Lord your God being carried by the Levitical priests, then you shall set out from your place and follow it.* (Joshua 3.3)

Devotional Thought: Following God is not easy. There are times when faith pushes us to do things that our minds resist. The Israelites experienced that as they prepared to pass over the Jordan River and enter into the Promised Land. God had said, "This is the way. Walk in it."

And so they set out...
- The priests set out with *confidence*. The waters remained high - at flood stage! - until the moment the priests got their feet wet. Going down to the water's edge, with thousands of eyes looking on, took confidence! Where is God calling you to set your feet?
- The people set out by the *influence* of their leaders. The waters of the Jordan had dried up, but how long would that be the case? Do these leaders really know what they are doing? When leaders are Spirit-filled and God-ordained, we can follow their influence.
- The men of war from the eastern tribes set out at their *expense*. Earlier, God had given these tribes permission to stay on the east side of the Jordan. But, they had to cross over and fight alongside their brothers. They did so at great personal risk and expense. Following God costs us everything!
- Twelve men set out in *obedience*. After everybody had gotten through the waters, one man from each tribe found himself back in the middle of the dry riverbed to obtain stones for a monument. They followed God obediently, even when others were not required to do so. Our obedience is a matter between us and God!

Have you set out to follow God?

Prayer: Thank you, Lord, that you lead me through the waters of life. Lord, I will not draw back in fear, doubt your leadership, deny the cost, or demand equal treatment. Instead, I am determined to follow you. Amen.

Psalm of the Day: 30.1-5

Shout!

Daily Reading: Joshua 5-6

So the people shouted, and the trumpets were blown. As soon as the people heard the sound of the trumpet, the people shouted a great shout, and the wall fell down flat, so that the people went up into the city, every man straight before him, and they captured the city.
(Joshua 6.20)

Devotional Thought: "Sometimes I feel like shouting." "Then shout!"

I've had that conversation with people before. We're so reserved in our worship. That's OK, but it's also OK to shout when the Spirit is moving and victory is coming. God instructed the Israelites to shout before the wall of Jericho. They did, and the wall of the city "fell down flat." God gave a great victory. What were these shouts?

There was the shout of *expectation*. In silence, Israel marched around the city once per day for six days and then seven times on the seventh day. They obeyed God completely. When it was time to raise their voices, when it was time to shout, they did so with confidence, expecting God to do what he said. In our own lives, there are times when the shouts we feel and the amens we raise are not in response to God's blessing, but in anticipation of his faithfulness!

There was the trumpet 'shout' of *exertion*. Standing on God's faithfulness, the Israelites sounded the trumpet's battle call. It was time to get the job done, to exert their best efforts. Have you ever watched a tennis match? Or how about a weightlifter dead lifting? Often the serve is made, or the weight is raised, with a loud grunt or shout. God is calling us to battle. Let us lift a great shout to arms!

There was the shout of *exaltation*. In the midst of the great victory, the people exalted God with a shout of triumph. God was on the move, and they joined their voices together, affirming that they were following in close behind their Leader.

God gave a great victory that day. I feel like shouting!

Prayer: Lord, we do not want shouting for shouting's sake. Our desire is not to make noise. Rather, Lord, we want to shout as your Spirit moves - shout in expectation, for exertion, and in exaltation. Give us a great victory, O God! Amen.

Psalm of the Day: 30.6-12

Root Out the Sin
Daily Reading: Joshua 7

The Lord said to Joshua, "Get up! Why have you fallen on your face? Israel has sinned; they have transgressed my covenant that I commanded them; they have taken some of the devoted things; they have stolen and lied and put them among their own belongings. (Joshua 7.10-11)

Devotional Thought: As Israel conquered her enemies, they were sometimes commanded to take the spoils of war, and sometimes were commanded to devote everything to the Lord, such as at Jericho. But Achan, of the tribe of Judah, had seen some of the devoted things in Jericho, and decided to take them for himself.

Though the other Israelites were not aware of Achan's sin and thievery, they had a big problem. Previously, the Lord had been giving them unlikely victories, but when they went up to Ai, a relatively small town, the Israelites were defeated in battle. "And the hearts of the people melted and became as water" (v. 5). Their leader, Joshua, fell on his face before the Lord, tearing his clothes in grief. The Lord reprimanded him, saying, "Get up! Why have you fallen on your face? Israel has sinned... they have taken some of the devoted things... therefore the people of Israel cannot stand before their enemies" (vv. 10-12). Joshua would now be forced to root out the sin that had put the whole nation of Israel at risk.

There is no sin that affects us in isolation, but the consequences and effects ripple out to touch our families, friends, and most importantly, our relationship with our Creator. But there is hope! Just as the Lord put to death the root of sin in Israel, he puts to death the root of sin in our own hearts when we come to him in repentance.

Jenny

Prayer: Lord, we know that sometimes we suffer because of the brokenness of the world around us. We also acknowledge that our own sin causes suffering as well. Please protect us from the temptations that surround us; give us your perspective of sin, that it would be repugnant to us, that we would find our delight in you instead. Amen.

Psalm of the Day: 31.1-8

Don't Go It Alone

Daily Reading: Joshua 8

So Joshua and all the fighting men arose to go up to Ai. (Joshua 8.3a)

Devotional Thought: Having suffered an unexpected and thorough defeat in battle at Ai, Joshua and his army were devastated. Had God left them? What had gone wrong? Could they ever 'win' again? Yes, they could, and so can we.

At the first battle of Ai, they took victory for granted. Underestimating their enemy, they took just a few thousand soldiers: "Do not make the whole people toil up there" (Joshua 7.3). Never underestimate the challenge, the temptation, or your enemy! The next time they went up, Joshua took 30,000 of his best fighting men. They gave their best. They prevailed in battle.

After the defeat at Ai, Joshua and the leaders searched their hearts, sought the Lord, and cleansed the sin out of their camp. The reason for the defeat at Ai was that Achan, a soldier in the victory at Jericho, harbored devoted things. The Israelites had to deal with that issue before they were fit for battle. When they did, God gave them victory.

Then, Joshua made a plan. Taking nothing for granted, their strategy even included listening to the Lord in the midst of the battle! Too often, I hear things like, "Whatever will be will be." No, whatever we work at with all our heart and soul, whatever we plan for, dream for, and pray for - those things will end in victory! Good plans include God!

Finally, we see that the army worked together. Two divisions cooperated in conquest. Too often, we neglect the partnerships that God provides us, and we suffer for it. If we want to defeat sin or accomplish a worthy goal in the Kingdom, we need to lean on our brothers and sisters. Don't go it alone!

Prayer: And now, Lord, look upon their threats and upon my fears and excuses, and grant that I may continue to speak your word with all boldness. Amen.

Psalm of the Day: 31.9-13

Causing a Stir
Daily Reading: Joshua 9

Then all the congregation murmured against the leaders. (Joshua 9.18b)

Devotional Thought: In Joshua 9, the enemies of God's people - the Gibeonites - became workers in the house of God! What a great turnaround. We need more turnarounds like that.

The Gibeonites entered into the covenant family under less than ideal circumstances - they actually lied! I am reminded of what I heard one preacher say, "You have to expect sinners to sin. That's what they are!" And, true to form, the Gibeonites dealt in the only diplomacy they knew - desperation and deception. But, when they followed through on their plan, they got more than they bargained for! God, in his grace, made them an integral part of the worshiping community. He gave them important jobs in the temple - providing the water and the wood for the altar.

Not everything went smoothly, of course. Does it ever? The entry of the Gibeonites into the covenant family caused quite a stir among the 'thoroughbreds'. "The congregation murmured against the leaders." Whenever new people come into an existing social structure, there is conflict and tension. But, Joshua and the leaders recognized a higher value than the comfort of the people. They saw the heart of God in reaching a people lost in darkness. Sometimes, a leader has to hold fast in the face of politically expedient winds.

I am reminded of how Jesus himself caused a stir when he included tax collectors and sinners in his kingdom and when he called uneducated fishermen to follow him. The 'thoroughbreds' of his day didn't much like it either.

Are you causing a stir?

Prayer: Jesus, help me to see that your Kingdom is bigger than my vision. You desire to save the lost of all stripes. You are building your church from the least likely raw materials. Help me to cause a stir by reaching out to those you died to save. Amen.

Psalm of the Day: 31.14-18

Do-Nots

Daily Reading: Joshua 10

Come up to me and help me, and let us strike Gibeon. For it has made peace with Joshua and with the people of Israel. (Joshua 10.4)

Devotional Thought: Yesterday, we saw how the Gibeonites made an alliance with the people of God, becoming an important part in the worshiping community. This threatened nearby kings who took up arms against them: "Let us strike Gibeon."

Some "Do-Nots" followed:

- *Do not relax.* Under assault, the Gibeonites turned to their new allies, sending word, "Do not relax your hand from your servants" (v. 6). In other words, "We've cast our lot with you. Don't abandon us now!" The Israelites honored the covenant that they had made, and protected their weak and vulnerable sisters and brothers. We need to be aware of the fact that Satan will attack new Christians to try to defeat them at the outset. And, they may struggle and stumble spiritually. We must not "relax our hand from" these new followers of God, but must come to their defense, proactively seeking and surrounding them.
- *Do not be afraid.* God told Joshua not to fear these enemies who would be unable to stand against Israel's army (v. 8). I am reminded of the assurance from God in 1 John 4.4: "Little children, you are from God and have overcome them, for he who is in you is greater than he who is in the world." When we come to the aid of our vulnerable sisters and brothers, we need to remember that God's got this!
- *Do not stop.* Joshua led his army on an all-night march. At great personal effort and cost, the Israelites pursued their enemies until they were destroyed. That is how we must be when we fight sin - in ourselves and in our fellow believers. We cannot stop until final victory is won!

Prayer: Lord, thank you for the promise of your help in our fight against sin. Grant that I may be faithful in offering my help to others who are struggling and stumbling. Amen.

Psalm of the Day: 31.19-24

Trials, Toil, and Time
Daily Reading: Joshua 11-12

In all, thirty-one kings. (Joshua 12.24)

Devotional Thought: I have reached a point in life when I have a tendency to look back over the victories God has given. It reminds me of the grace, power, and faithfulness of God. And, it gives me opportunity to express gratitude, praise, and fealty to him.

It was that way with the Israelites. They reviewed what God had done for them, how God had given them victory over thirty-one kings! But, it wasn't automatic: God worked through their...

- *Trials.* The Israelites did not arrive at their destination carried on beds of ease along paths of peace. There were scares and setbacks, defeats and disappointments. But, in every one of those trials, they learned of God's gracious work on their behalf. Their experience foreshadowed the New Testament proclamation, God works in all things for the good of those who love him (Romans 8.28).
- *Toil.* While God was working for their good, every one of those thirty-one victories required effort on their part as well. Plans had to be made, provisions gathered, risks taken, and battles fought. They were partners with God and with one another. Working partners. He still accomplishes his purpose and advances his Kingdom through us.
- *Time.* Reading Joshua, we can get the mistaken notion that it all happened quickly. It actually took over fifteen years for the kingdom to be established. As the old saying goes, "Rome wasn't built in a day." We need to be patient. Jesus used the analogy of a seed when he described the Kingdom. Seeds take time to germinate, to sprout and to grow.

Victory will cost us trials, toil, and time. Be steadfast.

Prayer: Thank you, Lord, for every one of the victories that you give me. Help me to endure trials, work hard, and be patient as you establish your Kingdom in my life, in my home, and in my church. Amen.

Psalm of the Day: 32.1-7

How Jesus Knows You
Daily Reading: John 1

How do you know me? (John 1.48)

Devotional Thought: As John Stuart Mill said, "He who knows only his own side of the case, knows little of that." I think that was Nathanael's problem. He could see things only from his perspective. When Nathanael met Jesus, he was shocked that Jesus already knew him. Jesus describe him as a true Israelite, one without deceit. I can almost picture Nathanael spinning around: "How do you know me?" I wonder if Nathanael was feeling somewhat threatened by Jesus' knowledge of him.

How about you? Do you wonder how Jesus knows you? Jesus knows us by...
- *Observation.* There is nothing hidden from God's sight. Nothing. Jesus knows us not only on the outside, but also on the inside: "in whom there is no deceit..." (v. 47). He knows our strengths and struggles, our joys and sorrows. He sees it all.
- *Creation.* "Through him all things were made..." (v. 3). We are not accidents in a cosmic game of chance. He designed us to work a certain way. When things get off-kilter, he knows why.
- *Identification.* "The Word became flesh and dwelled among us..." (v. 14). He came to be with us. He came to be us. Our experiences are not foreign to him, for he is like us in all things, except without sin.

Jesus knows us and still he loves us! May he find in each one of us "an Israelite indeed, in whom there is no deceit!"

Prayer: Lord, thank you that you know us and still you love us. Help me, O Lord, to know you and become more and more like you. Amen.

Psalm of the Day: 32.8-11

A Whip of Cords

Daily Reading: John 2

Making a whip of cords, he drove them all out of the temple. (John 2.15)

Devotional Thought: On two occasions in Jesus' ministry he had to get tough with people in the temple. They had transformed the temple into a place of profits rather than a house of prayer. He was not gentle in his approach.

As I read the story of Jesus clearing the temple, I couldn't help but think of how sometimes we need to get tough on ourselves. We are, after all, the temple of the Holy Spirit. If there are elements in us that detract from the purpose of God, and subtract from the praise of God, then we need to deal harshly with them, just as Jesus dealt harshly with those who profaned the temple in his day:

- Do we display attitudes that are not conducive to the praise of the Lord? We need to make a whip of cords and drive those attitudes - and the display of them - out of our lives!
- Do the words we say enhance or detract from our ability to pray? The Bible says that salt water and fresh water should not come forth from the same spring (James 2.11). The words we speak will condemn us or acquit us, for they show what's on the inside (Matthew 12.37). Let's clean up the inside with a whip of cords to drive all profanity, gossip, and discouraging words from our mouths.
- What about our habits and hobbies? Are those things drawing us closer to God or taking us further away from him? We must deal decisively with those things. Make a whip of cords and drive out all offending actions!

The Apostle Paul said he 'beat his body' to make sure he was living a disciplined life. Let's make a whip of cords to drive away everything that is not pleasing to Jesus!

Prayer: Jesus, you are so zealous for the temple of God! Help me to make sure that I am keeping this temple - my body, mind and soul - clean before you. Amen.

Psalm of the Day: 33.1-7

What We Know and See

Daily Reading: John 3

We speak of what we know, and bear witness to what we have seen.
(John 3.11)

Devotional Thought: I have a friend who until recently was childless. An amazing thing that I noticed about my friend was how freely he could give advice about raising children. He was an expert! Most people just took his expertise with a grain of salt. Then he and his wife began having children of their own. His wisdom suddenly was tested in the laboratory of life. His council changed drastically!

When Jesus spoke to Nicodemus, he told him, "We speak of what we know and bear witness to what we have seen." Jesus knew that advice given from a lack of education or experience was not all that reliable!

We have basically two sources for our knowledge. We speak of "what we know." We know something when we truly experience it. Jesus spoke of that experiential knowledge first, since it is the most important. If I want to speak authoritatively on the topic of Jesus, then I need to know him, to experience him as my Friend!

We also bear witness to what we have seen. This is a different form of knowledge. We 'see' things in the lives of other people either by witnessing them or reading about them. This form of witness is very important because it serves as a correcting influence on our experiences. Personal experiences are wonderful, but we need to test them against the combined experiences of God's people across the ages.

So, get out and testify! But do it from the basis of a personal experience with Jesus, informed by what you read in the Bible and what you see in the lives of others.

Prayer: Lord, help me to know you better and to be a better student of your Word. Then, help me to proclaim the wonderful news of God's love! Amen.

Psalm of the Day: 33.8-15

Upsetting the Apple Cart
Daily Reading: John 4

> *Jesus said to her, "Everyone who drinks of this water will be thirsty again, but whoever drinks of the water that I will give him will never be thirsty again. The water that I will give him will become in him a spring of water welling up to eternal life."* (John 4.13-14)

Devotional Thought: Jesus relished upsetting the apple cart - especially man-made rules meant to produce righteousness. That is why the religious leaders hated him. Jesus was upsetting all of their man-made rules. His actions at the well of Samaria really upset some apples!

For Jesus to stop and talk to a woman, especially a Samaritan woman, would have been unheard of and a serious social faux pas. The disciples, when they returned and saw him speaking to her, "marveled that he was talking with a woman" (v. 27), but at least they had the sense to refrain from questioning him. And not only was Jesus speaking to a woman, the woman he was speaking to was an adulteress and a five-time divorcee. The disciples were most likely concerned that Jesus was making a bad reputation for himself. But, Jesus knew exactly what he was doing.

Over and over Jesus upset man-made rules. Sinners from every walk of life, who had committed the most heinous sins, were welcomed to eat with him. He mingled with tax collectors. He called rough-around-the-edges fishermen to be his closest followers and then lowered himself to be a servant to them by washing their feet. He healed Jew and Gentile alike. He "violated" the Sabbath to feed his hungry disciples. For what reason did he do these things? Because he knows our need. "It is not the healthy who need a doctor, but the sick. I have not come to call the righteous, but sinners, to repentance" (Luke 5.31-32). Just like the Samaritan woman at the well, we come to Jesus stained with sin and desperate for the living water that only he can provide.

Jenny

Prayer: Thank you, Lord, for meeting us where we are. We are broken, sinful, and incapable of righteousness in our own strength and efforts. Thank you for sending your Son to enter into our brokenness, to love us, and to give his life as a ransom for many. Amen.

Psalm of the Day: 33.16-22

Journey of Growth and Holiness
Daily Reading: John 5

> *See, you are well! Sin no more, that nothing worse may happen to you.*
> (John 5.14)

Devotional Thought: I love the 'chance meeting' we read about in John 5. A man who is severely crippled "happened" to be in the right place at the right time. Then, Jesus just "happened" to pass by! With the presence of Jesus came healing. Later, Jesus found the man and started him on a journey of growth and holiness:

- *See.* Jesus had healed the man from a desperate situation. With that healing so fresh in his mind, it seemed unlikely that he would ever forget what Jesus had done for him. But, human nature being what it is, the wonder would begin to fade, so Jesus told him, "See." We, too, need to see what Jesus has done for us.
- *State.* This man heard the statement, "You are well." It was a testimony to his condition, brought about by the healing touch of Jesus. After we are saved, we, too, "are well." We have been brought from death to life, from darkness to light, from despair to hope. Just as that man was no longer an invalid, we are no longer slaves to sin.
- *Sin no more.* That's why Jesus says to us what he said to that man, and later what he said to the woman taken in adultery (John 8). Our state is no longer one of sinfulness, but is instead, one of righteousness. Christ has given us his righteousness! Now, let us sin no more!
- *Something worse.* Jesus gave a sober corrective to the man who thought he could go away from the encounter with no moral obligations. If we continue to sin, what remains? Something worse!

After healing our souls, Jesus starts us on our journey of growth and holiness!

Prayer: Thank you, Jesus, that you have healed my soul's disease, delivering me from sin and giving me your righteousness. Help me to live for you in holiness and soul health. Amen.

Psalm of the Day: 34.1-7

Left-Handed Power
Daily Reading: John 6

> *Perceiving then that they were about to come and take him by force to make him king, Jesus withdrew again to the mountain by himself.* (John 6.15)

Devotional Thought: I find it ironic that the people wanted to force Jesus to be their king. How can you force a ruler to rule? How can you force someone with the power of Jesus to do anything? But, that is the way of the world, isn't it? The world's kingdoms operate by force. The Kingdom of God operates in a different way. "Martin Luther called it 'left-handed' power. Right-handed power consists of the blatant demonstration of power over people. Left-handed power is the quiet demonstration of power in people..." (Larry Crabb, *Soul Talk*).

Politicians and interest-groups, employers and unions, pundits and ideologues - all exercise right-handed power. Threatening reprisal, withholding support, marching in protest, and shouting down speakers are all right-handed power-grabs. It is very disturbing to see this type of behavior multiplying in our society. But, it is all the more disturbing when we see that kind of power-wielding in the Church.

Jesus exercised left-handed power. He didn't clamor for attention. Instead, he withdrew by himself. He didn't force people to follow him. Instead, he invited them. He didn't insist on respect. Instead, he insisted on the right, leaving his reputation in God's hands. He didn't demand service. Instead, he served.

How do you handle power? Are you left-handed or right-handed?

Prayer: Jesus, ultimate power is in your hands. Help us to hold your hand, becoming like you more and more every day, laying down our lives so that others may enter your Kingdom. Amen.

Psalm of the Day: 34.8-14

Left-Handed Motives
Daily Reading: John 7

No one works in secret if he seeks to be known openly. (John 7.4)

Devotional Thought: Jesus' brothers didn't understand him. They didn't get his motives. They were frustrated by his seeming political obtuseness. On one occasion, urging him to go to a certain feast in Jerusalem, they said, "No one works in secret if he seeks to be known openly." In other words, "Don't waste all your good works by doing them in secret!" Sadly, that philosophy is not restricted to their day and time.

Jesus had a whole different way of looking at things; a refreshing way, an almost naive way. He said things like, "Don't let your left hand know what your right hand is doing, so that you will be rewarded by your Father in heaven." Good works don't need to be noticed by people. They are seen by God. If we seek to show our works off so that others will notice us, we have already received our reward.

Jesus likened the Kingdom of heaven to a seed. Nobody goes to a seed-growing exhibition. A seed doesn't need the spotlight or a cheering crowd. A seed grows secretly, doing its work in the dark, without fanfare, getting itself dirty, working in silence. But, the seed when it is full grown brings forth fruit - thirty, sixty, or even a hundred-fold.

Yesterday, we read of 'left-handed power.' Today, we discover 'left-handed motives.' Are we content to do the work of the Kingdom in Jesus' way? Left-handed and in secret?

Prayer: Jesus, I thank you that you came to do the Father's will - simply out of love. You did not demand attention and positive feedback. Even when the crowds deserted you, Lord, you finished the work the Father gave you to do. Help me, O Lord, to follow your example. Amen.

Psalm of the Day: 34.15-22

Left Alone With Jesus

Daily Reading: John 8

Jesus was left alone with the woman standing before him. (John 8.9)

Devotional Thought: Have you ever disappointed someone? Have you ever had to face that person later - just the two of you alone? Not an experience I relish!

But, that's what it was like for the woman in John 8. The adulteress, caught in the sinful deed, was dragged before Jesus, a man of spotless moral integrity, a man who was pure not only in deed but also in motive. Surely, this was not a comfortable place for a sinner. I imagine she was like all of us, wanting to "get this over with" and move on. Perhaps she was searching for ways to justify herself, or to redirect Jesus' attention to her 'partner in crime' or even to blame her accusers. But, Jesus cut short her defense with the simple words, "Neither do I condemn you. Go and sin no more."

We are afraid to be alone with Jesus, but that is exactly what we need. It is in our personal moments with him that we find the forgiveness, the freedom and the love that says, "Neither do I condemn you. Go and sin so more." When there is nowhere to hide, we find that we don't need to hide after all. Jesus loves us. Jesus forgives us. Jesus sets us free.

There is coming a time when it will be just you and Jesus, just me and Jesus, when "the books will be opened" and we will be judged. Standing alone before Jesus, we will thank him that our names are written in the Lamb's Book of Life!

Amen!

Prayer: Thank you, Lord, for your unfailing love! I come to you for forgiveness, for life, and for freedom. Help me to go out from this encounter to live a life of victory and purity. Amen.

Psalm of the Day: 35.1-8

Working the Day Shift

Daily Reading: John 9

We must work the works of him who sent me while it is day; night is coming, when no one can work. (John 9.4)

Devotional Thought: I used to work in a plant that had three shifts. A common question was, "Do you work days?" meaning, "Do you work the day shift?"

Recently, I received an email from a friend reminding me, "Tuesday is the vernal equinox in the Northern Hemisphere, otherwise known as the first day of spring. You probably already knew that." Yes, I did. I hadn't thought about it yet, but ever since the semi-annual ritual called "time change Sunday", I have been anxiously looking forward to the arrival of spring. I am enjoying the "longer" days, but I'm anxious for the weather to catch up. What good are later evenings if you can't get your outside work done?

Work and daylight go together, don't they? Jesus thought they did anyway! He said that "night is coming, when no one can work." There are days of opportunity in each of our lives. Sometimes, health concerns bring about the night. Sometimes, life situations slow us down. And, ultimately, the nightfall of death comes unwelcome and unbidden. Times of opportunity are also dictated by the circumstances of others' lives. Is the season right for you to do the work of the Kingdom in a loved one's life? That sun may set; that opportunity may pass - so we must work the works of God.

Jesus told his disciples, "As long as I am in the world, I am the light of the world" (John 9.5). Jesus is in us, shining his light in the world. May we be found faithful doing his work!

Prayer: Jesus, thank you for shining your light into my life. Help me to do your work, the work of him who sent you, while it is day. Then, Lord, when the night comes, may I hear the words, "Well done, good and faithful servant." Amen.

Psalm of the Day: 35.9-17

Feeling Sheepish
Daily Reading: John 10

He who enters by the door is the shepherd of the sheep. To him the gatekeeper opens. The sheep hear his voice, and he calls his own sheep by name and leads them out (John 10.2-3)

Devotional Thought: "I love that chapter in John that talks about the sheep and the Shepherd." Those were my wife Lana's words to me a few days ago. I was excited, because I love that chapter, and because I knew that it would be coming soon in *The Climb: Stay Focused*. Lana's always ahead of me!

In the early verses of this chapter, Jesus talks about the Shepherd, the Gatekeeper, and the sheep:

- *Jesus is the Shepherd.* Jesus identifies himself as the Shepherd of the sheep. Drawing from a long-understood metaphor in Israel, Jesus likened himself to the shepherd who "makes us to lie down in green pastures, who leads us beside still waters, who restores our soul." The Shepherd is our Provider, our Defender, our Guide. But, there is a problem. Our sins have separated us from the Shepherd (Isaiah 59.2).
- *The Holy Spirit is the Gatekeeper.* This is where the Holy Spirit enters the equation. He is the Gatekeeper that opens the door (which is, by the way, Jesus, but that is for another day...) so that the Shepherd and the sheep can be united. Jesus said that the Holy Spirit "will convict the world concerning sin and righteousness and judgment" (John 16.8). The Holy Spirit helps us in our infirmities to know how to pray to the Shepherd!
- *We are the sheep called by name who are led out.* Reunited with the Good Shepherd, we are led out from the bondage of sin to the freedom of those green pastures. Even when we walk through the valley of the shadow of death, we need not fear!

Amen!

Prayer: "Savior, like a shepherd lead us, much we need thy tender care. In thy pleasant pastures feed us; for our use thy folds prepare." Grant, O Lord, that we might be called out by name and led forth in grace. Amen.

Psalm of the Day: 35.18-21

Jesus Wept

Daily Reading: John 11

Jesus wept. (John 11.35)

Devotional Thought: Perhaps, you have had that wise-cracking person in your life who thinks they are clever to claim that they have memorized a Bible verse, and then promptly recited: "Jesus wept." While we may roll our eyes, this verse is profound.

When Jesus heard that Lazarus was ill, it was not a surprise. It was an opportunity "for the glory of God, so that the Son of God may be glorified through it" (v. 4). After hearing about it, Jesus purposely chose to stay away from Lazarus for two extra days. Jesus had a plan. He knew Lazarus would die and had a plan for that as well. So why, when he was on his way to the grave, was he so greatly troubled in his spirit? Why was he so deeply moved? Why did he weep?

The text is not specific, but we know the compassion and love of God is unending and unconditional. Seeing his friends grieve over the death of another of his friends, even knowing the celebration that was soon to come over his resurrection, caused him emotional pain. It is a reminder to us that death is indeed our enemy. God created us to live forever, until sin entered the world. Seeing the groaning of his creation when sin was introduced, God in his mercy limited the number of our days on this broken earth.

God grieves with us when we grieve. But praise God! We do not grieve as those who have no hope! Jesus has power over sin and death, defeating them at the cross and empty grave.

Jenny

Prayer: Lord, we have all been touched by death – we know that you grieve with us when one of our friends or family members passes out of this life. Thank you for your promises... you will not leave us in this state, but will resurrect all of the dead in Christ to eternal life! Amen.

Psalm of the Day: 35.22-28

Fall and Die

Daily Reading: John 12

Unless a grain of wheat falls into the earth and dies, it remains alone; but if it dies, it bears much fruit. (John 12.24)

Devotional Thought: A friend of mine recently sent me a time-elapsed video of a bean seed sprouting and growing. Twenty-nine days of growth were condensed to about 3 minutes. It was fascinating to watch. I noticed that in order for new life to come forth from that seed, however, the first thing it had to do was crack open and essentially die. All the growth that came after was preceded by this 'death.' No death = no growth.

The Savior had to fall to the earth and die as well. In order for new life to come to you and me, God ordained that his Son would suffer our death. It is only as Jesus dies that we can live. But, his death was not the end, it was the occasion for a resurrection! Now, because Jesus died and rose again, he is not alone. He has borne the fruit of our salvation.

In the same way, a soul must die to himself/herself in this life. If we are to bear fruit, we must be broken open on our own cross of consecration. As long as we remain unbroken, we will be unable to bear fruit. We will be alone. Other souls will be lost.

But, there is more fruit to be borne by the soul that dies. Jesus said in v. 25: "Whoever loves his life loses it, and whoever hates his life in this world will keep it for eternal life." Because we have been united to Jesus in his death, we will also be united to him in his resurrection (Romans 6.5). What comfort for those whose loved ones have passed through the veil of death into the next life!

How about you, dear friend? Have you fallen to the earth and died?

Prayer: Jesus, you are the firstborn from the dead. But, in order to be resurrected, you had to die. Help me to die to myself and live for you and so be united with you forever. Amen.

Psalm of the Day: 36.1-6

Afterward You Will Understand

Daily Reading: John 13

> *What I am doing you do not understand now, but afterward you will understand.* (John 13.7)

Devotional Thought: One evening, Jesus decided to wash his disciples' feet. Peter didn't want it to happen: "No, Lord! You will never wash my feet!" Jesus said, "You do not understand." There were many things Jesus did that they didn't understand:

- Doing his good works 'under the radar' instead of seeking credit and fame
- Refusing to call down judgment on his enemies
- Taking time to welcome, recognize, and bless children
- Talking with women
- Forgiving sinners
- Bypassing opportunities to establish an earthly kingdom - especially at the height of his popularity
- Laying down his life on a cross

At times, Jesus' disciples simply had to accept the fact that they did not understand what he was doing. Although one day they would understand, at the moment they did not and could not.

How many times I have wished I had "the answer" people were looking for! Whether in the courtroom or the living room, at the funeral home or the hospital, I have often struggled to understand with people what Jesus was doing now. Those were times when we just had to hear the words of Jesus, "Afterward you will understand."

Are you in a dark tunnel right now? Perhaps like Peter, you don't understand what Jesus is doing. It's not that Jesus is keeping it hidden from you. Rather, in those places we simply are not able to grasp it. Wait patiently, friend. "Afterward you will understand."

Prayer: Jesus, how thankful I am to know that in all things you are working for my good. Even though I don't understand it right now, I trust you, for "You've been faithful, faithful to me. Looking back your love and mercy I see. Though in my heart I have questioned, even failed to believe, you've been faithful, faithful to me." Amen. (Carol Cymbala)

Psalm of the Day: 36.7-12

Only One Way
Daily Reading: John 14

> *I am the way, and the truth, and the life. No one comes to the Father except through me.* (John 14.6)

Devotional Thought: There are times at the office when I need to be alone, and I tell Elaine, my assistant, "It's a DND [Do Not Disturb] morning. Unless it's an emergency, take a message." Nobody gets to me unless they come through her. Jesus said something similar about himself. "No one comes to the Father except through me." How is Jesus the way to God? Surprisingly, there are several answers...

The first and most obvious answer, is that we must have a personal faith in a personal Savior in order to be saved. Having heard the story of Jesus' life, death, and resurrection, we have believed it for ourselves. Repenting of our sins, receiving Jesus as our Savior, and confessing him as our Lord, we are born again. We have come to God through Christ.

But, what of worshipers before Christ? What about Noah, Abraham, Moses, and David? Were they lost? Of course not. But, their sacrifices alone did not atone for their sins. "For it is impossible for the blood of bulls and goats to take away sins" (Hebrews 10.4). Those sacrifices were only effective through the perfect sacrifice of Jesus.

What of children who die in innocence? Like David's child who went to heaven in 2 Samuel 12, those incapable of moral choice come to the Father through Jesus' sacrifice.

Is there room for others - who are walking in all the light that they have - to be saved, even if they don't know the name of Jesus? Didn't Jesus say, "I have other sheep that are not of this fold. I must bring them also" (John 10.16)?

Jesus is the only way. He is a Savior of mercy.

Prayer: In the words of the Psalmist I pray, "How precious to me are your thoughts, O God! How vast is the sum of them!" Lord, how great is the mystery of your love. It is higher, wider, broader, and deeper than I could ever understand, but with faith I receive it! Amen.

Psalm of the Day: 37.1-6

Grade-A Faith

Daily Reading: John 15

I am the true vine. (John 15.1)

Devotional Thought: My heart breaks when I see people make a start with Jesus, and then fail to make a relationship with him. I know how it will end... Jesus knew that simplistic faith in him was not sufficient. His disciples needed to re-orient their entire lives around him with "Grade-A" faith:

- The disciples were **A**lready clean (v. 3). Our life in Christ starts with sins forgiven and lives made new. If we never truly meet and surrender to Christ, then we absolutely cannot have a successful Christian life. We may not remember the exact moment, but there must be a birth in the Spirit in order for us to live a spiritual life.
- Further, the disciples were to undergo pruning in order to **A**bound in fruit-bearing (v. 2). Simply put, a follower of Jesus Christ will see their lives change. The old will pass away and the new will come. This process is progressive to be sure, but change is inevitable.
- Next, Jesus told his disciples that they must **A**bide in him and he in them (v. 4). The vitality, the wisdom, the joy and the power to live the new life has to come from somewhere. That somewhere is a Someone. If we are not attached to Jesus on a daily and ongoing basis, our spiritual lives will be dry and dead!
- The disciples had the incredible offer to **A**sk for whatever they needed (v. 7) in their new life. We have not because we ask not (James 4.2).
- The disciples then heard the good news that theirs was a life designed for significance, for meaning, for results. They were **A**ppointed to bear fruit (v. 16). We, too, are the friends of Jesus! He has chosen us to make a difference!

Do you have a "Grade-A" faith?

Prayer: Jesus, thank you that you have made me clean in the new birth and are daily making me new, pruning me and growing me to be like you. May I remain in close relationship with you, pray great prayers and bear much fruit. Help me, O Lord, to be a "Grade-A" Christian. Amen.

Psalm of the Day: 37.7-15

To Our Advantage

Daily Reading: John 16

It is to your advantage that I go away. (John 16.7)

Devotional Thought: Robby, a teen from my church, once did some yard work for me. Though I wanted to stay to supervise and advise, I knew it would be best for him and for me if I made myself scarce, for he was a responsible young man. How delighted I was when I returned to discover that he not only had done the job, but he exceeded my expectations! It was to his advantage that I went away.

When Jesus told his disciples that he needed to make himself scarce, he knew that they needed to depend on his spiritual presence and not his physical presence. As long as he was there to see, to hear, and to touch, they would not depend on the Holy Spirit to work through them. The spiritual initiative would always be with Jesus. And, they would remain spiritual infants.

I once read of a man who came through a dark hospital stay and shared this testimony: "'So many good friends came to visit me during those awful days. But, God never showed up. The One I wanted most to come never did. I never felt his presence for even a moment as I lay there in the hospital bed.' And, then I heard his voice choke: 'To think he trusted me to believe he was there just because he said he was, with no other evidence - I'm so grateful.'" [Soul Talk, Larry Crabb]

Perhaps you are struggling right now, wishing that Jesus' presence with you was more discernible. Have you considered that it may be to your advantage that Jesus is silent right now? It's a hard lesson, but one which will help you grow in faith and spiritual strength.

Prayer: Jesus, thank you that you came to this earth, that you walked among people, touching them, talking with them. But, thank you even more that you have gone to heaven to send the Holy Spirit to me, to silently walk with me, touch me, and talk with me. I trust you in the silence, O Lord. Amen.

Psalm of the Day: 37.16-24

Praying For the World
Daily Reading: John 17

So that the world may believe that you have sent me... (John 17.21b)

Devotional Thought: Last week, it was my pleasure to receive communion with and hear a message from my pastor, District Superintendent Bob Mahaffey. Bob commented from John 17, that Jesus prayed for himself, for his disciples, and for us. "Yeah, yeah," I thought, "I know that." But Bob went on, "What we sometimes miss is that he prayed for 'the world,' too." "He did?" I pondered. "I thought that he said, 'I am not praying for the world...'"

I went home and discovered what Bob was talking about. While he did say, at one point, he was not praying for the world, that was in relation to a specific request for his disciples, not a comment about his prayer overall. In each prayer - for himself, his disciples and for us - he prayed for the world:

- When Jesus prayed for himself, he expressed his confidence that he had been used by God to bring God's glory to the world (v. 4). Jesus always kept his mission in mind, didn't he? "For God so loved the world..."
- When Jesus prayed for his disciples (v. 11), he noted that they would remain in the world as witnesses. He wanted his disciples to keep his mission in mind, too! But, he didn't want them to be contaminated by the world, rather to infect the world with the love of God. They were set apart (sanctified) for God's purpose.
- When he prayed for us, for our unity, his motive was that the world may believe (v. 21). The overflowing joy we have as the united body of Christ, serves to make the world hungry to know the uniting Force of our lives - Jesus Christ.

Yes, Jesus prayed for the world, and we should, too!

Prayer: Thank you, Lord, for teaching me to pray for myself, for leaders in the church and for my brothers and sisters in the church. Help me, also, to pray for the world, that they "may believe that you have sent me..." Amen.

Psalm of the Day: 37.25-33

Truer Than We Know

Daily Reading: John 18

> *It was Caiaphas who had advised the Jews that it would be expedient that one man should die for the people.* (John 18.14)

Devotional Thought: My young children often say things that are truer than they know, and I find myself asking, "How did they know that?" My dad chalks it up to superior genes - received of course from their grandfather!

When Jesus was arrested, he was taken to Annas, the father-in-law of Caiaphas who was high priest that year. Caiaphas had once said something truer than he knew: "It was Caiaphas who had advised the Jews that it would be expedient that one man should die for the people." John 11, records this conversation between the Jewish religious council. "What are we to do? For this man performs many signs. If we let him go on like this, everyone will believe in him, and the Romans will come and take away both our place and our nation" (John 11.47-48). Caiaphas responded, "You know nothing at all. Nor do you understand that it is better for you that one man should die for the people, not that the whole nation should perish" (vv. 49-50). Caiaphas predicted that Jesus would be killed to save the Jewish people from the Romans.

What Caiaphas meant for evil, however, God turned into a glorious prophecy. Jesus was indeed the one man that would die for the people. Not to save them from the Romans, but to save them from themselves. To save them from their sin, their evil desires, their self-righteousness, even the guilt of carrying out this murderous plan against God's only Son. He does the same for all the undeserving who call upon the name of the Lord! That, my friends, is truer than we know!

Jenny

Prayer: What man meant for harm, you meant for good. Lord, we are so grateful that you are Sovereign over the sorrows of this life, that even the darkest of circumstances are a part of your unfolding plan for us; a plan to prosper and not harm us, a plan to give us hope and a future. Thank you that through it all, we have a Savior who loves us and whom we can trust. Amen.

Psalm of the Day: 37.34-40

Black Saturday
Daily Reading: John 19

Now in the place where he was crucified there was a garden, and in the garden a new tomb in which no one had yet been laid. So because of the Jewish day of Preparation, since the tomb was close at hand, they laid Jesus there. (John 19.41-42)

Devotional Thought: Black Saturday, the day between Good Friday and Easter, was "the darkest day in history." Jesus lay silent in the darkness of the tomb.

Reflect on the tomb of Jesus...
- It was in the place of death. Joseph's tomb was close to where Jesus died. It seems that death is not far off from where we live out our lives. The journey of life ends at the tomb. But is that the end?
- It was in a garden. There are two perspectives on this. Is the place of life (a garden) defined by the place of death (a tomb)? Or, is the presence of a garden in the place of death, the sign of a promise from God? In the midst of suffering and death, is it possible to hope in new life? Yes!
- No one had yet been laid there. Jesus' death is unique in kind. His death was the archetype for all spiritual death to follow. The good news, is that Jesus laid in the darkness of that tomb for you and for me!
- It was borrowed. The death Jesus died was not his to die. He willingly took on our death, so that he might give us his life. Hallelujah!
- It was close at hand. This reminds us in the words of the Apostle Peter, "The end of all things is at hand" (1 Peter 4.7). Each day we need to live with the end in mind.
- They laid Jesus' body there. It was your sin and mine that cost Jesus his life. "You were bought with a price. So glorify God in your body" (1 Corinthians 6.20).

Prayer: Thank you, Jesus, that your body laid in the still darkness of the tomb - for my sake and the sake of the entire world. Help me to remember this day and to dedicate my life to live for you. Amen.

Psalm of the Day: 38.1-8

While It Was Still Dark
Daily Reading: John 20

While it was still dark... (John 20.1)

Devotional Thought: Jesus' ministry had promised the dawning of a bright, new day. But now, he was dead and in the tomb. Mary, with love for Jesus, made her way to the grave "while it was still dark."

Mary was surrounded by *material* darkness. In the pre-dawn hour in that garden graveyard, there was little light. She had to get along the best she could under the circumstances.

Mary was lost in a *miserable* darkness. Jesus - who had delivered her from the darkness of demons, whom she loved with all her heart, and in whom she had put all her hope - was gone. She felt trapped. Alone. As dead on the inside as her Friend inside the tomb.

Unaware of what had happened, Mary was in a *mental* darkness. Mary did not have all the facts of the case yet. She did not know that Jesus was alive!

Mary labored in *mutual* darkness. Those with her, those who were left at home, those who had buried her Master - all of them - believed that Jesus was dead, never to be heard from again. Together, they just had to somehow go on.

Yes, it was still dark, but it was a *momentary* darkness. What she didn't know, in her personal darkness, was the fact that Jesus was alive! Yes, he had died and was buried, but God brought him back from the dead! The darkness fled as the dawn broke on a new day, not just then, but for all eternity!

May the light of the resurrection dispel all of your darkness!

Prayer: Hallelujah! Jesus, you are alive! The light of your living presence dispels all the darkness! I serve a risen Savior! Amen.

Psalm of the Day: 38.9-16

It's Always Dark Before Coffee!
Daily Reading: John 21

Just as day was breaking, Jesus stood on the shore; yet the disciples did not know that it was Jesus. (John 21.4)

Devotional Thought: We were just getting to the time of the year when it was light as I rose from sleep. Then time change hit, and I had to trudge out and turn on my coffee in the dark! But then, it's always 'dark' before coffee!

A few weeks after Jesus rose from the dead, he met several disciples one morning "as day was breaking." The disciples had been fishing all night on the Sea of Galilee. Their vision was blurred with weariness, darkness, and discouragement. They did not know it was Jesus.

When Jesus came to them, their work had been completed; their day was over. They had struggled all night to no avail. With each casting and drawing of the net, their spirits were deflated further and further. How disappointing to work with eager expectation, only to have your hopes dashed again and again. Yes, the day was over for them, both in the fact that the time had run out and their hope had dried up.

But then Jesus showed up and their day was about to begin! "Haven't you any fish? ... Throw your net on the right side of the boat and you will find some." When they did so, something miraculous and incredible happened. They caught so many fish they couldn't drag the net into the boat. They had to come to shore, pulling the net behind them. They left the weariness, darkness and discouragement behind them!

When Jesus shows up - no matter what time it is - the long night ends and a new day begins.

Prayer: Thank you, Jesus, that you are there to greet me every morning. As I begin my day today, may your presence chase away the weariness, the darkness and the discouragement with your strength, light, and joy. Amen.

Psalm of the Day: 38.17-22

Always Something to Do
Daily Reading: Joshua 13

Now Joshua was old and advanced in years, and the Lord said to him, "You are old and advanced in years, and there remains yet very much land to possess." (Joshua 13.1)

Devotional Thought: There is always something for the servant of God to do. The modern concept of retiring is not found in the Bible. A refocusing may come, however. Joshua underwent a refocusing. Having led the people in conquest, now Joshua began the job of allotting the territory. God told Joshua that though he was old, there was still very much to do. He went from being a leader of battles to a lister of boundaries.

There is always something for the servant of God to do.
- When Moses turned 82, he went from being an emancipator of slaves to a shepherd leading his 'sheep' through the wilderness.
- When David was in his 70's, he went from being a fighting commander-in-chief to the fund-raising architect of the temple.
- Late in life, Paul's circumstances dictated that he switch from being an itinerate preacher, planting churches, to a theologian, writing letters.

There is always something for the servant of God to do. Refocusing doesn't have to wait until late in life, either.
- Moses experienced it at age 40, when he became a nomad, leaving the courts of Pharaoh.
- David experienced it as a young man, when he was anointed king by Samuel, leaving the flocks of his father.
- Paul experienced it as a young rabbi, meeting Jesus on the road to Damascus.

There is always something for the servant of God to do. Perhaps God is calling you now to a new work, a new ministry. Are you willing to leave the comfortable, the familiar, the easy to pursue the call of God?

Prayer: Lord, the scripture says that you are transforming us 'from glory to glory.' Help me to refocus when you call, to remain with my hand on the plow, and to refuse to stop working for the Lord. Amen.

Psalm of the Day: 39.1-6

96

Impertinence
Daily Reading: Joshua 14

Now give me this hill country of which the Lord spoke on that day.
(Joshua 14.12)

Devotional Thought: Sometimes we think of the impertinence of youth, but Caleb had the impertinence of old age! At 85 he said, "Give me this hill country!"

It is not surprising that Caleb was so brash. He was a confident fellow! And why not? He served an awesome God. Forty years prior when he returned from the spying expedition into Canaan, Caleb brought a good report, but the other ten spies brought back a negative report. In response, God himself had promised that land to Caleb.

"That day" 40 years prior, Caleb displayed his...
- *Faith.* He believed what God told him. He had no reason to doubt the word of the God who had delivered the Israelites out from under the heavy hand of Pharaoh.
- *Fortitude.* He went against the flow and testified what was on his heart. He could not be dissuaded by the nay-sayers surrounding him.
- *Foresight.* Like his ancestor, Abraham, before him, Caleb was looking for "a city with foundations." He looked beyond the immediate circumstances and focused on the promised future.

"Now" Caleb received what he had long anticipated...
- *Length.* Caleb believed that in order for the promise to be fulfilled, God would have to keep him. God did just that! He kept Caleb alive those long years of wandering and warfare. While he watched his brothers die in the wilderness one-by-one, Caleb knew God would keep him.
- *Strength.* He testified that though he was advanced in years, he was still strong in mind and body. He was able to plan and then to execute the plan. Not many 85 year olds have that kind of stamina! He received it as a gift from God!

May we have Caleb's impertinence: "Now give me this hill country!"

Prayer: Lord, give me the faith, the fortitude and the foresight of Caleb, that I might live long and strong for you! Amen.

Psalm of the Day: 39.7-13   97

Boundaries

Daily Reading: Joshua 15

This is the boundary around the people of Judah according to their clans. (Joshua 15.12)

Devotional Thought: There is a lot of interest in the borders of America - and whether these borders should serve as boundaries to the movement of people into our nation. What does God say of boundaries?

God is interested in setting our boundaries for us. Boundaries helped Israel avoid conflict (both internal and external!) and will help us to do the same. He has equipped us to know and understand these boundaries through scripture. We can see his commands and expectations for us, and when we abide in the Spirit, these boundaries are pleasant and not burdensome. "The boundary lines have fallen for me in pleasant places; surely I have a delightful inheritance" (Psalm 16.6).

Boundaries are merciful. Those ancient boundaries were formed in mercy. The very fact that he gave the Israelites an inheritance, after all of their stiff-necked rebellion, is a testimony to his mercy and grace. In the same way, he shows us his justice and mercy by sending his beloved Son to die for our sins, fulfilling the requirements of justice while showing us tremendous mercy.

Boundaries are a safe refuge. After the Israelites had gained their inheritance, they failed to drive out all of the inhabitants as God had commanded them (v. 63). They called it "good enough" when they had driven most of them out. This "good enough" proved to be a deadly snare. Enticed by their gods, Israel was drawn away from the one true God. In the same way, we may not understand God's purposes in our lives, but we can trust that his will, his commandments, and his boundaries for us are our safest refuge.

Jenny

Prayer: Lord, we love you and we love your Word. Help us to see your commands for us as life-giving and soul-uplifting, rather than burdensome work. We are so grateful for your guidance, and ask that your Spirit would search our hearts and lead us in the way everlasting. Amen.

Psalm of the Day: 40.1-8

Determination and Courage Get the Job Done
Daily Reading: Joshua 16-17

> *To Machir the firstborn of Manasseh, the father of Gilead, were allotted Gilead and Bashan, because he was a man of war.* (Joshua 17.1)

Devotional Thought: The rights of the firstborn sons were an important entitlement in ancient Israelite culture. The firstborn was to receive a special portion, equal to twice that of the shares of the other sons. Machir, the firstborn descendant of Manasseh, was allotted Gilead and Bashan," two portions of land east of the Jordan. In one sense, this inheritance was an entitlement. But, that is not the whole story. The generous and challenging allotment was also given "because he was a man of war." There was work to be done in possessing and taming the land, requiring more than entitlement. Determination and courage were needed to get the job done.

The Christian life is a wonderful "entitlement," granted to us by the grace of God. But, that is not the whole story. Living out the life given us requires determination and courage. Ministry and service to God takes work! I've heard it said that "God always calls a busy person." Why do you suppose that is? Because serving God is more than an entitlement. It requires determination and courage to get the job done.

Jesus has the rights of the firstborn as the "only begotten of the father" and the "firstborn from the dead." But, the blessing of the firstborn brought with it the cross. Jesus was a man of war. He went to the cross and the grave, defeating sin and death, so that he could share the rights of the firstborn with us. Are we now willing to do whatever it takes to get the job done?

Prayer: Thank you, Jesus, that while you are the Prince of Peace, you also are a man of war. You defeated sin and death on my behalf. Help me to live for you today, with determination, vision, and courage. Amen.

Psalm of the Day: 40.9-17

Possess Your Possession

Daily Reading: Joshua 18

> *How long will you put off going in to take possession of the land, which the Lord, the God of your fathers, has given you?* (Joshua 18.3)

Devotional Thought: I love restaurant gift cards! Lana and I have received many of them from our generous and thoughtful friends. We are thankful for having a meal out together. But, did you know that over $1 billion in gift cards are left unused each year? That's a lot of cheese coneys!

Joshua confronted the people with the question of an unredeemed gift: "How long will you put off going in to take possession of the land, which the Lord ... has given you?" Joshua reminded them that the Promised Land was a *possession*. They had to *possess* it!

The sanctified life is like that. It is a possession. And, we need to possess it, just as the Israelites needed to possess their promise from God. Joshua tells us how:

- *Go in.* A true and vital relationship with God cannot be had from a distance. We need to come into complete harmony with the Lord and consecrate our lives fully to him. Half-hearted religion will not cut it. Joseph of Arimethea discovered that being a secret disciple of Jesus was not satisfying. Confronted with the Lord's sacrifice on the cross, he surrendered himself completely to Christ.
- *Take.* God will give us the fullness of the Spirit as our possession, but will we take it? If we don't believe it, will we ever claim it?
- *Possess.* Don't let circumstances rule you. Claim the life God has for you. By faith receive the blessing.
- *Do not put off.* Why wait another day? Blessed are those who hunger and thirst for righteousness, for they shall be filled.

Prayer: Jesus, you have promised me the Holy Spirit. By faith I receive the Spirit in fullness and power. This is a gift I will redeem today! Amen.

Psalm of the Day: 41.1-9

Partnering in God's Work

Daily Reading: Joshua 19

Because the portion of the people of Judah was too large for them, the people of Simeon obtained an inheritance in the midst of their inheritance. (Joshua 19.9)

Devotional Thought: I just finished a "grandchild bunk house" in my basement. It is a simple room with a futon and a mattress for when the kids are home to see Nana and Pahpooh. I had been wanting to do this for a while, but had never gotten started because the room was such a mess. I didn't know where to begin! One day I asked our friend Hannah to come over and help me clean the room up. That got me started.

Simeon was one of the tribes who had not yet possessed their inheritance in the Promised Land. Joshua had asked them, "How long are you going to wait?" Sometimes we need a little push to get started, don't we? Not only so, we may need some help, too! That's what the people of Judah provided for the people of Simeon. And, the help they provided turned out to be just the thing they themselves needed, for "the portion of the people of Judah was too large for them."

By coming together, both Simeon and Judah were helped in receiving God's promise and achieving God's purpose.

What promise and purpose from God are you waiting to see fulfilled? Is there somebody with whom you need to partner to help you get started? Don't hesitate to ask for help. It will not only help you, it will be a blessing to them as well!

Prayer: Lord, thank you for the promises and purposes you have for me. Help me to receive and achieve them as I partner with others in the work of the Kingdom. Amen.

Psalm of the Day: 41.10-13

Ask

Daily Reading: Joshua 20-21

> And they said to them at Shiloh in the land of Canaan, "The Lord commanded through Moses that we be given cities to dwell in, along with their pasturelands for our livestock." (Joshua 21.2)

Devotional Thought: You have not because you ask not. That's a principle of prayer expressed in James 4.2. The Levites weren't going to be left in that position. God had commanded that they receive cities and pastures in the midst of the tribes, and they intended to get them!

The Levites were responsible for the public worship of God. Out of their ranks came the priests and ministers at the altar. Since they gave themselves to the work of the Lord on behalf of the people, God provided them land in the midst of the people. They still had to work the fields and flocks, they still had to develop and manage the cities, but God gave these things as their possession.

So they went boldly to Joshua and reminded him of what the Lord had commanded. I notice several things about this story...

- Nobody else went to the leader asking this. When it comes to praying for the promise of God, we are responsible for ourselves. The Bible doesn't say, "You have not because someone else didn't ask..."
- Neither did anybody find fault with them. Instead, they received what they asked for. In another place, James says we can ask God for wisdom because God "gives generously to all without reproach" (James 1.5). God is pleased when we ask him for what he has promised.
- The Levites didn't receive the promise until they asked for it. We need to remember this. Just because we have been promised abundant life in Christ, does not mean we will possess it. We must go boldly to the throne of God and ask for what he has promised. The promise does not nullify the need for asking; it just gives us boldness!

Prayer: Thank you, Lord, for the "cities and pasturelands" that you have promised me. I now ask that you give them to me, helping me to do the work that needs to be done. Amen.

Psalm of the Day: 42.1-7

Open Lines of Communication
Daily Reading: Joshua 22

And the people of Israel heard it said... (Joshua 22.11)

Devotional Thought: Have you ever been misunderstood? Not fun. Even worse, is to be misrepresented. Even worse than that, is to do something stupid and then have that misrepresented! That's where the "Eastern Tribes" (Reuben, Gad and the half tribe of Manasseh) found themselves. As they returned home, they built a monument at the Jordan to ensure that they were not alienated from the faith and family of their fathers. The monument, however, was misunderstood. The eastern tribes were accused of deserting the faith and of putting the 'family' at risk. What they were really guilty of was being poor communicators. When they explained their motives, their western brothers understood and even accepted their action.

This story, I believe, can serve as a warning to the risk of poor communication in the church.
- The eastern tribes should have communicated with their western brothers before they started the huge imposing memorial. Even better, they should have *consulted* with them. I have brought many problems and complaints on myself, simply by not communicating.
- The western tribes almost seemed to be *eager* to find fault with their eastern brothers. I'm not sure how and why, but an environment of suspicion and fear had been fostered. Whisperings, innuendos, and jealousy should not be allowed to gain traction among God's people. It leads to civil war!
- There was also another party which played a part. The source of the information - those who brought the story back to their western brothers - should have dug a little deeper before spreading the dirt! Anonymous and unverified sources are never a good idea!

Let's all do our part to keep the lines of communication open in the church!

Prayer: Father, help us as your family not to deal in innuendo and in unverified accusations. Rather, enable us to communicate clearly and openly with one another, to preserve the peace and unity of the church. For Jesus' sake we pray. Amen.

Psalm of the Day: 42.8-11

Working Partners with God
Daily Reading: Joshua 23

> *You shall cling to the Lord your God just as you have done to this day.* (Joshua 23.8)

Devotional Thought: At the end of his life, Joshua took great pains to impress upon the Israelites the importance of clinging to God in the Promised Land. The people of God, he said, were working partners with God:

- God will push them back; you shall possess their land (v. 5). The Israelites never were intended to depend upon their military might and strategy. Instead, they were to follow the lead of God and enter the doors he opened. That does not imply inactivity. After God pushed their enemies back, then they were to do the work of taming and occupying the land.

- God has written it down; you shall live it out (v. 6). Their moral and legal code was not a mystery. It was founded in the Ten Commandments - principles that God had etched in stone with his own finger. They partnered with God in knowing and doing his will in his way. Being hearers of the Word is not enough. We must be doers of the Word.

- God shall fight for you; you shall love your God (vv. 10-11). This aspect of their partnership with God was a reminder that not everything would be easy and automatic. There were barriers to be overcome, battles to be fought. But, they would not be alone. God would be fighting for them. Their part was to always remember that God loved them, and to love him in return.

- God has not failed you; you shall not transgress his law (vv. 15-16). In all things, they had found that God was faithful to them. Now, he was asking that they remain faithful to him. God went first, but they had to be faithful in turn.

Prayer: Thank you, Lord, for your grace that goes before us. Help us to respond to that preceding grace in faith and in faithfulness. Make us full partners with you for your glory and our good. Amen.

Psalm of the Day: 43.1-5

Cross-Stitched Wisdom
Daily Reading: Joshua 24

Choose this day whom you will serve. (Joshua 24.15)

Devotional Thought: Joshua 24 contains a phrase that has become a well-known, cross-stitched ornament in many Christian homes: "As for me and my house, we will serve the Lord."

In its context, this verse contains even more meaning. Joshua had just recapped everything the Lord had done for the Israelites, all of the reasons they could put away their false gods and idols and trust solely in him. He then gave them something of an ultimatum: "Choose this day whom you will serve" (v. 15). In other words, you cannot serve both the true God and false gods. There was a choice to be made.

In the same way, we must also choose whom we will serve. It is becoming increasingly "evil" to serve the Lord. The world sees Christians as mindless, irrational, misogynistic, intolerant, backwards-thinking bigots. Some Christians have been pulled away from God's truth as it is revealed in scripture, to a twisted version of the truth which is actually the enemy's lie. This lie is disguised as progressive thinking, inclusiveness, tolerance for all. In reality, it is a normalization of sin.

We all must choose whom we will serve. Every person on earth must decide who Jesus is/was. As Paul says in Romans 1:20, "For his invisible attributes, namely, his eternal power and divine nature, have been clearly perceived, ever since the creation of the world, in the things that have been made. So they are without excuse."

His existence is cross-stitched on creation. Is serving him cross-stitched on your heart?

Jenny

Prayer: Lord, our hearts ache for the lost around us, even as they mock us for our most dearly held beliefs. Help us to show love and forgiveness towards those who see us as foolish, and use us to draw unbelievers to yourself. Amen.

Psalm of the Day: 44.1-8

Taking Responsibility
Daily Reading: James 1

> But each person is tempted when he is lured and enticed by his own desire. Then desire when it has conceived gives birth to sin, and sin when it is fully grown brings forth death. (James 1.14-15)

Devotional Thought: We live in a 'blaming culture'. People say that what they do is not their fault, and therefore it is not their responsibility to fix, change, or even try to control it. Some people in James' day went so far as to blame God for their failures. James would have none of that. He laid the blame right where it belonged: allowing sin to progress in our lives:

- *Desire.* We all have desires. God made us that way. Desires are not evil in and of themselves, and they are different for each one of us. What gets our attention? We need to know so that we can properly control our appetites.
- *Temptation.* The things that get our attention, soon get our affection. Temptation comes when we consider fulfilling our desires in ways that are not legitimate, compromising our integrity to get what we want. We must say no to temptation just as Jesus did.
- *Conception.* When we say yes to temptation, we have taken the next step in the progression of sin. What temptation conceives is the assent of the mind to do the thing we know we shouldn't. That is just as sinful as the act itself.
- *Sin.* Having granted mental assent, it is just an easy step to actually do the thing forbidden. The action cements the decision.
- *Death.* Each sinful step takes us further away from God. "In him was life", so when we are moving away from God, we are moving toward death.

James gives a solution in v. 21, and it is our responsibility: "Therefore put away all filthiness and rampant wickedness and receive with meekness the implanted word, which is able to save your souls."

Prayer: Lord, help me to discipline my desires, turn down my temptations, and master my mind so that I might live according to your will. Amen.

Psalm of the Day: 44.9-16

Justified by Works
Daily Reading: James 2

> *And in the same way was not also Rahab the prostitute justified by works when she received the messengers and sent them out by another way? For as the body apart from the spirit is dead, so also faith apart from works is dead.* (James 2.25-26)

Devotional Thought: James chose two Old Testament examples of how faith and deeds work together in our salvation. Abraham's faith resulted in his journey to Mount Moriah, to offer his son Isaac to God. Rahab's faith was proven real when she helped the messengers. James said that both were "justified by works." What does that mean?

Let's look at Rahab's experience...

She received the messengers. This is a picture of grace working. Joshua sent the messengers into the land without any invitation from Rahab. She had done nothing to deserve their arrival. She simply responded to their presence. And, when they spoke words of grace to her, she accepted their offer. In the same way, God sends the Holy Spirit to convict us and to give us saving faith. It is up to us to decide if we will receive the gift offered, but clearly we have done nothing deserving of the messenger. Receiving the message of salvation is not a work that brings us merit.

She sent them out by another way. This is a picture of faith working. Rahab's life changed in that encounter with Joshua's messengers. Her faith caused her to do something. She believed in them and their message. She staked her safety and her future on them. When we accept the Holy Spirit's message of salvation, we too are changed. We go out another way. Faith is real when it results in us living a different life, the Jesus life. Receiving the message of God's salvation, we are like the woman in John 8, whom Jesus told to "Go and sin no more."

Unless our faith changes our lives, it is not real. For, in the words of James: Faith without works is dead.

Prayer: "Lord, I believe. Help my unbelief." Help me that I won't substitute the hollow faith of an unchanged life for the full faith of a changed life. May my faith and deeds work together!. Amen.

Psalm of the Day: 44.17-26

Tongue Tamer
Daily Reading: James 3-4

No human being can tame the tongue. It is a restless evil, full of deadly poison. (James 3.8)

Devotional Thought: Is there enough 'noise' in the world to suit you? And, with Facebook, Instagram, Twitter, and Snapchat, there will be no shortage of words in the foreseeable future. People have a lot to say: "No human being can tame the tongue!" The real problem, however, is not the amount of the 'noise.' It is the evil character of what is being said. It doesn't take long, listening to the news, to discover that people struggle to say good things about people they don't agree with.

Why is that? The tongue is...
- *A restless evil* (v. 8): These two words are very strong in the original language. "Restless" means unstable to the point of anarchy. There is nothing able to restrain it. "Evil" is malice flowing out of a morally rotten character.
- *Full of deadly poison* (v. 8): This phrase indicates that words are like the venom of adders and can bring about spiritual as well as physical death.

Is there hope in this 'noisy' world? Yes! Jesus said that the words we speak reveal the character that is within us: "You brood of vipers! How can you speak good, when you are evil? For out of the abundance of the heart the mouth speaks" (Matthew 12.34). When the heart is overflowing with the love of God, then the words we speak will be full of love.

While no man can tame the tongue, God certainly can! The question is, "Will we let him?"

Prayer: Lord, please sanctify my tongue. May the words of my mouth and the meditation of my heart be acceptable in your sight, O Lord. Amen.

Psalm of the Day: 45.1-7

Simple Honesty
Daily Reading: James 5

> *But above all, my brothers, do not swear, either by heaven or by earth or by any other oath, but let your "yes" be yes and your "no" be no, so that you may not fall under condemnation.* (James 5.12)

Devotional Thought: Recently, I visited the bank with two other members of our homeowners' association. We had been appointed by the association as signatories for our road maintenance account. What I thought should have been a two minute job, turned into two hours. And then, we had to go back for 30 more minutes on another day! I was more than a little dismayed over all the 'legalese' required for such a simple thing.

What has become of our society to cause us to feel the need to protect ourselves with all this legal jargon? Too many people have become experts at twisting words and making them say what was not intended. Attorneys have to be extremely careful and redundant because yes and no are no longer adequate! I guess it is nothing new, is it? James had to deal with it in his letter to the church. James was basically quoting Jesus who said, "Let what you say be simply 'Yes' or 'No'; anything more than this comes from evil" (Matthew 5.37).

Does this mean that we shouldn't swear an oath in court or pledge our honesty? Quite the opposite. In Jesus' day, people circumvented their religious duties by adding elaborate oaths, obscuring the meaning of what was said. We need to remember that context. Then we will see that James and Jesus were advocating for honest, simple communication which assured everyone involved that they were being treated fairly and honestly.

Prayer: Lord, thank you that your words give life. Help me to speak plainly and honestly, so that I can bring the life of God into every conversation that I have, and so that others can have confidence in what I say. Amen.

Psalm of the Day: 45.8-17

The Superiority of Christ
Daily Reading: Hebrews 1

In the past God spoke to our ancestors through the prophets at many times and in various ways, but in these last days he has spoken to us by his Son, whom he appointed heir of all things, and through whom also he made the universe. (Hebrews 1.1-2)

Devotional Thought: The book of Hebrews argues that Christ is superior in all things:

- Christ is superior to angels (chapter 1).
- Christ is greater than Moses (chapter 3).
- Christ, our Great High Priest, is superior to the priests who officiated under the Levitical system (chapter 7).
- The covenant of Christ is superior to the Old Covenant given to the Jews at Sinai (chapter 8).

There are more than 100 references to angels in the Bible from Genesis to Revelation. Angels are featured throughout the Old Testament and mentioned in the book of Hebrews. We generally think of angels of being messengers for God; they did serve that purpose. They ministered to Jesus (Matthew 4:11), and they protect and minister to us in our time of need. Angels are wonderful creatures, but the difference between Christ and angels is clear. Jesus is not an angel; he is the Son of God (v. 5). Jesus is not an angel; he is worshiped by angels (v. 6). Jesus is not an angel; he is God (v. 8). Jesus is not an angel; he is the eternal Creator of all things (vv. 10–12).

So, here is the whole summary of Hebrews in one sentence. Ours is the High Priest of high priests, and he is *seated*. His work is done - completely finished for all time and for all people. So, what does the superiority of Christ mean for us? That Christ is the Son of God means that Jesus is the greatest person in the universe alongside his Father. Therefore, all he taught is true, and all he promised will stand firm, and all his soul-satisfying greatness will never change.

Pastor Dale

Prayer: Jesus, thank you for being my great High Priest, Creator and all sufficient Savior. I acknowledge your superiority in all things. Amen.

Psalm of the Day: 46.1-7

God's Help for Salvation
Daily Reading: Hebrews 2

> *For surely it is not angels that he helps, but he helps the offspring of Abraham.* (Hebrews 2.16)

Devotional Thought: Anytime you unpack scripture, there's way more than can be done in just five minutes. Hebrews 2, does not disappoint.

God has created all things, and everything is marvelous. Nothing would be created or continue to exist without God. All creation needs God's help in some manner to continue to be. This is very true in the specific cases of angels and of human beings. The Bible doesn't have many details about angels, but then, the Bible is not written for angels. It is written for us, the offspring of Abraham, the believers in Christ. It is written to us and for us.

The focus of Hebrews 2 is the salvation of mankind. No big surprise. Salvation is the focus of the entire Bible. But, it is not the angels who need God's help for salvation, it is mankind itself.

God's specific help for our salvation is Jesus. Hebrews 2 shows how it is so helpful. Jesus had to be made just like us so he could be the perfect mediator and the perfect sacrifice. He knows what it is to be human and to be God.

Thank God that he has created human beings and angels. Thank God that he has provided the help that sinful man needs for salvation and reconciliation to him. And beware for, "How shall we escape if we neglect such a great salvation? " (Hebrews 2.3).

John Wade

Prayer: Thank you, Lord, for providing the way. I'll take all the help I can get. Amen!

Psalm of the Day: 46.8-11

Life-Giving Word
Daily Reading: Hebrews 3-4

> For the word of God is living and active, sharper than any two-edged sword, piercing to the division of soul and of spirit, of joints and of marrow, and discerning the thoughts and intentions of the heart. (Hebrews 4.12)

Devotional Thought: Jesus is called the Word throughout the New Testament. The gospel of John begins with this assertion: "In the beginning was the Word, and the Word was with God, and the Word was God." Knowing this gives even more meaning to Hebrews 4:12: "For the word of God is living and active... piercing to the division of soul and of spirit.... and discerning the thoughts and intentions of the heart." The Word is indeed living and active. It is living and active in our hearts if we are followers of Jesus, convicting us and changing us with its power. It is dreadful for those who do not believe... "And no creature is hidden from his sight, but all are naked and exposed to the eyes of him to whom we must give account" (v. 13).

When we are in the Spirit, we have nothing to fear from the two-edged sword. As we are faithful to read God's Word and strive for spiritual wisdom and understanding, we simply ask the Spirit to do the refining work in our hearts. The Lord has promised that his Word will not return to him empty, but it shall accomplish that which he purposes, and shall succeed in the thing for which he sent it (Is. 55:11). None will escape the power of the Word, as we must all give an account on our day of judgment. The wages of sin is death... (Rom. 6:23). The only question is, whose blood will pay for your sins? Romans 6:23 continues, "...but the free gift of God is eternal life in Christ Jesus our Lord." This life is by faith, and faith comes by hearing, and hearing by the Word. Amen!

Jenny

Prayer: Lord, we are overwhelmed with gratitude that you, in your great mercy, would allow your Son's blood to cover our transgressions. Thank you that we can approach you, not with terror and trembling, but with confidence in your Son's righteousness that has been given to us! Amen.

Psalm of the Day: 47.1-9

Are You Sure?

Daily Reading: Hebrews 5-6

We feel sure of better things—things that belong to salvation.
(Hebrews 6.9b)

Devotional Thought: Several years ago, when I completed Clifton's Strengthsfinders evaluation, I discovered that one of my signature strengths is 'positivity.' I tend to view things optimistically. So, I can identify with the writer of Hebrews when he writes, "We feel sure of better things..." But, certainty is not limited to those who are naturally positive. Certainty is rooted in "things that belong to salvation."

What gives us certainty?
- When our hearts are clear. The Holy Spirit convicts of sin, righteousness and judgment. We can be thankful when the Spirit convicts us, because he brings us to repentance and faith. This, of course, relieves the conviction. So, the first gauge of our certainty is a clear conscience before God. But, that is not enough because our hearts can deceive us.
- When our lives have changed. Faith without deeds is dead! We know that our faith is real and life-giving when our lives have been changed by the power of God! We no longer live in the same way that we did when we were slaves to sin. Our language is softer, attitude kinder, behavior more Christ-like. Even that is not enough, though, for we can fall into self-righteousness.
- When our testimony is affirmed - when others see the change that we feel. But, in the final analysis, even that is not enough to make us sure of better things.
- Because God is faithful! Our certainty is not in ourselves, in our feelings, in our performance, in our reputations. Our certainty is in Jesus! The Son of God has saved us according to his Word. God said it. I believe it. That settles it!

Prayer: Thank you, Lord, for the certainty of better things that belong to salvation. I rest in your faithfulness. Amen.

Psalm of the Day: 48.1-8

The Guarantor of a Better Covenant
Daily Reading: Hebrews 7

This makes Jesus the guarantor of a better covenant. (Hebrews 7.22)

Devotional Thought: In Hebrews 6, we encountered the certainty of better things. In the final analysis, we are sure of those things that belong to salvation because of the faithfulness of Jesus. In Hebrews 7, we see how and why Jesus is the guarantor of this better covenant:

- *Permanence* (vv. 23-24). We know the vagaries of changing leadership in our own culture and politics, don't we? When one administration goes out and another comes in, changes are inevitable. Jesus superseded an old priesthood which had ever-changing high priests. But, Jesus is the same "yesterday, today, and forever." We know where we stand in this covenant, because we know who our High Priest is.
- *Perseverance* (v. 25). Several years ago, I experienced some 'trouble' with the leadership of the church I served. To make matters worse, my district superintendent, who was an advocate interceding on my behalf, retired. I felt very vulnerable. The good news is, that Jesus is always living to intercede for me! He saves to the uttermost!
- *Personal* (vv. 26-27). Unlike other priests who offered impersonal sacrifices, Jesus offered himself! Jesus came to us, descending into our darkness, suffering our sickness, dying our death. He personally became what we are, sin excepted, to make us into what he is.
- *Perfection* (28). The old covenant required the inspection of the sacrifice to assure it was without blemish. Jesus' offering of himself was perfect because he was personally holy and righteous! There is no question about the integrity and efficacy of the Lamb of God who takes away the sin of the world!

Prayer: Thank you, Lord Jesus, that you are the Guarantor of a better covenant. I trust in you, O Lord. Amen.

Psalm of the Day: 48.9-14

A Good Deal More
Daily Reading: Hebrews 8

For this is the covenant that I will make with the house of Israel after those days, declares the Lord: I will put my laws into their minds, and write them on their hearts, and I will be their God, and they shall be my people. (Hebrews 8.10)

Devotional Thought: God takes something good and makes it even better. Or, he takes away one thing and gives us something better in return. That's what he did with the Old Covenant. He took it away and replaced it with something better - the New Covenant in Jesus Christ!

Consider what God says he will do...
- *Put my laws into their minds.* Since their foundation, the Jews had been concerned with keeping the law of God near: "You shall bind them as a sign on your hand, and they shall be as frontlets between your eyes. You shall write them on the doorposts of your house and on your gates" (Deuteronomy 6.8-9). God says in Hebrews, "I have something better for you. I will make my Word a part of your very thought process." The Word of God is called the sword of the Spirit. It is the Spirit who makes our minds sharp with the Word.
- *Write my laws on their hearts.* Not only will you know the Word, you will love the Word! Through the grace of the indwelling Spirit, God will cause us to love his ways. He changes us from the inside out when we surrender our affections to him!
- *Be their God.* God will make himself the ruling principle and power in our lives. Oh the wonder that he wants to be identified with us! He is casting his lot in with ours; his reputation depends on us.
- *They shall be my people.* I'm not saying this is easy. Jesus never said it was. It takes giving ourselves completely to him. But, we get all of him in return!

Prayer: Thank you, Father, for the New Covenant in Jesus Christ! Please put your Word deep in my mind and my heart and be my God. I give myself completely to you. Amen.

Psalm of the Day: 49.1-9

Seconds, Anyone?

Daily Reading: Hebrews 9

Behind the second curtain was a second section called the Most Holy Place. (Hebrews 9.3)

Devotional Thought: Hebrews 9, takes us "behind the second curtain", where we find the "second section."

In the original tabernacle, and later in the temple, there were two sections, the Holy Place and the Most Holy Place (the Holy of Holies). The two were separated by a curtain. (It was that curtain, or veil, that was torn in two from top to bottom when Jesus died on the cross.) The first section was holy and was a place for the worship of God and fellowship of the saints. The second section, however, was accessible only to the high priest and required blood for entrance. These two sections are representative of the two experiences of grace that are ours in Christ.

In addition we find in this chapter...

- *A second covenant* (15). This covenant is better than the first, in that it is now written not on tablets of stone, but on tablets of the human heart. It is signified by circumcision of the heart by the Spirit.
- *A second sacrifice* (23). The blood of bulls and goats was not enough to take away sin. There needed to be a better sacrifice, a perfect sacrifice. That sacrifice behind the second curtain is the Son of God himself, who entered in once and for all. No further sacrifice is needed other than the Lamb without blemish, who was slain from the foundation of the world.
- *A second appearing* (28). The Lamb who was slain, however, has risen! He is ascended to heaven, and will open the scroll that will mark the beginning of the new heaven and new earth. He is coming again to take us to be with him forever and ever.

Yes, I'll have seconds!

Prayer: Thank you, Jesus, that you entered behind the second curtain, and you now invite me to go with you there in a new covenant. I long for your appearing, O Lord! Amen.

Psalm of the Day: 49.10-15

Taking the Old and Making It New

Daily Reading: Hebrews 10

He does away with the first in order to establish the second.
(Hebrews 10.9b)

Devotional Thought: In the first two churches that I pastored, I was privileged to serve older, established congregations. In that role, I led in remodeling efforts and building projects. It was demanding work while shepherding a flock. I remember one day, in the midst of a remodeling effort, when God came to reassure me of the importance of what I was doing. The thought clearly came to me that God had called me to take what was old and make it new. The more I thought about it, the more excited I got!

God does just that, doesn't he? He is in the transforming business. He takes what is old and makes it new:

- *Old covenant.* God entered a blood covenant with Abraham and circumcision, then codified it through Moses and the Ten Commandments. Now, however, there is new covenant. This covenant is through Jesus. It is a covenant in his blood. We commemorate it in the Lord's Supper.
- *Old community.* The old community, Israel, was established around The Law and Sabbath. The new community, The Church, is established around the Royal Law (of love) and around the Sabbath rest for the people of God. The old community was done away with in order to establish a new and better community of faith.
- *Old character.* In Christ we are all new creations. We are no longer sinners, but we are saints. Then, in grace and through the Holy Spirit, God enables us to grow in the likeness of Christ. "From glory to glory he's changing me!"

God is in the transforming business. Be transformed through Christ today!

Prayer: Lord, thank you for taking this sinner and making him/her into a saint. Help me to live out what you have made me within, to grow more like you daily. Amen.

Psalm of the Day: 49.16-20

Will You Be a Hero?

Daily Reading: Hebrews 11

...in reverent fear constructed an ark. (Hebrews 11.7)

Devotional Thought: Who are your heroes - people who shaped - maybe even "saved" - you? I have many who showed me the way. Some showed me life skills: my childhood neighbor, Si Siler; my Uncle Cedric; my father-in-law, Nick Moore. These men taught me a work ethic and the value of saving. There are other heroes, men who constructed spiritual values: my first pastor, Nelson Perdue; the district superintendent who gave me my first church, Eugene Simpson; an older friend who spent time with me, Don Ekis. These men led me to God. They, among many, many others, are my heroes.

Hebrews 11, is all about heroes of faith. Noah was one such man in this "Hall of Faith." Noah, in reverent fear, constructed an ark, and...

- *Condemned the world.* Noah was not afraid to name sin for what it was. He stood in stark contrast to the evil of his day by his faith and obedience. The world today needs women and men who will stand against the evils of pornography, human trafficking, economic oppression, loose morality, and all other forms of sin.
- *Inherited righteousness.* Noah was not righteous by his own efforts; he inherited it from God. Noah then claimed his inheritance and went to work to possess it. Today, we need people who will take God at his Word, receive the righteousness of Christ, and build their lives according to his pattern.
- *Saved his family.* Noah's faith not only saved him, but also his family. When men and women of God give themselves to works of righteousness, the generation following them will benefit. We need parents who will put faith above sports, generosity above materialism, and holiness above pleasure.

Will you be a hero?

Prayer: Thank you, Father, for the "Hall of Faith" in Hebrews 11. Help me, O Lord, to be a hero of faith, so that others may find their way to you. Amen.

Psalm of the Day: 50.1-6

Receiving and Revering

Daily Reading: Hebrews 12

Therefore let us be grateful for receiving a kingdom that cannot be shaken, and thus let us offer to God acceptable worship, with reverence and awe, for our God is a consuming fire. (Hebrews 12.28-29)

Devotional Thought: In our faith walk, most of us have not endured persecution to the extent of First Century believers. That persecution was real. It was widespread. It was life-threatening. So, when the author of Hebrews instructs his readers to "run with endurance the race that is set before us" (v. 1) and "consider him who endured from sinners such hostility against himself, so that you may not grow weary or fainthearted" (v. 3), these exhortations were greatly needed.

To what end were these believers (and today's believers) enduring? To what end did they hold on to their faith? For the joy of "receiving a kingdom that cannot be shaken" (v. 28)! The original Hebrew readers would have read the last section of this letter, remembering the stories of God as he descended onto Mount Sinai in the desert to establish the covenant, with awe and reverence. God's terrifying holiness caused every Israelite to tremble with fear, and no person on earth is exempt from the standard of holiness that God has set forth for his creation.

What is the result of receiving a Kingdom that cannot be shaken? "Acceptable worship with reverence and awe." Acceptable worship is worship on God's terms. Before, under the old covenant, this included very specific rules about sacrifice; only certain people could "worship" under this covenant, at certain times, under certain conditions. Under the new covenant, we can approach the throne with confidence, on God's terms, for Jesus has reconciled us to him.

Jenny

Prayer: Lord, we thank you for the new covenant established by your Son. We thank you for our promised inheritance, as heirs to the Kingdom, the Kingdom that cannot be shaken. We anticipate the glorious day of your return! Amen.

Psalm of the Day: 50.7-15

Sisterly Love

Daily Reading: Hebrews 13

Let brotherly love continue. (Hebrews 13.1)

Devotional Thought: I love to see my daughters enjoying one another as friends. Holidays at our home are wonderful, because our kids really like each other!

The Lord feels that same way about his children. He delights in the love and fellowship that we enjoy. Jesus commands us, "love one another: just as I have loved you, you also are to love one another" (John 13.34). The writer of Hebrews reinforced that thought when he wrote, "Let brotherly love continue." In the following verses, we see some of the 'recipients' of that brotherly love:

- *Strangers.* Some people are stranger than others! I've heard it said, "Everybody is normal - until you get to know them!" But, the fact of the matter is, we are to love people who are different from us. Jesus certainly did. We must not isolate ourselves from those not like us. That means we do what Jesus did - go where the 'sinners' are.
- *Angels.* The word angel means messenger. There are times when messengers bring us words that encourage and inspire. At other times, they must speak the hard truth in love. We must love them then, too.
- *Prisoners.* We tend to write people off when they fail. Remember that before a person is incarcerated or is imprisoned by addiction, bitterness, or fear, they have become prisoners to Satan. We should love the one who is bound by sin!
- *Spouses.* I am amazed by the couples I see that don't seem to like each other, but instead 'use' one another - even in the church. The Bible teaches we are to love and respect our spouses. Lana is my best friend, and I can't imagine it any other way!

Let brotherly *and sisterly* love continue!

Prayer: Thank you, Lord Jesus, that you love me - that you laid down your life for me - even when I was a stranger to grace. Help me to love others the way you love me. Amen.

Psalm of the Day: 50.16-23

120

Master Your Circumstances
Daily Reading: Judges 1

> *After the death of Joshua, the people of Israel inquired of the Lord.*
> (Judges 1.1)

Devotional Thought: Do you remember those picture riddles that we used to get when we were in school? The challenge was to find out "What's different between these pictures?" I used to love them!

The people of Israel were faced with something different between the book of Joshua and the book of Judges. It was the same type of difference faced between the books of Deuteronomy and Joshua: the death of a beloved leader. Just as they had counted on Moses to lead them to the Promised Land, so they had depended on Joshua to lead them through the Promised Land. But now, Joshua was gone. What were they to do?

The people of Israel inquired of the Lord!

When we go through changes, when things are different in our lives, we sometimes forget to inquire of the Lord. But, every change is an invitation from God to look unto him, for he is the author and finisher of our faith (Hebrews 12.2). Innumerable changes come in life: The birth of a child, the purchase of a home, a change in jobs - At these intersections, God is waiting for us to inquire of him, "Which way should I go, Lord?"

It's tempting to do life on auto-pilot, to let our circumstances lead us through life. But, God does not want us to be mastered by our circumstances. Instead, he invites us - with his wisdom and strength - to master our circumstances by following the Master!

Prayer: Lord, every day I face changes and choices, some big, some small. Help me, in the changes of life, to choose the path that you have for me. Amen.

Psalm of the Day: 51.1-6

Invite. Invest. Involve.
Daily Reading: Judges 2-3

> *Then the Lord raised up judges, who saved them out of the hand of those who plundered them* (Judges 2.16)

Devotional Thought: How often we hear things like, "What's this generation coming to?"! That certainly was true in the time of the Judges. The charismatic, foundational leaders of two generations prior - Moses and then Joshua - had "gone the way of the fathers," and the nation languished under the oppression of their enemies. God did not forget his people, but he "raised up judges, who saved them..."

The Lord still raises up judges. One generation moves on into history, and the Lord calls new leaders to take their place. But, do we have any role in the process? I believe we do. Our part in passing on leadership to those whom God raises up is simple. I call it i[3].

- *Invite.* This is a critical part of leadership development, even of evangelism and disciple making. We need to prayerfully take the initiative to invite younger (less experienced) people to "spread their wings and fly." Are they going to make mistakes? You bet! We sure did, but God used us in spite of it. Our part of invitation is to choose them, cherish them, and challenge them. Who are you inviting?
- *Invest.* There is more to it than simply inviting. That is hard work, but there is harder work to be done. We must invest in the next generation of leaders. We do this when we intercede for them in prayer, instruct them in Kingdom truth, and introduce them to other leaders and to the Holy Spirit.
- *Involve.* Then comes the risky part. We have to trust them with responsibility, involving them in the work of the Kingdom. To do that, we serve with them, send them to serve, and supervise them in their service.

The Lord raises up judges. Will you take part in the process?

Prayer: Lord, thank you for the leaders who came before me. Thank you that they invited me to follow you; that they invested in me and involved me in the work of the Kingdom. Help me to do the same for others whom you are calling today. Amen.

Psalm of the Day: 51.7-15

Unlikely Heroes

Daily Reading: Judges 4-5

> *Most blessed of women be Jael, the wife of Heber the Kenite, of tent-dwelling women most blessed.* (Judges 5.24)

Devotional Thought: We pray regularly in our church for the end of human trafficking. As I prayed this past Sunday, I was overcome by anger. I asked God, "How could anybody do this to a child or to any human being?" There are some crimes so horrible that we can only think of the justice they demand. Judges 4-5, is like that. We may be put off by the gruesome details, but the fact of the matter is that the enemies of Israel were terrorizing innocent people: They "oppressed the people of Israel cruelly for twenty years" (Judges 4.3).

The Israelites needed deliverance and the terrorists needed justice. God worked salvation through the most unlikely of means:
- *Barak.* Here was a man with skills for warfare, yet he lacked courage, drive, and a sense of destiny. God, however, was able to wake him out of his stupor and use him. He did it through...
- *Deborah.* It was very unusual for a woman to be a prophet and a political and military leader in that generation. Yet, Deborah did not shrink from her task. As unlikely as it seemed that God would use her, he did! And, she was able to goad the more experienced Barak into action.
- The most surprising of all was *Jael.* She had no skills, no particular call from God and no history of bravery in battle. Yet, this "behind the scenes" player was a true hero in the work of deliverance for God's people. Using no strategy but the enemy's weariness, no weapons but a mallet and tent peg, Jael sealed the victory.

The enemy is terrorizing God's children. His crimes are so heinous, that justice must be done. Will you be used of God to help bring about deliverance?

Prayer: Lord, help me to overcome my lethargy, my excuse-making and my lack of resources. Instead, help me to use what is at hand and bring about your glorious Kingdom for those who need to be delivered from sin. Amen.

Psalm of the Day: 51.16-19

Shalom

Daily Reading: Judges 6

> *Then Gideon built an altar there to the Lord and called it, The Lord Is Peace.* (Judges 6.24)

Devotional Thought: Judges 5 shared the story of the unlikely heroes - Barak, Deborah, and Jael. Today's scripture tells the story of another one: Gideon. When the enemy was plundering God's people, the angel of the Lord came to Gideon and called him a mighty warrior. Gideon thought he was mocking him. After all, he was hiding in a winepress trying to eke out a living for his impoverished family.

But, something changed in the heart of this quiet, fearful, self-doubting man. God came on the scene! Gideon became convinced in his heart that God *would* use such a one as he. After that encounter, Gideon knew God by a new name: The Lord is Peace, or "Jehovah Shalom."

Shalom means so much more than simply the absence of trouble and conflict. The Hebrew word conveys a sense of "completeness, soundness, welfare, and peace."

As you read this chapter, you will discover what Gideon discovered...
- In the midst of turmoil, the Lord is peace.
- In the midst of suffering, the Lord is peace.
- In the midst of fear, the Lord is peace.
- In the midst of doubt, the Lord is peace.
- In the midst of a great challenge, the Lord is peace.
- In the midst of idolatry, the Lord is peace.
- In the midst of uncertainty, the Lord is peace.

Shalom!

Prayer: Thank you, Lord, for giving me your peace. The scripture says you will keep in perfect peace the one whose mind is stayed on you (Isaiah 26.3). Lord, I fix my mind upon you just now and walk in your peace. Amen.

Psalm of the Day: 52.1-9

Don't Do That

Daily Reading: Judges 7

> ... *lest Israel boast over me, saying, 'My own hand has saved me.'*
> (Judges 7.2)

Devotional Thought: I know I've told this story dozens of times, but it never grows old in the telling. Years ago, when I was a younger man, I used to travel quite a bit for the company I worked for. I would park my car at the airport, be gone a day or two, and then come back, jump in the car and head home. The airport was about 50 miles from home. We had 3 children at home - young babies. Lana did not work outside the home, so it worked out OK - most of the time - to have just one car. When I was gone, she was busy at home.

It usually went without incident, but on one trip I had been having trouble with our car. I often found myself either getting a jump or 'push-starting' it - you know, pushing it in neutral, jumping in, and popping the clutch. I tried to park it in places where I could push it down a little grade.

I was coming home from a trip and I remember praying, "Lord, would you please help me start my car..." Then I did something crazy. I prayed, "But if you don't, that's OK. I parked it on a grade, and I can push start it."

Ummm... Don't do that.

God let me push start it. Once...it didn't start. Again...nope. I was running out of room. One more push was all I had left on that little grade. I prayed a different prayer. "Oh, God! I need you. Please help me start my car!" It started.

I learned a valuable lesson that day. Always remember "Our help is in the name of the Lord, who made heaven and earth" (Psalm 124.8).

Prayer: Lord, like Gideon, help us always remember that our help is in you. Let us never think that it is our own hand that saves us. Thank you, Lord, for your faithfulness to deliver, whether by many or by few. We trust in you. Amen.

Psalm of the Day: 53.1-6

Snared

Daily Reading: Judges 8

> And Gideon made an ephod of it and put it in his city, in Ophrah. And all Israel whored after it there, and it became a snare to Gideon and to his family. (Judges 8.27)

Devotional Thought: Gideon was a great warrior, judge, and leader whom God used to deliver his people from the oppression of Midian. He had understandably become something of a hero among the Israelite people. They said to him, "Rule over us, you and your son and your grandson also, for you have saved us from the hand of Midian" (v. 22). Even then, Gideon refused this honor, knowing that the Israelites had elevated him to the Lord's position of authority. However, Gideon made a fatal mistake. He requested that they make an ephod (which was a priestly garment) out of gold. He then displayed it in his city - to give honor and glory to him and his family, not to the Lord. "And all Israel whored after it there, and it became a snare to Gideon and to his family" (v. 27).

It is sad to see this great man of God go from faithful and humble to prideful and self-righteous. The men of Israel appealed to his sense of pride, and Gideon created a snare, not only for himself, but for his entire family and all of Israel. It seems incredible to us. Are we guilty of the same sin that led to Gideon's downfall? How often do we enter into service to God with good intentions, but then let praise and accolades fall onto us, instead of onto the God who equips us for every good work? How often do we steal the glory that rightly belongs to our Creator? Let us learn a lesson from the story of Gideon. Let us heed the words of Jesus in Matthew 5:16, "Let your light shine before others, that they may see your good deeds and glorify *your Father in heaven.*"

Jenny

Prayer: Lord, we want you and you alone to receive the glory for our good works. We know as believers that any talents or skills we have are from you. Any blessings are gifts from our Father. Help us to remember this, and boast only in the cross. Amen.

Psalm of the Day: 54.1-7

Who's Your Boss?
Daily Reading: Judges 9

> *Which is better for you, that all seventy of the sons of Jerubbaal rule over you, or that one rule over you?* (Judges 9.2)

Devotional Thought: I was talking with some friends the other day, and they asked who my boss was. Some thought it was my district superintendent. I said, "No, not really. He's my pastor, but he's not my boss." What about the church board? "No, not them either. I actually am the chairman of the board." Well then, the congregation? "Um, no, not them either. I am the shepherd of the flock." Well who *is* your boss? "After God, it's the district assembly! The Church Manual says I'm 'amenable to the district assembly.'" Then I looked at my friends, "Oh no! Most of you are members of the district assembly! That means you're all my boss!"

That was all said in fun, but have you ever had a job where you had more than one boss? It's not pleasant, is it? You never really know what to do. And, Abimelech, although godless, ruthless and thankless, shows the logic and wisdom of having only one boss - of having only one defining principle, only one God.

We have only one God, don't we? The scripture says, "The Lord our God, the Lord is one. You shall love the Lord your God with all your heart and with all your soul and with all your might" (Deuteronomy 6.4-5), and "You shall have no other gods before me" (Exodus 20.3). Our one God will crush all other gods under our feet (Romans 16.20).

Which is better? Is it not better to have the one true God as our God? Nobody needs two bosses, "for either he will hate the one and love the other, or he will be devoted to the one and despise the other" (Matthew 6.24).

Who - or what - rules over you?

Prayer: "King of my life, I crown thee now. Thine shall the glory be! Lest I forget thy thorn-crowned brow, lead me to Calvary." Jesus, no other God would pour out his life for me. I gladly own you as my King! Amen.

Psalm of the Day: 55.1-8

"No Theology" Is Bad Theology

Daily Reading: Judges 10-11

> And Jephthah made a vow to the Lord and said, "If you will give the Ammonites into my hand, then whatever comes out from the doors of my house to meet me when I return in peace from the Ammonites shall be the Lord's, and I will offer it up for a burnt offering."
> (Judges 11.30-31)

Devotional Thought: I know people who say, "I don't like all this stuff about doctrine." Some even neglect doctrine in the choice of their church. That is a mistake. Doctrine is important! Judges 11, contains the tragic story of Jephthah, a judge in Israel who had bad doctrine. He didn't understand God and made his own theology.

Not understanding the covenant nature of God, Jephthah made a rash vow, saying that if God would give him the victory, then he would sacrifice the first thing that came out of the door of his house. Tragically, his daughter was the first thing he saw. We are not certain if Jephthah actually sacrificed his daughter (the text is unclear), but at a minimum, he did prevent her from leading a normal life. In those days daughters were considered the property of their fathers until they were married, and Jephthah was within his rights to prohibit marriage, though not to make a human sacrifice of her.

Jephthah's daughter lost her future because of her father's bad theology and stubborn pride. He thought he had to bargain with God, but God was ready to help him even before he called out to him. His pride prevented him from repenting, confessing his sin and seeking release from his vow. But, his daughter paid the price.

It is true that God used Jephthah to win deliverance for his people Israel. God uses imperfect vessels. How much better it would have been for his family, however, if he had cared about doctrine!

Prayer: Lord, help me to "watch my life and doctrine closely", so that I live and believe in a way that is pleasing to you and helpful to those around me. Amen.

Psalm of the Day: 55.9-15

Bluster or Battle

Daily Reading: Judges 12-13

The men of Ephraim were called to arms, and they crossed to Zaphon and said to Jephthah, "Why did you cross over to fight against the Ammonites and did not call us to go with you? We will burn your house over you with fire." (Judges 12.1)

Devotional Thought: You've known people who have said, "You should have called me! I would have helped!" Or even the ones who get mad at you for not including them in the work. The men of Ephraim were like that. They complained against Gideon, "'What is this that you have done to us, not to call us when you went to fight against Midian?' And they accused him fiercely" (Judges 8.1). Gideon was able to appease these hot-tempered Ephraimites by stroking their vaunted egos.

Here in Judges 12, we again see the Ephraimites "up in arms" for being overlooked by Jephthah. This time, however, they are not appeased, they are punished. Jephthah called their bluff, basically saying, "I did call you. You just didn't come." Then, having been threatened with violence, he turned the table on the Ephraimites, and 42,000 of them were killed in war.

Looking back on the history of Ephraim, we find that they were not as fierce and brave as they led people to believe. "Ephraim did not drive out the Canaanites who lived in Gezer, so the Canaanites lived in Gezer among them" (Judges 1.29). They were more bluster than battle, interested more in comfort than conflict.

Ephraim allowed their enemies to live among them. I believe that was part of their problem. Then to compensate, they picked 'safe' battles with those who wouldn't retaliate. Jephthah showed them the error of rash words.

Do I allow spiritual 'enemies' such as anger, pride and fear to dwell in my life? Am I more bluster than battle when it comes to spiritual things? Do I lash out at the 'safe' ones in my life?

Prayer: Lord, deliver me from arrogance and anger. May my words and actions reflect the courage, resolve and humility of Christ. Amen.

Psalm of the Day: 55.16-23

Super Hero
Daily Reading: Judges 14-15

> *[Samson] was very thirsty, and he called upon the Lord and said, "You have granted this great salvation by the hand of your servant, and shall I now die of thirst and fall into the hands of the uncircumcised?"*
> (Judges 15.18)

Devotional Thought: When I was a little boy, my siblings and I used to play super-heroes. We would argue over who could be Hercules or Atlas or Tarzan. If those were taken, sometimes I had to be Samson. We knew about the others from black and white TV shows. And, we had heard enough about Samson in Vacation Bible School that we knew he was a strong hero, too, but he didn't always win.

The story of Samson is a mixed bag, isn't it? He was a hero in Israel, delivering his people from Philistine oppression. God gave him strength and victory in battle. But, he was immoral and impetuous. I wonder sometimes if he isn't a picture of some modern Christians.

Whether it was eating honey from the carcass of a lion or engaging the services of a prostitute, he constantly struggled to keep his fleshly appetites in check. When he saw a Philistine virgin, he just had to have her as his wife, even though it was strictly forbidden him as a Nazarite. When his pride was damaged, he sought vengeance on those who mocked him and brought trouble on himself and others. When he grew weary and thirsty, he accused God of leaving him. Samson was indeed a super-hero, but he was also a spiritual infant.

Samson needed the New Testament principle: "All that is in the world—the desires of the flesh and the desires of the eyes and pride of life—is not from the Father but is from the world. And the world is passing away along with its desires, but whoever does the will of God abides forever" (1 John 2.16-17).

Prayer: Lord, help me to be a spiritual super-hero. Not for the praise of man, but for the pleasing of my heavenly Father; not to master people, but to master my passions. Help me to be a hero like Jesus! Amen.

Psalm of the Day: 56.1-6

Don't Be Triggered!
Daily Reading: Judges 16

> *And when she pressed him hard with her words day after day, and urged him, his soul was vexed to death. And he told her all his heart... She made him sleep on her knees. And she called a man and had him shave off the seven locks of his head. Then she began to torment him, and his strength left him.* (Judges 16.16-19)

Devotional Thought: One of the most important ingredients to successful sobriety is to avoid being 'triggered' by circumstances and friends. The sad, but irrefutable truth is that some friends will have to be left behind. That is true for more than just addiction. The wrong friends can drag you down.

Delilah was like that in Samson's life. Her tactics seem only too familiar as we deal with sin. The spiritual slide in Samson's life is a textbook case:

- *She pressed and urged him.* Temptation to sin increases in proportion to its proximity. The closer we are to it, the more pressing are its demands. "Sin is crouching at your door, but you must master it" (Genesis 4.7).
- *Day after day.* Delilah didn't take a break. She wanted Samson's defeat and kept working at it. That's why we are told to throw off the sin that so easily entangles (Hebrews 12.1).
- *His soul was vexed.* That was a good thing! It was God telling him "Get out!" God sends the Holy Spirit to convict us when we are getting too close to sin. We do well to heed those promptings.
- *He told her his heart.* Giving in to sin is giving away something most precious, something reserved for God!
- *Sleep.* We need to stay awake spiritually!
- *Shaved off his hair.* He never meant for it to happen, but while he slept, he was defeated.
- *Strength left him.* When we give in to one temptation, the others gain strength in our lives.
- *She tormented him.* You think sin is your friend? Satan will torment you, shame will grip you, and despair will rule you.

So, run from sin and do not play around the edges of temptation!

Prayer: Father, help me to be strong in the face of temptation. Thank you that you have made a way of escape for every sin that I face. Help me, O Lord, to take that escape route! Amen.

Psalm of the Day: 56.7-13

Dangerous Substitutes
Daily Reading: Judges 17-18

> *Then Micah said, "Now I know that the Lord will prosper me, because I have a Levite as priest."* (Judges 17.13)

Devotional Thought: Have I mentioned that sound doctrine is important? Some people prefer to substitute superstitions and feelings for strong biblical theology. It is easier and just feels better! Micah was fooled by such quasi-religious principles.

Micah was a thief and a scoundrel. He stole money from his mother and then expected a reward when he brought it back. When he returned the stolen silver, he and his mother decided that it sounded like a good idea to make the coins into an idol. (It's pretty clear where Micah got his misguided theology!) To compound his error, Micah decided that when a Levite presented himself in need of employment, it would be a good idea to employ him as a priest. Then, the coup de grace: "I know that the Lord will prosper me because I have a Levite as a priest."

What?

Was Micah serious? He apparently didn't have enough doctrine to understand that he shouldn't steal (the 8th commandment) or that he shouldn't have an idol (2nd commandment). The fact that the priesthood was reserved for Aaron's line (not the Levites *in toto*), would never have occurred to him. He simply had some vague memory that Levites were sacred people.

This story that began with thievery and continued through spiritual confusion, ended with defeat and disgrace! Micah's 'god' and his priest were stolen by others whose theology was just as bad! "But the people of Dan took what Micah had made, and the priest who belonged to him" (Judges 18.27).

Later, we will read sad words that reflect the spiritual confusion of these times: "Everyone did as he saw fit." Superstitions and feelings are dangerous substitutes for sound doctrine!

Prayer: Father, you have deigned to give me your Word, the Bible. Help me to read it and to understand it. Then, help me to live according to your Word. Protect me from error, O Lord. Amen.

Psalm of the Day: 57.1-5

Live and Let... *Die*?
Daily Reading: Judges 19

And all who saw it said, "Such a thing has never happened or been seen from the day that the people of Israel came up out of the land of Egypt until this day; consider it, take counsel, and speak." (Judges 19.30)

Devotional Thought: A horrible crime against a vulnerable woman, the story of the Levite's concubine, shows the complete depravity to which man will sink when left to his own moral code and conduct.

While this specific account may shock us, we are surrounded by the same type of evil in our current culture. "And since they did not see fit to acknowledge God, God gave them up to a debased mind to do what ought not to be done. They were filled with all manner of unrighteousness, evil, covetousness, malice... envy, murder, strife, deceit, maliciousness. They are gossips, slanderers, haters of God..." (Romans 1.28-30). Paul's words give the cause and effect relationship between rejection of God and the evil that exists in our world. They are equally applicable to Old Testament times, New Testament times, and current times. "Though they know God's righteous decree that those who practice such things deserve to die, they not only do them but give approval to those who practice them." This is eerily on the mark for today's "live and let live" morality.

When we see a new depth of depravity emerge in our culture, it should not surprise us, but should spur us to prayer. We should not bend with the flexible morality of the progressive masses, but stand firm on the Lord's definition of sin and his warnings of its consequences. The world will hate us, just as it hated and rejected God's own Son. But, acceptance of sin is acceptance of death for those who do not yet know the truth. May we show love as Jesus did, never compromising the truth, but full of love and compassion for the lost.

Jenny

Prayer: Lord, help us to understand how to be full of grace and truth. We know we will not be loved by the world for speaking the truth about sin and our need for a Savior. We will be hated, mocked, and reviled. Give us the ability to love our enemies and win them to your Kingdom. Amen.

Psalm of the Day: 57.6-11

Where Do You Go for Advice?

Daily Reading: Judges 20

Behold, you people of Israel, all of you, give your advice and counsel here." (Judges 20.7)

Devotional Thought: I appreciate my daughter, Jenny, writing yesterday's devotional. When she saw her assignment, she wasn't exactly thrilled with her dad! Judges 19, is tough, and I was just as glad that she had it! (She did a great job BTW.) Then I came to Judges 20! (Spoiler alert: it doesn't get easier tomorrow!)

Judges reminds me that just because someone in the Bible does it, that doesn't make it right. Most people in the Bible are just as ignorant as we are today. That's why I highlighted today's verse. The people compounded the problem by seeking a solution in the wrong place. They had a human council, instead of seeking godly counsel. Instead of humbling themselves, broken and desperate before God, they scratched their heads and looked at each other asking, "What do you think we should do?"

Confusion, death, and destruction sometimes come when God allows us to have what we ask for... I believe that God would rather this whole sordid affair had never happened. I believe that God would have preferred that the tribe of Benjamin take care of it. Self-righteous, hyper-critical judges do not normally come to sound conclusions - especially when they don't know the Bible! I believe that God would have preferred that Israel seek peaceful resolution, not make threatening demands. Blessed are the peacemakers, not trouble makers! I believe that God would have preferred for Benjamin to turn over the guilty murderers, rather than protect them illegally. God had made cities of refuge for that purpose.

Once again, we see how dangerous it is when everybody does as he sees fit. Where do you go for advice and counsel? Let the Word of God be your counsel and advice.

Prayer: Lord, forgive me when I substitute men's advice for God's truth, political correctness for biblical counsel. Help me to know the difference and to seek your wisdom. In the name of Jesus who is the Way, the Truth and the Life. Amen.

Psalm of the Day: 58.1-8

Ugly

Daily Reading: Judges 21

And they said, "O Lord, the God of Israel, why has this happened in Israel, that today there should be one tribe lacking in Israel?"
(Judges 21.3)

Devotional Thought: Whew! We are finally reaching the conclusion of Judges. It's not that this book is bad. It's just that it is depressing to see how bad things can get when people choose to ignore the commands of God. I'm glad that God gave us Judges. I just wish we didn't need it! As I mentioned yesterday, this chapter doesn't get any better. The people of God are solving their problems their way instead of God's way. When we do that, people get hurt. People get lost. People turn ugly.

Ugly. That's a good word to describe these closing chapters of Judges. The people lapse into sin, and sin is ugly.

The incident in Judges 21, shows that sin is ugly in its...
- *Inception.* This whole ugly scenario never needed to happen. It goes back to the ugliness of what happened in Gibeah, when the man gave up his concubine to be raped and murdered to a horde of degenerates. Sin starts out in ugliness.
- *Impact.* The sin at Gibeah did not stop there. Eventually, it worked its way all through society, touching everything and everybody with its ugliness.
- *Irresponsibility.* There is something particularly ugly about the failure to assume responsibility and take blame. What is the mantra? "Admit nothing, deny everything, demand proof, and make counter accusations."
- *Increase.* Multiplied among the people of God, it becomes uglier. There's a saying that catches that ugliness, too: "Sin will take you farther than you want to go, keep you longer than you want to stay and cost you more than you want to pay."

"In those days, there was no king in Israel. Everyone did what was right in his own eyes" (Judges 21.25). We need to make Jesus King!

Prayer: Lord, please give me the wisdom and humility to acknowledge my sin, admit my mistakes and assume my responsibility. I trust in Jesus. He is my King! Amen.

Psalm of the Day: 58.9-11

Joy Unspeakable

Daily Reading: 1 Peter 1

Though you have not seen him, you love him. Though you do not now see him, you believe in him and rejoice with joy that is inexpressible and filled with glory, obtaining the outcome of your faith, the salvation of your souls. (1 Peter 1.8-9)

Devotional Thought: When Jesus first appeared to the apostles after his resurrection, Thomas was not there. He stated emphatically, "Unless I see... I will never believe" (John 20.25). A week later, Jesus appeared before them again, and Thomas was there. That convinced him! But, Jesus had a different take on it: "Blessed are those who have not seen and yet have believed" (John 20.29). Peter was there on both occasions, and it made a deep impression on him. Years later, he wrote these words to second generation Christians - who had been saved after Jesus' ascension into heaven: "Though you have not seen him, you love him" (1 Peter 1.8). In these two verses, Peter reminds us...

That love is able to overcome any obstacle. Just like us, those early Christians had never seen Jesus face-to-face. Yet, they were willing to give him their devotion and allegiance. When new life is given to us through the forgiveness of sins, our love knows no bounds!

That faith is more powerful than sight. Skepticism says, "Show me and I'll believe it." God says, "Believe it and I'll show you." The Bible is full of stories of those who believed God without seeing it with their own eyes. Those are the ones who obtained the promise.

That joy can exceed our ability to describe. You've heard the expression, "It just doesn't get any better than this." Usually, that is an overstatement. But, with Jesus we obtain the salvation of our souls, and it literally doesn't get any better than that. I am reminded of the old hymn: "It is joy unspeakable and full of glory! Oh, the half has never yet been told!"

Prayer: Thank you, Jesus, for your undefeatable love! Thank you for the faith to believe, even when I can't see. Thank you for sending your Spirit to speak to me. I love you, I believe in you, and I rejoice in my salvation. Amen.

Psalm of the Day: 59.1-9

Grow Up into Salvation
Daily Reading: 1 Peter 2

Grow up into salvation. (1 Peter 2.2)

Devotional Thought: What a joy to watch our children grow! They were not born to remain infants, but to grow in the life that they have received. The same is true of spiritual life. In 1 Peter 2, we see that spiritually we are to...

Grow up in salvation (v. 2). Too often we view salvation as a transaction, so that when we are 'saved' the deal is completed. End of story. Biblical salvation, however, is about so much more than being born again. God has saved us, is saving us, and will save us. Salvation is not a legal status, but a living relationship. We are always growing in it.

Be built up (v. 5). This indicates that our growth is the work of God, not ourselves. Just as a plant grows because of the sun, rain and soil, so we grow in the Lord because he shines his love on us in our worship, he refreshes us with the Word, and he plants us in the nourishing environment of the Church. Grace always is at work in our salvation!

Refuse to cover up (v. 16). Some, in Peter's day, were using freedom in Christ as a cover up for doing evil. Peter said that's not what freedom is all about. Rather, we are set free from sin in order to become servants of God. What a trade that is! No longer under the tyranny and misery of sin, we are liberated to "put on the new self, created after the likeness of God in true righteousness and holiness" (Ephesians 4.24).

Let us grow up into our salvation!

Prayer: Thank you, Lord, for saving me. Help me, I pray, to grow up into this salvation. I have so much growing to do, and I'm so excited about the possibilities of grace before me. Amen.

Psalm of the Day: 59.10-17

Be Prepared

Daily Reading: 1 Peter 3

...prepared to make a defense to anyone who asks you for a reason for the hope that is in you. (1 Peter 3.15)

Devotional Thought: Ever the optimist. That's how I want to be known. And, Peter - at least somewhat - assumed that optimism would be the disposition of the Christian. He took it for granted that people would wonder about the hope that is in us. But, he reminds us of what we read about in Romans 8.24: "Hope that is seen is not hope." In other words, people see our hope through the trials we endure.

We are 'prepared' to defend hope when we...
- Are zealous for what is good (13). Often the good is not popular. But, when we are steadfast in our support for the good, people will be take note of our hope.
- Suffer for righteousness' sake (14). The Apostle Paul was moved in his spirit by the Spirit he saw at work in Stephen, who was martyred for his faith. Stephen's hope did not waver even when the stones struck him. This is indeed a costly testimony of hope.
- Honor Christ the Lord as holy (15). Does your life bring honor to the holiness and love of Christ? That kind of living exudes hope.
- Treat others with gentleness and respect (15). It is easy to strike out at our accusers. If people feel judgment and condemnation from you, however, they have little reason for hope.
- Keep a clean conscience when we are slandered and reviled (16). Peter shows us how Jesus is the prime example of not striking back. His accusers, and even his executioners, found hope in the mercy he showed.

We've all heard the expression, "Be careful what you wish for. You may get it!" And, so it is with our testimony of hope. We all want to have it, yet getting it is costly. Be prepared!

Prayer: Lord, I know that you suffered so that I might find hope. Help me to be willing to pay the price so that others, too, may experience the hope that I have found in you. Amen.

Psalm of the Day: 60.1-5

Revealed Glory
Daily Reading: 1 Peter 4-5

...as a partaker in the glory that is going to be revealed. (1 Peter 5.1)

Devotional Thought: Have you ever thought you knew what was going on, only to have it turn out that you didn't have a clue? It's worse when you add speech to your thoughts! I've done that more times than I care to admit. In 1 Peter, the apostle reminds us that we are "partaker[s] in the glory that is going to be revealed..." We just don't know the whole story.

In a practical sense, what does that mean?
- First, we need to remember that we are not privy to all the workings of God in someone else's life. There is a *partial* revelation of a *hidden* glory. God has a glorious plan and is at work in others' lives. Instead of judging, celebrate the journey so far, and patiently await the unveiling of God's plan in their future.
- Then, we need to personally live today with tomorrow in mind. We don't want to short circuit our futures. Tomorrow may be – no, probably **will** be - different - from today. I had a friend who told me once, "I don't buy the car I need today. I buy the one I need tomorrow." In other words, a two-seater may be fine for a newly married couple, but if they are planning on having a child soon they better get a sedan.
- And of course, we need to live today with eternity in view. This world is not our final home. We are heirs of eternity. We need to live today in such a way as to partake of his divine glory forever.

As God reveals his glory, may you partake of it!

Prayer: Thank you, Lord, for the unfolding of your divine plan. Thank you that you have included me and those I love as partakers of the glory to be revealed. Help me to remember that I don't have the full story just yet, but to live with the end in mind. Amen.

Psalm of the Day: 60.6-12

Glory Realized

Daily Reading: 2 Peter 1

> *He has granted to us his precious and very great promises, so that through them you may become partakers of the divine nature.*
> (2 Peter 1.4)

Devotional Thought: Yesterday, we read about how we are partakers in the glory to be revealed - the glory of tomorrow. Today, we read how we can be partakers of the realized glory of today. How? Through the promises of God!

God make *promises* to us. He promises his love and faithfulness. He promises to answer our prayers. He promises to fill us if we are hungry and thirsty for him. He promises that if we seek him with all our hearts, we will find him. He promises that no good thing will he withhold from us. He promises that nothing will ever separate us from his love.

God's promises are *precious*. To be precious has two aspects. First of all, it is to be **valuable**. God's promises are valuable because they are sealed with the blood of his only Son. We were redeemed from our empty way of living by the blood of Jesus! But, to be precious also means to be **valued**. God's promises are precious because we cherish them. They remind us of his love. Last week was my Mom's birthday. She has been in heaven for 13 years now, but I still have some of her things tucked away in a safe place: her Bible, her old thick glasses, some unusual gifts. Are they precious? Not according to this world's economy, but they are cherished by me, so that makes them precious.

We are *partakers* of those promises. The promises of God are not simply universal or hypothetical. They are personal. What he promises, he promises to me. Most precious of all, of course, is that I can become a partaker of his nature. By the blood of Jesus, I am adopted into the family of God! My soul has a home!

Prayer: Thank you, Lord, for your great and precious promises. I believe them, and I receive them for myself and my loved ones. Amen.

Psalm of the Day: 61.1-8

False Teachers
Daily Reading: 2 Peter 2

> *But false prophets also arose among the people, just as there will be false teachers among you, who will secretly bring in destructive heresies, even denying the Master who bought them, bringing upon themselves swift destruction. And many will follow their sensuality, and because of them the way of truth will be blasphemed.* (2 Peter 2.1-2)

Devotional Thought: Paraphrasing today's scripture, we could say, "False teachers are preying upon the true believers, and they bring destructive teaching, even denying that Jesus is the only way to heaven. Many will follow their emotion-based, self-centered philosophy, and because of them the truth will be compromised and blasphemed." How?

- *Secretly...* God's enemy rarely shows himself in his true form – ugly, destructive, sinful, and always set against truth and goodness. He will use deception to trick God's image-bearers into believing a lie, and will spread that lie to draw as many as possible away from the truth of the gospel.
- *Sensuality...* The condition of being pleasing or fulfilling to the senses. Could this be seen as "seeker-friendly"? These "seekers" are seeking nothing more than a feel-good, self-congratulatory, we-are-all-basically-good-people emotional high, as they hear sermons without a single mention of sin or our need for a Savior.
- *Blasphemed...* The gospel message can be corrupted, twisted, and treated with irreverence - in short, blasphemed. Those who despise God's authority are bold and willful; they do not tremble as they blaspheme; they revel in their deceptions; they are insatiable for sin and entice unsteady souls.

Our only defense comes from knowing and embracing the truth. "If you shall confess with your mouth that Jesus is Lord and believe in your heart that God raised him from the dead, you will be saved" (Romans 10.9). Embrace the wonderful, saving news of the gospel!

Jenny

Prayer: Lord, we ask that you guard our hearts and minds in Christ Jesus. Preserve us blameless until your coming. Give us wisdom and discernment to recognize and reject falsehoods and lies from the enemy. Amen.

Psalm of the Day: 62.1-4

God's Theory of Relativity
Daily Reading: 2 Peter 3

The Lord is not slow to fulfill his promise as some count slowness, but is patient toward you, not wishing that any should perish, but that all should reach repentance. (2 Peter 3.9)

Devotional Thought: The special theory of relativity postulates that as speed increases, time slows, until you reach the point when time stands still - the speed of light. I say that as age increases, time speeds up... When I was a child, it was a year between Christmases. Now, it seems to be just a few weeks!

Time also is different as we age in Christ...

- *The Lord is not slow.* From the very beginning of creation in Genesis to the end of history in Revelation, we see that God is timing everything out in order to work all things together for our good.
- *His promises are sure.* God made a promise to Abraham that his descendants would be as numerous as the sand on the seashore and the stars in the sky. He promised David that he would not fail to have a descendant on the throne. History has shown us that these promises pointed to Jesus! What promises has he made to you? They are certain in Jesus!
- *His patience is steady.* I've noticed all my friends are getting older - so much older than me it seems! With their age, they seem to be gaining patience, waiting for God to do his work. When I think how old God is, I realize he must have tremendous patience. But, to what end?
- *His goal is salvation.* God is walking at just the right speed, working all things for our good, waiting on stubborn hearts for one purpose - to bring souls to repentance. God has planned to populate his kingdom with those whom he loves, those for whom his Son died. Thanks be to God for this wonderful love!

Prayer: Thank you, Lord, that you are not slow and that your promises are sure. Help me to remain steady as you are working out salvation for me and for those I love. Amen.

Psalm of the Day: 62.5-12

A Famine in the Land

Daily Reading: Ruth 1

There was a famine in the land, and a man of Bethlehem in Judah went to sojourn in the country of Moab. (Ruth 1.1)

Devotional Thought: I love the story of Ruth and of Boaz, her 'kinsman-redeemer,' and how his love is a picture of the love of Christ for his Bride, the Church. I love how Ruth shows trust, love, and utter abandonment to Boaz as her redeemer, and how that is a picture of the church's faith in and dependence on Christ. I love how Naomi cares more for her foreign daughters-in-law than for her own safety and well-being, and how that is a picture of the church's concern for the lost.

The book of Ruth, however, starts with famine. There was a famine in the land of Judah, and Elimelech - a citizen of Bethlehem - left his home to go to Moab. Taking his wife and two sons with him, he went to a foreign land. The story that began with famine went from bad to worse. Elimelech and his two sons died in Moab, leaving behind three widows. There was no safety net in that society, and Naomi decided she better go home. How good it is when the church realizes the need to get back to her roots!

Naomi departed, and Ruth, who had fallen in love with Naomi and with her God, jumped at the chance to become a part of God's family, eventually even becoming an ancestor to the Messiah.

Centuries later there was another famine in the land. This time God sent his Son to Bethlehem to sojourn in the land of darkness and despair. And, God worked salvation through this Man, Jesus Christ.

Prayer: Lord, thank you that you came to this land of famine and darkness and despair. Thank you that you became our Redeemer. Help us to share your love with a world lost in sin. Amen.

Psalm of the Day: 63.1-7

Favored Foreigners
Daily Reading: Ruth 2

> *Why have I found favor in your eyes, that you should take notice of me, since I am a foreigner?* (Ruth 2.10)

Devotional Thought: "GBTO - We full." Those words were printed on a bumper sticker - over the image of a Johns Island, SC map. I was riding with my friend Gerry, who asked, "What's that?" I snickered and said, "Go back to Ohio. We're full." Gerry was from Ohio. Ouch.

Contrast that to the welcome Ruth received when she found herself an outsider. Boaz, a distant relative of her mother-in-law, saw her in his fields and told her, "Now, listen, my daughter, do not go to glean in another field or leave this one, but keep close to my young women. Let your eyes be on the field that they are reaping, and go after them" (Ruth 2.8). That kindness moved Ruth to exclaim, "Why have I found favor in your eyes?"

Are there not parallels in this story to the story of our lives?
- We were *foreigners* to hope. Ruth was not an Israelite, but rather an alien. Our sin alienates us from God. We are "separated from Christ... and foreigners to the covenants of the promise, without hope and without God" (Ephesians 2.12).
- Our Redeemer *found us.* Boaz noticed Ruth among the crowd of harvesters and gleaners. He went to her with an amazing offer of grace. Jesus "came to seek and to save the lost" (Luke 19.10).
- God has shown us *favor.* While allowing beggars to glean was expected, Boaz didn't have to show this extravagant kindness. God has shown us extravagant kindness as well: "You who once were far away have been brought near by the blood of Christ... no longer foreigners and strangers, but fellow citizens with God's people and also members of his household" (Ephesians 2.13, 19).

Prayer: Lord Jesus, thank you that you came in love to redeem me from sin and hopelessness and despair. You have welcomed me into your family. Help me to have the mind of Christ and welcome others. Amen.

Psalm of the Day: 63.8-11

You Are a Redeemer
Daily Reading: Ruth 3-4

Spread your wings over your servant, for you are a redeemer. (Ruth 3.9)

Devotional Thought: Have you ever needed to just have someone in your corner, someone to believe in you, someone to rescue you? There are times in life when it seems that everything has gone wrong and you need a friend. Ruth had gone through such a time.

A foreigner to Israel, Ruth found herself destitute and homeless when her husband died. Not only so, but her father-in-law and brother-in-law died, too. She needed rescued. But, there was hope. According to the custom of the day, a widow and her family had a redeemer. The nearest relative was instructed by law to buy the widow's property, care for the widow, and take her into his home. Boaz was that person for Ruth.

So what did she do? She boldly - yet discreetly - went to him and orchestrated a way to make it all happen. Having made known her plight to the kind-hearted Boaz, Ruth said, "Spread your wings [the corner of your garment] over me, for you are a redeemer." Boaz was thrilled! He would gladly redeem her and provide a home for her. Not only that, he would do one better than rescue her. He would marry her!

We all need rescued, for "all have sinned and fall short of the glory of God." We try to do things to save ourselves, but that just isn't possible because "all our righteous acts are like filthy rags." We need someone to spread his wings over us. We need a Redeemer.

Do you realize that you have a Redeemer? It is Jesus! Come with boldness to him and pray as Ruth said to Boaz, "Spread your wings over me, for you are my Redeemer."

Prayer: Jesus, I need your help. My sins are as scarlet, and there is nothing I can do to wash them away. Will you spread your wings over me, for you are my Redeemer? Amen.

Psalm of the Day: 64.1-10

With Pain - Great Gain!
Daily Reading: Acts 1

He presented himself alive to them after his suffering... (Acts 1.3a)

Devotional Thought: No pain, no gain. Without the valleys, there would be no mountain tops. If there were no rainclouds, there would be no rainbows. The darkest hour comes just before dawn. If you want to marry a prince, you gotta kiss a few frogs... Wait, I don't like that last one. I've got granddaughters! Be that as it may, there are many ways to say that suffering is a part of life, and that without it there will not be much progress. We're used to the concept.

We see the truth of 'no pain, no gain' in Jesus' life, don't we? Today's scripture proclaims that Jesus "presented himself alive to them after his suffering."

Jesus' pain was his death. The disciples witnessed his suffering - the beating, the crucifixion, and the last cry of death. They knew he was dead. I don't think it would have been as impressive to the disciples for Jesus to show up at their prayer meetings and potlucks, if he had not suffered as he did. His dying gave significance to his appearing.

We know Jesus' pain, but what was his gain? By dying, Jesus gained many things:
- He became the firstborn from the dead.
- He was exalted to the highest place.
- He irrefutably demonstrated the love of God.
- He was given a name that is above every name.
- He conquered death forever.
- He paid the price for our sins.
- He was given the keys to death and life.

Jesus suffered pain for each of us. May his death not be in vain. Instead, may it be with great gain!

Prayer: Lord, thank you for taking my place on Calvary's cross. As the song says, you paid a debt you did not owe. May your life bring me, and those I love, abundant life evermore. Amen.

Psalm of the Day: 65.1-8

146

What Are You On?
Daily Reading: Acts 2

For these people are not drunk, as you suppose... (Acts 2.15a)

Devotional Thought: Some years ago, I received a call from a man whose little girl attended my church. He was, as they say, "feeling no pain." After talking with him for a few minutes, and not being able to make heads or tails from what he was saying, I asked him, "John, have you been drinking?" I thought he would deny it, but his answer surprised me, "Preacher, I'm drunk as a monkey!"

There you have it. I didn't get much more out of that conversation, but there were better days ahead.

In Acts 2, some people thought that the disciples of Jesus were drunk. Their problem was that they *did* understand! They weren't supposed to be able to understand these unschooled speakers. They were foreigners! What was going on? The answer lay in the fact that those speakers were filled with the Holy Spirit.

That story makes me ask the obvious: "Am I so full of Jesus - so full of the Holy Spirit - that people struggle to understand what's wrong with me?" Are you? Like the Apostle Paul, does your joy know no bounds? It's funny that in Ephesians 5, Paul compares being Spirit-filled with being drunk. There must be some similarities. We are not to get our buzz with alcohol or with drugs. We are to get it with Jesus!

I've never been accused of being drunk as a monkey, but I have had people ask me, "What are you on?" I like that.

So, what are you on?

Prayer: Lord, you have said that the joy of the Lord is my strength. Help my joy to know no bounds. Fill me to overflowing with your Spirit, so that others will ask me what is going on with my life, so that I can tell them about you. Amen.

Psalm of the Day: 65.9-13

Who Did That?

Daily Reading: Acts 3

> *And his name—by faith in his name—has made this man strong.*
> (Acts 3.16)

Devotional Thought: I've had people tell me that they could never do this or quit that. But, I've seen those same people give up lifelong habits because they have done so in the power of Jesus' name. A friend of mine came to Jesus a few years ago. She was a heavy drinker. One day she told me, "I quit drinking." What? "Yes," she said. "It just didn't taste good anymore." She never thought she could quit. She's been sober a couple years now. Now, she's working on smoking, and I believe she will whip that by the powerful name of Jesus!

Peter and John came across a man who thought he would never walk again. He didn't have the strength. Medical treatments were not available. He was reduced to begging. But, when Peter and John came by, he was in for the surprise of his life: "I have no silver and gold, but what I do have I give to you. In the name of Jesus Christ of Nazareth, rise up and walk!" He went walking and leaping into church!

Peter and John were quick to testify that they didn't do it. It was only by the name of Jesus that the man became strong enough to walk. And, it's only the name of Jesus that can make a person stand strong in their faith.

What are your weaknesses? What are your struggles? In the name of Jesus - by faith in his name - you can be strong enough to defeat every foe.

Prayer: Lord, I bring you my weaknesses, my struggles. Please make your power perfect in them. By faith in your name, I claim victory! Amen.

Psalm of the Day: 66.1-7

Go Out and Annoy Someone
Daily Reading: Acts 4

...greatly annoyed because they were teaching the people and proclaiming in Jesus the resurrection from the dead. (Acts 4.2)

Devotional Thought: Did you know that there are websites filled with ideas about how to annoy people? Ha! Who needs a website? I know what to do: Just be happy! That doesn't always work, but the sad reality is that it works too often. Many people are just not happy unless others around them are unhappy!

Did you ever wonder why the stiff shirts were annoyed with the apostles for proclaiming Jesus? Besides the fact that they didn't want to see anybody else happy, I think it's because they didn't think they needed Jesus. They didn't need any resurrection. They had this life mastered, thank you, and that was enough.

Those spiritual leaders in Jerusalem were in denial. Like many today, they denied their need to be raised from...
- *Spiritual death.* They saw themselves as righteous, not needing what Jesus has come to give: new birth. Today, the concept of sin, and subsequent alienation from God, is seen as archaic. Everybody has to find their own way. If it seems right to you, then it is legitimate.
- *Cultural death.* Those leaders couldn't grasp the fact that their nation was dying from rot within. Our culture shows obvious signs of disease and death. Yet, many are in denial about it, or they think that the solution is in more government and more laws - and less Jesus!
- *Eternal death.* Some of those leaders didn't believe in life after death, so they had no need for a resurrection. It greatly annoyed them that Jesus offered eternal life!

Go out and annoy Satan today. Proclaim hope in Jesus!

Prayer: Jesus, I don't really want to be annoying, but I do want to bear witness to the hope, the joy, the peace, and the love that you give me. If that annoys someone, may you convict them of their need of you. And, help me to always be caring and respectful. Amen.

Psalm of the Day: 66.8-15

Deceit and Death
Daily Reading: Acts 5

> *While it remained unsold, did it not remain your own? And after it was sold, was it not at your disposal? Why is it that you have contrived this deed in your heart? You have not lied to man but to God.* (Acts 5.4)

Devotional Thought: The early church had jointly decided to share their wealth with one another. Many people were selling their land and houses, giving the proceeds to be distributed according to need (Acts 4). When Ananias and Sapphira sold their property, they kept back a portion of their proceeds, but acted as though they were giving it all. Because of their deceit, judgment was passed on them, and they dropped dead on the spot.

On the surface of this story, it is hard to understand why this would have happened, but Peter's statement makes it more obvious. He declared, "You have not lied to man but to God," (v. 4). Satan had filled the hearts of this couple, and they had lied to the Holy Spirit (v. 3). They were not full of the Spirit, but rather full of themselves.

We don't normally hear of cases where people drop dead mysteriously. Yet, there is a lesson here for us as well. First, it should remind us of the holiness of the Lord. There is no room for deceit in the heart of a believer. Second, it should renew in us a sense of awe and wonder as we think about the power of the Lord. As the writer of Proverbs states, "The fear of the Lord is the beginning of wisdom" (Proverbs 9.10). Third, the Lord expects us to keep our vows, especially to fellow believers. James echoes the words of Jesus when he says, "Simply let your 'Yes' by yes, and your 'No,' no, so that you will not fall under judgment" (James 5.12).

Jenny

Prayer: Lord, protect us from being full of ourselves. We are prideful by nature, and desire praise from man above praise from our Father. Fill our hearts with a desire to bring you glory, to make more of you as we make less of ourselves. Amen.

Psalm of the Day: 66.16-20

Irresistible

Daily Reading: Acts 6

They could not withstand the wisdom and the Spirit with which he was speaking. (Acts 6.10)

Devotional Thought: I would like to have an irresistible testimony, wouldn't you? How can we do that? As we look into the life of Stephen, we find some clues...

- Stephen was full of the Spirit and wisdom (v. 3). He did not depend on his own personal charisma or opinions. His testimony was grounded in God.
- Stephen was full of faith and the Holy Spirit (v. 5). When he took on the job of 'compassionate ministry director', he knew he was getting into a hornet's nest. But, he took it anyway, believing that God would help him do it.
- Stephen was operating under the authority of the church (v. 6). He was willing to submit to the combined wisdom and experience of the church.
- Stephen was full of grace and power (v. 8). Power is a good thing, when used with grace!
- Stephen was doing great wonders and signs (v. 8). Stephen just didn't talk about service. He served!
- Stephen was versed in the Bible. He was clearly a student of the Word.
- Stephen was respectful (7.2). He addressed his accusers properly and with dignity.
- Stephen was courageous (7.51-53). He didn't back down from the truth. He stood upon the truth, speaking it in love.
- Stephen kept his gaze upward (7.56). Had he focused on his accusers, he may have grown discouraged. But, he saw Jesus, and that was enough!
- Stephen was forgiving (7.60). It was this attitude that had such an impact on Paul.
- Stephen trusted Jesus with his life (7.59). Do you?

Prayer: Lord, I want to be an effective witness for you. Fill me with the Holy Spirit and wisdom, and help me to live out my faith when the pressure is on. Amen.

Psalm of the Day: 67.1-7

It's Never Too Dark!
Daily Reading: Acts 7

> *But he, full of the Holy Spirit, gazed into heaven and saw the glory of God, and Jesus standing at the right hand of God.* (Acts 7.55)

Devotional Thought: Stephen's testimony for Jesus was powerful, in spite of opposition. One of the reasons for this was that he "gazed into heaven and saw the glory of God." Most of us, I believe, have a desire to see God's glory. So, how and when did Stephen see it?

Not in a worship service. Do we depend on musicians, lyrics and melodies to reveal to us the glory of God? Don't get me wrong. Worship is a wonderful time to experience the presence of God. I wonder, however, if we don't depend too much on a third party to manufacture an experience for us.

Not in a time of fellowship with other believers. Jesus did say that he would be with us when we gather in his name, didn't he? But, when Stephen saw the glory of God, his 'small group' was nowhere to be found.

Not even in his personal devotions. Now, I do believe that when we draw near to God, he draws near to us, but Stephen was not enjoying his 'quiet time' when he saw Jesus.

Stephen saw the glory of God in the midst of persecution and pain.

Should we be surprised? Isaiah saw God in bereavement and anxiety. Paul saw him in a storm at sea. Peter saw him in a cold dark jail. John saw him on a lonely, forsaken island. Seven fishermen saw him in the dim dawn, after a night of failure.

No matter what you are going through, it is never too dark to see the Light!

Prayer: Lord, thank you for showing up, even in the most unlikely of places. Help me to see your glory and find your grace - evident in the simple fact that you are here. Amen.

Psalm of the Day: 68.1-10

Do You Trust Jesus Alone for Salvation?
Daily Reading: Acts 8

> *But Peter said to him, "May your silver perish with you, because you thought you could obtain the gift of God with money!"* (Acts 8.20)

Devotional Thought: In Acts 20, we encounter a man, Simon, who came to know Jesus through the preaching of Philip. Yet, having been saved by faith, he was trying to be filled with the Spirit by finances. He offered Peter cash money in order to get the gift of the Spirit, and the ability to impart the Spirit to others. Peter did not look favorably upon the offer, saying, "May your silver perish with you... you have neither part nor lot in this matter..."

In the book of Revelation, Jesus is described as the Lamb who was slain from the foundation of the world. When God looked forward through time and saw the need of humanity, he planned that Jesus would be the sacrificial Lamb who would take away the sin of the world. It is by grace we are saved, through faith in what Jesus did on the cross.

Yet, people have always struggled to accept that salvation is a free gift of grace. We have tried somehow to earn or work or pay our way in. But, grace always points to the cross.

What about you? Do you trust him, and him alone, for salvation? Are you tempted to substitute anything for Jesus? Social status? Family relationships? Church attendance? Generous giving? When we, like Simon, try to buy our way in, we grieve the heart of God and Spirit of grace. If we find ourselves in that position, there is, however, no need to despair. As Peter counseled Simon, we can repent of our wickedness and be forgiven by God.

Prayer: Thank you, Jesus, that you paid the price for my sins. I have been redeemed from my empty way of life by the precious blood of the Lamb. If I forget that, remind me and bring me to repentance. I pray in Jesus' name, amen.

Psalm of the Day: 68.11-18

Sponsored By...

Daily Reading: Acts 9

But Barnabas took him and brought him to the apostles. (Acts 9.27)

Devotional Thought: Sometimes, people need a little extra help to make it into the church. When we have been hurt, it is extremely difficult to trust somebody simply at their word. Saul (Paul) found himself in that unenviable position. He had hurt a lot of people in the church, even presiding over the execution of the first Christian martyr. Now, he wanted to join the church. The church rightfully exercised caution to protect the flock. Just because he said he was changed, didn't make it so! Now, the church was at risk of losing the greatest evangelist, missionary, and theologian of the first century.

Saul needed a sponsor.

Enter Barnabas. Whether it was through personal observation, relying on the testimony of others, or spiritual discernment, Barnabas was able to tell the church how Saul had seen and heard the Lord, how he had immediately and effectively begun preaching boldly in the name of Jesus.

Barnabas stuck his neck out for this upstart. He sponsored him, taking him to the disciples and personally vouching for him. I'm sure that Barnabas also agreed to 'keep his eye on him' and make sure that Saul was growing in the Lord, acting in ways that confirmed his Christian testimony. Saul did, after all, bear some responsibility for whether or not the church accepted him.

Look around you. Are there people who are struggling to break into the circle of fellowship at your church? Go to them. Bring them to others. Agree to sponsor them, until they can stand on their own. God will bless you for it, and the church will gain the addition of another laborer for the work of the kingdom.

Prayer: Lord, I sometimes judge people solely on their past, and fail to recognize their potential in you. Help me to be discerning, yet accepting. Help me to include new people in the family of God. Amen.

Psalm of the Day: 68.19-27

Everybody's a Sinner.
No One Wants to Be Called One.

Daily Reading: Acts 10

Everyone who believes in him receives forgiveness of sins through his name. (Acts 10.43)

Devotional Thought: Cornelius and his household were virtuous and respectable citizens. Yet, Cornelius sensed a spiritual need. Prompted by the Holy Spirit, he sent for Peter to tell him and his family about Jesus. Peter came and shared the gospel. He preached forgiveness of sins.

I'm wondering what Cornelius thought when Peter began to share his message. We are not told, but it would be easy to imagine that Cornelius was at first insulted. "Hey! I'm just as good as this guy! Why is he preaching about forgiveness of sins to me?" The Holy Spirit was faithful to Cornelius, and as Peter preached, Cornelius' heart was opened. His life was changed! What if Peter had hesitated to obey God?

Are we hesitant to tell people about Jesus, because we think that they don't need him? They are good people, after all, wonderful members of the community. Who am I to tell them that they need forgiveness of sins through Jesus Christ?

We need to remember the words of the Bible, "There is none righteous, no not one" (Romans 3.10). And, "All have sinned and fall short of the glory of God" (Romans 3.23). And, "All of us have become like one who is unclean, and all our righteous acts are like filthy rags" (Isaiah 64.6, NIV).

No, nobody wants to be called a sinner. But yes, everybody needs the forgiveness of sins through Jesus Christ. We are not to condemn, but to share the love of God. It is the work of the Holy Spirit to convict and to save.

Prayer: Lord, help me to remember that outside of your saving grace, everyone is lost - even the good, respectable and moral people I know. Then, help me to be bold to share forgiveness in Jesus' name. Amen.

Psalm of the Day: 68.28-35

Standing in God's Way
Daily Reading: Acts 11

Who was I that I could stand in God's way? (Acts 11.17)

Devotional Thought: God in a box... Sometimes, we think we have God figured out. Like a jack in the box, God will jump out and do what we say when we turn the crank. But, then he does something totally unexpected that just blows up our boxes. That happened to the church in Acts 11.

Peter had gone to the house of Cornelius to share the good news of Jesus with the Centurion and his household. He even ate with them! In those days, it was considered irreligious for a Jew to eat in the home of a Gentile. So, there were those in the Jewish church in Jerusalem who took it upon themselves to correct Peter. What they didn't realize, however, was that in correcting Peter, they were attempting to correct God, too, for God was the one who had sent Peter there in the first place. For his part, Peter recognized what was happening, and he subtly brought the church to see that they were standing in God's way.

Yes, we must always "earnestly contend for the faith." Yes, God has a plan to reach the entire world with the gospel of his Son, Jesus Christ. But, when we hold on to traditions, methods, and preferences, we may find ourselves standing in God's way. If we have tried to keep him neatly tucked away until we turn the crank, he may just need to blow up our boxes!

God desires to do a great work in and through you. He is on the move in the church and in the world. Let's make sure that we are not standing in his way!

Prayer: Father, forgive me when my vision is narrow and my prejudices prevent me from seeing the new things you are doing. Help me to be a willing partner in your mission to reach the lost. In Jesus' name I pray. Amen.

Psalm of the Day: 69.1-5

Earnest Prayer

Daily Reading: Acts 12

> So Peter was kept in prison, but earnest prayer for him was made to God by the church. (Acts 12.5)

Devotional Thought: Believers were being persecuted, even unto death. The church was losing members to religious persecution. Christians faced constant scorn and physical threats. The Roman government seemed to feed on the fury of the Jews. This is why Peter was arrested in the first place. Herod... "saw that it pleased the Jews, and proceeded to arrest Peter also" (v. 3). Peter was kept in prison under heavy guard, even being chained to two sentries.

What could his friends and fellow believers do? They most certainly felt helpless, but their faith doesn't seem to waver in the face of this impossible situation. The church doesn't gather to bemoan the unfairness of the situation, nor does it try to concoct a rescue plan. "So Peter was kept in prison, but earnest prayer for him was made to God by the church," (v. 5).

These early believers understood that with God all things are possible. It's as if they were recalling the words of Jesus in Matthew 19.26: "...with men this is impossible; but with God all things are possible." Do we have the same perspective on prayer? When speaking to a friend in crisis, have you ever said something like, "I wish I could help you, but I will be praying for you." Comments like this reflect our heart's skeptical attitude towards prayer, and a God with whom anything is possible.

Peter was rescued miraculously. Sometimes, God answers our prayers in a way that feels and looks miraculous, even to the world. But, more often he works his miracles in unseen ways, in the hearts of those who love him and those whom he is drawing to himself.

Prayer: Lord, give us boldness when we pray! Help us to not view prayer as a poor second choice for those who are suffering, but rather as our first line of defense and our highest privilege as children of God. Amen.

Psalm of the Day: 69.6-12

Holy Ought

Daily Reading: Acts 13

I have made you a light for the Gentiles, that you may bring salvation to the ends of the earth. (Acts 13.47)

Devotional Thought: Do you have a sense of "holy ought"? The Apostles Paul and Barnabas did. In Acts 13, Paul was preaching to the Jews in the synagogue. The Jews had rejected him and the message of Christ. They were jealous over Paul's success in ministry. Paul made a bold move. He applied Old Testament scriptures - meant for the people of Israel - to himself! As he later would write to the Corinthians, "Woe to me if I do not preach the gospel!" (1 Corinthians 9.16)

Paul had been a jealous Jew at one point, too. Until, that is, Jesus Christ appeared to him on the road to Damascus. From that time forward, Paul was compelled to preach the gospel, to proclaim Jesus as the Messiah. God had made him a light for the Gentiles. God had called *him* to bring salvation to the ends of the earth.

The same thing is true of all of us. When we meet Jesus on the road of life, he not only brings us salvation, he sends us with salvation that we may bring it to others. Jesus fills us with his Spirit in order for us to be witnesses (Acts 1.8). He commissions us to make disciples (Matthew 28.18-20). He sends us to preach the gospel to the whole world (Mark 16.15). He authorizes us to cast out demons, dispel darkness, and heal the broken.

But, does my life shine the light of his love to those around me? Am I ready to share the reason for the hope that I have? (Do people see me as a person of hope?) In short, do I have a sense of "holy ought"?

Prayer: Thank you, Lord, for saving me and for making me a light for those in darkness. Help me to bring news of your salvation to all whom I encounter today. Amen.

Psalm of the Day: 69.13-21

Do You Have Rose Garden Faith?

Daily Reading: Acts 14

But the unbelieving Jews stirred up the Gentiles and poisoned their minds against the brothers. (Acts 14.2)

Devotional Thought: Some of us remember the Lynn Anderson song: "I beg your pardon. I never promised you a rose garden. Along with the sunshine. There's gotta be a little rain some time..." I wonder if Barnabas and Paul ever felt like singing that tune. It seems that wherever they went, there were hardships and persecution, suffering and rejection. When they arrived at Iconium, there were people who didn't like their message. These jealous unbelievers, poisoned the minds of their fellow citizens - Gentiles - against the church. Sound familiar?

GQ magazine once said the Bible is over-rated and not worth reading, attempting to stir up some controversy and perhaps spark magazine sales. I'm not sure that it worked, but one thing it showed me - *GQ* is not worth reading! To call the most published book in the history of the world over-rated, shows that all critical thinking has gone out the window, and what is espoused is purely personal opinion and animus. After all, what could 5 billion readers know?! But, obvious truth does not often hinder the purveying of revered prejudices!

Are you suffering rejection and ridicule for your Christian faith? Do not despair. While God has not promised you a rose garden, the Bible says that he will not keep silent (Psalm 50.3). You can be assured that the last voice heard will be the voice of God. When he calls for an end of all things, every doubting voice will be silenced.

Prayer: Father, help me to be firm in the face of opposition. When popular culture rejects the message of God's love, help me to stand on the truth of the Bible. Amen.

Psalm of the Day: 69.22-28

Shutting Down Debate

Daily Reading: Acts 15

> *After there had been much debate, Peter stood up and said to them...*
> (Acts 15.7)

Devotional Thought: One thing I know about the Church... it's not perfect. Why? Because there are imperfect people in it! How do I know that? Because I'm in it! (And because you are in it, too!)

Even the New Testament church was not perfect. The Bible is pretty frank about its imperfections, one of which was its resistance to Gentiles. There were some who insisted that Gentiles convert to Judaism before they be accepted as members of the church. It was a huge blind spot that came to a head in Acts 15. The church arrived at the right conclusion, however, "after there had been much debate."

In mass media, social media, political forums, and even on university campuses, we see just the opposite. Instead of engaging in debate, people simply want to shut each other down. It should never happen, however, in the church. We should be willing to explore the scriptures together, as did the Bereans in Acts 17 who: "received the word with all eagerness, examining the Scriptures daily to see if these things were so. Many of them therefore believed." Healthy, respectful debate does not weaken our faith, but leads to stronger faith!

What are some things we should avoid so that we don't shut down debate?
- Impugning motives. We don't know what is in another's heart. Only God judges that, so we should not make it a part of our discussions.
- Making light. When we devalue another's opinions, they will not be willing to share in the future, and we will lose valuable perspective.
- Calling names. That just devalues people and makes them angry.
- Instilling fear. People who are afraid will simply repeat what is being said. This leads to group think.

Do you shut down debate?

Prayer: Lord, thank you that the early church, though imperfect, was able to reach good conclusions through earnest and respectful debate. Help me to encourage, and not stifle, communication. In Jesus' name, amen.

Psalm of the Day: 69.29-36

Go Light

Daily Reading: Acts 16

They attempted to go into Bithynia, but the Spirit of Jesus did not allow them. (Acts 16.7)

Devotional Thought: Have you ever heard someone giving directions say something like, "Go to the second stop light and make a right?" Why is it that people use the term 'stop light'? Isn't it green as much as it is red? Why not call it a 'go light'?

The Apostle Paul usually operated under the idea of a 'go light.' He was always on go for Jesus! As Paul and his fellow missionaries travelled around Asia Minor, they encountered obstacles. And, they weren't just normal obstacles. They were Holy Spirit obstacles! We don't know how the Spirit spoke, but it is obvious that Paul and his companions clearly understood that the Spirit was closing certain doors. Did that stop them? No! They just tried other doors! Paul had a 'go light' mentality.

Now, I understand that there are times to wait upon the Lord, to stop and contemplate what's next. In this same chapter, we encounter Paul waiting in Philippi "some days" until God opened the door (v. 12). But, I think that the bigger problem for Christians is that we hesitate to do *anything*, because we don't know *everything*. It is so hard to overcome spiritual inertia.

I once heard a preacher say, "If you're not sure what to do, try something. If it's wrong, don't worry. God will stop you. The worst thing you can do is nothing." I heard another one say, "God always calls a busy person." And, one more preacher quote: "It's harder to get a ship moving, than it is to turn one in a different direction."

So, let's be bold and try something for Jesus! He won't be upset if you don't get it right the first time! He's giving you a go light!

Prayer: Jesus, forgive me for being timid and shy about my work for you. Help me to have a 'go light' mentality, so that you can use me for your purposes. Amen.

Psalm of the Day: 70.1-5

Head of the Table
Daily Reading: Acts 17

> *Being the Lord of heaven and earth...* (Acts 17.24)

Devotional Thought: I love to repeat this story that I heard many years ago. A young executive was attending a meeting, and the CEO showed up a few minutes after everyone else was seated and found a seat in the midst of the group. The young man, wanting to make a good impression, said to the CEO, "Sir, you should be seated at the head of the table." The CEO's response was priceless: "Young man, where I sit *is* the head of the table." I've told that to my kids many times at dinner...

In preaching to the Athenians in Acts 17, Paul presents God just in that manner. The Athenians were particularly superstitious and wanted to make sure that they had all their spiritual bases covered. So, they built many altars and shrines to make sure that the right god had a seat at the table. Paul said, in essence, "The true God doesn't need all this."

In Acts 17.24-26, Paul explains that where God sits is the head of the table for...
- He made the world and everything in it.
- He is the Lord of heaven and earth.
- He does not live in temples made by man.
- He is not served by human hands, as though he needed anything.
- He himself gives to all mankind, life and breath and everything.
- He made, from one man, every nation of mankind to live on all the face of the earth.
- He determined allotted periods and the boundaries of their dwelling place.

Where God sits is indeed the head of the table! As Paul told the Athenians, let us "seek God, and perhaps feel [our] way toward him and find him" (v. 27).

Prayer: Lord, you are sovereign over earth and heaven, over time and eternity. I seek you with all my heart today and recognize that in my own life, you are indeed seated at the head of the table. Amen.

Psalm of the Day: 71.1-8

Looming Large
Daily Reading: Acts 18

I have many in this city who are my people. (Acts 18.10)

Devotional Thought: Several years ago I went through a very difficult time in my life and ministry. During this time I let those problems grow way out of proportion. I lost my focus on God and could only see the problems around me. God helped me to get refocused on him, however, and to regain my spiritual perspective.

In Acts 18, Paul was in danger of doing that, as he ministered to the Corinthians. And, just as God did for me, he did for Paul. He spoke to Paul one night and reminded him that he was with him, and more than that - that God had many other people who were with Paul as well. Paul took courage from that message from the Lord, and stayed another 18 months, preaching the gospel and establishing the church.

I am reminded of the story in 2 Kings 6, where the servant of Elisha could only see the Syrian army surrounding them in Dothan. He despaired, crying, "Alas my master! What shall we do?" Elisha had the perfect answer: get your eyes off the enemy of man and on the army of God... "O Lord, please open his eyes that he may see." When the servant opened his spiritual eyes, he saw indeed that "the mountain was full of horses and chariots of fire all around Elisha."

Are problems looming large in your life? You need to make sure that you have the right spiritual focus. He has not left you, and he also gives you helpers all around. "Turn your eyes upon Jesus. Look full in his wonderful face. And the things [problems] of earth will grow strangely dim in the light of his glory and grace."

Prayer: Lord, when troubles surround me, help me to keep my spiritual focus on you - to fix my eyes on Jesus, and to find courage and comfort in those whom you send to help me. Amen.

Psalm of the Day: 71.9-16

Are You Reasoning Daily?
Daily Reading: Acts 19

> *But when some became stubborn and continued in unbelief, speaking evil of the Way before the congregation, he withdrew from them and took the disciples with him, reasoning daily in the hall of Tyrannus. This continued for two years.* (Acts 19.9-10)

Devotional Thought: Paul was unmatched in zealousness, both before and after his conversion. As a *Jewish* leader, he came from the right family, had the right education, and possessed a passion for righteousness under the Law. Thus, he persecuted Christians with zeal. As a *Christian*, Paul's entire life and perspective was changed, but his personality remained intact. The Lord used Paul's zeal, his boldness, and his passion for righteousness to advance his Kingdom.

In Ephesus, he unabashedly entered the Jewish synagogue and "for three months spoke boldly, reasoning and persuading them about the kingdom of God" (v. 8). However, when the Jews "became stubborn and continued in disbelief, speaking evil of the Way" (v. 9), Paul knew that his efforts would be more fruitful in a different arena, "reasoning daily... This continued for two years..." (v. 9-10).

Wow! Daily ministry for two years... it doesn't get more zealous than that! We know that God was "doing extraordinary miracles by the hands of Paul," (v. 11), but we also know that Paul's preaching came at a great cost to him personally. He was mocked, beaten, thrown in prison, even stoned. But, his message to the world – the message of salvation through faith in Jesus – was one that simply had to be spread, whatever the cost.

So it is for us as well. There is no passive faith in Jesus. The good news we have for a lost and hurting world is too important to keep to ourselves. Let us proclaim the truth with zeal!

Jenny

Prayer: Jesus, give us boldness! We are too often embarrassed to speak of you, afraid of rejection or of harm to our reputation. Fill our hearts with love for those who need to hear the truth, and then empower us by your Spirit! Amen.

Psalm of the Day: 71.17-24

Finish What You Start
Daily Reading: Acts 20

If only I may finish my course and the ministry that I received from the Lord Jesus... (Acts 20.24)

Devotional Thought: My wife, Lana, is a finisher. When she says she's going to do something, she starts it. When she starts a job, she finishes it. And, not only finishes it, but she is going to do it right. In a day when commitment to the church is waning, Lana is a shining example of following through for the Lord.

The Apostle Paul felt that way about his life and ministry. As he made his way toward Jerusalem, for what he sensed would be his last visit there, he called together the elders of the church in Ephesus. He wanted to clear some things up for them, but along with his instructions, he also used the meeting as an opportunity to teach about finishing the course.

When Paul was saved, he received a ministry from the Lord. He was to be the Apostle to the Gentiles. Paul never wavered from that calling. He told the Ephesian elders that that was the most important thing to him. He didn't care about hardships and persecution. He worried not about acceptance or rejection. He only want to finish his course and do what Jesus had given him to do.

All of us have been given a job in the Kingdom (see 1 Corinthians 12), but are all of us fulfilling that calling? How about you? Are you passionate about fulfilling the ministry that Jesus has given you? Is your desire reflected in the words of the old hymn: "What He says we will do; Where He sends, we will go; Never fear, only trust and obey." (John Sammis)

Prayer: Thank you, Lord, for giving me purpose and significance in this life and for eternity. Help me, Lord, to remember the wisdom in these words: "Only one life; 'twill soon be past. Only what's done for Christ will last." Amen.

Psalm of the Day: 72.1-7

A Citizen of No Obscure City
Daily Reading: Acts 21

> *I am ... a citizen of no obscure city.* (Acts 21.39)

Devotional Thought: My wife and I tease about how we are homebodies... We love our home in the country. We love life in a small town. Living in a city is not something that comes natural to me, so when I read Paul's words about being a citizen of no obscure city, I have to carefully reflect on their significance.

As I think about it, however, I am able to rejoice that I am a citizen of no obscure city!

In the beginning, God created people to be together. At the tower of Babel (Genesis 11), God separated them, giving them boundaries and borders, in order that they might seek him and find their way to him (Acts 17). People are looking for foundations. The history of humanity, from that first scattering until now, is a story of movement to cities. And, innate within the human population, there seems to be a seeking of "a city with foundations whose builder and maker is God" (Hebrews 11). The good news is that we can find that city, and that God will be there to greet us! As the writer of Hebrews goes on to say, "God is not ashamed to be called their God, for he has prepared for them a city" (11.16).

Is there a yearning in your heart for home? Is there a loved one calling you home? Rejoice, child of God! You have been invited to come home, to come to the city that Jesus has prepared for you. For all eternity, you will dwell in that city and behold the glory of God.

Prayer: Thank you, Lord, for preparing a place for me. Thank you for my citizenship in heaven. Help me to live in this world with an eye on the next, so that I will be ready when you call me home. Amen.

Psalm of the Day: 72.8-16

Time for a Family Meeting?

Daily Reading: Acts 22

And when they heard that he was addressing them in the Hebrew language, they became even more quiet. (Acts 22.2)

Devotional Thought: Yesterday I had a gratifying conversation with my daughter, Jenny. We were discussing these devotional articles that we work on together. We were able to communicate in a 'language' that we both understood and appreciated. It's great to be on the same wavelength with someone you love, isn't it?

It wasn't always like this. I remember when my daughters were teenagers. We sometimes had to have conversations to discuss behavior and attitude. I called them 'family meetings.' And, as often as not, it seemed like we were talking two languages. But, we somehow managed to communicate in spite of the frustration. God's grace!

Communication is enhanced when we take the time and make the effort to speak in the same language, isn't it? When, in Acts 22, Paul spoke to the crowd in Jerusalem, he adopted their language and got on their wavelength. Immediately, the raw nerves were soothed and they were able to hear what Paul had to say. As it turned out, they didn't like what he had to say, but at least at this point they were willing to listen to him.

As we communicate the love of God to those around us, it is good to address them in their own 'language,' to get on their wavelength. If we will make the effort to do that, we will have a much better chance at being heard. And, even if they don't accept our message, we have at least planted a seed that may one day bring forth life. If we don't bother to speak their language, then there will be no seed to spring to life.

So, give attention to not only what you say, but how you say it. Speak their language.

Prayer: Father, as I communicate your love to a broken and hurting world today, help me to take on their perspective and to speak their language. May my words be seeds of your love to mend and heal. In Jesus' name - the one who came to speak my language - I pray, amen.

Psalm of the Day: 72.17-20

Struck on the Mouth

Daily Reading: Acts 23

The high priest Ananias commanded those who stood by him to strike him on the mouth. (Acts 23.2)

Devotional Thought: The Apostle Paul spoke in the language of his listeners, and thereby gained a hearing. Yet, people did not necessarily like what he had to say. Paul discovered that quickly, as he testified before the high priest concerning his relationship to Jesus. Ananias ordered that he be struck on the mouth! The enemies of the gospel were striking out at the very instrument of communicating the gospel - the mouth. What Paul was saying was a threat to their worldview and their way of life. He had to be silenced!

Shocking to us, such conduct was quite normal in that day. The power of rulers was taken much more seriously, and the rights of subjects were not taken into account. But, as we consider today's political and social climate, are things that different? The message of Christ is not popular, and there are cultural powers that would strike out at the very instrument of communicating the gospel. Satan would silence the message if he could. Even eating at a chicken restaurant is seen as threatening to those who would silence the truth, so they strike it on the mouth!

Jesus said that when we follow him, we will make enemies. They hated the Master, they will hate the student... But, threats, jeers, reprisals, and accusations of intolerance must not silence the message of love. "In this world you will have trouble, but take heart, I have overcome the world" (John 16:33).

Prayer: Jesus, you are the Way, the Truth, and the Life. But sadly, there are those who oppose truth. Help me today to lovingly stand on the truth of your Word, even if the culture lashes out at me in fear, anger and hatred. Amen.

Psalm of the Day: 73.1-11

Ringleader

Daily Reading: Acts 24

A ringleader of the sect of the Nazarenes. (Acts 24.5)

Devotional Thought: I'm a pastor in the Church of the Nazarene. I feel like I'm in good company, for the Apostle Paul was accused of being a ringleader in the sect of the Nazarenes. Even better, Jesus himself was called "the Nazarene" (Mark 14.67).

As part of the sect of the Nazarenes (not the denomination, but the followers of Jesus), what do we believe?

- We believe in the *humiliation* of Jesus. The Bible says that Jesus humbled himself in order to come to this earth to save the lost. He emptied himself of all his rights, privileges, wealth and honor in order to identify with his broken creation. He was born to a humble family, in a lowly setting, in a subjugated nation. He left his crown for a cross.
- We believe in the *crucifixion* of Jesus. Jesus was rejected by those in authority in his day. Religious and civil authorities conspired to execute him. He was illegally tried, mercilessly beaten, nailed to a cross, and hung out to die. But, his blood was not shed in vain. He was crushed for our iniquities.
- We believe in the *resurrection* of Jesus. As the old Easter hymn goes, "Death could not keep its prey, Jesus my Savior. He tore the bars away, Jesus my Lord. Up from the grave he arose!" (Robert Lowry) God did not abandon his Son to the grave. He raised him in power and victory!
- We believe in the *redemption* of Jesus. All of this took place - the humiliation, the crucifixion, and the resurrection - for a reason: to redeem fallen and sinful humanity from the curse and control of sin. Jesus came and died and rose again that you and I may have life - life here and life hereafter!

Prayer: Lord, as the song goes, "I stand amazed in the presence of Jesus the Nazarene, and wonder how he could love me, a sinner condemned, unclean. How marvelous, how wonderful is my Savior's love to me!" (Charles Gabriel). Amen and Amen!

Psalm of the Day: 73.12-20

No Good Deed Goes Unpunished
Daily Reading: Acts 25

They were planning an ambush to kill him on the way. (Acts 25.3)

Devotional Thought: "No good deed goes unpunished..." Have you ever felt that way? I'm sure the Apostle Paul did in the latter chapters of Acts. He was bringing the message of salvation to the lost, and for his efforts he was arrested, beaten and jailed. Finally, so strong was his adversaries' hatred toward him, that they were plotting his murder! And, they didn't seem to care what might be the impact on themselves or others.

Recently, it seems that no good deed of President Trump goes unpunished either. I'm by no means a Trump loyalist, but I've actually been appalled at the actions of some in the press, in politics, and in the entertainment world when it comes to our president. So strong is their hatred against him that they are actually rooting for a recession or for failure in negotiations with North Korea! Anything, to see Trump fail! I would think that the people whose lives would be impacted by an economic recession or nuclear aggression might see things differently, but that is another story.

When hatred gets to such a fevered pitch, common sense goes out the window. The hated, the haters and the innocent bystanders all suffer.

What is the solution to such hatred? There is only one I know: love. The love God poured into our hearts by the Holy Spirit. We may disagree about politics, about policies and about presidents, but let us love one another for love comes from God (1 John 4.7).

Prayer: Father, there is so much anger and hatred in the world today. Help me to be an instrument of your love today, so that others may know the freedom and joy that come from you. Amen.

Psalm of the Day: 73.21-28

You're Crazy!

Daily Reading: Acts 26

And as he was saying these things in his defense, Festus said with a loud voice, "Paul, you are out of your mind; your great learning is driving you out of your mind." (Acts 26.24)

Devotional Thought: When brought before King Agrippa and Governor Festus, Paul gave a heartfelt account of his conversion to faith in Jesus. In an impassioned but well-reasoned speech, he testified of his background, his education, his sincerity, and his determination. Even though he was on trial defending himself, he could not help but testify.

Festus, however, had a hard heart towards the gospel. Exasperated, he interrupted Paul's defense, "Paul, you are out of your mind; your great learning is driving you out of your mind" (v. 24). This Roman ruler could not understand how such an intelligent and educated man, as Paul had undoubtedly proven himself to be, could believe in such nonsense as a man rising from the dead.

In the same way, today's world is befuddled that reasonable, intelligent people could believe in the "fairy tales" of the Bible. There is a biblical explanation for this: "The person without the Spirit does not accept the things that come from the Spirit of God but considers them foolishness, and cannot understand them because they are discerned only through the Spirit" (1 Corinthians 2.14).

Paul, recognizing Festus's hard heart, turned his attention to King Agrippa. In the same way, we should be testing the hearts of those around us. Sadly, there are some in whom the Spirit has yet to work. The seeds that we sow will fall on the path, never taking root in their hearts. They will be ever hearing, but never understanding; ever seeing, but never perceiving (Isaiah 6.9). When we sense the Spirit's work in a heart, may we always be ready and anxious to scatter the seeds of the gospel.

Jenny

Prayer: Lord, help our ears to hear and our eyes to see your truth! Thank you for giving us a Helper, without whom we could not comprehend the wonderful mystery of the gospel. Prompt us and equip us to respond to the Spirit-softened hearts of those around us. Amen.

Psalm of the Day: 74.1-8

Toss It Overboard!

Daily Reading: Acts 27

> *Since we were violently storm-tossed, they began the next day to jettison the cargo.* (Acts 27.18)

Devotional Thought: I have some friends who have long since passed retirement age, and are now beginning to make plans to move into a senior citizen apartment complex. It is not easy for them. One of the most difficult things is letting go of the 'stuff' that they have accumulated over the years. Garages, closets, attics, and extra bedrooms have been cleaned out. Their 'stuff' has been given away or sold in garage sales. But, as they have come to realize, they can't take it with them!

Those who were aboard the ship with Paul, discovered how 'stuff' suddenly becomes less important in times of change or danger. The storms threatened their ship and they gladly got rid of the cargo to save their lives. Eventually, "even the ship's tackle" (v. 19) was tossed overboard. Who needs to steer a sunken ship?

Sometimes 'stuff' gets in the way, even when seas are serene and sailing is smooth. 'Stuff' can get in the way of our spiritual growth. Jesus told us that we are not to have our treasures on earth, where moth and rust destroy and where thieves steal. Instead, our treasure is to be in heaven, for where our treasure is, there our hearts will be also. If in our pursuit of goods and pleasures, we neglect the matters of the heart and spirit, we will find ourselves bereft of the important things. Periodically, we need to take an inventory and see what might be weighing us down.

Where is your treasure?

Prayer: Jesus, you are the treasure of my heart. Your love, O Lord, is sweeter than all the pleasures that this world affords. It is sweeter than life itself. I cling to you, and you alone. Amen.

Psalm of the Day: 74.9-17

Home!

Daily Reading: Acts 28

And so we came to Rome. (Acts 28.14)

Devotional Thought: As I have mentioned in the past, Lana and I are homebodies. But in recent weeks, we have been away from home quite a bit. Some of our excursions were for pleasure, others for family needs, and a sad and victorious journey for a funeral. But, how sweet it has been to go through the little valley, round the bend, and top the ridge to see our home. Home!

Coming home fills our hearts with peace, with satisfaction, and with hope. I wonder if that is what Paul felt when he came to Rome. While it was not home to him, there seemed to be a yearning, a sense of destination to his missionary travels. Rome! He longed for it in his spirit (Acts 19.21, Romans 15.24) and was comforted by it in his trials (Acts 23.11).

Those simple words in Acts 28 - and so we came to Rome - reflect a much deeper experience than simply the end of a journey. Paul came to Rome through great trials: rejection by his countrymen, hard work, sleepless nights, unjust beatings, accusation and arrest, three plots to kill him, unlawful arrest and imprisonment, rejected appeal, and finally a shipwreck. The sight of Rome filled his heart with a sense of arrival, of fulfillment, of destiny. In his spirit, he was home.

One day, we will lay aside our burdens and trials, our hurts and our struggles. We will come through the valley, round the bend, and top the ridge to see the lights of heaven. The gates will swing open, and Jesus will greet us. We will be home.

Prayer: Lord, at times we feel the burdens and perplexities of life pressing against us so hard, that we struggle to believe. But, we do believe, Lord, and we know that one day we will be home. Thank you for preparing a place for us. Help us to be faithful to the end. Amen..

Psalm of the Day: 74.18-23

Pouring Out My Soul

Daily Reading: 1 Samuel 1

> *I have been pouring out my soul before the Lord... speaking out of my great anxiety and vexation.* (1 Samuel 1.15-16)

Devotional Thought: Being unable to bear children is a heavy burden on many in our day. I have prayed for many friends and parishioners who want to have children, but seem unable to. Their hearts are heavy, and their souls long for children. Thankfully, I have seen God answer those prayers – some I didn't even know about until later! At times the answer came through medical science, while at other times God just orchestrated the process. Either way, the announcement of the pregnancy was a joy-filled occasion.

Hannah was barren, a condition which was almost unbearable in that culture and time. While we have medical treatments for infertility, Hannah did not. Her only recourse was God, so the scripture says that she had been "pouring out [her] soul before the Lord, speaking out of [her] great anxiety and vexation." So intense were her prayers, that she seemed like a drunken woman to Eli the high priest. But, verses 19 and 20 reveal that out of those intense longings and prayers, "the Lord remembered her. And in due time Hannah conceived and bore a son, and she called his name Samuel, for she said, 'I have asked for him from the Lord.'"

What intense longing do you carry in your soul? Be encouraged, child of God! Others may misunderstand you and even impugn your motives, but God sees your heart and has not forgotten you! And, while it is perfectly legitimate to take steps humanly to solve your problems and to satisfy your soul, what is most needed is prayer! Do not give up. Keep pouring out your soul.

Prayer: Lord, you know the desires - the intense longings - of my heart. Hear my prayers as I lift them to you out of my great anxiety and vexation. Amen.

Psalm of the Day: 75.1-5

To Whom Honor Is Due

Daily Reading: 1 Samuel 2

> *Those who honor me I will honor, and those who despise me shall be lightly esteemed.* (1 Samuel 2.30)

Devotional Thought: As God pronounced his judgment on the sons of Eli, he made a powerful statement: "Those who honor me I will honor, and those who despise me shall be lightly esteemed." I've had countless conversations with people who wonder why God is not blessing them. They are angry at God for not answering prayer or for not giving them what they want. They often fail to realize that it is their behavior blocking the blessings of God. For some reason, people think that they can live any old way they please and God is still obligated to answer their prayers. God sees it differently, though. In today's American culture – and sad to say this exists even in the church – we are ignoring God's commandments, replacing them with our new enlightened version of things.

And, this principle applies not just to individuals. It extends to churches and even to nations. A church that does not honor the Lord through prayer, faith, and compassion, will not be honored by the presence of the Lord. Oh, they may be able to gather a crowd and to stir up emotional excitement, but there is a vast difference between human excitement and the Holy Spirit's presence. A nation that turns its back on God's principles will not enjoy the protection and favor of the Lord. It is as simple as that.

What about you? Are you honoring the Lord through obedience? Through witness? Through holy living? Through tithing? Through prayer? Through faith? Through worship? If we desire to receive the honor of the only One who really matters, then we must honor him in our lives.

Prayer: Lord, forgive me for those times when I have failed to honor you in my actions, my attitudes, or my words. "In my life, Lord, be glorified today." Amen.

Psalm of the Day: 75.6-10

Speak, for Your Servant Hears
Daily Reading: 1 Samuel 3

And the Lord came and stood, calling as at other times, "Samuel! Samuel!" And Samuel said, "Speak, for your servant hears." Then the Lord said to Samuel, "Behold, I am about to..." (1 Samuel 3.10-11)

Devotional Thought: In our post-pastoral life, my wife Lana and I have developed a routine of working at home. Her work desk is in our bedroom at the back of the house. I study and write in the office at the front of our house. I have found that when Lana comes to talk to me, I am usually quite distracted by what is on my computer screen. So, I have developed a habit of pushing back from my desk and getting up out of my chair to disengage from my work. Otherwise, there's no way I can focus on what she is saying. (As you can imagine, that has gotten me into trouble a time or two!) When I stand up, that is an indication for her to go ahead and speak, for I am ready to hear.

When Samuel was a boy, in the service of God's house at Shiloh, God came to speak to him. At first he didn't give God attention, instead going to Eli. Finally, through the gentle instruction of Eli, Samuel realized God was calling him. The next time that God spoke, Samuel responded, "Speak, for your servant hears."

Some "takeaways" from Samuel's encounter with God...
- We need to stay engaged in God's work: "The boy Samuel was ministering to the Lord..."
- The Lord initiates conversations with us, and he does so repeatedly.
- At times, God has a specific and individual message for us, calling us by name!
- When God speaks, we must stop and purposefully listen.
- God reveals to us his plans. It's up to us to respond to his call.

Is the "word of the Lord rare" in your life? Do you need a fresh vision from God? Tell him, "Speak, for your servant hears."

Prayer: Lord, I need a fresh word from you, but I know that my life is full of demands and distractions. So, I put all of them aside right now and say, "Speak, for your servant hears." Amen.

Psalm of the Day: 76.1-7

Why?

Daily Reading: 1 Samuel 4-5

> *When the soldiers returned to camp, the elders of Israel asked, "Why did the Lord bring defeat on us today before the Philistines?"*
> (1 Samuel 4.3)

Devotional Thought: Why did defeat come to the Israelites? Why does defeat come to the church?

We had a hint in the last chapter: "In those days the word of the Lord was rare; there were not many visions" (1 Samuel 3.1). The people had lost sight of the Lord! Even Samuel, raised in the house of the Lord, "did not yet know the Lord: The word of the Lord had not yet been revealed to him" (v. 7). Should not this boy have been exposed to God's Word as he worked in the tabernacle?

In these days, the word of the Lord is rare, and it is becoming rarer as Christianity faces religious persecution as never seen in America before - and done in the name of tolerance! Christians are singled out for their beliefs, and punished for staying true to their convictions – from pastors to bakers to sisters of mercy. To make matters worse, many churches have watered down the gospel and compromised the truth, leaving their members either confused and unsatisfied, or worse – confident in an eternal security that will not belong to them.

I am grateful for the churches that remain true to God's Word. There are still many of them, but I wonder: For how long? They face increasing pressure to conform to the world, rather than proclaim the truth of sin and the hope of the gospel. We need to stand firm in the truth, and most importantly, we need to pray. Without the Truth and without prayer, we go into the battle without the Ark of the Lord!

Jenny

Prayer: Lord, we must remain faithful in these days of moral relativism, but we cannot do so without you, so help your church to be strong in Truth and vigilant in prayer. Amen.

Psalm of the Day: 76.8-12

A Sense of the Holy

Daily Reading: 1 Samuel 6

> *And he struck some of the men of Beth-shemesh, because they looked upon the ark of the Lord... Then the men of Beth-shemesh said, "Who is able to stand before the Lord, this holy God?"* (1 Samuel 6.19-20)

Devotional Thought: Years ago, I had an "older pastor" (Yikes! I'm one of those now!) lament to me that the church lacked a sense of the holy. He wondered if it was because our people were coming into the sanctuary flippantly and irreverently. I think he was on to something.

The people of Beth-shemesh had a solution to their flippant inspection of the ark of the Lord: Send the ark away! I don't like that solution. I want the presence of God in our midst! I think the better solution is to consider how we can reverence and worship a holy God, how we can invite his presence into our midst.

Perhaps you recall the story about Uzzah, a seemingly innocent person, who was struck dead by the Lord when he reached up to steady the ark of the covenant while it was being transported (2 Samuel 6). Uzzah acted in an improper and irreverent way. What was the big deal? The big deal was that God had given very specific instructions about how to handle, how to transport, and who could see the ark of the covenant. This was done in order to instill reverence among the people of God, concerning the presence of God in their midst.

Do we take the presence of God lightly? In our enlightened and liberated day, are we approaching God too casually? In our "come as you are" approach to God, have we lost a sense of the holy? I am not opposed to making people feel welcome – Jesus himself teaches that. But, there is something to be said for the awesome presence of God to be real and reverenced in our midst. If we are not reverent before God, can we expect to be moved by his holy presence?

Prayer: Forgive me, Lord, for my casual approach to you. Though you are my Father, and you invite me to call you "Daddy," you also are my Creator, Redeemer, and Lord. I reverence you, O Lord. Help me to sense your holy presence in worship. Amen.

Psalm of the Day: 77.1-9

Hitherto Hath the Lord Helped Us
Daily Reading: 1 Samuel 7

Then Samuel took a stone, and set it between Mizpeh and Shen, and called the name of it Ebenezer, saying, Hitherto hath the Lord helped us. (1 Samuel 7.12, KJV)

Devotional Thought: I served as the pastor of a church whose cornerstone at the front door of the church building read, "Hitherto hath the Lord helped us." I always liked going in that door, and being reminded that the Lord had helped us yesterday, and that he would be faithful to help us today. I also wondered, "What, if anything, can I do to receive the help of the Lord?"

As I studied that passage of the Bible and the event it described, I came to see, we can expect help from the Lord when we...

- *Call* for him: "All the house of Israel lamented after the Lord" (v. 2). The word lament means to mourn for, to grieve after. The people had godly sorrow in their hearts that they had forsaken God. They now returned to him with all their hearts. Will we?
- *Consecrate* to him: "So the people of Israel put away the Baals and the Ashtaroth, and they served the Lord only" (v. 4). Are we willing to surrender the things that keep us from serving God?
- *Cry* out to him: "And Samuel cried out to the Lord for Israel, and the Lord answered him"(v. 9). The leader prayed, but the people also joined with him in earnest appeal for God's help. They gathered together to pray, and their prayers were accompanied by fasting. Are we that zealous for the Lord's help?
- *Contend* for him: "And the men of Israel went out from Mizpah and pursued the Philistines and struck them, as far as below Beth-car" (v. 11). The people were not satisfied with going part way, but went even beyond Beth-car, or "the place of the lamb." Are we willing to join the Lamb of God in sacrifice and service?

Prayer: Lord, thank you for your faithfulness. Day after day, I receive grace and strength, wisdom and direction, comfort and instruction. Grant that I would continually receive your help. In the name of Jesus, amen.

Psalm of the Day: 77.10-15

Where Do You Get Directions?

Daily Reading: 1 Samuel 8

> *But the people refused to obey the voice of Samuel. And they said, "No! But there shall be a king over us, that we also may be like all the nations."* (1 Samuel 8.19-20a)

Devotional Thought: Travelling from Sturgis, Michigan to Canton, Ohio, I thought it would be fun to drive on US 6 – a highway from my childhood. I had briefly consulted a map, but it soon became apparent that I did not have enough information. I turned on the GPS, but instead of following the instructions, I kept trying to figure out a way to make my original plan work – to follow US 6 as far as I could before turning south. I ended up backtracking and crisscrossing all the way across northern Ohio, spending at least an extra hour on the trip – all because I refused to listen to the information that was within my reach.

Several years ago, Lana and I had the privilege of hosting Christian and Monica Boseff in our home. The Boseffs are pastors from Romania, and they also run a shelter to rescue ladies and children from human trafficking. I was curious about the mood of Romanians concerning same-sex marriage. They told me that Romanians are staunchly against redefining marriage. They went on to say, however, that the European Union was putting pressure on Romania to come to Western Europe's way of thinking – to accept and validate homosexual marriages. There is intense economic and social pressure for Romania to be "like all the nations."

The people of Israel in Samuel's day, wanted to be like the nations around them. Those nations had a king over them. God warned them what a king would do to them, but they insisted: "There shall be a king over us!"

Where are you getting your guidelines for what is proper and moral behavior? From the nations and people around you? Or are you getting them from the Lord?

Prayer: Forgive me, Lord, when I turn to sources other than you. It is so easy to live by sight and not by faith. Help me to block out the voices of worldly wisdom, and follow your true wisdom. Amen.

Psalm of the Day: 77.16-20

Stop and Listen

Daily Reading: 1 Samuel 9

> *Stop here yourself for a while, that I may make known to you the word of God.* (1 Samuel 9.27)

Devotional Thought: Have you ever tried to converse with someone who wasn't paying attention to you? I've visited in homes and hospitals where the person I have come to see doesn't turn off the TV. It's a very frustrating experience!

Saul had to stop what he was doing, in order to hear the Word of God. Samuel wasn't about to tell Saul this important message from God while Saul was otherwise occupied. We need to stop and listen. It will take intentional effort and investment of time, but it is the only way for God to make known to us his Word.

Saul's mission was not yet complete. But, he was told to "stop here yourself for a while." Saul's family was waiting to hear from him. But, he was told to "stop here yourself for a while." Saul had other obligations to see about. But, he was told to "stop here yourself for a while." Saul had a long way to travel. But, he was told to "stop here yourself for a while."

Saul had been awakened by the prophet to hear the Word of God. We must wake ourselves up. It is your responsibility and mine to rub the sleep from our eyes to read our Bibles. There were lots of other things Saul could have been doing, but in order to hear the Word of God, he needed to stop for a while. The same is true for you and me. God desires to make known the Word of God to us, but we must be willing to stop long enough to hear it!

Prayer: Lord, I over-schedule my day and overstuff my mind. Help me to stop and listen. Reveal your Word to me, I pray. Amen.

Psalm of the Day: 78.1-8

What About My Son?

Daily Reading: 1 Samuel 10

The donkeys that you went to seek are found, and now your father has ceased to care about the donkeys and is anxious about you, saying, "What shall I do about my son?" (1 Samuel 10.2)

Devotional Thought: Kish had sent Saul to find some lost donkeys. There was a lot at stake in Saul's search. But, as time wore on and Saul didn't return, Kish came to worry about more than his lost donkeys. He started worrying about his lost son!

How do we set our priorities?

When crises come, many things that we felt were important cease to hold sway over us. The time to set our priorities isn't when the donkeys are missing. It's when the donkeys are found! So many times we will make promises to God in the storm, only to forget those promises when fair weather arrives. That pattern must be broken if we are to have spiritual victory and strength. The fact of the matter is that we need to make even more effort to serve God in prosperity than we do in adversity!

Something else I noticed in this story is that financial profits do not define the worth of a person. When Saul was delayed in coming home, Kish discovered that the donkeys were not nearly as important to him as he thought. His son was much more important! We all know how Kish felt. We tend to neglect our loved ones until we think we are at risk of losing them. Too many decisions are based on "the bottom line", rather than on the importance of family and dignity and love. What is a life worth? Is one life worth more than another? Jesus Christ died to save all people, not just the successful, the talented, the attractive, and the wealthy. God sees all life as valuable. Do we?

Prayer: Lord, I don't want to wait until the next crisis, the next storm, to make you my priority. I crown you as Lord of my life now, and I surrender my will to yours. Amen.

Psalm of the Day: 78.9-16

Let Us Go to Gilgal

Daily Reading: 1 Samuel 11

> Then Samuel said to the people, "Come, let us go to Gilgal and there renew the kingdom." (1 Samuel 11.14)

Devotional Thought: There are times for all of us when we all need a "Gilgal," a renewing of the Kingdom of God in our lives.

What can we learn about renewal from Gilgal?

- Gilgal was the first camp that Joshua and the Israelites established, after they crossed the Jordan River into the Promised Land. It was there that they set up a monument of remembrance - twelve large stones taken out from the Jordan's dry riverbed. When we need renewal, it is good to go back to our Gilgal of deliverance. Jesus told the church in Ephesus to "Remember therefore from where you have fallen; repent, and do the works you did at first" (Revelation 2.5).
- It was at Gilgal that the people of God renewed the covenant under Joshua. They observed the rite of circumcision and the celebration of the Passover. When you need renewal, revisit the spiritually high times in your life and recommit to the Lordship of Jesus.
- Gilgal was a base of operations for military conquests. From there, the people marched around Jericho. From there, they extended the kingdom. When you are longing for renewal, take the battle the enemy. Step out in faith. Do the things that God has called you to, and accept the victories God has promised you.
- The prophet Samuel had a three-city preaching circuit that included Gilgal. On these circuits, Samuel taught the words and way of God. You can find renewal by studying the Word of God and walking in the way of obedience.
- Saul was crowned king at Gilgal. If you are in need of renewal, make Jesus the King of your life - of every decision, every word, every attitude, every action.

Let us go to Gilgal and there renew the Kingdom!

Prayer: Lord, whether my soul is on fire or I have lapsed into a coldness of heart, I need a Gilgal of renewal! Fan the flames of revival in my spirit so that I can love and serve you with passion and zeal. Amen.

Psalm of the Day: 78.17-31

Instruction and Assurance
Daily Reading: 1 Samuel 12

Do not turn aside from following the Lord, but serve the Lord with all your heart. And do not turn aside after empty things that cannot profit or deliver, for they are empty. For the Lord will not forsake his people, for his great name's sake, because it has pleased the Lord to make you a people for himself. Moreover, as for me, far be it from me that I should sin against the Lord by ceasing to pray for you, and I will instruct you in the good and the right way." (1 Samuel 12.20b-23)

Devotional Thought: As Samuel passed on the mantle of leadership, he instructed and assured the people:

Instruction:
- Do not turn aside from following the Lord. It is so easy to do. Unless we are diligent, we lose our focus. I have known many people who have made a good start, only to turn aside.
- Serve the Lord with all your heart. Turning aside is a byproduct of split loyalties. When we try to serve two masters, we will fail.
- Do not turn aside after empty things. An "empty thing" is anything besides God - wealth, pleasure, power - that we think will satisfy us. Chasing empty things actually leaves us emptier.

Assurance:
- The Lord will not forsake his people. Nothing can separate us from God's love. God will never leave us nor forsake us.
- The Lord has made you a people for himself. Our redemption from slavery has been paid through the sacrifice of Jesus. God has given his very best for us.
- I will pray for you. How comforting! We need to assure one another of our prayers, and follow through on that assurance.
- I will instruct you. In our jobs, our homes, and our churches, we need spiritual guidance. And, it is available in God's Word, in the Holy Spirit, and in the saints!

Follow this instruction and have this assurance today!

Prayer: Lord, I need your instruction. Lead me in the way I should go. I need your assurance. In the pressures of life, I tend to forget your steadfast love. So, instruct me and assure me, I pray. And, Lord, help me to help others along the way. Amen.

Psalm of the Day: 78.32-39

Where Are the Blacksmiths?

Daily Reading: 1 Samuel 13

> Now there was no blacksmith to be found throughout all the land of Israel... So on the day of the battle there was neither sword nor spear found in the hand of any of the people. (1 Samuel 13.19, 22)

Devotional Thought: When Saul began his reign as king, the Philistines were in a position of strength over the Israelites. The Philistines subjugated Israel by preventing them from having spears and swords. How did they do that? By stopping the work of blacksmiths. The Philistines knew that if they controlled the blacksmiths, they controlled the weapons. And, if they controlled the weapons, they controlled the battle.

I believe that Satan has the same strategy today.

The sword represents the Word of God. It is designed for close-in battle. The Word is powerful. The Word penetrates into the minds of people. The Word lays bare the secrets of the heart. The spear represents prayer. It is designed for longer-range use. Prayer is the tip of the spear in our fight against evil. With it we hold our enemy at bay. The spear also represented the authority of the commander. Without prayer, we operate on our own authority. That's a recipe for disaster!

So, how do you think Satan uses the strategy of the Philistines? He knows if he controls the blacksmiths, he controls the weapons. If he controls the weapons, he controls the battle.

The people of God need more blacksmiths, those who are capable of forging the weapons of battle. It seems that it is getting more and more difficult to find blacksmiths in the church. People want to "be fed," but not feed others. They covet the prayers of others, but do not stand in the gap themselves. We need more people to teach the Word of God, and help people - especially young Christians - apply it. We need more people to teach the way of prayer, and to lead in the work of prayer.

Will you be a blacksmith?

Prayer: Lord, the Bible talks about how the Word of God can be rare, how there can be a famine of the Word of God. Is that famine due to the fact that we lack blacksmiths? Here I am. Send me. The Bible speaks of no one to intercede. Here I am. Send me. I will be a blacksmith. Amen.

Psalm of the Day: 78.40-49

To Pray or To Do?

Daily Reading: 1 Samuel 14

Saul said to Ahijah, "Bring the ark of God here." For the ark of God went at that time with the people of Israel. Now while Saul was talking to the priest, the tumult in the camp of the Philistines increased more and more. So Saul said to the priest, "Withdraw your hand." Then Saul and all the people who were with him rallied and went into the battle... (1 Samuel 14.18-20)

Devotional Thought: As the Philistines closed in on the Israelites, Saul wanted to seek guidance and blessing from God. "Bring the ark of God here." But, no sooner than the ark of God was set up, activity in the Philistine camp heated up. That was enough for Saul! "Withdraw your hand." In other words – "We need to stop praying and get to work!"

The next day, though, something quite different happened. Saul and the Israelites had handed the Philistines a devastating defeat, and Saul was ready to press the battle. This time, however, it was the priest who said stop, "let us draw near to God here." When they prayed, God remained silent. The silence was due to something else entirely, but the point I am trying to make is that Saul was ready for immediate action, but God was saying wait – just the opposite of what had happened the prior day.

There is danger in assuming that God is going to lead us the same every time. There will be times when immediate action is called for. There will be other times when we want to take immediate action, but God will say, "Stop and pray." This matter of following God is not wooden and predictable. We must always be ready to pray and to act. That means we should be prayed up! Jesus told his disciples to "Stay dressed for action and keep your lamps burning" (Luke 12.35).

Prayer: Father, help me to have a bias for prayer, but also to be ready to act at a moment's notice when you say, "Move." Help me to be dressed for action with my lamp burning! Amen.

Psalm of the Day: 78.50-55

God's Great Mercy

Daily Reading: 1 Samuel 15

> Then Saul said to the Kenites, "Go, depart; go down from among the Amalekites, lest I destroy you with them. For you showed kindness to all the people of Israel when they came up out of Egypt." So the Kenites departed from among the Amalekites. (1 Samuel 15.6)

Devotional Thought: The Amalekites had shown themselves to be irreconcilable enemies to Israel (Exodus 17). The Kenites - who were living among the Amalekites - were warned ahead of time, so that they might escape the coming destruction. These Kenites had shown kindness to Israel during their journey from Egypt through the wilderness. They heeded Saul's warning, and escaped the judgment that came upon the Amalekites who were utterly destroyed.

Judgment like this may sound extreme to us, until we consider the fact that we are all deserving of death, for indeed, "The wages of sin is death" (Romans 6:23). The truly remarkable thing is that God has extended the grace to spare any of us from the judgment we all deserve.

We see God's great mercy over and over again in Scripture – He spares Noah's family from the flood, Lot's family from the firestorm that destroyed Sodom and Gomorrah, Rahab and her family from the destruction of Jericho, the Kenites from the judgment of Amalek.

And, we see it most clearly in the death and resurrection of Jesus, "who gave himself for us to redeem us from all wickedness and to purify for himself a people that are his very own, eager to do what is good" (Titus 2:14). When you put your faith in him, "you are a chosen race, a royal priesthood, a holy nation, a people for his own possession, that you may proclaim the excellencies of him who called you out of darkness into his marvelous light" (1 Peter 2:9). Rejoice today in the Lord's great mercy!

Prayer: Thank you, Father, that you are a kind and merciful God. When people reject you, they must do so over your objections and in spite of your reaching out to them. I praise you for your great love! Amen.

Psalm of the Day: 78.56-64

When Leadership Changes
Daily Reading: 1 Samuel 16

> For we saw his star The LORD said to Samuel, "How long will you grieve over Saul?" (1 Samuel 16.1)

Devotional Thought: When we elected a new District Superintendent in NC, how difficult it was for me to transfer my loyalty to the new DS. The former DS had given me my first opportunity in ministry, and I considered him a friend. I was grieving over the loss that this change represented.

Samuel's heart was grieved over a change of leadership. Having been personally involved in Saul's rise to power, Samuel took it hard when Saul fell from grace.

What can we learn from this incident?
- *God instructed Samuel to get over it!* God had a plan, and Samuel needed to come into alignment with God, not the other way around.
- *Samuel wanted to replace Saul with someone like Saul.* Samuel had instinctively chosen Eliab because he reminded him of Saul – tall and strong, an impressive figure. It is only natural when we change leaders to look for someone who is just like the former leader, whom we have loved. But, if God wants someone like the present leader in place, he would have left him/her in place!
- *The Lord looks on the heart.* Samuel couldn't see what God saw – Eliab's heart. Eliab was a petty and jealous big brother. Can we trust God to reveal his will based on what he sees?
- *God chose the smallest.* Most translations refer to David as the "youngest," but the Hebrew word can also mean the "smallest." There is some irony in this. Samuel had been impressed by the height and appearance of both Saul and Eliab, but God chose exactly the opposite.

God said to Samuel, "I have provided for myself a king." It's good to know that God has a plan. Let us always seek to discover and follow that plan!

Prayer: Lord, you have said that you will provide shepherds after your own heart. Help me to trust in you, even when I don't understand changes in leadership. In the name of Jesus, the Great Shepherd, I pray. Amen.

Psalm of the Day: 78.65-72

Run to the Fight

Daily Reading: 1 Samuel 17

> *When the Philistine arose and came and drew near to meet David,*
> *David ran quickly toward the battle line to meet the Philistine.*
> (1 Samuel 17.48)

Devotional Thought: I recently officiated at the funeral of a very dear friend of mine. Problems arose to meet him, his wife and family. Cancer... surgery... chemo... radiation... recurrence... sickness... Then, death. Others I know, have lost jobs and homes, savings and security. Divorce and disappointment have drawn near to my family. Life is not always easy, is it?

Just as Goliath "arose and came and drew near to meet David," problems will arise in our lives. They draw near to us. But, just as David "ran quickly toward the battle line," we too can have confidence to face our problems head on.

Where did David's confidence come from?
- David remembered how God had helped him in the past.
- David rested in the fact that he was part of God's chosen people.
- David had received the anointing of God from the prophet Samuel.
- David relied on the fact that he was there on assignment from God.

When God assigns you to do something, are you confident? The odds were against David. The Philistine was a trained and experienced warrior; David was only a shepherd. The Philistine was a giant; David was a man. The Philistine was protected with the best armor; David was wearing street clothes. The Philistine was armed with a spear and sword; David had a sling and some pebbles. Yet, David was so confident that he "ran quickly toward the battle line to meet the Philistine."

When problems come, how do you meet them? Run quickly to the fight! You can do all things through Christ who gives you strength.

Prayer: Lord, I know that problems and battles will come my way. The enemy will oppose me. But, in the name of Jesus, I run into the battle, confident that you will do immeasurably more than I can ask or imagine. Amen.

Psalm of the Day: 79.1-7

As His Own Soul

Daily Reading: 1 Samuel 18

> Then Jonathan made a covenant with David, because he loved him as his own soul. (1 Samuel 18.3)

Devotional Thought: In the ancient world, covenants were very important. Today we have contracts. Contracts are designed to benefit us and protect us from each other. Contracts are temporary and can be dissolved. Covenants, however, were based upon something more than law and protection. Covenants were agreements that each would care for the other for life.

Jonathan's covenant with David was based upon love: "He loved him as his own soul." There is something mysterious about love, isn't there? We are not sure where it comes from or how it originates, but we know it when we see it, and we are controlled by it when we feel it. I have some friends that are like that in my life.

When I was the pastor at Bethel Nazarene Church, I developed a friendship with Dick. He lived next door to the church. He always had a bountiful garden in the back and beautiful flowers all around. When I came to Bethel, however, Dick was not a member of the church. So, I got to know him first as a friend and only later as his pastor. Our friendship was based upon love. He did so much for me – for no other reason than because he loved me. I wish I could have done more for him, but I cherish all the times we spent together.

We all have a Friend like Jonathan was to David. We all have a Friend like Dick was to me. Jesus is a Friend who sticks closer than a brother. He has sealed the covenant of friendship with you and me in his own blood. He loves us as his own soul.

Prayer: Jesus, thank you that you no longer call us servants, instead you have called us friends. What a friend we have in you, O Lord! Amen.

Psalm of the Day: 79.8-13

Not Open Indefinitely

Daily Reading: 1 Samuel 19

If you do not escape with your life tonight, tomorrow you will be killed.
(1 Samuel 19.11b)

Devotional Thought: There is one road onto and off Folly Beach, South Carolina. That road is a designated hurricane route. When a hurricane threatens, people are to take that road off the island as soon as possible. If they wait too long, the storm swell is too great, the winds are too high, and the route is closed. The opportunity to escape is not open indefinitely.

Did you know that the door of spiritual opportunity does not stand open forever? There comes a time in everyone's life, when the words of the prophet ring true: "my people know not the rules of the LORD… The harvest is past, the summer is ended, and we are not saved" (Jeremiah 8.7, 20). As the Lord made clear in the days of Noah, God will not always strive with the heart of man. There is the season in each of our lives, when we can hear and respond to the voice of the Lord. But then, there comes a season when "the keepers of the house tremble, and the strong men are bent, and the grinders cease because they are few, and those who look through the windows are dimmed, and the doors on the street are shut—when… desire fails, because man is going to his eternal home… and the dust returns to the earth as it was, and the spirit returns to God who gave it." (Selected from Ecclesiastes 12.3-7)

I think that the name Folly Beach is interesting. What was the folly at that beach? I wonder if it got its name because there were some people who delayed too long in leaving the island. Let's not be fools when it comes to our eternal salvation, but let us act today while there is still opportunity.

Prayer: Lord, thank you for making a way of escape for me. That way is for everybody. I pray that not only myself, but that many others will travel that way before it is too late. Amen.

Psalm of the Day: 80.1-3

Your Steadfast Love

Daily Reading: 1 Samuel 20

> *"Show me the steadfast love of the Lord, that I may not die; and do not cut off your steadfast love from my house forever"... And Jonathan made David swear again by his love for him, for he loved him as he loved his own soul.* (1 Samuel 20.14-15a, 17)

Devotional Thought: It was an expected practice in David's day, for an incoming regime to wipe out all vestiges of the old regime. As part of the old regime, all that Jonathan could expect from David was death.

In this story, Jonathan represents you and me – sons and daughters of the old kingdom, the dying kingdom, the kingdom of Saul. Just as Jonathan came to David, we can come to Jesus with confidence:

- Jonathan's confidence was due to the steadfast love of the Lord. Our confidence is due to the fact that God loves us! He gave his one and only Son for us.
- Jonathan pressed his claim not only for himself, but also for his family. Remember the foreign mother, who brought her daughter to Jesus and was not turned away, then press your claims for your family!
- Jonathan made David promise to remain true to the original covenant. What an amazing thing – Jonathan had no power over David, yet he *made* him swear by his love! As Jacob of old wrestled with the Lord, do not let go until you receive the blessing you seek.
- Jonathan loved David as his own soul. Jonathan's demands were not one-sided. Had he not loved David, had he not trusted him, then he would not have been able to come before him in this manner. When we press our claims before God, we must do so in complete love and trust.

Oh wonderful grace of Jesus!

Prayer: Show us your steadfast love, that we may live and not die. Do not cut us off from your love, we pray, for we love you as we love our own souls, O Lord. Amen.

Psalm of the Day: 80.4-7

There Is None Like It

Daily Reading: 1 Samuel 21

And the priest said, "The sword of Goliath the Philistine, whom you struck down in the Valley of Elah, behold, it is here..." And David said, "There is none like that; give it to me." (1 Samuel 21.9)

Devotional Thought: When my lifelong friend, Keith, returned from Kenya, Africa, he gave me a Maasai warrior's club. For years, I displayed it on my bookshelf as a pleasant reminder of our friendship, and as encouragement to "fight the good fight of faith." When we moved to South Carolina, I packed it away. Recently I came across it, packed away with some other things from my office. I hadn't been looking for it, but when I "found" it, I felt a surge of joy and satisfaction.

When David "found" the sword of Goliath in the safe-keeping of Ahimilech, the priest of Nob, what memories did it press into David's mind? Years before, when Goliath threatened the army of Israel, David had put his life on the line and had single-handedly gone out to face and defeat the giant. After he had slain Goliath, David had taken his sword. That sword had found its way to Ahimilech, the priest at Nob.

Years later, David found his way to Ahimilech, too. But, now he was on the run from Saul, who had turned on him in a jealous rage. Finding that sword must have been a source of great joy and satisfaction to David. He said, "There is none like it."

What sword do Christians have? Is not the Word of God called "the sword of the Spirit" in Ephesians 6? There is none like it! The Word of God is...
- *Imposing* - Having been wielded not by a worldly giant, but by our heavenly Lord!
- *Available* - The Spirit of God opens up its truth to us.
- *Precious* - It comes to us from the heart of God. It has been sanctified by the martyrs of the faith.

The Word of God. Indeed, there is none like it!

Prayer: Lord, I thank you for your Word. There is nothing else like it! I will hide it in my heart, that I might not sin against you. Amen!

Psalm of the Day: 80.8-19

All the Strength of Heaven
Daily Reading: 1 Samuel 22

And everyone who was in distress, and everyone who was in debt, and everyone who was bitter in soul, gathered to him. (1 Samuel 22.2)

Devotional Thought: The rift between David and Saul was growing, and many marginalized people found their way into David's circle:

- *In distress...* This comes from a root word that means to be constrained or oppressed. Romans 6, tells us that those who serve sin are slaves to sin. But, through Jesus "sin shall not be your master."
- *In debt...* Not only are we in bondage to our sins, we all are in debt for our sins. It is a debt we cannot hope to pay. But, Jesus has paid the price by his death on the cross!
- *Bitter in soul...* Bitterness of soul comes when our circumstances rule over us. Yet, we do not need to reside in our bitterness. Jesus offers us a way that we can rise above the circumstances that hold us down.

What did these distressed, indebted, and bitter souls do? They "gathered to him." One of those who came to David was Abiathar, the son of the priest whom Saul had killed, due to his helping out David. David said to him, "Stay with me; do not be afraid, for he who seeks my life seeks your life. With me you shall be in safekeeping." Those were bold words! David had only a ragtag militia against Saul's organized military. Yet, he was confident that he could protect not only himself, but also Abiathar. Why? Because he had been given a promise by God himself. David wasn't bragging about his military might. He was confident in the promises of God. You can be, too, for all the strength of heaven is on your side!

Prayer: Lord, in my distress... Lord, in my debt... Lord, in my bitterness... I come to you. Thank you for giving me a safe haven, a final payment, and a place of refuge. I receive your grace with gladness of heart. Amen.

Psalm of the Day: 81.1-7

Knit to the Soul

Daily Reading: 1 Samuel 23

David saw that Saul had come out to seek his life. David was in the wilderness of Ziph at Horesh. And Jonathan, Saul's son, rose and went to David at Horesh, and strengthened his hand in God. (1 Samuel 23.15-16)

Devotional Thought: We have many different types of friends these days, don't we? Our definition of friendship is perhaps a little too expansive if we are honest. After all, who could possibly maintain relationships with all 500 of their "friends" on social media? And yet, our modern culture seems to thrive on this new and shallow definition of friendship – which offers connection without cost. When we see the example of friendship through David and Jonathan, it should make us stop and think. What is a true friend? In Proverbs 17:17 we find an answer: "A friend loves at all times, and a brother is born for a time of adversity."

While David was hiding from jealous King Saul, his friend Jonathan, the son of Saul, came to comfort David and renew his covenant with him. "The soul of Jonathan was knit to the soul of David" (chapter 18). Jonathan provides an example of true friendship when he went to David to "strengthen his hand in God."

We need to recognize our deep and true friendships and nurture them. These are the friends who strengthen one another in the Lord. They remind us of God's faithfulness in the past, and his reliability in our current situation. They take to heart the words of Jesus in John 15:12-13, "My command is this: Love each other as I have loved you. Greater love has no one than this, that he lay down his life for his friends."

The writer of Ecclesiastes, reminds us of the importance of having and being a friend: "Two are better than one, because they have a good return for their work: If one falls down, his friend can help him up. But pity the man who falls and has no one to help him up!"

Prayer: Dear Jesus, thank you for your friendship and for placing other friends in my life to strengthen me in God. Help me to be a good friend to you and to them. Amen.

Psalm of the Day: 81.8-16

My Hand Shall Not

Daily Reading: 1 Samuel 24

> *May the Lord judge between me and you, may the Lord avenge me against you, but my hand shall not be against you.* (1 Samuel 24.12)

Devotional Thought: Yesterday, I was speaking with Toni, one of my prayer partners, who shared her story of how the mercy of the cross became real for her. That realization, along with the tragedy that preceded it, changed her life forever.

While the father of Toni's two grandchildren was caring for the children, the baby – three months old – unexpectedly died. Her daughter was away from the house. No one was there except the father, the three year old and the three month old. A week later, it was determined that the baby had died of "shaken baby syndrome" and that the father was guilty of murder. Toni shared with me, "I was broken. But, in that moment I realized what the cross meant. Jesus died so that even the most heinous sin could be forgiven. Even a senseless murderer could find mercy because of the cross." And, in that realization, Toni knew that she too must forgive the murderer of her grandbaby. She even reached out to the family of the father to help them find peace.

I must admit to you, that I was humbled by that story. I remembered how angry I was when my daughter was going through a bitter custody dispute. I had struggled to find forgiveness in my heart, to not wish ill upon those involved. I dreamed of ways that they would "get theirs."

We are familiar with the adage: "I don't get angry; I get even." Aren't you glad that God doesn't live by that adage? Aren't you thankful that God has mercy on those who least deserve it? Aren't you glad for the cross of Jesus Christ, which brings us forgiveness in place of judgment?

Jesus died for us all. For every sinner.

Prayer: Our Father in heaven, hallowed be your name... Forgive us our trespasses as we forgive those who trespass against us. Amen.

Psalm of the Day: 82.1-8

Intercede for Them

Daily Reading: 1 Samuel 25

> *"On me alone, my lord, be the guilt. Please let your servant speak in your ears, and hear the words of your servant... Please forgive the trespass of your servant.* (1 Samuel 25.24, 28a)

Devotional Thought: Fleeing from the murderous Saul, David and his men found themselves in the vicinity of Nabal's estate. Instead of demanding what he wanted from Nabal, David asked a favor from him. Nabal, however, refused David's request. David became furious and threatened to wipe Nabal and his household from the face of the earth. Something happened to prevent that. That something was the intercession of Nabal's wife, Abigail.

Abigail's plea to David is a picture of intercessory prayer:
- *Identified with the sinner.* Abigail knew that her future was all tied up with Nabal's destiny. She did not try to distance herself from the sinner, but rather acknowledged that she too needed mercy. When we pray for lost souls, let us always remember that we too need the grace of God in our lives.
- *Recognized her position.* Abigail was in no position to make demands. She recognized that David simply hearing her out was perhaps more than she could hope for. While we are urged to come boldly, we must do so humbly – recognizing that it is not any merit of our own that gives us boldness, but only the merits of Jesus and his blood!
- *Sought the salvation of the wicked.* It could have been tempting for her to say to David, "I'll tell you where he is and how to get to him, so that he finally gets what is coming to him." Instead, she said, "Please forgive..." What is our attitude toward the lost? Do we want God to zap them? Or, are we praying for their salvation?

Think about someone you know who is lost. Intercede for them, as Abigail pled for Nabal.

Prayer: "Lord, lay some soul upon my heart and love that soul through me. And may I humbly do my part to win that soul for thee." Amen. (Leon Tucker)

Psalm of the Day: 83.1-8

The Lord's Anointed

Daily Reading: 1 Samuel 26

> *The Lord forbid that I should put out my hand against the Lord's anointed.* (1 Samuel 26.11)

Devotional Thought: Every day, you and I are placed in circumstances that will test our faith in God and our obedience to his principles. We may justify acting in ways that violate our principles: "He did it to me first..." "God wouldn't put this feeling in my heart if he didn't want me to act on it..." "No one will get hurt..." "Nobody will ever find out..." Yet, we discover something very satisfying when we stand on our principles.

On two occasions, God gave Saul into David's hands. But, in his heart, David knew that it would not be right to strike Saul. On each occasion, David refused to put out his hand against the Lord's anointed.

For David, the principle was that King Saul had been anointed by God himself to rule over Israel, and it would have to be God who removed him; David wouldn't lift a finger against him. Many issues were involved: the political ramifications, his friendship with Saul's son, Jonathan, the strife in his own family that would inevitably come when Michal – David's wife and Saul's daughter – found out her husband had killed her father. All of these were important factors, but paramount in David's mind was the fact that Saul was anointed by God. David couldn't violate this.

David recognized an important principle, but Saul missed it. Saul did not want to accept the fact that David was anointed, too. How much better things could have gone for Saul and for the nation if only he had operated by the same principle David held. The Bible says that believers are the anointed of God (1 John 2.20). Let's be very careful how we treat the Lord's anointed!

Prayer: Thank you, Lord, for the anointing I have received from you. Other believers share that privilege as well. When I am tempted to "put out my hand against" brothers and sisters in Christ, stay my hand by allowing me to see that they are your anointed. Amen.

Psalm of the Day: 83.9-18

The Way of Escape

Daily Reading: 1 Samuel 27

> *And when it was told Saul that David had fled to Gath, he no longer sought him.* (1 Samuel 27.4)

Devotional Thought: I have known people who have beaten addiction. Many factors brought about deliverance, but common to all of them was putting distance between them and the temptation. And, not just the substance itself, but the situations, people, and places that trigger their insatiable desire.

David wanted to get out from under the pressure of Saul's ongoing, almost obsessive, pursuit. David's life was in constant danger if he stayed where Saul could reach him. So he fled to Gath, where Saul no longer sought him.

From David's experience, we can learn some things about temptation:
- First of all, we must be aware that the threat always exists. We never get too old, too strong, or too wise for temptation. Until we open our eyes in heaven, we must always be on our guard.
- Particular temptations - besetting sins of Hebrews 12 - are unique to us and our personality. My Christian friends may not share this weakness, but for me to avoid falling, I must get completely away from things that would trip me. I must not make it easy for temptation to lure me.
- Go to a safe place, where you can find support and encouragement. For David in his situation, it was Gath. He had to immediately flee. The moment sin comes against us to tempt us, we must take action. Find a safe place in God's Word, in prayer, in truth.

1 Corinthians 10.13 says, "No temptation has overtaken you that is not common to man. God is faithful, and he will not let you be tempted beyond your ability, but with the temptation he will also provide the way of escape, that you may be able to endure it."

Prayer: Thank you, Lord, that you have made a way of escape for me. Help me to turn to you and obtain strength from your Spirit, that I may endure and defeat temptation. Amen.

Psalm of the Day: 84.1-7

Have It Both Ways

Daily Reading: 1 Samuel 28

And when Saul inquired of the Lord, the Lord did not answer him, either by dreams, or by Urim, or by prophets. Then Saul said to his servants, "Seek out for me a woman who is a medium, that I may go to her and inquire of her." (1 Samuel 28.6-7)

Devotional Thought: Saul's life and reign were nearing the end, and he knew it. The Philistines pressed the battle against him, but in his desperation he tried to "have it both ways." At first, "Saul inquired of the Lord." He tried dreams. He tried Urim (a type of dice used to determine God's answer). He tried the prophets. It seems that he was exhausting all possible avenues. I wonder, though, how much effort he made.

"You will seek me and find me when you seek me with all your heart" (Jeremiah 29.13). Saul's heart was not set on seeking the Lord alone. He turned to a medium even though he himself had "put all the mediums out of the land" (v. 3). In desperation, he tried to have it both ways - answers from the Lord and answers from forbidden sources.

Are we any different today? We are seeking our answers in all the wrong places. Instead of doing the hard work of building godly relationships, we turn to sex. Instead of consistently working hard, we skate by and then buy a lottery ticket. Instead of planning for our future, we spend everything we've got and count on Uncle Sam to take care of us when we're old. Instead of pushing away from the table and going for a walk, we buy diet pills. (Or cholesterol medicine! Ouch!) Instead of spending time reading the Bible and praying, we count on the preacher's message on Sunday to give us all we need to stay spiritually fit.

Like Saul, do I "hedge my bets" and leave a little wiggle room to get my answers somewhere else? Do I try to have it both ways?

Prayer: Lord, forgive me when I try to "supplement" your way with ways of my own, when I seek answers from sources that are not grounded in you, when I try to have it both ways. Help me now as I trust in you, and you alone, for the answers I need. Amen.

Psalm of the Day: 84.8-12

201

Camp by the Spring
Daily Reading: 1 Samuel 29

> *Now the Philistines had gathered all their forces at Aphek. And the Israelites were encamped by the spring that is in Jezreel.* (1 Samuel 29.1)

Devotional Thought: In 1 Samuel 29, God delivered David from a potentially career-ending alliance with a Philistine ruler named Achish. (God's grace is amazing!) What struck me from this chapter, however, is a phrase we find in verse 1: "The Israelites were encamped by the spring."

The Philistines were a large and imposing military force. Israel's army paled in comparison. This was the military expedition that would eventually claim the life of Saul and his sons. Yet, here in the face of impossible odds, we find the Israelites encamped by the spring. The spring would provide water for the battle-weary army.

When we are battle-weary, we too can camp by the Spring! Jesus gives us living water when we are...
- *Trapped in the hopelessness of sin.* Jesus offered living water to a woman whose life had spiraled out of control (John 4). At the well of Samaria, he gave her hope for a new life.
- *Overwhelmed by our circumstances.* I remember a period in my life when I could see nothing but my "opposition." Time and again, I found myself drinking from the Spring himself!
- *Convinced we are all alone.* The Apostle John was exiled to Patmos. Isolated from friends and family, he decided to worship in the Spirit. He heard the voice of his Master and realized he was not alone.

Camp by the Spring!

Prayer: Lord, you are the Spring of Living Water. When the enemy comes against me, I will not be overwhelmed for I am camped by the Spring! Amen.

Psalm of the Day: 85.1-7

Stay by the Stuff!
Daily Reading: 1 Samuel 30

For as his share is who goes down into the battle, so shall his share be who stays by the baggage." (1 Samuel 30.24)

Devotional Thought: Oh, no! Returning from battle, David and his men discovered that their families had been taken as spoils of war. David led his men on a successful campaign to reclaim all that had been taken. There were some men, however, who were simply too exhausted to go on. If they had, they would have been a hindrance and not a help. So, they stayed and guarded the equipment. When the battle was won, those who had pressed the battle to its successful completion were not willing to share the spoils of war with these brothers.

David would have nothing to do with that attitude. He said, "but as his part is that goeth down to the battle, so shall his part be that tarrieth by the stuff" *(KJV)*. The biographer goes on to note that this became "a statute and a rule for Israel from that day forward to this day" (v. 25).

In the church, we are in a battle, too. It is not a physical and military battle, but it is a spiritual battle. There are some who press the battle at the front lines: attacking hell through their prayers, engaging in the political process, working in recovery centers, protecting the unborn, preaching the gospel, teaching children and adults the Word of God, and so on. There are others who "stay by the stuff," doing the things necessary for the efficient and effective work of the church: administering the church, communicating between workers, raising funds, writing books, and other things. We all share alike in the success and the rewards of the Kingdom.

So, whether you press the battle or stay by the stuff, you are doing your part. And remember, "in due season we will reap, if we do not give up" (Galatians 6.9).

Prayer: Lord, my labor may go unnoticed, my work may receive no praise, but help me "stay by the stuff" today, tomorrow, and always. Amen.

Psalm of the Day: 85.8-13

Are You Defined by Your Past?

Daily Reading: 1 Samuel 31

> But when the inhabitants of Jabesh-gilead heard what the Philistines had done to Saul, all the valiant men arose and went all night and took the body of Saul and the bodies of his sons from the wall of Beth-shan, and they came to Jabesh and burned them there. And they took their bones and buried them under the tamarisk tree in Jabesh and fasted seven days. (1 Samuel 31.11-13)

Devotional Thought: Saul and his sons had died in battle. The valiant men of Jabesh-gilead came to retrieve their bodies in order to give them a proper burial. In the past, Jabesh-gilead was severely punished for failing to respond to the civil war against the Benjamites (Judges 21). Did that failure, and the subsequent disgrace, define them? No! They rose above their past.

Some things we can learn from this story:

- *We have things from our past to overcome.* Jabesh-gilead carried the stigma of being a place of slackers and cowards. They had paid dearly for their sin in pain and suffering. The sins of our past haunt us and cost us dearly.
- *Jesus rescues us from our pasts.* Why did Jabesh-Gilead risk life and limb to retrieve the bodies of Saul and his sons? The answer is simple. Regardless of their past, Saul considered them "savable" and had once rescued them (See 1 Samuel 11)! Jesus did not give up on us, either. Thank God for our Redeemer, who counted us worthy of his sacrifice!
- *No matter how bad our past is, by the grace of God we can rise above it.* Jabesh-gilead could have adopted the attitude that society tried to force upon them: "You'll never amount to anything." But, they refused to be defined by their past failures and instead chose to rise above them. God is still in the business of making valiant men out of cowards, victorious women out of society's losers.

Prayer: Lord, my past failures have been buried in the sea of your forgetfulness, never to be remembered against me again! Hallelujah! You have set me free! Amen.

Psalm of the Day: 86.1-10

Who's Your Daddy?
Daily Reading: Matthew 1

The book of the genealogy of Jesus Christ, the son of David, the son of Abraham. (Matthew 1.1)

Devotional Thought: "Genealogy! Ugh! I needed something more inspiring today!" Admit it. You've felt that way!

But, as you read the genealogy of Jesus, you will encounter some familiar names. Remember Tamar, the woman who posed as a prostitute to entice her father-in-law to impregnate her? Frankly, that story doesn't really shine a good light on any of the characters. What about Ahaz, the wicked king who participated in the pagan traditions of sacrificing children to the fires of Molech, a demon god? Or Mannaseh, whose wickedness finally resulted in the Babylonian captivity of the Israelites? This is the family tree of the Messiah, God's Son who was sent to redeem and save the world. And, you thought your family was embarrassing!

God doesn't use people who have their acts together. He isn't interested in sharing his glory with a "righteous" person. Throughout scripture, we find that he uses the weak, the sinful, the timid, and the poor to accomplish his purposes. He showcases his mercy and his faithfulness, by using ordinary people to do extraordinary things for his Kingdom. It should give us hope, as we recognize that we too are unrighteous, weak, and ineffective without him. What God calls us to do, he will surely equip us to accomplish through his power. "Now may the God of peace... equip you with everything good for doing his will, and may he work in us what is pleasing to him, through Jesus Christ..." (Hebrews 13.20-21).

Jenny

Prayer: Father, equip us! We are unequal to the task of spreading your gospel to our friends and family. But, by your grace, you have given us power through your Spirit to accomplish your good purposes! Amen.

Psalm of the Day: 86.11-17

Shine!

Daily Reading: Matthew 2

Herod is about to search for the child, to destroy him. (Matthew 2.13)

Devotional Thought: After hearing about Jesus from the Wise Men, Herod set about to destroy the Baby Savior. Was this a potential "downside" to the Wise Men's best-intentioned efforts at worship?

Have you ever thought about how our best-intentioned efforts, could actually do damage to the cause of Christ? How can we destroy the impact of the Child Jesus?

We destroy / damage the effort of Jesus when we try to...

- *Combine* his message with other ways of salvation. Jesus is the way, *the* truth, and *the* life. No one comes to the Father except through him. When we try to combine the Kingdom of God with other kingdoms, with other ways, then neither kingdom will stand.
- *Enshrine* him in a museum. Jesus didn't intend his message to be encased. He wants it to be lived and proclaimed! He is alive!
- *Design* him in our image. When we make Jesus to be like us, or like what we want him to be, he is weakened and rendered powerless. The people in Nazareth defined him down to their level, and he couldn't do many miracles there.
- *Confine* him to certain areas of our lives. Jesus doesn't take up part residence. If we don't deny ourselves, take up our cross, and follow him, then we are putting up a "Do Not Enter" sign in front of him.
- *Refine* him to meet society's expectations. Jesus doesn't meet culture's demands for tolerance and inclusivity. Jesus has a stern message. He said that the way is narrow and few will find it.

Let's not make these mistakes! Instead, let's come in line with the Kingdom and set Jesus free to be Lord in our lives!

Prayer: Father, help me to align myself with your Son, for he is Lord of all. Amen.

Psalm of the Day: 87.1-7

Get In, Get Out, or Get Out Of The Way
Daily Reading: Matthew 3

Bear fruit in keeping with repentance. (Matthew 3.8)

Devotional Thought: Society is slow to give people a second chance. It's up to them to turn around, but if we don't give them an opportunity to prove themselves, how will they ever become contributing members of society?

John the Baptist had people coming to be baptized by him, who were irredeemable, according to the prevailing culture. These sinners were finding their way into the Kingdom of God. The religious elites - trendsetters and gatekeepers - were aghast! How could these 'lowlifes' be a part of the Kingdom?

John answered, "The same way you must enter the Kingdom of God - through repentance." And, John wasn't talking about a clean and easy process. He said to the leaders coming to him, "If you want to get in, you need to 'bear fruit in keeping with repentance.'" In other words, it had to be more than show. It had to be real.

What fruit of repentance was John the Baptist looking for? What fruit of repentance is God looking for from us? There are many, but I can think of a few right off the bat...
- *Humility.* God saves those who are of a humble and contrite heart. The proud he turns away.
- *Honesty.* If we aren't willing to own up to our mistakes, he can't wash them away. But - and this is the good news - if we confess our sins, he is faithful and just to forgive us our sins!
- *Mercy.* The Bible is plain: Blessed are the merciful for they shall obtain mercy. If you don't forgive your brother's sin, God won't forgive yours.

God gives us opportunity to turn our lives around. Are we bearing the fruit of repentance?

Prayer: Lord, help me to bear the fruit of repentance. It is only by grace that I am saved, but I am not truly saved unless my heart has so thoroughly changed that this fruit can grow in it. Help me, O Lord, to bear this fruit. Amen.

Psalm of the Day: 88.1-5

207

Lead Us NOT into Temptation

Daily Reading: Matthew 4

Jesus was led up by the Spirit into the wilderness to be tempted by the devil. (Matthew 4.1)

Devotional Thought: Doesn't the Bible say that God cannot be tempted with evil, and that he does not tempt anyone with evil (James 1.13)? Doesn't the Lord's Prayer teach us to say "Lead us not into temptation but deliver us from evil" (Matthew 6.12)? So, why did God lead his Son into the wilderness to be tempted?

Why indeed did God lead Jesus into the wilderness to be tempted *by the devil*? Ah... I see! God did not tempt his Son, but the devil did! But still... why did God lead him where he knew he would be tempted? And, why does he allow me to go through temptations and trials?

First of all, notice when this happened. It was right after a great spiritual high (his baptism) and right before Jesus embarked on his earthly ministry. This temptation prepared Jesus for his life's work, by reminding him to continually trust in God! Spiritual highs are not enough. We need grace to get us through the valleys!

This temptation helped Jesus answer the deep questions of motivation. Am I serving the Father because everything is easy and comfortable? Jesus had to get past his "delight of sonship" to the "demands of surrender." We, too, need to examine our motives for serving God. Am I serving God because it's fun and easy, or because I love him supremely?

Also, this temptation prepared Jesus for greater trials. The cross loomed before him, and he would need to grow stronger and stronger to say, "Not my will, but yours be done." Temptation develops our "Yes-to-God" muscles!

This temptation gave Jesus the 'credentials' he needed to fulfill his ministry. We serve a God who has been tempted just like us, so we can trust him!

Prayer: Lord, lead us not into temptation, and when we are tempted, deliver us from evil. Help us to grow in every trial and temptation, so that we become more and more like Jesus. Amen.

Psalm of the Day: 88.6-12

Who's Your Daddy - II
Daily Reading: Matthew 5

> *Blessed are the peacemakers, for they shall be called sons of God.* (Matthew 5.9)

Devotional Thought: Political enmities, national enemies, and business entities all strive to assert their control and superiority. Strife and stress abound. But, children of God are called to be peacemakers. How are we to be peacemakers? Look no further than the rest of this chapter...

We make peace when we...
- Are salt in a decaying and tasteless world. Salt is used both as a preservative and a flavoring. When the salt of the Kingdom is present in our lives, we help others "taste and see that the Lord is good."
- Light the way for others. When I get lost or am uncertain of my way, I experience anxiety which comes out in terse words. I can reduce the internal stress of others by helping them find their way.
- Fulfill the law of God. Most interpersonal strife comes from people failing to obey the 10 Commandments in their relationships. The Royal Law of God is to love others. When we fulfill that law, we are making peace.
- Seek reconciliation. Instead of hiding and denying our faults and our offenses, we need to be reconciled to those whom we have offended - whether intentional or not! The Psalmist said, "How good and pleasant it is when brothers dwell together in unity!" (Psalm 133)
- Refuse to use people. Marriage is not an occasion to dominate, but to serve. Lusting after another is a form of using them for your own ends. We need to refuse these things.
- Engage in communication not 'trickeration.' Simple communication enhances trust and openness. Uncertainty breeds strife. Clarity brings peace.
- Turn the other cheek. Don't strike back. It's hard to sustain an argument alone!
- Love your enemies. That disarms them, defusing their anger.

Are you a peacemaker, a child of God?

Prayer: Lord, help me to live according to your teachings in the Sermon on the Mount. May peace multiply in me and around me that I might ever live as a child of God. Amen.

Psalm of the Day: 88.13-18

Look At Me! Look At Me!
Daily Reading: Matthew 6

In order to be seen by them... (Matthew 6.1)

Devotional Thought: In Matthew 6, Jesus assumes something striking: that his followers, as well as others, can do the righteousness of God - that our righteousness includes doing, as well as believing. After all, even the demons believe... and tremble! But, Jesus' real purpose is to go behind these acts of righteousness to the motives that inspire them. In particular, he says that we must always be vigilant not to do good deeds in order to be seen and praised by others.

Jesus cites three examples:

- *Charity.* Jesus said that we will always have the poor with us. We will always, therefore, have opportunity to share our blessings with them. We should do that. At times it is hard to maintain anonymity, even impossible, but that is not the point. The point is don't do it to get noticed. (Note - sometimes this scripture is misapplied to giving to the church, but that is not what Jesus had in mind at all. That, however, is a story for another day!)
- *Prayer.* Jesus wasn't saying here that you should never pray in a public way. Often, Jesus' disciples knew he was praying. We read of public prayers of the early Christians. Prayer can be very public, but its motive must not be to get attention.
- *Fasting.* Some in Jesus' day liked to put their piety on display. When they fasted, they wanted others to know just how hard they had it. So, they put on sad faces. Jesus said they were wasting their time! Strict secrecy in fasting is not commanded here, however. There are many instances of public fasts in the Bible. Jesus was simply pointing out that true fasting does not seek to be praised.

Are you doing acts of righteousness? What is your motive?

Prayer: Jesus, help me to do deeds that accompany my testimony of faith in you. But, help me to do them with an eye on you and not be concerned if others see me. Amen.

Psalm of the Day: 89.1-4

A Little Fruity

Daily Reading: Matthew 7

You will recognize them by their fruits. (Matthew 7.20)

Devotional Thought: "You can't judge me. You don't know my heart." Have you ever heard that?

It's not entirely true. We can know a good deal about people by observing their actions. Or, as Jesus said, "You will recognize them by their fruits."

- Many people can make their **case**. They can say the right words, but words are probably the least reliable indicator of their hearts.
- We also cannot judge people by the **face** they put on. It is too easy to put on a mask. We can sustain an aura of spirituality for brief periods. Jesus had a name for people who wore masks, however: hypocrites.
- Nor can we know people by their **race**. People may feel that they have special privileges, and deserve special treatment because they have a special status. Jesus was never impressed with people's pedigrees!
- We can't judge others by their **place**. Many people elevate their own importance. Jesus advised us to "take the lowest place."
- We cannot judge others by their intentions, by what they **chase**. As a child, I often told my mother, "I was going to..." She very lovingly reminded me that the road to loss is paved with good intentions. We need to be doers of the Word!

Not only can we know others by their fruit, but we can know ourselves by our fruit. Paul said, "Examine yourselves, to see whether you are in the faith. Test yourselves. Or, do you not realize this about yourselves, that Jesus Christ is in you?—unless indeed you fail to meet the test!" This is more than introspection. He was urging us to be objective - to see what kind of fruit our faith is producing.

Does your fruit pass inspection?

Prayer: Lord, Lord... I don't want to just talk about the Kingdom of God. I want to be in - fully in - the Kingdom. Help me to produce the fruit of the Kingdom. Amen.

Psalm of the Day: 89.5-13

The Ones at the Table

Daily Reading: Matthew 8

> *I tell you, many will come from east and west and recline at table with Abraham, Isaac, and Jacob in the kingdom of heaven, while the sons of the kingdom will be thrown into the outer darkness.* (Matthew 8.11-12)

Devotional Thought: The centurion, a high-ranking official in the Roman army, was a "Gentile of Gentiles," representing the intrusive Roman power that the Israelites hoped to crush with the coming of their Messiah.

What must the Jewish people have thought about Jesus, when he not only healed the centurion's servant, but then marveled at his faith? "Truly, I tell you, with no one in Israel have I found such faith. I tell you, many will come from east and west and recline at table with Abraham, Isaac, and Jacob in the kingdom of heaven, while the sons of the kingdom will be thrown into the outer darkness. In that place there will be weeping and gnashing of teeth" (vv. 10-12). Jesus' words of commendation to this Gentile would have been heresy to the religious Jews. This Roman oppressor eating with the father of the Jewish faith, while the Israelite blood descendants are thrown into outer darkness? It becomes clear why the religious leaders sought opportunity to kill Jesus.

Are we as exclusive with our faith as the Jews were then? Do we reserve the good news of the gospel for those who we feel are worthy to partake in it? Or, do we offer it to the same ones Jesus offered it to – the hopeless, downcast, outcast, unrighteous sinners? Jesus says in just the next chapter of Matthew, "It is not the healthy who need a doctor, but the sick... I have not come to call the righteous, but sinners." Look around you for the sick and unworthy – for they are the ones to whom Jesus calls.

Jenny

Prayer: Lord, give us eyes to see the hearts in which your Spirit is working. Give us courage and boldness to proclaim your praises and your redemption. Help us to swallow our pride and recognize that we were all children of darkness before your saving grace redeemed us. Amen.

Psalm of the Day: 89.14-18

Flattened by Life

Daily Reading: Matthew 9

Rise, pick up your bed and go home. (Matthew 9.6)

Devotional Thought: One cool summer evening, I was riding along in my convertible, returning from a visit with a friend in NE Ohio. Suddenly, my tire blew and I found myself on the side of a country road. Opening the trunk, I discovered that my spare was flat. Uh oh. State Farm to the rescue! They sent a tow truck operator who pumped up my spare, told me to get the full size tire back on ASAP, and sent me on my way home.

What a parable for how Jesus healed the lame man! The lame man in Matthew 9 found himself out of options, just like me. State Farm to the rescue! Well, not exactly, but he did have four friends who took him to Jesus. He got pumped up, cleaned up and sent home.

I like what Jesus said to the man...
- *Rise.* Jesus doesn't leave us in our broken condition. He helps us to our feet. He pumps up our deflated lives, so we can go on our way. Most importantly, he forgives our sin!
- *Pick up your bed.* The lame man's bed represented all of his crippled past. Jesus was saying, in effect, "Your past paralysis does not define you. Your present circumstances don't control you. Your future challenges will not limit you. With my help, you are able to overcome!"
- *Go home.* The crippled man had a life to live. He had friends and a family who loved him. He needed to go home. Even if you don't have that, when you come to Jesus you have a family and a home - a place and a people where you belong. You are part of God's family, the Church.

Prayer: Jesus, thank you for forgiving my sins, for helping me to my feet, for cleaning up my mess, and for giving me a 'home' in your family. Amen.

Psalm of the Day: 89.19-26

My House Is Full

Daily Reading: Matthew 10

Behold, I am sending you out... (Matthew 10.16)

Devotional Thought: Many years ago, there was a popular song by the Lanny Wolfe Trio that included the lines, "My house is full, but my field is empty... It seems my children all want to stay around my table. But, no one wants to work in my fields." That song has stuck with me. And, it is needed more today than it was then.

God has always had a work for his children. Adam was placed in a garden of life and beauty, but God also called him to tend to his creation. Noah and his family were saved from the flood waters. But, God gave Noah the assignment of building the ark of salvation. Abraham was to be blessed by God, who then gave Abraham the work of being a blessing to the nations.

The Bible is a story of God partnering with people to accomplish his purposes. So, when Jesus sent out his disciples in Matthew 10, he was simply continuing this long-established pattern. Do you think that God's methods have changed? Does he not still call people and send them out to do the work of the Kingdom? Should you be surprised that God's call and sending includes you? Are we to think that serving God is only about going to church on Sunday, and getting our spiritual appetites fed and our spiritual fancies tickled?

Before he sent the disciples out, the Bible says that Jesus called them to him (Matthew 10.1). Each week, God calls us to him for worship, for inspiration, for encouragement - but also for instruction. We receive our 'marching orders' and are to go out with a mission - to let the world know of God's great love. Where is God sending you?

Prayer: Lord Jesus, thank you for blessing me. But, help me to go from being blessed to being a blessing. May I not be simply a consumer, but also a conveyor of your great grace. Amen.

Psalm of the Day: 89.27-39

Get Some Rest

Daily Reading: Matthew 11

Come to me, all who labor and are heavy laden, and I will give you rest. Take my yoke upon you, and learn from me, for I am gentle and lowly in heart, and you will find rest for your souls. For my yoke is easy, and my burden is light." (Matthew 11.28-30)

Devotional Thought: Lana commented to me just a day or so ago: football will be starting back up in about 4 weeks! We love our college football. Go Mountaineers! Someone once defined football as 22 guys desperately needing rest, playing their hearts out in front of 50,000 people, desperately needing exercise.

We need both exercise and rest in life, don't we?

Jesus recognizes that life is filled with burdens, and he invites us to come to him, to lay down our burdens, and to find rest.

The work of life takes various forms, depending on the seasons and circumstances of our lives. Last week Emily, my middle daughter, had to 'work' through the night because Ellis, our baby granddaughter, got sick during the night. Being a parent is not easy! Another precious friend of mine is laboring under the burden of a past filled with pain and abuse. Even though the past is covered by the blood, it has left scars, and she needs grace to work through feelings of abandonment and fear. I know another man who is struggling with a disability, and feeling isolated. The burden of being alone is sometimes overwhelming.

I could go on and on and on, but you get the picture. You understand. How do I know that? Because everyone has burdens to bear. Life can be hard work.

But, Jesus has a solution for that. When you are in the trenches and desperately need rest, come to him. He will take your burdens and carry them - and you!

Prayer: Jesus, I sometimes feel overwhelmed, and the burdens seem too heavy to bear. Remind me, O Lord, to come to you and find rest for my soul. I do not have to carry these burdens alone. Thank you!

Psalm of the Day: 89.40-45

Restoration

Daily Reading: Matthew 12

And it was restored, healthy like the other. (Matthew 12)

Devotional Thought: My friend, Dan, 'flips' houses. He buys run-down houses and restores them to homes. Another friend, Tom, buys and restores old cars, then sells them to provide transportation to others. Jesus is in the restoration business, too. He buys old, run-down lives, fixes them up, and puts them back into circulation!

In Matthew 12, Jesus met a man at church (in the synagogue) "with a withered hand." That in itself is a lesson to us that not everybody in church is in mint condition. The man didn't let his withered hand keep him away from the place of spiritual worship and learning. Some people let their sins or their faults keep them away from the church, away from God. "When I get my life straightened up, then I'll come to God." That is a lie from Satan! No person can straighten up their lives to the point that they can come to God. The man with a withered hand recognized that the very place he needed to be was in church!

Other people will let the sins and faults of others keep them away from church, away from God. They reason, "Why should I go there? They are no better than me." That is the truth from Satan! It is true that the people in the church are no 'better' than those away from God. But, if we used that same logic, we would not go to the doctor or hospital, because the people there are just as sick - or sicker! - than we are.

But, Jesus has purchased us all with his blood, so that he can restore us to the image of God, make us healthy in spirit, and use us for his purposes.

Thanks be to God!

Prayer: Thank you, Jesus, for shedding your blood on the cross of Calvary. You have redeemed me and you are even now restoring me, so that I can rediscover the life I was always meant to live. Amen.

Psalm of the Day: 89.46-52

Did Not or Could Not?

Daily Reading: Matthew 13

> And he did not do many mighty works there, because of their unbelief.
> (Matthew 13.58)

Devotional Thought: Well, it's almost August, and as I mentioned a few days ago, college football starts soon! Some of you are really excited, and others are thinking, "So?" Lana and I are in the former group! With my mind on football, I thought of an analogy for today's scripture. Imagine a quarterback sending his wideout downfield for a deep pass. The receiver, however, doesn't run the route because he does not believe that the QB can make the throw. No matter how long and accurate the QB might be, he cannot make a completion without the receiver's faith and cooperation.

That's what happened to Jesus in Matthew 13. The people of his hometown did not believe that he could do mighty works, so they did not run their routes. Jesus "did not do many mighty works there, because of their unbelief." This same account in Mark, says that Jesus "could not." But, is there any difference? Jesus could not because they would not.

Wow! Did you realize that your faith, or lack thereof, is key to what Jesus does?

God has chosen to work through and with our faith, hasn't he? I thought of two examples of this. In 2 Kings, Naaman the Syrian went to the prophet of God for healing of his leprosy. At first, Naaman refused to believe and healing was withheld. But, when his faith took hold and he entered the muddy waters of the Jordan River, his leprosy was healed! Later in Matthew, Jesus said, "How often would I have gathered your children together, as a hen gathers her brood under her wings, and you were not willing!"

Are we willing to run our routes? What 'passes' are being left incomplete in our lives, because we are not?

Prayer: Father, forgive us for our unbelief. We know that you are able to do "immeasurably more than all we could ask or imagine," but we are slow to act on that knowledge. We believe. Help our unbelief! Amen.

Psalm of the Day: 90.1-6

There Alone

Daily Reading: Matthew 14

When evening came, he was there alone... (Matthew 14.23)

Devotional Thought: Do you ever get worn out by people? There are times we just want to be alone. And, there are times we need to be alone. Jesus had those times. The crowds wore him out. Even his closest friends could tax him to the limit. Then he would go off by himself. In Matthew 14, he experienced such a time, and went up on a mountain to be alone. To be with God.

Jesus was intentional about this. First, he sent the disciples away. Jesus didn't just dismiss them, but he gave them a destination and a purpose. They were to go "to the other side" where more meaningful ministry awaited them. He also planned to rendezvous with them. But, the fact of the matter is, he needed to very specifically say to them, "I want to be with you, but not now. I have something else that I just have to take care of." Are you in the habit of sending your 'friends' away, so you can be with God?

Then, Jesus dismissed the crowds. These crowds were those who needed his constant attention. They were very demanding. They were important to Jesus, just as were his friends, and they were the reason he had come - God's purpose for him. But, even the crowds had to take a back seat at times, waiting while Jesus communed with his Father. There are times in all our lives when even legitimate demands must give way.

Finally, Jesus went up the mountain where he would not be disturbed. He needed quiet, undistracted time where he could not only talk to, but also hear from God. In modern parlance - no TV, no phone, no internet.

What are your plans for being alone with God?

Prayer: Sweet hour of prayer! Sweet hour of prayer! That calls me from a world of care... Lord, I long for those times with you. Help me to purposefully plan to pray. Amen.

Psalm of the Day: 90.7-12

Employees Must Wash Their Hands...

Daily Reading: Matthew 15

So for the sake of your tradition you have made void the word of God. (Matthew 15.6)

Devotional Thought: I am a huge stickler for washing hands. Ask any of my three daughters (and their friends)... if we have been out of the house, I always insist on a nice thorough hand-washing once we return. Even a trip to my mailbox will result in a hand-washing. In my van, there is a giant hand sanitizer pump, and my kids are trained to get a squirt every time they load up. I could keep going. After all, who wants the flu?

The Pharisees and religious leaders confronted Jesus with a similar concern. They came criticizing the eating practices of his disciples. They were not following the "tradition of the elders," and were not washing their hands when they ate. Keeping in mind that Louis Pasteur would not develop his germ theory of disease for 1800 more years, this was not an argument over hygiene. Rather, for the Jews, these commandments and traditions of man had become equally important (and maybe more so) to the actual Law given to them by Yahweh. Jesus is quick to point out their hypocrisy, quoting the prophet Isaiah: "This people honors me with their lips, but their heart is far from me; in vain do they worship me, teaching as doctrines the commandments of men" (vv. 8-9).

While this seems like a minor argument, Jesus recognized the attempts of these religious Jews to obtain righteousness by themselves, while imposing their traditions on others. Their hearts were far from him. Do we do the same in our communities of believers? In the church? Do we impose our non-core beliefs and convictions on others? Paul has much to say about this in Romans 14, but the bottom line is that we should "pursue what makes for peace and for mutual upbuilding" (Romans 14.19).

Jenny

Prayer: Lord, keep my heart from judgment, and incline my heart towards grace and mercy. Help me to stand firm on the indisputable truth of the gospel, and not on prideful tradition. Amen.

Psalm of the Day: 90.13-17

Have You Seen My Keys?

Daily Reading: Matthew 16

I will give you the keys of the kingdom of heaven, and whatever you bind on earth shall be bound in heaven, and whatever you loose on earth shall be loosed in heaven. (Matthew 16.19)

Devotional Thought: When I was 24 years old, I served as the Youth President in our local church. As such, I was on the church board. I still get the shakes when I remember the board meeting right after we moved into our new church building. Keys to the new facility were on the agenda. We spent 45 minutes trying to decide who should and who should not get keys. I noticed that those who had been around the longest got the keys.

In their book *Growing Young*, the authors (Powell, Griffin and Mulder) talk about how important it is to give away keys, "the capabilities, power, and access to empower young people." If we are willing to entrust our keys to young people, they will trust us with their hearts, their energy, their creativity, and even their friends.

Jesus recognized this. He did not horde keys, but rather gave them away. And, the keys were not to a church building, but to the Kingdom of heaven! Eternal consequences hung on those keychains! Jesus knew that, but he gave the keys away anyway. And, he gives them away to us still today.

With those keys, we can either bind or loose things. We can make things accessible or inaccessible. We can keep things safe or put them in jeopardy. Keys can lock or unlock. It's important to understand this, and to know that when we lock some things up, we may also be locking up things we don't intend to lock up!

May God give us wisdom in using the keys he has placed in our hands, and may we be willing to share them with others so that they too can do the work of the Kingdom!

Prayer: Lord, it is overwhelming that you should entrust to us the keys to the Kingdom of heaven. Help us to be wise in opening and shutting, in binding and loosing, the things of eternity. Amen.

Psalm of the Day: 91.1-8

Where Are the Elijahs of God?

Daily Reading: Matthew 17

> *Elijah has already come, and they did not recognize him.*
> (Matthew 17.12)

Devotional Thought: Elijah has already come?

People of Jesus' day believed Elijah, the prophet, *was* to come. He had come in the Old Testament, but he was to come again. In Malachi 4, God had said he would send the prophet Elijah before the day of the Lord. From this, Jewish scholars understood that Elijah would come before the Messiah. So, when Peter and John saw Elijah with Jesus on the mountain, they were very excited about what that could mean. Jesus surprised them saying, "Elijah has already come." Jesus was speaking of John the Baptist.

From days of antiquity, people had been asking, "Where is 'Elijah'?" God's people began looking for God to raise up a prophet like Moses, who would speak the word of the Lord to them (Deuteronomy 18.15). In 2 Kings 2, Elisha asked, "Where is the God of Elijah?" Today, I would ask, "Where are the Elijahs of God?"

The Elijahs of old bravely proclaimed justice and righteousness in their days of governmental injustice and personal sin. But, is it wrong to ask, "Where are the Elijahs of God?" today? Where are the heralds of God's Kingdom, those who will face the evil powers of injustice and immorality and then courageously call them out?

Would people recognize you as an Elijah of God?

Prayer: Father, thank you for sending your prophets to proclaim the Kingdom of God. Help me to be an Elijah in my day, so that people can hear the good news of God's love revealed in Jesus. Amen.

Psalm of the Day: 91.9-16

What Do You Think?

Daily Reading: Matthew 18

What do you think? If a man has a hundred sheep, and one of them has gone astray, does he not leave the ninety-nine on the mountains and go in search of the one that went astray? (Matthew 18.12)

Devotional Thought: Put yourself in this situation. You have a flock of 100 sheep. Ninety-nine of them are safe in the fold with you. You are there to provide for them, to protect them, to guide them. But, one of your helpers comes to you and says, "That sheep that keeps wandering off... Well, she's done it again..." What would you do? Would you leave the 99? Would you risk the many to save the one? Would you be able to explain it to the doubters and detractors? What do you think?

We know what Jesus, the Good Shepherd, thought. He left the comforts of heaven, he left the house of his Father, to "go in search of the one that went astray." I'm glad that he did, for I was that one. I was lost and had no way of finding my way back into the fold. As the old Squire Parson's song goes, "When I could not come to where he was, he came to me." What do you think?

In this day of disinterest - and even animosity - toward Christ and the Church, it is tempting to circle the wagons, to look inward, to count our losses and lick our wounds. But, Jesus didn't adopt that attitude, did he? And, he doesn't allow us that option either. We are to enlarge the Kingdom, not enclose it, we are to seek the lost sheep, not forget them. What do you think?

Prayer: "You came to me. O, you came to me. When I could not come to where you were, you came to me. That's why you died on Calvary. When I could not come to where you were, you came to me." Thank you, Lord! (from "He Came to Me" by John Starnes)

Psalm of the Day: 92.1-9

I Hate Divorce

Daily Reading: Matthew 19

If such is the case of a man with his wife, it is better not to marry.
(Matthew 19.10)

Devotional Thought: With tears, an elderly parishioner once confided in me that she believed her son could never be saved. "What? Why?" "Well, as long as he is married to a woman who was not his first wife, he is committing adultery, and there is no place in heaven for adulterers." If such indeed is the case, he would have been better not to marry!

In years past, divorce was a lot stickier subject in the church than it is today. In one sense, that is very sad. Marriage is God's plan for a lifelong relationship of mutual encouragement, love, and joy. Today, it has become an expendable arrangement, if entered into at all. But in another sense, I've seen circumstances that absolutely prevent a relationship from being what God intended it to be, when the only option was divorce. Perhaps, it would have been better to never have married, but staying married was not a possibility.

Jesus, in answering questions about divorce, said, "Have you not read that he who created them from the beginning made them male and female, and said, 'Therefore a man shall leave his father and his mother and hold fast to his wife, and the two shall become one flesh'? So they are no longer two but one flesh. What therefore God has joined together, let not man separate" (Matthew 19.4-6). Clearly, God is not for divorce.

But, there are other things God is not for, either. Through the Old Testament prophet Malachi, God said that he hates divorce, but he also hates violence and the withdrawing of affection and protection. So, instead of making divorce the unpardonable sin, we should understand that some circumstances are really no-win situations, and extend grace to the broken.

Prayer: Father, thank you for giving us the joy and intimacy of marriage. Thank you that we are indeed the bride of Christ! Help our marriages to be strong and loving and filled with your Spirit. Amen.

Psalm of the Day: 92.10-15

True Equality

Daily Reading: Matthew 20

You have made them equal to us. (Matthew 20.12)

Devotional Thought: In Matthew 20, Jesus told a parable that I have always read as if it were directed against his detractors. Reading it more carefully, however, I came to realize that Jesus taught this lesson while speaking to his disciples - *alone*! And what did he say? That those who come to him at the end of life will experience the same glorious eternity, as those who have worked hard and served Jesus all their lives.

That's a tough pill to swallow. Think about those men who followed him first, who travelled with him when he had no place to lay his head, who suffered deprivation and disregard alongside Jesus. Surely, this teaching was an affront to their sense of fairness. It is evident that James and John didn't buy into this philosophy. Just a few verses later, we find them jockeying for position to get the prime seats in the Kingdom. They must have felt that they deserved special treatment.

Are we any different? How can it be fair when "These last worked only one hour, and you have made them equal to us who have borne the burden of the day and the scorching heat"? If I'm honest, I would admit that it doesn't seem fair to me. But it's the truth, isn't it? Jesus has made us all equal.

It is human nature to want to be among the privileged, the special, the favored. Yes, we are glad that these others come in at the eleventh hour, but we want to believe that we deserve something more, for we have served God faithfully. The truth of the matter is, however, we don't deserve any of God's gracious gifts. Yet, in his love he brings us all into his family. Thanks be to God!

Prayer: Thank you, Jesus, for giving me what I could never deserve - a place in the Kingdom of heaven. Help me to always show to others that same generous spirit that you have shown to me. Amen.

Psalm of the Day: 93.1-5

Healing and Health

Daily Reading: Matthew 21

And the blind and the lame came to him in the temple, and he healed them. (Matthew 21.14)

Devotional Thought: The blind and the lame. Have you ever seen them healed? Have you been in a church service where people came and found healing? I must confess, that I have never seen one who was physically blind or lame healed miraculously at church. I was praying at church with a friend once, and his wife - who was not there - was instantly healed of cancer. I remember him stopping and shouting - God's touched Jan! Sure enough, she was healed. Another time, I had been praying for a young man who had a broken bone as they took him to surgery. They X-rayed it before surgery, and the bone was healed!

Pretty amazing stuff. But, as I said, I've never seen the blind and the lame come to Jesus in church and be healed.

Or, have I?

I've seen people that I've prayed for - too blind for hope and too lame to cope - be miraculously delivered! One young lady was so far gone, that she couldn't see anything but her addiction. Jesus healed her mind and addiction. I prayed with a young man who later ended up flat on his back in a jail cell. Jesus came and saved him. He's now out of prison and serving the Lord. There is another who has been addicted to opiates for years. After playing games and gaming the system for years, he went to a faith-based recovery center. There he found freedom. Yes, Jesus still works miracles!

Jesus heals! We need to get people to come to him. I also would urge them to keep coming to church, where they found the Healer - for if coming to church for healing is good, staying in church for health is even better!

Prayer: Jesus, thank you that your power is able to do immeasurably more than we could ask or imagine. Help us to believe you, O Lord. And, when you work healing in our lives, may we not forget to serve you wholeheartedly! Amen.

Psalm of the Day: 94.1-7

Government and God
Daily Reading: Matthew 22

> *"Therefore render to Caesar the things that are Caesar's, and to God the things that are God's."* (Matthew 22.21)

Devotional Thought: There is something satisfying about watching those Pharisees, Sadducees, scribes and religious leaders try to one-up Jesus, only to be stunned into speechlessness by his wisdom and his "comebacks." In one such encounter, the Pharisees have approached Jesus about the lawfulness of paying taxes to Caesar. The Jews resented the Roman government's control over them and longed for their Messiah to overthrow the government. They were still so blind as to who Jesus was, and what he had come to do.

As usual, Jesus responds with a zinger that left them marveling. After pointing out Caesar's inscription on the denarius (a Roman coin), Jesus says, "Render to Caesar the things that are Caesar's, and to God the things that are God's" (v. 21). In other words, yes, you are accountable to the governing authorities placed over you. Both Paul and Peter go into more detail later, with Paul's instruction being quite clear. "Let every person be subject to the governing authorities. For there is no authority except from God, and those that exist have been instituted by God" (Romans 13.1).

Depending on the ebbs and flows in our political system, that command can sometimes rankle! No less so for the early church, facing intense persecution under Roman government. Also, don't forget the last phrase in Jesus's command! Render to God the things that are God's. If we profess faith in Jesus, our hearts, minds, souls, and bodies belong to him. Do we act as though we believe that? Do we behave as those who have been brought out of darkness into marvelous light? As Paul would beseech his fellow believers, "By the mercies of God... present your bodies as a living sacrifice, holy and acceptable to God, which is your spiritual worship" (Romans 12.1).

Jenny

Prayer: Father, help us to remember that we belong to you. We are no longer conformed to the patterns of this world, but transformed through your Spirit. Help us to present ourselves as a pleasing sacrifice to you. Amen.

Psalm of the Day: 94.8-15

Snapchat Dysmorphia

Daily Reading: Matthew 23

They do all their deeds to be seen by others. (Matthew 23.5)

Devotional Thought: I read an interesting article recently. It seems that some young people are developing something called "Snapchat Dysmorphia." They want to change their appearance (plastic surgery) to look like their filtered and edited selfies. It is a symptom of the social media world, where people capture and post pictures and videos of whatever it is they are doing. If you are around it, you soon get the impression that these selfie-driven people are more interested in sharing the moment than experiencing it. It's almost as if they are doing "all their deeds to be seen by others." Wait, that's our scripture for today!

Jesus indeed dealt with people who were more interested in appearances than reality. There were religious folks - the scribes and the Pharisees - who had lost all the joy of their religion because they were doing it for all the wrong reasons for the response of the group - and not for a relationship with God. Jesus revealed the emptiness of that way of living.

We've all seen it, and probably (if we were honest) done it ourselves: performed a good deed, put on a spiritual face, or practiced a spiritual discipline with an eye on others' eyes - to see if they are noting just how good we were! The competition to appear spiritual is just as fierce as the competition to present the perfect image of ourselves in social media.

What can we do about it? Psychologists recommend that patients with "Snapchat Dysmorphia" be treated with psychological interventions like therapy and medication. For those who have "Spiritual Dysmorphia", the treatment is to repent of our pride, humble ourselves, and ask God to purify our hearts!

Prayer: Father, forgive me for any pride that I have a tendency to display in spiritual endeavors. Help me, like Jesus, to "empty myself" and become a beacon that points to you. Amen.

Psalm of the Day: 94.16-23

Not One Stone

Daily Reading: Matthew 24

> *There will not be left here one stone upon another that will not be thrown down.* (Matthew 24.2)

Devotional Thought: I'm not as fascinated with the sensational events that many expounders of scripture define and describe. When it comes to the "End Times," there are two certainties: 1) Jesus is coming again, and 2) I need to be ready. Everything else is speculation! (OK, that's hyperbole, but not by much!)

In Matthew 24, the disciples were concerned about the End Times, and they asked Jesus a threefold question: "Tell us, when will these things be, and what will be the sign of your coming and of the end of the age?" They were concerned about the destruction of the actual physical temple that Jesus had just described, the indications of his return to establish the Kingdom, and what things would look like at the end of the age.

In response, Jesus said, "There will not be left here one stone upon another that will not be thrown down" (Matthew 24.2). We can understand Jesus' statement on at least three levels:
- First, the temple before them was destroyed. In AD 70, the Roman commander, Titus, besieged Jerusalem and razed the temple. Not one stone was left upon another. Jews still mourn this at the Wailing Wall.
- Second, we can understand Jesus' statement in the fact that "the day of the Lord will come like a thief, and then the heavens will pass away with a roar, and the heavenly bodies will be burned up and dissolved..." There is a day in the future when the stones of the temple - along with all other stones - will pass away.
- Finally, these words remind us that whatever you and I build, if we're not building on Jesus, it will be destroyed at the last day (Matthew 7). Not one stone will remain.

He's coming. Are you ready?

Prayer: Lord Jesus, thank you for the assurance that you are coming again and that your Kingdom will be established forever. Help me to be ready for that day and to help others be ready as well. Amen.

Psalm of the Day: 95.1-5

Well Digging Time!
Daily Reading: Matthew 25

Truly, I say to you, I do not know you. (Matthew 25.12)

Devotional Thought: Last week, I was going through my library and came across: *Dig Your Well before You're Thirsty*, by Harvey Mackey. As I remember, the premise of the book was to work on relationships before you needed them. Then when the need came, they would be in place. There's nothing quite as awkward as trying to get close to someone from whom you need something - especially when you haven't been close before.

In the first of the three parables of Matthew 25, the story of the wise and foolish bridesmaids, Jesus shows us that we need to *stay* close to him. The five wise ones had their oil before they needed it. The five foolish ones waited until the last minute and then got caught unprepared. The response of the bridegroom was interesting. When the five foolish bridesmaids begged to come into the wedding, the bridegroom said, "I do not know you." The time to get to know *the* Bridegroom, Jesus Christ, is not when he returns to take us all to heaven. We need to have that relationship in place long before that!

I've always marveled at (and felt sorry for) people who do not take care of their relationships with family and friends. Those are the kind of people who are left alone at the end of life. When need comes, they have no one on whom they can call. They usually get angry when the people, whom they have ignored for a lifetime, turn around and ignore them.

That is sad enough in human terms, but it is eternally devastating in our relationship with Christ. The worst words we could ever hear would be to hear Jesus say, "I do not know you." Then who will we turn to?

Prayer: Lord, help me to keep my jar filled with oil - to keep my relationship with you current! How great is the joy of friendship with you. It would be tragic to miss out on a single hour! Amen.

Psalm of the Day: 95.6-11

Me? Fall Away?
Daily Reading: Matthew 26

> *You will all fall away because of me this night. For it is written, 'I will strike the shepherd, and the sheep of the flock will be scattered.'* (Matthew 26.31)

Devotional Thought: Something as small as a preposition can make a huge difference, can't it? Think of these two phrases: He works *for* me... She works *with* me... There is a huge difference. That's what caught my eye in today's verse. Jesus said, "You will all fall away *because* of me this night..." He didn't say, "You will all fall away *from* me..." which we would expect, but rather he said *"because of* me..."

Fall away *because of* Jesus? Well, then *from* what were the disciples going to fall away?" From the faith? That didn't seem to happen, except perhaps momentarily out of fear. From their God? Again, evidence does not bear that out. I think it meant that they were going to fall away from their certainty and strength. Speaking directly to Peter, Jesus said, "I have prayed for you that your faith may not fail. And when you have turned again, strengthen your brothers" (Luke 22.32).

That brings up in my mind the image of Jesus, falling under the weight of the cross... When burdens grow heavy, we may stumble and fall. "Even youths shall faint and be weary, and young men shall fall exhausted" (Isaiah 40.30). The disciples lost their strength, stumbled and fell - *because of* their connection to Jesus.

Jesus did not leave them to despair. He had warned them, so that they would recognize what was happening and return to him. As Isaiah had written 700 years prior: "They who wait for the Lord shall renew their strength; they shall mount up with wings like eagles; they shall run and not be weary; they shall walk and not faint" (40.31).

Prayer: Lord, thank you for the invitation, "Come to me all who are weary and burdened..." And, should I stumble and fall, please renew my strength as I wait for you. Amen.

Psalm of the Day: 96.1-6

What Are You Asking For?

Daily Reading: Matthew 27

He went to Pilate and asked for the body of Jesus. (Matthew 27.58)

Devotional Thought: I've been 'packing up' my office the last few weeks, moving library and files to my home office. I quickly discovered that I have accumulated a lot of books and papers in over thirty-one years of ministry! And, I have also found that I need to be selective about what to keep. There's just not space for everything. Lana certainly doesn't want me to clutter up the house with all my 'work stuff'!

Times come when we have to ask ourselves, do I want that? Do I need it? Those questions are hard, but necessary.

In Matthew 27, Joseph of Arimethea wanted something - the body of Jesus. So, he went to Pilate and asked for it. I'm sure Pilate found that an unusual request. Often the bodies of condemned criminals were simply discarded in a pit near the place of execution. When they were taken, it was by grieving family members. But, here was a respectable and well-to-do Jewish citizen - unrelated to Jesus - asking for the body of the Lord. Why would he want the body of the Lord? "Oh well," Pilate thought, "I guess he can have it."

How about you? Do you want the body of Jesus? Will you identify with the stigma of the cross? The sign of weakness? The symbol of death? It is easy to want the *resurrected* body of Jesus. But, the body of death? The Apostle Paul said that we are "always carrying in the body the death of Jesus, so that the life of Jesus may also be manifested in our bodies" (2 Corinthians 4.10).

Prayer: Jesus, how incredible that you, the Son of God, would die for me. I gladly identify with you in your death so that your life may be manifested in me. Amen.

Psalm of the Day: 96.7-13

But First, This...
Daily Reading: Matthew 28

> *Come, see the place where he lay. Then go quickly and tell...*
> (Matthew 28.6b-7a)

Devotional Thought: I'm not sure we ought to be in the business of 'rating' various scriptures, but here in Matthew 28, the Great Commission seems very important. But, is it the most significant thing in this chapter?

On that first Easter morning, the two Marys were greeted at the tomb by an angel. He told them the tomb was empty, the body of Jesus gone. Then he gave them these instructions...

- *Come.* Though these two had come a long way, they needed to go further still. They had an insufficient concept of Jesus. They saw him as a teacher who had taught the way of life, and a friend who had died a tragic and undeserved death. They needed to come into the understanding that this One, who had healed bodies and forgiven sins, could also defeat death.
- *See.* It was not enough to take the angel's word for it. They needed to see for themselves. We, like them, must be willing to "Taste and see that the Lord is good" (Psalm 34.8). Like the Hebrews in the wilderness, if we are not willing to look, we will not live (Numbers 21).
- *Go.* Before the Church could be given the Great Commission, these ladies had a job of their own to do. They could not stay at the tomb. In the same way, the Church today will not fulfill her destiny unless we are willing to go.
- *Tell.* The ladies had some explaining to do... The disciples didn't have all the truth. They needed to be instructed. In the same way, the Church today needs to be taught "sound doctrine in accordance with the truth." An erroneous witness can be worse than no witness at all!

Prayer: Lord, I want you to use me to make disciples. But first, I need to come and see, to go and tell. Give me grace and open doors, I pray. Amen.

Psalm of the Day: 97.1-7

Pray for Those Who Persecute You

Daily Reading: 2 Samuel 1

You daughters of Israel, weep over Saul. (2 Samuel 1.24a)

Devotional Thought: David was the greatest King in Israelite history, but his rise to power was not without problems. Saul's insecurity and jealousy stood in the way of David coming into the kingship. Though Saul threatened and pursued David to kill him, David always remained loyal to Saul, whom he considered the Lord's anointed. At one point, when David had the opportunity to slay Saul, David had said, "The Lord forbid that I should put out my hand against the Lord's anointed" (1 Samuel 26.11). Now, when David heard of Saul's demise, he was genuinely grief-stricken.

David had known Saul in his vigor and strength. He had served in Saul's military. He was familiar with all that Saul had done to unite and protect the 12 tribes of Israel. He had heard the story of Saul's anointing as king. While David benefitted from Saul's death, he did not rejoice in it. He even wrote a lament, a eulogy, to be sung about Saul. Perhaps it was used at a state memorial service. Even though David and Saul were in "rival parties," David acknowledged all the good Saul had done. He encouraged people to remember the good things of Saul's reign.

In this simple gesture, we discover something about David' character. Though far from perfect, he wanted to do the right thing. He had a heart for God. And, as we shall see later, when David failed, disappointing himself and God, he did not assert his power and privilege, nor did he hide behind a veil of self-justification. He repented and returned to his values.

May God help us to be like David, men and women after God's own heart (1 Samuel 13.14).

Prayer: Lord Jesus, when I consider your words, "Father forgive them..." I realize I come up short. Help me to have a heart like yours, a heart that forgives even my enemies and prays for those who persecute me. Amen.

Psalm of the Day: 97.8-12

After This, What?

Daily Reading: 2 Samuel 2

After this David inquired of the Lord. (2 Samuel 2.1)

Devotional Thought: Saul and Jonathan were dead. David was grief-stricken for his friend (Jonathan) and his foe (Saul). But, after this, what?

David had been told about God's plan to elevate him to the throne, but how was it going to happen? Uncertain, David did a good thing. He "inquired of the Lord." He had an idea of what he was to do – go up into a city of Judah – but he did not assume that his idea was correct. Even after God told him that he was indeed to go, David wanted further assurance that he was moving ahead in the will of the Lord. So, he asked him, "Which one?" God told him to go up to Hebron, a city with a rich spiritual and political history.

David's inquiring of the Lord illustrates:
- *The value of action.* As we follow the Lord, it is important for us to "keep moving." I believe that when we take the initiative in faith, God is pleased. We are not to be presumptuous, but we must actively seek to follow God. David had an idea what he was to do, and he presented it to God.
- *The value of patient listening.* Following the Lord also demands obedient and submissive spirits. Having received direction from God, we must be careful to continue following him. Experience has taught me that I need God to guide me *after* I start out, just as much as I need him to guide me *before* I begin.

Like David, let us inquire of the Lord – both in our action and in our patient listening.

Prayer: Lord, you promised that you would walk beside us to guide us. Help us to walk with you, but also to listen for your instructions as we go. In the name of Jesus, amen.

Psalm of the Day: 98.1-9

Somewhere to Go

Daily Reading: 2 Samuel 3

> *David made a feast for Abner and the men who were with him.*
> (2 Samuel 3.20)

Devotional Thought: In 2 Samuel 3, today's chapter, we read about the re-uniting of Israel under King David. Abner, the military commander for Saul's son Ish-bosheth, was instrumental in bringing the tribes of Israel into the fold of David. When Abner came to David, who was then the King of Judah only, David welcomed him gladly. David honored Abner and those who were with him, grateful for the help in restoring peace and unity to the fractured nation. The scripture says "David made a feast" for them.

How welcome that feast was for Abner! Abner found himself under attack from both sides. A general in David's army sought revenge for Abner's slaying of his brother. Saul's son accused him of unseemly behavior with one of Saul's concubines - an act of treason. Abner had nowhere to go.

Judah's army rejected Abner. Israel's army was torn from him. Where could he go? He went to the king!

Have you ever been in that situation? Have you ever felt like you had nowhere to go? I've been there. Though you know it's not true, you feel like you don't have a friend in the world. The good news is this: We do have somewhere to go. We can go to the King! Like David, our King is in the feast-making business! I'm so glad that our King, Jesus, has made a feast for us! He welcomes us to his table and into his inner circle. When we, with sincerity, go to him, we discover that he has prepared a feast for us. We are loved, appreciated, and valued. There's always room at the King's Table for one who comes!

Prayer: Thank you, Jesus, that in you I have somewhere to go! I am not an orphan, a foreigner, or a stranger. I am accepted at your table to feast on your goodness and grace. Amen.

Psalm of the Day: 99.1-9

Shall I Go? Will You Give?

Daily Reading: 2 Samuel 4-5

David inquired of the Lord, "Shall I go up against the Philistines? Will you give them into my hand?" (2 Samuel 5.19)

Devotional Thought: A house next to our church property was being auctioned. We thought it was a "no-brainer" for us to get it. We paused, however, and asked the Lord to direct us. The church met and voted. When we went to the auction, we were prepared to bid up to $41,000. We were outbid. We did not press the issue, but left it in the Lord's hands. We had asked "Shall I?" and had received our answer: "Not now." We concluded it was not the time and place for us to act.

David faced something of a "no-brainer" early in his reign. Before acting, however, he "went down to the stronghold." Aren't you glad for the Stronghold! When the enemy comes against us, the Lord is our refuge and strength, an ever present help in the day of trouble!

There, before the Lord, David asked two things:
- *Shall I go?* David wanted to be certain that God was leading him. Though it seemed obvious what he needed to do, he did not want to assume that this was the time and place for him to act. So too with us: when we are faced with "obvious" decisions – so-called no-brainers – we need to pause and let God direct us.
- *Will you give?* Not only did David want to know his part, he wanted to know what God would do. That's always a good thing for us to know, isn't it? Working in partnership with God, we know his promises are certain! When we have a clear idea of what God will do, we are able to work with confidence and faith and boldness.

Oh, about the house... Six months later, we were able to purchase that very property for $13,000! The Lord is good!

Prayer: Lord, your ways are not our ways and your thoughts are not our thoughts. Help us always to "go to the stronghold" so that we will know what we are to do and what you will do. Amen.

Psalm of the Day: 100.1-5

237

How Indeed

Daily Reading: 2 Samuel 6

> *And David was afraid of the Lord that day, and he said, "How can the ark of the Lord come to me?"* (2 Samuel 6.9)

Devotional Thought: The ark represented the holy presence of God with his people. When David was king, the ark had been disregarded. The regulations for handling it were forgotten. Careless, Uzzah - a servant of the king - was struck down by the Lord for his irreverence when bringing the ark to Jerusalem. David lamented, "How can the ark of the Lord come to me?"

I'm like David. I want "the ark" with me and my church! I desire God's presence and blessing upon me, and in the midst of his people! How can "the ark" of the Lord come to me?

- *Faith:* "Whoever would draw near to God must believe that he exists and that he rewards those who seek him." (Hebrews 11.6)
- *Resolve:* "You will seek me and find me, when you seek me with all your heart." (Jeremiah 29.13)
- *Humility:* "This is the one to whom I will look: he who is humble and contrite in spirit and trembles at my word." (Isaiah 66.2)
- *Holiness:* "I will make my dwelling among them and walk among them, and I will be their God, and they shall be my people. Therefore go out from their midst, and be separate from them, says the Lord, and touch no unclean thing; then I will welcome you, and I will be a father to you, and you shall be sons and daughters to me, says the Lord Almighty." (2 Corinthians 6.16-18)
- *Prayer and Unity:* "Again I say to you, if two of you agree on earth about anything they ask, it will be done for them by my Father in heaven. For where two or three are gathered in my name, there am I among them." (Matthew 18.19-20)

Come, Lord Jesus!

Prayer: "Holy Spirit, you are welcome here. Come flood this place and fill the atmosphere. Your glory, God, is what our hearts long for, to be overcome by your presence, Lord." Amen. (Katie Torwalt / Bryan Wilson)

Psalm of the Day: 101.1-8

God Doesn't Play Fair
Daily Reading: 2 Samuel 7

Who am I, O Lord God, and what is my house, that you have brought me thus far? (2 Samuel 7.18)

Devotional Thought: You've heard it before - when kids are playing - "Mom! He's not playing fair!" Have you ever considered how God doesn't "play fair"?

Think about what God did for David, who wanted to build a house for God in 2 Samuel 7:

- He took him out of the pasture and made him prince (v. 8).
- He went with David, cutting down David's enemies and making David's name great (v. 9).
- He appointed a place for David's people and gave them rest from their enemies (vv. 10-11).
- He built David a "house" and raised up offspring to establish David's throne and kingdom (vv. 11-13).
- He promised David that his steadfast love would not be withdrawn from David's offspring (v. 15).

What was David's response? Basically, "God, you don't play fair! I wanted to build you a house, instead you have promised to build one for me!" Instead of getting puffed up, David was humbled! "Who am I ... that you have brought me this far?" David recognized his modest origins and his own failures. He was overwhelmed that God would give him, of all people, such promises.

The tendency is to get a little proud when we consider how God has blessed us. The reality is, however, that we are all of humble origins and do not deserve the goodness and kindness of God. If he gave us what we deserved, we would be lost. Honesty compels us to say, "God, you don't play fair! And, I'm so thankful!"

Is God not playing fair with you? Have you thanked him for it?

Prayer: Help me, O Lord, to be faithful in all my trouble, toil and labor so that my deeds will follow me - in the form of ransomed souls! - all the way to heaven's throne. Amen.

Psalm of the Day: 102.1-11

What Will You Do with It?

Daily Reading: 2 Samuel 8

And David made a name for himself. (2 Samuel 8.13)

Devotional Thought: Aaron was given a great opportunity. "Would you like to open a store in South Carolina?" That was seven years ago. He accepted the offer, invested the capital, and got started. That was just the beginning. Hard work, long hours, and personal sacrifices were needed to get the business off the ground. But, he did it and made a business for himself. Some looked on with envy: "He had that business given to him..." No, he was given an opportunity and made something of it.

David was like that. God had promised to build a house for David. God made him an offer completely out of divine and infinite grace. But, that wasn't all the story. David had to accept the offer! David had to accept the terms of the offer. David had to work hard and wise to take advantage of the offer. And, that's what he did.

David made a name for himself. He was given the opportunity, but he had to do something with it.

All of us are like David in God's eyes. He loves each one of us with an infinite love. He makes us an offer that seems too good to be true: Exchange your poverty for my riches, your guilt for my forgiveness, your obscurity for my name, your death for my life. What an offer!

But then, we have to do something with it. With his strength and by his grace, we have to work hard to live into the name that he gives us. Self-denial, suffering, surrender, and obedience are all needed to form a character worthy of the gift.

Are you making a name for yourself?

Prayer: Thank you, Father, for the unsearchable riches of your kindness, for the gift of life in Jesus, your Son. I receive your love and consecrate myself to achieve your purposes for me. Amen.

Psalm of the Day: 102.12-17

The King's Table

Daily Reading: 2 Samuel 9

And Mephibosheth lived in Jerusalem, because he always ate at the king's table. (2 Samuel 9.13)

Devotional Thought: King David and Jonathan had a friendship like no other. After Jonathan's death, David remembered a promise he had made to Jonathan.

The Promise. David promised Jonathan he would always care for his family. In David's heart, that promise was inviolable. We must remember the promise God has made. John 3:16 tells us that "God so loved the world that he gave his only son that whoever believes in him shall not perish but have eternal life." The King's Table has no maximum seat capacity. It doesn't have any prerequisites. There is a seat for any who come to the King's table.

The Restoration. When Mephibosheth arrived at the table, there is a vision of him sinking as low as he can to the ground before King David. In no way did Mephibosheth feel that he deserved the gift that King David was about to bestow on him. It's no different for us. We are not worthy of the life we live in Christ, but he makes us worthy. Scripture tells us that Christ came for us. Just as King David offered Mephibosheth complete restoration, Christ has the same gift for us.

The Life Change. His encounter with King David left Mephibosheth forever changed. He no longer would eat anywhere else. In fact, verse 13 tells us he lived in Jerusalem because he always ate at the king's table. When we give people an opportunity to encounter Christ, their lives will change.

Pastor Kenny McQuitty

Prayer: Jesus, you have set a table for me and for all people. Help me and everyone to come to that table and eat to our full satisfaction of your love and grace. Help me also to invite others to the table of our King! Amen.

Psalm of the Day: 102.18-28

Casualties of War

Daily Reading: 2 Samuel 10

When it was told David, he sent to meet them, for the men were greatly ashamed. (2 Samuel 10.5)

Devotional Thought: A candidate for public office once said, in reference to a former prisoner of war: "I like people who weren't captured." That seems harsh, doesn't it? A decorated veteran spent 5 years in a Vietnamese prison, and that's the thanks he gets? We don't all win all the time, do we? And, what is to be done for those who become a "casualty of war"?

David's men found themselves in a position of being "greatly ashamed." Having been sent on a mission of peace and consolation, their motives were impugned and their beards were shaved half off. To "top" it off, their uniforms were cut off half way up, bringing great shame. David could have said, "Those guys are losers! They never should have gotten caught!" But, he didn't. Instead he sent a contingent of men to meet these "greatly ashamed" soldiers.

Some things we can learn about casualties of war from this story:
- They are not necessarily blameworthy.
- They can happen to anybody.
- Only those not engaged in the battle are immune to them.
- There is no shame in experiencing them.
- Those who experience them need our encouragement and support, not our judgment and rejection.
- I can be a part of the healing process.

We are in a spiritual war, and inevitably, there will be casualties of war. Let's prevent the casualties from becoming fatalities! Do you know someone who has experienced failure or who has become a casualty of war? Offer understanding, patience, mercy, and help. One day you may need the same.

Prayer: Father, I was destined to become not just a casualty of war, but a fatality of the spiritual battle that raged for my soul. In loving kindness, you came and rescued me! Help me to show that same loving kindness to others who may become casualties of war. In Jesus' name, amen.

Psalm of the Day: 103.1-5

Springtime

Daily Reading: 2 Samuel 11

> *In the spring of the year, the time when kings go out to battle, David sent Joab... But David remained at Jerusalem.* (2 Samuel 11.1)

Devotional Thought: When he was a college student, Evan began to sell things on eBay part time. After college, the eBay business was doing fairly well, and he made a decision to quit his job and go "full time" with it. In the springtime of his business, there were hurdles: nay-sayers to tune out, financing to acquire, inventory to build, paperwork to slog through. With purpose, he fought every one of those battles, and is now operating a successful eBay enterprise called E-Money. It wasn't easy (and it isn't easy), but he stuck with it.

The springtime of an endeavor is filled with excitement and energy. But, the truth of the matter is - we have to work hard at it, we have to keep a springtime attitude.

David didn't do that. In the spring of the year, he sent Joab. David remained in Jerusalem. And then, his troubles with Bathsheba began. Think of the trouble that he could have avoided had he kept the springtime excitement:
- A family would not have been torn asunder.
- A valued commander would not have died in a set-up.
- The name of God would not have been impugned.
- A baby would not have been born, only to die after seven days.

God redeemed the situation, but it came at a great price. God redeems all our mistakes if we turn to him, but wouldn't it be better if we simply did what we were supposed to do, if we kept up a springtime relationship with him?

Do you need spring to return to your walk with God?

Prayer: Lord, thank you that you are in the business of redeeming our failures! You have redeemed so many of mine. Help me, Father, to keep my relationship with you in springtime condition and so avoid failures that need redeemed! Amen.

Psalm of the Day: 103.6-14

Arise and Worship
Daily Reading: 2 Samuel 12

> *Then David arose from the earth and washed and anointed himself and changed his clothes. And he went into the house of the Lord and worshiped.* (2 Samuel 12.20)

Devotional Thought: Tragic! The only innocent people in this story - a newborn baby and a loyal soldier - are the ones bearing the burden for David and Bathsheba's sin. The wisdom of the Lord is beyond our grasp at times. The Lord operates on an eternal timetable, of which we have merely a snapshot, and that is why it is essential to trust in his mercy, love, and compassion for all mankind.

David trusted. Even after Nathan delivered his crushing news, David knew to whom he must turn. He cried out, fasted, prayed, and poured his heart out in anguish before the Lord, pleading for the life of his child. He is laying flat on the floor and refuses to get up, until he hears the news that his son is dead. At this point, "David arose ... and he went into the house of the Lord and worshiped" (v. 20). David knew that God could have answered his prayers to spare his son. When God chose not to do that, David immediately goes into the house of the Lord to worship him. Not because he was happy with what had happened, not because God answered his prayer in exactly the way he had wanted, but because he is God. No other reason is needed.

What is our reaction when our prayers are not answered in the way we think is best? We are told that his ways are higher than our ways, and his thoughts higher than our thoughts (Isaiah 55.9). So, why are we surprised when he chooses to answer our prayers in his own way?

Regardless of how God chooses to answer our prayers, may our response be like David's: to worship him.

Jenny

Prayer: Lord, I confess that I do not understand your ways. But, I trust in you! I worship you, for you are God and your ways are best. In the name of Jesus, who died for my sins, I pray. Amen.

Psalm of the Day: 103.15-22

Anger
Daily Reading: 2 Samuel 13

> *When King David heard of all these things, he was very angry.*
> (2 Samuel 13.21)

Devotional Thought: Amnon, the king's son, raped his half-sister Tamar, the sister of Absalom. King David heard of it but did nothing about it. It was simply said of him, "He was very angry." The anger of the king was understandable. It was justified. But, it was not enough. Absalom, seeing justice frustrated, decided to take the matter into his own hands and murdered his brother.

The anger of the king accomplished nothing. That's generally how anger works, isn't it? Not always, but generally.

The Bible says "the anger of man does not produce the righteousness of God" (James 1.20). Anger may serve the purpose of getting us motivated, but anger by itself does not accomplish anything. That's why James also wrote, "Be quick to hear, slow to speak, slow to anger" (v. 19).

The Apostle Paul instructs us to "Be angry and do not sin; do not let the sun go down on your anger, and give no opportunity to the devil" (Ephesians 4.26-27). Instead, we are to direct our anger into godly responses. If we use our anger as a catalyst for correction, then it is transformed into good. If we simply seethe in our anger, letting it live on in our hearts from day to day, we give the devil repeated opportunities to tempt us and to defeat us. Jesus himself was angry at the money changers in the temple, and he "cleaned house"! In another place, Jesus was angry at the hard hearted attitude toward suffering that he found in the synagogue, and he healed a man on the Sabbath. Anger directed at a godly solution can be productive.

David paid a huge price for his anger. He lost Amnon to murder and Absalom to exile.

What price are you paying for your anger?

Prayer: Lord, I know that my anger does not produce the righteousness of God. If righteousness, however, bids me to be angry, then help me to channel my anger into a godly solution. Amen.

Psalm of the Day: 104.1-9

Do Not Remain an Outcast

Daily Reading: 2 Samuel 14

> *We must all die; we are like water spilled on the ground, which cannot be gathered up again. But God will not take away life, and he devises means so that the banished one will not remain an outcast.*
> (2 Samuel 14.14)

Devotional Thought: An unnamed woman from Tekoa, came before King David to plead for the return of Absalom. The wisdom of her words is appropriate for all ages.

We must all die. The Bible says that it is appointed unto man once to die. With the sin of Adam, death came into that beautiful garden. Ever since that invasion, all people who live have also died – or they face an inevitable death in the future. There are two scriptural exceptions to this: Enoch who walked with God and was no more, and Elijah who ascended into heaven on a chariot of fire. None of us can claim to be an Enoch or an Elijah. Even Jesus himself experienced death.

Physical death is final. Just as spilled water cannot be gathered up again from the ground, so life that is spilled out cannot be gathered again into the physical body. There is coming a resurrection in which we will be given new bodies, but the Bible says the "plant" that comes (the heavenly resurrection body) is different from the "seed" that is sown (the earthly physical body) in burial. I have stood at many graves, laying to rest the final remains of saints who have died. There is no hope for those remains to be reanimated, but there is a greater hope!

God's grace goes beyond the curse of death. Two thousand years ago, Jesus defeated death and sin on an old rugged cross. Death is not our master. It is not our destiny. We are no longer outcasts, for God has devised a means to bring banished souls back. Praise the Lord!

Prayer: Our Father in heaven, thank you that we are no longer outcasts. Your Son, Jesus, is the firstborn from the dead, and because of his death and resurrection, our sins are forgiven and we have been given life - eternal life! Amen.

Psalm of the Day: 104.10-15

There Also Will Your Servant Be

Daily Reading: 2 Samuel 15

Ittai answered the king, "As the Lord lives, and as my lord the king lives, wherever my lord the king shall be, whether for death or for life, there also will your servant be." (2 Samuel 15.21)

Devotional Thought: King David was at times wildly popular, and at other times mildly tolerated. There were people who readily rejoiced when he came to power and others who silently seethed. But, until Absalom deposed his father the king, it was generally a good thing to be a supporter of the king. At that time, people's true colors were revealed. Ittai was one of those people.

Ittai was a Gittite, a "foreigner," yet he fully supported the king – even when the king had lost popular support. Redeemed from the enemies of God to become an ally of God and his people, Ittai was determined to stay with David, no matter what. His decision would have meant certain death if Absalom had prevailed.

What about us and our determination to "stay" with our King? Are we willing to say, as did Ittai, "wherever my lord the king shall be, whether for death or for life, there also will your servant be?" The way may lead to sickness: I'm sticking with Jesus. The path may be through persecution: I won't leave Jesus. Others may reject, neglect or ridicule me: I want Jesus' approval.

There are those who follow Jesus at the peril of their lives. In the New Testament, their homes were confiscated, their businesses were boycotted, and their families were threatened. These things are still a reality in today's world, where antagonistic religions persecute Christians. Even in "The Land of the Free," holding Christian values can be very costly. Churches, pastors, even businesses are subject to persecution for acting on their faith.

In this day of darkness, may we be like that foreigner Ittai: "Wherever my Lord shall be, there also will your servant be."

Prayer: Lord, as Ittai told David, so I say to you, "Wherever my lord the king shall be, there also will your servant be." I have decided to follow Jesus, and there's no turning back! Amen.

Psalm of the Day: 104.16-23

Repay Me with Good
Daily Reading: 2 Samuel 16

It may be that the Lord will look on the wrong done to me, and that the Lord will repay me with good for his cursing today. (2 Samuel 16.12)

Devotional Thought: The mayor of Bethel, Ohio, is a friend of mine. He attends a sister church in our community. We sing in the community choir together. I know that he has had to make decisions unpopular with some members of the community, but I was quite surprised last fall when he was running for reelection in our little town. His opponents came out swinging. I would think that people would be grateful for anybody willing to take that responsibility. But, the negative things that were said, the misrepresentations that were advanced, were hurtful. I thought, "What a thankless job! I wouldn't take that kind of abuse!" I was impressed with the mayor's spirit, however. He was not hateful. He was not vindictive. He simply pursued the office he felt compelled to fulfill.

David had to go through verbal abuse as a leader. Shimei confronted David and cursed him as a man of blood, a usurper, and a worthless man. Shimei illustrated what one person told me: "It's easy to throw rocks at the people in charge!" One of David's generals sought permission to kill Shimei, but David would not allow it. He responded that he would rather trust in the Lord to right this wrong.

Have you ever been wronged? Of course! We all have. Perhaps you have even been cursed. Where should we turn when we are made to feel worthless by our adversaries? Or worse yet, when the Shimeis – our own countrymen – defame us? It's so tempting to take the matter in our own hands, but the Bible teaches us: "Do not repay evil for evil or reviling for reviling, but on the contrary, bless, for to this you were called, that you may obtain a blessing" (1 Peter 3.9).

Prayer: O Lord, help me to heed the words of Paul in Romans 12.20: "If your enemy is hungry, feed him; if he is thirsty, give him something to drink; for by so doing you will heap burning coals on his head." In the face of abuse, may I show love in the name of Christ. Amen.

Psalm of the Day: 104.24-35

Help in the Wilderness

Daily Reading: 2 Samuel 17

> *The people are hungry and weary and thirsty in the wilderness.*
> (2 Samuel 17.29)

Devotional Thought: As I write this devotional, it is time for March Madness. This year, however, March Madness has been delayed by COVID-19. Just when we need sports, we aren't able to watch any! I have a feeling that this corona virus is going to extend for not only NCAA March Madness, but also for a good part of the major league baseball season. I'm already "hungry and weary and thirsty" in this wilderness! On top of all that, some of the basic necessities are flying off the shelves, as people horde things in fear.

David and his men had fled a rebellion in the capital city. They were ill-prepared for their emergency flight. They needed help. Shobi, Machir, and Barzilla to the rescue! Not knowing if their aid would be punished as sedition, these men brought the weary refugees "beds, basins, and earthen vessels, wheat, barley, flour, parched grain, beans and lentils, honey and curds and sheep and cheese from the herd, for David and the people with him to eat, for they said, 'The people are hungry and weary and thirsty in the wilderness.'"

Rest, cleansing, sustenance, and encouragement - just what the doctor ordered!

I wonder how the corona virus will play out. Will it be a time of selfish hoarding or generous sharing? Will we reach out our hands to help, even at great cost to ourselves?

There is another virus going around. It is called sin. It makes people suffer with hunger, weariness, and thirst in a great wilderness of fear and doubt. How will we respond to that?

Prayer: Father, thank you for placing people in my life who have helped me when I'm hungry, thirsty, and weary. Lord, show me someone today who could use my help and encouragement. I pledge to act upon that need. In the name of the One who left heaven's comfort to give me all I need, amen.

Psalm of the Day: 105.1-6

Consider Jesus

Daily Reading: 2 Samuel 18

And the king was deeply moved and went up to the chamber over the gate and wept. And as he went, he said, "O my son Absalom, my son, my son Absalom! Would I had died instead of you, O Absalom, my son, my son!" (2 Samuel 18.33)

Devotional Thought: In David's great anguish over Absalom, was there a measure of guilt? After all, Absalom has gotten away with murder, literally, when he killed his half-brother Amnon. David had looked the other way. The consequences of his disobedience were severe for him, his family, and the entire nation.

Do we ever compromise on what we know is right? We sometimes do it in the name of love and mercy, but in reality it is often driven by our own feelings of guilt or fear ("I'm in no position to judge", or "I don't know the specific circumstances"). We should be prayerful in our convictions, and careful to avoid self-righteousness, but I wonder if we are sometimes too quick to excuse, or turn a blind eye to blatant sinfulness, to avoid tension in our close relationships. Isn't it within these loving relationships that we must speak, if we see a fellow believer straying from the security of the Father? As one of my precious friends so wisely reminds me, "Iron sharpens iron, so one man sharpens another," (Prov. 27:17).

David could have been instrumental in helping his son pursue righteousness, rather than his own sinful desires. Instead, he hid his head in the sand and failed to call his son into account for his sin. Consider Jesus, however. He didn't turn his back on justice, but he loved us enough to pay the tremendous debt for our sin. May God give us the courage of our convictions to point the way to righteousness, but to do so in mercy and love.

Jenny

Prayer: Thank you, Jesus, that you paid the penalty for my sins, fulfilling the just requirements of the Law. Help me to have such an attitude for righteousness that I do not gloss over sin, but instead point to you as the atoning sacrifice for our sins. Amen.

Psalm of the Day: 105.7-15

Go to Meet the King
Daily Reading: 2 Samuel 19

> *Then the king returned and came to the Jordan. And Judah came to Gilgal, to go to meet the king.* (2 Samuel 19.15)

Devotional Thought: After the death of Absalom, who had usurped the throne, King David returned to Jerusalem. The people went out to meet him and to welcome him. Three men stand out:

- *Shimei* had previously sinned against David and was first to ask for his forgiveness. "My lord the king, please forgive me," he pleaded. His repentance was sincere. This is what we all must do in coming to the King – acknowledge our sin, repent and humbly seek forgiveness. Our sin demands a penalty, but Jesus paid the price for us and we are spared.

- *Mephibosheth*, the grandson of Saul came down to meet the king. He was the son of David's friend, Jonathan, and was actually next in line for the throne of Saul. He was so humble. In verse 28 we read, "All my relatives and I could expect only death from you, my lord, but instead you have honored me by allowing me to eat at your own table! What more can I ask?" David showed unique kindness to Mephibosheth. So it is with us.

- *Barzillai* was another who came to welcome David and escort him across the Jordan. Barzillai was the ultimate old-timer. David invited him to come and live with him in Jerusalem. But, Barzillai replied that he was too old. He felt useless. Do we sometimes feel that way because we are getting too old? We need not feel that way! There is always opportunity for service, no matter our age.

We shall go to meet the King someday. I look forward to that day! Do you?

Pastor Dale

Prayer: Jesus, my heart leaps within me when I think of your return. Help us to be ready, O Lord, when you split the eastern sky and come to take us home! Amen.

Psalm of the Day: 105.16-22

Deceitful Whispering
Daily Reading: 2 Samuel 20

He blew a trumpet, and said: "We have no share in David, Nor do we have inheritance in the son of Jesse; Everyman to his tents, O Israel!" ... But the men of Judah, from the Jordan as far as Jerusalem, remained loyal to David. (2 Samuel 20.1-2)

Devotional Thought: Are we like the man who hit a parked car? He left the following note on the car's windshield: "Everybody looking at me right now thinks I'm leaving you my name, address and phone number. But, I'm not......" We want to look like we are doing the right thing to those watching.

What did Sheba think as he was about to cause a wreck in the already shaky kingdom? He certainly thought he was right. I'm pretty sure he wanted others to think he was right. But, was he right?

I have seen this happen in churches and business and even in families. But, in almost every case, the devil has been able to once again exchange the truth for a lie, and has found someone to buy into his lie.
- Could a pastor have a Sheba in his church who feels the pastor is showing favoritism, and then whispers deceitfully about it in the church?
- Maybe it's at work, where the boss picks someone else over you to head up a big visible project. Or, it's just because someone else got the promotion. Then, the whispers of deceit and disloyalty begin.

Many times loyalty is purchased - what do I get out of it? That's what Sheba was basically saying here. But, the men of Judah had true loyalty and honor. At the end of purchased loyalty, you will often find deceit. But, when you find true loyalty, it's normally structured from a magnanimous heart - a heart full of God's love and God's Truth, which will bring honor to the one to whom you are loyal.

Pastor Bruce

Prayer: Lord, help me to be a person of honor, loyalty and truth. Help me to refrain from deceitful whispering that tears down another's reputation. Amen.

Psalm of the Day: 105.23-36

Weary

Daily Reading: 2 Samuel 21

And David grew weary. (2 Samuel 21.15)

Devotional Thought: Recently, I was cutting, splitting and stacking firewood with my sons-in-law. I grew weary more quickly than they did, and though my man-pride was damaged, I stopped while they continued working. I recognized that it's not a good thing to operate a chain saw when you are exhausted!

A brave warrior who led by example, David had gone "down together with his servants, and they fought against the Philistines." David's stamina, however, was not what it had been in his prime. He grew weary. As David was about to be slain in battle, one of his battle companions had to come to his rescue.

Consider two things we learn from this scenario:
- It is not a shame to grow weary. David's age and exertion combined to make him weary before the younger soldiers. But, as the Bible says, "Even youths shall faint and be weary" (Isaiah 40.30). I suppose it would be a shame to never grow weary, to never exert yourself to the point of exhaustion.
- Not only do we need to recognize our own weariness, we also should watch for signs of weariness in others. David's men probably waited too long to do something about it, but they did act when they saw David in danger. We should observe the workers around us. Are they showing signs of weariness? If so, we ought to step in and help them or find someone else to do so.

Are you weary? One way to prevent that is to recognize our limits and take the steps to properly rest our bodies, minds, and spirits. Are you getting the rest you need? Do you see another who is weary? Lend a helping hand and encourage them to rest.

Prayer: Jesus, when you were so weary that you fell beneath the load of the cross, Simon of Cyrene helped you. Grant that I may be a helper to those who have grown weary. Give me strength for the battle myself, also. I come to you to find rest for my soul. Amen.

Psalm of the Day: 105.37-45

Exalted Be My God!

Daily Reading: 2 Samuel 22

The Lord lives, and blessed be my rock, and exalted be my God, the rock of my salvation. (2 Samuel 22.47)

Devotional Thought: This story was told to me by Missionary, Harmon Schmelzenbach. I am relating it by memory, so I ask forgiveness for any inaccuracies...

Outside the king of Mozambique's palace walls, a warrior danced, singing the praises of the king. On and on he went, until the king thought he would wear himself out with exhaustion. He gave the warrior food and drink. "Food from the king's table? Water from the king's cistern? How could it be?" The warrior just redoubled his efforts! Dust and feathers flew everywhere. Perspiration gleamed from the warrior's dark skin.

To show his appreciation of the warrior's exuberant praise, the king ordered that goats be brought as a gift to the warrior - as a way to bring his exhausting tribute to an end. "A gift from the king's flocks?" The warrior danced and sang and shouted all the more in the African heat. To get the warrior out of there, the king called his servants to get his car and take him home, giving him a gift of cattle as well. As he was driven off down the road, with his gifts of cattle and goats following, the warrior had his head out the window, shouting the king's praises!

Who was that warrior? He had been framed for a crime he had not committed. The king had investigated the case, reversed the sentence, and given him justice. The man had come all the way across the country on foot to praise the king.

That's how David felt about the Lord, in 2 Samuel 22. He just couldn't praise God enough!

What about you and me? Do we feel that way about our King? Jesus Christ has taken our guilt upon himself!

Prayer: Blessed are you, O Lord, my rock! May you be exalted, O rock of my salvation! Amen.

Psalm of the Day: 106.1-5

I Thirst!
Daily Reading: 2 Samuel 23

> *Oh, that someone would give me water to drink from the well of Bethlehem that is by the gate!* (2 Samuel 23.15)

Devotional Thought: In today's chapter, 2 Samuel 23, we find the mighty men of David, men who distinguished themselves by their courageous and selfless service to the king. Among them were three men who "broke through the camp of the Philistines and drew water out of the well of Bethlehem that was by the gate and carried and brought it to David." They did this because David longed to be refreshed from the waters of that well. Consider David's words as if they were being spoken today by our King, Jesus.

Just as the Philistines had captured the city of Bethlehem, wielding control over its inhabitants, so the enemy of God's people has ensnared and captured the world today. Our nation is in the grip of an insidious enemy. As I watched the news last night, my heart was broken by the sad stories of how heroin is capturing, controlling and ultimately killing people. Every year, thousands lose their lives to heroin overdoses. Besides the deaths, there are thousands more who have fallen under the control of the drug and are in great despair. The heart of Jesus is thirsty for the rescue of these souls.

On the cross, Jesus cried out, "I thirst!" Yes, he was physically thirsty, but I believe, too, that his soul within him longed with love for those souls bound for hell, trapped by sin. Many of these souls, are trapped behind enemy lines, held by addiction, crime, and futility. They don't even know how to choose right. They are waiting, and Jesus is calling, for mighty men and women of God to break through the enemy lines and bring them to Jesus.

Who will be a mighty man/woman of Jesus?

Prayer: O Lord, help me to feel your thirst and to know your hunger for the souls of the lost. Help me to break through the enemy lines and bring them to you. Amen.

Psalm of the Day: 106.6-12

Minimum Impact
Daily Reading: 2 Samuel 24

I am in great distress. Let us fall into the hand of the Lord, for his mercy is great; but let me not fall into the hand of man. (2 Samuel 24.14)

Devotional Thought: Sometimes even godly leaders make mistakes. Against the advice of his military and spiritual leaders, David had decided to conduct a census. In this account, you could come away with the thought that God originated the idea of a census. In reality, God *allowed* it. You might read verse 1 as "OK. Go ahead and number Israel if you are intent on doing it." Nowhere in David's defense does he say to God, "You told me to do this!" (Reading the account in 1 Chronicles 21, will help bring understanding to your reading.)

Though censuses had been permitted in the past, for some reason what David did was displeasing to the Lord. We get some indication of why in verse 3: "Joab said to the king, 'May the Lord your God add to the people a hundred times as many as they are, while the eyes of my lord the king still see it, but why does my lord the king delight in this thing?'" It seems as though David was feeding his pride with this census.

The real lesson from this chapter, is David's confession that it is better to fall into the hands of a merciful God than it is to trust your future destiny into the hands of chance or other people. David had come to know the mercies of God. He knew that what he had done was wrong, but he also knew the best way to right the wrong was to go directly to God in trust and confession. Yes, there would be consequences to his actions, as there are with all actions, but David knew that by going to God now he would minimize the negative impact of the consequences.

Prayer: Lord, help me to have the wisdom and humility to minimize the impact of my mistakes, by quickly confessing them and turning to you. Thank you for your great mercy! Amen.

Psalm of the Day: 106.13-18

Division of Labor

Daily Reading: Galatians 1

Paul, an apostle—not from men nor through man, but through Jesus Christ and God the Father, who raised him from the dead...
(Galatians 1.1)

Devotional Thought: Paul was an apostle. Yet, Paul had not met Jesus while Christ walked on this earth in his incarnate body. A careful reading of Acts 1, reveals that an apostle had to be an eyewitness of Jesus - to have personally known Jesus - not just heard about him through the witness of others. So, how could he make the formal claim of apostleship?

Paul's apostleship wasn't from man. Paul was careful to point out that his authority did not rest on any ecclesiastical body. Human authority had actually caused him to persecute Christ and Christians. Nor was his apostleship through man. While Paul had heard about Jesus through the Christians he had persecuted, none of those testimonies had convinced him that Jesus was the Son of God.

So, how did Paul become an apostle?

It was through Jesus Christ. Though Christ had ascended to the Father, and no longer walked on this earth in his human body, he appeared to Paul on the road to Damascus. And, when he appeared, he commissioned him in his apostleship! But, it was also through God the Father. The same power that raised Christ from the dead, also raised Paul from spiritual death. That power was from God.

The same thing is true today. We need to remember that when we testify to others about the grace of God. The power to convince them does not rest in us. That power is from God. We want our family and friends to know Jesus, so we bear witness to his saving grace. But, we must pray and depend on God to do the work of convincing and converting. When we try to do it, it becomes coercion - never a good thing!

Let's honor the "Division of Labor."

Prayer: Lord, thank you for saving me, and for giving me the wonderful privilege of bearing witness to your amazing grace. Help me to allow you to do your work of convincing and converting the lost. Amen.

Psalm of the Day: 106.19-23

Along with Me

Daily Reading: Galatians 2

> *I went up again to Jerusalem with Barnabas, taking Titus along with me.* (Galatians 2.1b)

Devotional Thought: "Never go alone." That piece of advice was given to me many years ago by a veteran pastor. He was referring to when I went out to do ministry - hospital calls, nursing homes, other visits and functions of the pastorate - I should always take someone with me. The 'never' and 'always' are impractical, of course, but it is a good principle.

The Apostle Paul modeled this principle in his ministry. On almost every recorded occasion of ministry, Paul had someone else with him. He learned that practice, of course, from the Master himself! Jesus took his disciples with him wherever he went, and he let them stretch their apostolic wings under his tutelage.

When Paul had to go to Jerusalem to settle a dispute with the elders of the church, he went with Barnabas, taking Titus along as well. Barnabas was a Jew. He was probably older than Paul and had been a Christian a lot longer than Paul. As a matter of fact, Barnabas had been instrumental in Paul's spiritual and ministerial development. Titus, on the other hand, was a Greek. He was younger - both in physical years and in spiritual experience - than Paul, who had served as an instructor and supervisor to him. This shows that Paul was always learning, and always teaching.

I have been taught to ask myself two important questions: "Who is discipling me?" And, "Who am I discipling?" How would you answer those questions? If you don't have a mentor who is leading you to higher heights, ask God to provide someone! Seek out relationships that will enhance your understanding and broaden your perspective. And, if you aren't discipling someone else, open your eyes, for - as Jesus said - "The fields are white unto harvest."

Prayer: Lord, thank you for the people whom you have sent into my life to help me grow in spirit and in service. Help me to be a positive influence in someone else's life, too, that they may grow in wisdom and knowledge and grace. Amen.

Psalm of the Day: 106.24-31

Law and Promise

Daily Reading: Galatians 3

> *Is the law then contrary to the promises of God? Certainly not!*
> (Galatians 3.21a)

Devotional Thought: Evangelicals tend to struggle with the tension between grace and law. We, like our Protestant forebear, Martin Luther, know salvation is by grace alone, through faith. Those of us raised in a 'legalistic' environment, tend to overcompensate to avoid being seen as judgmental. Paul, however, was perfectly content to live with the tension. Yes, we are saved by grace. Yes, our salvation is inexorably linked to obedience. Certainly, the Law was not contrary to grace.

Paul would say following the Law does not bring us salvation, but he would also say the Law brings us to salvation. The Law is our schoolmaster, teaching us of the need of grace. The Law is our prosecutor, proving to us that we cannot be saved by works. And, the Law is our trainer, helping us to know the will and way of the Lord.

Is the Law, then, 'contrary to the promises of God'? Certainly not!

The Greek word translated contrary is "kata", and means down from, against, or throughout. The context helps determine the meaning of the word in particular usage. In this case, all the meanings apply:
- Is the Law *down from* the promises of God? Certainly not! The way of the Law must come first, or there is no need for grace.
- Is the Law *against* the promises of God? Certainly not! The Law's very purpose is to lead us to grace.
- Is the Law *throughout* the promises of God? Certainly not! The Bible says that God has made a new way. The old way of the written code has passed away, and we no longer serve according the Law, but by the Spirit of grace.

We're not afraid of the Law because we are under grace!

Prayer: Thank you, O Lord, for the wonderful grace of Jesus! And, thank you for the Law that leads me to grace. Amen.

Psalm of the Day: 106.32-39

Meet in the Middle
Daily Reading: Galatians 4

I entreat you, become as I am, for I also have become as you are. You did me no wrong. (Galatians 4.12)

Devotional Thought: Have you ever used the website, "Meet in the Middle"? I use it frequently, when I'm trying to set up points of rendezvous with family and friends. It's a great tool when you don't know exactly where the middle is, and when you don't know what's in the middle!

The Apostle Paul wrote to the Galatians to urge them to meet him in the middle: "Become as I am, for I also have become as you are." In other words, "Let's compromise. Let's meet in the middle." Often, we think of Paul as being inflexible and dogmatic, and at times he could be. But, I think he gets a bad rap in that regard. Paul was very flexible when it was advantageous to be so. On one occasion, he wrote, "To the Jews I became as a Jew... To those under the law I became as one under the law... To those outside the law I became as one outside the law... To the weak I became weak... I have become all things to all people that by all means I might save some" (1 Corinthians 9.20-23). If compromise furthered the mission of the gospel, Paul was all for it! If, however, compromise undermined the cause of Christ, he was against it.

John Wesley, the great English preacher of the 18th Century who began the Methodist movement, followed the maxim, "In the essentials, unity. In the non-essentials, liberty." I guess the trick is to determine what the essentials are. That's not easy, but I would venture to say that too often, we probably name things essential when they really are not.

How about you? Are you willing to meet in the middle?

Prayer: Lord, help me to hold on loosely to my ways, but to hold on tightly to yours. Help me to discover the difference, as I become a student of your Word and a vessel of your Spirit. Amen.

Psalm of the Day: 106.40-43

Freedom

Daily Reading: Galatians 5-6

For freedom Christ has set us free; stand firm therefore, and do not submit again to a yoke of slavery. (Galatians 5.1)

Devotional Thought: Almost from the beginning of history, some form of slavery has existed. In Galatians 5, Paul speaks of freedom in Christ. He instructs the Galatians to "not submit again to a yoke of slavery" (v. 1). What is this slavery to which Paul refers? Jesus answers plainly in John 8:34, "Truly, truly, I tell you, everyone who sins is a slave to sin."

Paul has much to say about this subject, and not just in this letter. He knows that the human heart is bent towards legalism, towards religious activities that will supposedly save us from our sins. In Paul's day, this attitude manifested itself in the "circumcision sect," those who would have the new believers follow the old Jewish law in order to be saved. Paul argues, "If you accept circumcision, Christ will be of no advantage to you" (v. 2). In other words, it's either the grace of God through Jesus that saves you, or it's your ability to adhere to the whole law. The latter is impossible, and there is no middle ground.

Today, we see that the "circumcision sect" way of thinking is still alive and well. We hear and are glad for the news of the gospel, yet we feel like we must somehow supplement his grace with our own atoning works. This is heresy. Nor should we accept the grace of God and abuse it, continuing in unrepentant sin. When we accept the grace of Jesus, we do so to the exclusion of all else. We throw off the yoke of slavery to sin, but we take up another yoke. We become "slaves of righteousness" (Romans 6.18), and the fruit we get "leads to sanctification and its end, eternal life" (Romans 6.22).

Jenny

Prayer: Lord, you have created our hearts - so that we long to be free. Set us free indeed, that we would happily become slaves to righteousness!

Psalm of the Day: 106.44-48

Living the Dream!

Daily Reading: Jude 1

To those who are called, beloved in God the Father and kept for Jesus Christ: May mercy, peace, and love be multiplied to you. (Jude 1.1b-2)

Devotional Thought: The book of Jude has but one chapter, and it is mostly about false teachers. It can be a bit discouraging, but the salutation is very uplifting! It tells us we are "living the dream."

Who we are...

Called - Life can be very lonely. A call goes a long way in lifting someone's spirit. God doesn't leave us wondering if there's anybody who knows we exist. He sent his Son to be our Savior and his Spirit to be our Companion. He calls us!

Beloved - I love to watch my children with their children. Even when things aren't convenient or easy, I see how they love those babies. God loves us even when it's not easy. He loved us when it was the hardest thing in the world to do!

Kept - On September 2, 1978, I asked Lana to be my bride. It was in June of 1979, that we were married. But, in those intervening months, we kept ourselves for each other. In the same way, we are espoused to Jesus and there is a great wedding day coming!

What we're given...

Mercy - Not getting something we deserve - the sentence of our sin. That is multiplied daily in our lives!

Peace - Getting something we don't deserve - the assurance of knowing that it is well with our souls!

Love - The greatest gift of all! And, this from the One whose love is infinite and eternal!

May these things be multiplied in you!

Prayer: Thank you, Lord, for calling me, loving me, and keeping me. Thank you for forgiving my sins, for giving me peace, and for loving me unconditionally. Help me, O Lord, to multiply these things to others. Amen.

Psalm of the Day: 107.1-3

Fear Not

Daily Reading: Revelation 1

> *Fear not, I am the first and the last, and the living one. I died, and behold I am alive forevermore, and I have the keys of Death and Hades.* (Revelation 1.17b-18)

Devotional Thought: Last week in church, a duet presented the song "Known" by Tauren Wells. Consider the lyrics: "You see right through the mess inside me. And you call me out to pull me in. You tell me I can start again. And I don't need to keep on hiding. I'm fully known and loved by you."

Did you catch that? "I don't need to keep on hiding!" God knows me, and yet loves me unconditionally!

That was the message of Jesus to John in Revelation, when he said, "Fear not." The Greek word for revelation is *apocalypsis*. It means unveiling. As Jesus is revealed – unveiled - we have less and less reason for fear, for he...

- Is the First and Last. All of creation is the work of his hands, and all of history is lived within his existence. Jesus is therefore the perfect Judge, for he knows all truth; nothing is hidden from him. What he pronounces clean is clean. What he writes is certain. When we dwell in him, we are connected with the Ultimate Reality.
- Is the Living One. He died, but is "alive forevermore." Jesus, the eternal living one, entered into our sphere so that he might taste death for us all. Neither death nor the finitude of this world could hold him. By his power, he conquered his own death and is alive forever.
- Holds the keys of death and Hades. Having conquered his own death and grave, he has wrested the keys out of the hands of our captor, and sets us free!

Jesus has done all this for you and me, even though he knew us. He did it *because* he knew us. So, fear not. You are fully known and loved by him!

Prayer: Thank you, Jesus, that you are the First and Last. You are the Living One. You are alive forevermore. And, you hold the keys to eternity! I follow you with confidence and praise. Amen.

Psalm of the Day: 107.4-9

Remember, Repent, Repeat
Daily Reading: Revelation 2

Remember therefore from where you have fallen; repent, and do the works you did at first. (Revelation 2.5a)

Devotional Thought: Recently, I have been preaching a series of messages I entitled "Where's the Church?" These are messages from the book of Revelation and include Jesus' words to the Seven Churches in Asia. The first church he addressed was the church in Ephesus. Where was this church? "In Denial."

Jesus commended the church in Ephesus. They were hard-working and patient. They endured persecution. They had maintained morally and doctrinally. They refused to grow weary, but just kept on going.

In this church of purity, morality, and consistency, however, Jesus found a tragic flaw. So deep was the flaw, that he told them to "Remember. Repent. Repeat." What was the flaw? They had abandoned their first love. And, they were living in a state of denial.

It is tragic when we put orthodoxy and duty in the place of love and passion for Christ. It is tragic when we would rather follow the rules than love Jesus with all our heart, soul, mind and strength. It is tragic when we have forgotten how much Jesus means to us. No matter how perfectly performed, dry dead religion does not please the heart of the Lover of our Souls.

In Luke 7, Jesus was eating in the home of a respectable "church member." A scandalous woman crashed the dinner party and wept profusely at the feet of Jesus. Jesus' host was indignant. Jesus, however, saw things differently. He said that her great love was due to her recognition that her great sins had been forgiven. He received that kind of love with joy, but the church member left him feeling cold.

How about you? Is your love for Jesus still red hot? If not, "Remember. Repent. Repeat."

Prayer: Lord, you have given me so much. Forgiveness! New life! Unconditional love! Cleansing! Forgive me, O Lord, when I take these things for granted, and reignite a passionate love for you in my soul! Amen.

Psalm of the Day: 107.10-16

Come In! The Door's Open!
Daily Reading: Revelation 3

Behold, I have set before you an open door, which no one is able to shut. I know that you have but little power, and yet you have kept my word and have not denied my name. (Revelation 3.8)

Devotional Thought: Yesterday, we considered Ephesus, a church that had lost their first love. In today's chapter, we read about a church at the opposite end of the spectrum: Philadelphia, "The Church of Brotherly Love."

In these messages to seven churches of Revelation, Jesus expressed a variety of concerns for the various congregations. For the church in Philadelphia, Jesus had three concerns...
1. Expulsion from the synagogue. Many of their neighbors, friends, relatives, and business associates were undoubtedly a part of the Jewish synagogue. When the Christians were expelled from the synagogue, those relationships suffered.
2. An open door. Although the synagogue had been closed to them, the church was in a unique position to spread the gospel of Jesus. Philadelphia was in a strategic location - culturally, commercially, and politically - an open door for evangelism.
3. Waning strength. The church had been working hard in the midst of disappointment. That had sapped them of strength. Jesus knew that they were under tremendous burden.

In all of the pain of severed relationships, and in the face of daunting challenges, the Christians in Philadelphia...
1. Kept the word of Christ. I have found the Word of God to be such a resting place. In the midst of the storm, the Word keeps us as much as we keep his Word. Hold on!
2. Had not denied his name. Jesus promises us that when we acknowledge him before men, he will acknowledge us before the Father!
3. Would themselves be acknowledged. Not only would Jesus acknowledge them, but those who had rejected them would come to the place that they would have to confess that these Christians were the real deal.

May Jesus give us the strength to go through the open door!

Prayer: Thank you, Lord Jesus, for the love that we share as brothers and sisters in Christ. Help us, as you helped the Christians in Philadelphia, to acknowledge your name and be acknowledged by you. Amen.

Psalm of the Day: 107.17-22

Come Up Here!

Daily Reading: Revelation 4-5

> *Come up here, and I will show you what must take place...*
> (Revelation 4.1b)

Devotional Thought: Yesterday, we considered an open door on earth. Today, we see the "door standing open in heaven." Through that door, John heard a voice saying...

Come up here. We sullenly wonder why God does not speak to us. Often, it is because we have contented ourselves to live in the lowlands. When Moses received the Ten Commandments, he went up on the Mountain. When the disciples saw Jesus transfigured, they went up on the Mountain. God longs to show us his glory. But, when we live in the lowlands - mists and shadows, fears and doubts, sin and self - we can't see him. We need to get down on our knees, so we can climb up to our God!

I will show you. Another reason we may not hear from God, is that we're tuned in to everything else! Instead of seeking the face of God, we seek the wisdom of man. I once heard a preacher say, "We spend hundreds of dollars and spend countless hours at conferences, when God is giving seminars all the time." I'm not opposed to learning and training - I do it for a living! - but when we neglect the Master Trainer, all the other training is just clatter and confusion.

When I was a young man, I was asked to serve as the youth director at our church. I declined the nomination, telling the pastor that I wasn't really where I needed to be spiritually, so I probably shouldn't accept it. Later, however, the Lord asked me gently, "Don't you think the better choice would be to get where you need to be so you can serve me?" I went back to the pastor and accepted the nomination.

Do you hear that? God is calling, "Come up here..."

Prayer: I can hear my Savior calling... Lord, help me to respond to your call, to come up the mountain, to listen to your voice, and ultimately to do your will. Amen.

Psalm of the Day: 107.23-32

These Are They

Daily Reading: Revelation 6-7

These are the ones coming out of the great tribulation. They have washed their robes and made them white in the blood of the Lamb. (Revelation 7.14)

Devotional Thought: I was amused by Nike's recent ad for the opening game of the NFL season - and the backlash - that featured Colin Kaepernick saying, "Believe in something, even if it means sacrificing everything." Most of the backlash, was actually wondering just what Kaepernick had sacrificed, in his much-publicized kneeling for the National Anthem. (I guess every person's sacrifice is costly to him/herself in ways immeasurable by others.)

That, along with today's scripture, got me to thinking, "What am I sacrificing for Jesus?"

In Revelation, John saw "a great multitude that no one could number ... crying out with a loud voice, 'Salvation belongs to our God!'" John was amazed at the multitude's vociferous praise. His question, "Who are these people?" was answered by an angel: "These are the ones coming out of the great tribulation."

The passage seems to indicate that all those who have been blood-washed have come "out of the great tribulation." I wonder how we live up to that description. Again, "What am I sacrificing for Jesus?"

Jesus said that since he was ridiculed, his followers would be ridiculed too; since he was misunderstood, his followers would be misunderstood too; since he was persecuted, his followers would be persecuted too; since he was rejected, his followers would be rejected, too. The student is not above the teacher.

But, we want to make Christianity a means to peace, prosperity, and popularity. Paul's sentiment that he "filled up in his body that which was lacking in the sufferings of Christ" is foreign to us. We don't want to have anything to do with tribulation, with suffering, with sacrifice. Or, we make our inconveniences seem like great sacrifices.

Are you coming out of great tribulation? Again, "What am I sacrificing for Jesus?"

Prayer: Lord, thank you for sacrificing everything for me. Help me to believe in you, even if it means sacrificing everything for you. My desire is to be completely yours, no matter what the cost. Amen.

Psalm of the Day: 107.33-38

And There Followed

Daily Reading: Revelation 8-9

The first angel blew his trumpet, and there followed... (Revelation 8.7)

Devotional Thought: Several months ago, I noticed a squeal coming from under my convertible hood. I knew it was the belt, but I hardened my ears to it, trying to ignore it. One morning I went to take it out with Lana, and not only was there a loud squeal, but there was a significant loss of power. I pulled it back in the garage, and finally decided it was time to listen to those foreboding sounds. A few minor adjustments by my mechanic, and the problem was taken care of. If I hadn't listened though, the troubles would have multiplied. I should have taken care of it much sooner, but I have a tendency to ignore such 'warning sounds,' hoping that they will go away.

In Revelation, there is a warning sound: the blowing of heavenly trumpets. The scripture says that after each trumpet sounded, "there followed..." The trumpets served as harbingers to what was to come. When the trumpet blew, things inevitably and predictably came to pass.

There is coming a day when the heavenly trumpet will sound once again - in the twinkling of an eye. Certain things will follow the sounding of this last trumpet: "The dead will be raised imperishable, and we shall be changed" (1 Corinthians 15.52). "And the dead in Christ will rise. Then we who are alive, who are left, will be caught up together with them in the clouds to meet the Lord in the air" (1 Thessalonians 4.16-17).

The trumpet will sound, but we must not wait for the last trumpet. We should respond now to the call of God. "Today if you hear his voice, do not harden your hearts" (Hebrews 4.7).

Prayer: Thank you, Lord, for the warning 'sounds' of your return. Help us to heed the trumpet call of God, and to make sure we are ready! Amen.

Psalm of the Day: 107.39-43

And He Shall Reign...

Daily Reading: Revelation 10-11

> *Then the seventh angel blew his trumpet, and there were loud voices in heaven, saying, "The kingdom of the world has become the kingdom of our Lord and of his Christ, and he shall reign forever and ever."* (Revelation 11.15)

Devotional Thought: The book of Revelation is not for the faint of heart. The events prophesied by John are terrifying, but they are meant to extend mercy to those who have yet to repent. God is giving the wicked one last chance, and he uses many of the same methods and symbolism that he used in Israel's history to once again showcase his glory. He leaves little room for doubt in the minds of the unbelievers as to Who is in control. Yet, sadly, not all will accept this mercy and grace.

Then enters the seventh angel. He blows his trumpet, and voices from heaven proclaim, "The kingdom of the world has become the kingdom of our Lord and of his Christ, and he shall reign forever and ever" (Revelation 11.15). Finally, God will reclaim his Kingdom! He will cleanse his creation of all sin and unrighteousness, and he will reign on his throne forever. Thousands of years after the first man and woman introduced sin into God's perfect world, he will restore it to perfection.

For thousands of years, he has shown his power and glory. He has shown his beauty, as evidenced in creation. He has shown his love, as he sent his only Son to earth to provide us with a way back to him. He has given countless opportunities to the wicked to repent, and to accept the free gift of eternal life through Jesus. "The Lord is not slow to fulfill his promise... but is patient toward you, not wishing that any should perish, but that all should reach repentance" (2 Peter 3.9). As believers, we anxiously await the day that the Lord reclaims the world as his own, and we pray for the unsaved to have eyes to see and hearts to believe.

Jenny

Prayer: Oh Lord, how we long for the day when you make all things new again! When you come to earth to perfect it and cleanse it from sin, to dwell with us forever. Come quickly, Lord Jesus!

Psalm of the Day: 108.1-6

Hear. Heed. Hang On.

Daily Reading: Revelation 12-13

> *If anyone has an ear, let him hear: If anyone is to be taken captive, to captivity he goes; if anyone is to be slain with the sword, with the sword must he be slain. Here is a call for the endurance and faith of the saints.* (Revelation 13.9-10)

Devotional Thought: In Revelation 13, there is a beast who has authority over the nations of the earth. This beast will force all whose names are not written in the Book of Life to worship him. John issued a threefold warning to the church:

Hear. "If anyone has an ear, let him hear." I watched with dismay as the confirmation hearings for Brett Kavanaugh progressed. Or, should I say did not progress? Those who had made up their minds before the first hearing, did everything in their power not to hear what he had to say. And, they wanted to prevent anyone else from hearing it, too. Satan uses the same strategy - silence the truth. The truth is available to us, if we would but hear. Our culture has turned a deaf ear to God and we will pay the price for it. Worse yet, I fear that there are those in the church who have tuned God out, not wanting to face the plain truth of Scripture. They would rather be in the dark and do what they want!

Heed. "With the sword must he be slain." Those who refuse to heed what they hear from God and his Word, face a judgment. Taken captive by their own lusts, these rejecters of God will receive the due consequences of their decisions. We cannot be simply hearers of the Word, we must be doers of the Word! (James 1.22)

Hang on. "Here is a call for the endurance and faith of the saints." You've heard the expression, "That's why they play the game." The outcome of the sporting event is not predetermined. They play to see who wins. In the same way, the saints have to endure and believe to the end.

Prayer: Thank you, Lord, for giving me spiritual ears. Help me to hear. Thank you for giving me truth. Help me to heed it. Thank you for giving me the ability to hang on. Help me to do so, in your power and by your grace. Amen.

Psalm of the Day: 108.7-13

Sing to the Lord
Daily Reading: Revelation 14-15

> And they sing the song of Moses, the servant of God, and the song of the Lamb, saying, "Great and amazing are your deeds, O Lord God the Almighty! Just and true are your ways, O King of the nations! (Revelation 15.3)

Devotional Thought: Retirement was bittersweet. Lana and I left behind a wonderful church family - bitter - but we moved to John's Island, SC - sweet. We love the ocean. It communicates a sense of God's glory to us. Though we don't sing on the beach, we feel like it!

According to Revelation 15, the multitude of worshipers in heaven will find themselves on the shore of "a sea of glass mingled with fire" (v. 2). "With harps of God in their hands," they will sing...

- *The song of Moses, the servant of God.* This is the song of **deliverance**. After the children of Israel were delivered from Egyptian slavery, Moses wrote a song (Exodus 15). He praised God for bringing them safely out of Egypt and through the Red Sea. In heaven, we will be able to look back at the troubles and obstacles of life, and see how God delivered us. We will sing of his great salvation!

- *The song of the Lamb, the Son of God.* This is the song of **redemption**. The Bible says that we have been redeemed from the curse of sin. The price of redemption? The blood of Jesus, the Lamb of God! So, in heaven we will sing a new song to the Lamb: "Worthy are you ... for you were slain, and by your blood you ransomed people for God from every tribe and language and people and nation" (Revelation 5).

Lana and I can't wait to sing in that choir with our friends and former choir members, standing side-by-side, praising our Lord together!

Prayer: "We praise thee, O God, for the Son of thy love, for Jesus who died and is now gone above. Hallelujah! Thine the glory! Hallelujah! Amen! Hallelujah! Thine the glory! Revive us again." Amen. (William Mackay)

Psalm of the Day: 109.1-5

Is Papaw in Heaven?

Daily Reading: Revelation 16

> *And God remembered Babylon the great, to make her drain the cup of the wine of the fury of his wrath.* (Revelation 16.19b)

Devotional Thought: A few weeks ago, I was asked the question, "Is Papaw in heaven?" That's tough - especially at a funeral. What do you say when 'Papaw' was obviously not a Christian?

As a young pastor, I was scared to death of doing funerals, especially when the deceased was not a Christian. Eugene Simpson, my District Superintendent, helped me so much. He told me, "Scott, remember that your funeral sermon cannot preach one person into heaven, nor can you preach one person out of heaven." That is reflected in the words of a graveside committal: "This body we commit to the ground. The spirit we leave with God, the just and merciful judge of the earth."

You see, it isn't our job to judge anybody. Our information, at best, is inaccurate and incomplete. Often, it is biased. But, there is One who is not subject to our biases, who sees perfectly and forgets nothing (except confessed sins!). God remembers.

Babylon, in the book of Revelation, is a metaphorical reference to Rome and the oppressive systems of this world. At times, the government - or other powerful sources, such as media, business, and Hollywood - line themselves up against the children of God. As a matter of fact, Jesus said that the world would hate us because it hated him. The good news is, we don't have to seek vengeance or try to mete out the correct punishment for the crime. We don't even have to keep track of it. God remembers.

So, is 'Papaw' in heaven? We will leave it in the hands of the Lord, for God remembers.

Prayer: Lord, forgive us for failing to think about the eternal destiny of lost souls. Stir our hearts to bear witness to the salvation of the Lord. And then, Lord, having done all we can, help us to leave their spirits with God, for you remember. Amen.

Psalm of the Day: 109.6-15

And the Winner Is...

Daily Reading: Revelation 17

> They will make war on the Lamb, and the Lamb will conquer them, for he is Lord of lords and King of kings, and those with him are called and chosen and faithful. (Revelation 17.14)

Devotional Thought: Coexist! I've read that many times on bumper stickers, and I appreciate its sentiment. But, are there not some things that by their very nature cannot exist together? Where there is light, darkness must flee. Where there is contamination, purity is compromised. Where there is truth, deception cannot survive. Where there is war, peace is gone. Where there is love, hatred has no home. We can cover the world with bumper stickers, but the fact remains that some things are mutually exclusive.

In today's verse, there are three distinct groups or individuals:
- *The Lamb.* Jesus is the Lamb who was slain from the foundation of the world. But, he has overcome the world. By defeating the despair of death and conquering the darkness of the grave, Jesus has won over all that is an enemy of life and light. The Lamb will conquer, for he is Lord of lords and King of kings!
- *Those with the Lamb.* Jesus is not the sole Victor. He brings with him those who trust in him. At the end of all things, we are victorious because we are called, chosen and faithful!
- *Those against the Lamb.* Rallied by powerful God-haters and truth-deniers, there will be those who make war on the Lamb. In the words of that ancient hymn: "Lo their doom is sure. One little word shall fell them."

A Mighty Fortress is our God! Jesus said that those who are not with him are against him. There is no neutral ground and there is no default position. Are you with or against him?

Prayer: Thank you, Jesus, O King of kings and Lord of lords, for the victory that you have won. I trust in you. I am with you, Lord! I am for you, Lord! I am in you, Lord! Amen.

Psalm of the Day: 109.16-20

Permanent Residence
Daily Reading: Revelation 18

So will Babylon the great city be thrown down with violence, and will be found no more. (Revelation 18.21b)

Devotional Thought: A few weeks ago, I was riding through town with a friend. We drove by an old, dilapidated house on her street. The house had a bright orange 'X' on an outside wall. She remarked, "I thought they were going to tear that house down." I thought to myself, "If they leave it much longer, they won't need to. It's going to fall down!" That's kind of sad to think about, isn't it? When that house was built many years ago, it was a source of satisfaction and pride. Today, it is ready to be torn down to "be found no more."

John the Revelator saw that future for Babylon. In chapter 16, of Revelation, we saw Babylon as symbolic of this world's corrupt powers. Today, we see in it another comparison: Babylon as the temporal city vs. The New Jerusalem as the eternal city.

The New Jerusalem is a city coming down from heaven (Revelation 21). It is destined to host the marriage supper of the Lamb (Revelation 19). It is an eternal city, where those who enter shall never go out (Revelation 3). Abraham sought a city with foundations, whose builder and maker is God (Hebrews 11).

I've had a hand in the construction of 4 new homes. I've loved those homes - been proud of them – but, I recognize that they will not be there forever. Through the ravages of time, everything is destined to destruction. There is a house that will remain strong through all the storms of life. It will also last through all eternity. That is the house built on the Rock which is Jesus Christ.

Are you building your life on Jesus?

Prayer: Lord, I am looking for a better city, an eternal city, the abode of God. I purpose to so live in this world that I may dwell in that world forever. Amen.

Psalm of the Day: 109.21-25

Wedding Planner

Daily Reading: Revelation 19

> *The marriage of the Lamb has come, and his Bride has made herself ready; it was granted her to clothe herself with fine linen, bright and pure" — for the fine linen is the righteous deeds of the saints.* (Revelation 19.7b-8)

Devotional Thought: In a few weeks, I will be performing a wedding for some friends. Preparations are being made. One of the most important preparations and one I always stress: "You need to get your marriage license now! Bring it to me at least a week before the wedding." I want to be sure - because if they don't do that, all the other preparations will be in vain. That's the stuff of wedding nightmares!

There is coming a day for another marriage. The angel told John, "The marriage of the Lamb has come." The date is set. It is known only to the Father, but Jesus has been preparing ever since the foundation of the world when God looked down the corridors of time and saw a perfect and eternal setting where we would be with him. The Kingdom of God comes. He will be our God, and we will be his people.

The bride must make herself ready. First of all, by saying yes to his proposal, we take on the garments of Christ - his righteousness! As the song goes, "Not our own righteousness, but Christ within!" Having been clothed in the righteousness of Christ, then we can start putting on "fine linen, bright and pure ... the righteous deeds of the saints." Notice that the bride of Christ is always singular. Jesus does not have many brides, but only one. It is the Church. But, each one of us are a part of the body of the bride. And, each one of us can do something to effect the beauty of the bride. Those are our righteous deeds.

Are you putting on fine linen, bright and pure?

Prayer: Thank you, Lord Jesus, for clothing me in your righteousness. Help me, O Lord, to enhance the beauty of the Church and to glorify your name, as I live out this life of righteousness with my deeds. Amen.

Psalm of the Day: 109.26-31

Summary Judgment

Daily Reading: Revelation 20

> *And I saw the dead, great and small, standing before the throne... and the dead were judged by what was written in the books, according to what they had done.* (Revelation 20.12)

Devotional Thought: In this scene of the Lord's revelation to John, we read of the White Throne Judgment. Those whose names are written in the Lamb's Book of Life will be judged according to the gospel, justified and acquitted by Christ, and will enter into eternal life with God.

What of those who are not found in the Lamb's Book of Life? They will stand before the throne of God, and be judged according to what is found in the other books, in which all of their past actions, thoughts and deeds are written. What a terrifying thought, for all of what has been done openly and in secret will be laid bare before our holy Creator. There is none who can stand before him in our own merit. All who try will be thrown into the lake of fire (v.15).

What do we do with this knowledge? How do we process this terrible imagery? First, it should give us renewed determination to reach others with the saving news of the gospel. Like us, their only hope is to have their names written in the Lamb's Book of Life. Second, it should renew in us a sober-mindedness regarding the tremendous cost of our sin, and of the Lord's contrasting holiness. We have no hope apart from God's grace. Third, the appropriate response of those who have trusted in Jesus for their salvation, is wholehearted worship and praise. At the end of time, there will be a blood sacrifice required by the Lord. The only question is: whose blood will pay the price? Praise God, for he has provided the perfect Lamb, whose blood is sufficient for all of our sins!

Jenny

Prayer: Lord, without the Lamb of God, we would be hopelessly lost. None can stand before your throne of judgment. Praise your holy Name for the atoning blood of your Son! Amen.

Psalm of the Day: 110.1-4

In With the New

Daily Reading: Revelation 21

Then I saw a new heaven and a new earth, for the first heaven and the first earth had passed away. (Revelation 21.1)

Devotional Thought: My friend, Fuad - manager and owner of Gold Star Chili in Bethel, OH - told me that his store is scheduled to be rebuilt in 2019. The process is simple: tear down the old one, build a new one.

Some things have to be torn down or taken away before new things can come to life...

The first heaven and earth will pass away. This world will not last forever. This is nothing new. Scientists have been telling us for generations that the universe is headed to oblivion. It will either keep expanding, until things are so spread out that it cannot sustain life. Or, it will expand to a certain point and then start contracting, until it draws completely into itself and 'dies' in the unimaginable pressure and temperature of its creation.

There will be a new heaven and earth. This will be different from the first heaven and earth. Will it be made using the same 'stuff' of today's world? That depends. Do you believe in evolution? Can God use existing ingredients to make something new? He can do what pleases him! But, as I said, it will be different. It will be eternal. We are coming to "an inheritance that is imperishable, undefiled, and unfading" (1 Peter 1.4). It is a "city that has foundations, whose designer and builder is God" (Hebrews 11.10b).

Prayer: Lord, I know that creation, as we know it, is on a timer. One day - however far in the future, only you know - this world will pass away. Help me to live my life so that I go to dwell in that new place with you forever and ever. Amen.

Psalm of the Day: 110.5-7

For the Healing of Nations
Daily Reading: Revelation 22

The leaves of the tree were for the healing of the nations.
(Revelation 22.2b)

Devotional Thought: There is a lot of debate going on concerning the status of immigrants and refugees. Fear, prejudice, terrorism, and irreconcilable cultural differences have made for a much divided world. Though there is little agreement about the solutions to the problems, there is near universal consensus that the nations need healing. Sadly, as long as there is sin in the world, there will be wars and rumors of wars; there will be power struggles and oppression; there will be greed and exploitation.

But, there is coming a day when sin will be erased from our existence. We will live in a place of perfect beauty and love. We will be like Jesus, for we shall see him as he is! And, there will be a healing of the nations. That place is beautifully depicted in Revelation.

In the midst of the heavenly city, there will be the River of the Water of Life. On each side of that river, will be a tree. It is the Tree of Life. It shall bear fruit every month. There will never be any lack. In that place - delivered from want, from disease, from death, from separation, from sorrow - there will be perfect healing for the nations.

The word for nations indicates people who practice similar customs or common culture. All those customs and cultures will be perfectly blended together in heaven. We will not lose our identity, but we will rejoice together in the fact that Jesus can save a Spanish-speaking capitalist, as much as he can save an English-speaking socialist. Those who come from cultures subdued and formal, shall worship alongside those who are boisterous and informal. I believe that even Democrats and Republicans will get along in that place. What a work of healing!

Prayer: Lord, in the early history of humanity, you spread mankind apart through diverse languages and customs. But, the day is coming when we will all be united in worship at your feet. What a day that will be! Amen.

Psalm of the Day: 111.1-5

Dear Sir or Madam

Daily Reading: 1 Corinthians 1

> *To the church of God that is in Corinth, to those sanctified in Christ Jesus,*
> *called to be saints together with all those who in every place call upon*
> *the name of our Lord Jesus Christ, both their Lord and ours.*
> (1 Corinthians 1.2)

Devotional Thought: I recently heard a friend complain about a negative email: "And there was no, 'Hey, how ya doin?' or anything like that. It was just bang..." Most of us are turned off by - or simply turn off! - impersonal or contrived communication. I used to tell my staff members, "Whenever you communicate with somebody - even email or text - say something genuinely kind and personal. A simple salutation works wonders!"

Paul gave careful attention to his salutation to the Corinthians. With deliberate precision, Paul taught a lot of theology in these words, writing that Christians are to be...

- *In Corinth...* Paul's address immediately reminded the Corinthians that they were, indeed, in Corinth. As Christians, we must never lose sight of our surroundings! We are to be good neighbors and citizens.
- *In Christ Jesus...* Not just in Christ Jesus, but **sanctified** in Christ Jesus. The word sanctify simply means to make holy or set apart. While living in the world, remember who you are living for - Jesus!
- *In the Church...* They were in Corinth and in Christ **together**! Sainthood is not a solitary activity. As a matter of fact, when we try to be saints without the Church, we have only a whisper of the influence that Jesus intends for us. When people isolate themselves from the people of God, eventually they find that they are isolated from the company of God!
- *In prayer...* Paul 'accused' the Corinthians of calling upon the name of our Lord. Would that accusation stick with you? Would the evidence of your life convict you of being a woman or man of prayer? Food for thought!

Prayer: Thank you, Lord, that while I am in you, I am also in the church and in the world to make a positive difference! Help me, therefore, to be a person of great prayer and faith and obedience. Amen.

Psalm of the Day: 111.6-10

A Know-Nothing

Daily Reading: 1 Corinthians 2-3

For I decided to know nothing among you except Jesus Christ and him crucified. (1 Corinthians 2.2)

Devotional Thought: In the 1850's, the Know Nothing movement was born. Nativist, intolerant, and anti-Catholic, it began as a secret society. It later became a political party, but did not live long, dying out in 1860. Those who adopt those kinds of views, are destined to become not only know-nothings, but to become unknown as well.

Was Paul a know-nothing? He testified to the Corinthians that he "decided to know nothing... except Jesus Christ." Paul said that he did not depend on the effectiveness of human efforts - current methods of logic and debate. He didn't rely on his great learning and superior knowledge. None of that was good enough for Paul. He came preaching Jesus: Jesus in weakness, Jesus in death. It's not that the other things were without use and merit. It's just that they were not powerful enough, in and of themselves, for the all-inclusive message of the gospel. For Paul, the gospel of God was too important to depend on the methods of man.

So, in that sense, Paul was indeed a know-nothing, a know-nothing-but-Jesus! Paul's message was full of the Spirit and power! Lives were changed - brought from darkness to light, from death to life, from the power of Satan to God. They received a place among the holy ones of God!

Paul's know-nothing approach was not narrow-minded and exclusive, like the Know Nothings of the 1800's. No, it was so wide, so broad, that it included all people - Jews and Greeks, male and female, slave and free. Whosoever will may come!

What about you? Are you a know-nothing? A know-nothing-but-Jesus? That's the only way the power of God will rest upon you!

Prayer: Father, I know that you have a work for me to do, a life to live. Help me to set aside the methods of man for the gospel of God, so that Christ's power may rest on me. Amen.

Psalm of the Day: 112.1-5

Bluster or Blessing

Daily Reading: 1 Corinthians 4

> *The kingdom of God does not consist in talk but in power.*
> (1 Corinthians 4.20)

Devotional Thought: "Bluster, *n* - loudly boastful or threatening speech; syn.: babel, blare, cacophony, chatter, clamor, clangor, din, discordance, noise, racket, rattle, roar." (Webster's dictionary)

Looking at that definition, there is a lot of bluster these days, isn't there? But, the Bible says the Kingdom of God is not like that. The Kingdom is not bluster, but rather blessing.

It is tempting to make the Kingdom all about 'talk': preaching, debating, and winning arguments. That is bluster. Bluster theorizes about love, but lives to dominate. It talks about holiness, but lives under the dominion of sin. It talks a big game, but wilts under pressure. Bluster refuses to go out on a limb, to take risks or to make sacrifices. That's not the Kingdom way of doing things.

When the Kingdom of God is about power, things look different. By the power of the Spirit, we can love others without conditions. We are enabled to live holy and godly lives. We can stand for Jesus when we face opposition. We can testify, "In the name of Jesus rise up and walk." The Spirit gives us power to be generous, to live free from addictions, to forgive the sins of others. In power, we testify to the life and resurrection of Jesus. We love those not like us, and treat others with dignity and respect. We sacrifice our own personal comforts and causes for the sake of others.

I would rather operate *in* the power of the Kingdom, live *by* the power of the Holy Spirit - than to talk about it. How about you?

Prayer: Lord, thank you for making me a part of your Kingdom. Help me to live out this Kingdom life with power. Forgive me when my talk doesn't match my walk. In the name of Jesus, amen.

Psalm of the Day: 112.6-10

Dismissed without Prejudice

Daily Reading: 1 Corinthians 5-6

For what have I to do with judging outsiders? (1 Corinthians 5.12)

Devotional Thought: Recently, I found myself in court with an anxious family. It was for a preliminary hearing in a legal matter. After discussion with the prosecutor and the defendant's counsel, the judge dismissed the charges without prejudice. That sounds good, right? Prejudice is bad, so without prejudice is good, isn't it? Sadly, it doesn't work that way in court! After asking the prosecutor, we discovered that if a matter is dismissed without prejudice it can be brought up again. If it is dismissed with prejudice, then it can never again be re-filed. The judge had left the door open for judgment in the future!

In 1 Corinthians 5, Paul wrote about judging someone in the church vs. outside the church. Paul made it plain that, at this time, we can't judge outsiders. It's not that we can't say an action is wrong or right - for we have to be able to discern good from evil. But, we cannot condemn sinners. We dismiss their case without prejudice, leaving it up to God, whose ultimate judgment is in the future.

In the case of a human court, charges are dismissed without prejudice in order to give the state opportunity to build their case for prosecution. With God, however, just the opposite is true. The Bible says that God is not willing for any to perish, but for all to come to repentance. He dismisses without prejudice in order to give the *defense* time to build their case - for the lost soul to come to Jesus and have his or her sins forgiven! "Therefore do not pronounce judgment before the time, before the Lord comes, who will bring to light the things now hidden in darkness and will disclose the purposes of the heart" (1 Corinthians 4.5).

Amen!

Prayer: Thank you, Lord, that in your mercy you gave me opportunity to believe in Jesus, and to receive him as my Savior. Help me not to give up on anybody. May my loved ones and friends respond to you in the time of decision. Amen.

Psalm of the Day: 113.1-3

Do the Hard Work

Daily Reading: 1 Corinthians 7

But because of the temptation to sexual immorality. (1 Corinthians 7.2)

Devotional Thought: I got myself in trouble once... (Yeah, yeah, yeah... I hear you thinking, "Only once?") Well the one time that I'm thinking about, had to do with a young boy and his sister in the church fellowship hall. She was picking on him and he came crying to his mom. I happened to be sitting there and piled it on: "What? I thought you were a big boy! Be a man!" He went and hit his sister. "Whoa! I didn't mean that! Just man up and work it out..." Mom didn't buy it. She wasn't too happy with me.

I recently read an article about the demise of masculinity. The author - a female - bemoaned the fact that men were unwilling - or unable - to do the hard work of being a man. It seems that conversation and relationships are being surrendered by 'emasculated' males, cowed by the current climate of political correctness. Even intimacy is giving way to the three p's: porn, prostitution, and puppets! That's not healthy. It's neither good for men or women.

Paul wrote that intimate, monogamous relationships (marriages) are important, because of the temptation to sexual immorality. Being a man was not about having sex with as many partners as possible, or about surrendering sexual satisfaction. To Paul, being a man meant doing the hard work of remaining pure until marriage, and faithful within marriage. That sounds to me like doing the hard work of relationships.

What does it mean to be a man? Jesus, of course, was the perfect Man. His manhood was expressed by doing the hard work of laying down his life for his Bride - the Church. To be real men and women today, we need to do the hard work of relationships.

Prayer: Jesus, thank you for being the example of the perfect man. And, thank you for giving us the power to be the man or woman you created us to be. Help us to live into that potential! Amen.

Psalm of the Day: 113.4-9

Balancing Act
Daily Reading: 1 Corinthians 8-9

Thus, sinning against your brothers and wounding their conscience when it is weak, you sin against Christ. (1 Corinthians 8.12)

Devotional Thought: Paul spends much time in his letters convincing Jewish converts of their freedom from the law. It must have been extremely difficult for those devout, law-following Jews to grasp, that the grace offered to them by Jesus should replace their efforts to make peace with God through the law. But, Paul argues the other side of that scenario as well. Eating food offered to idols has no spiritual significance under the new covenant; however, believers should be aware that doing so could become a stumbling block to the weak, and should therefore abstain.

And so today, it also goes both ways. The Church is made up of people from all different backgrounds, ways of thinking, and deeply ingrained beliefs that are secondary in importance to the core beliefs of the saved. There is freedom in Christ, but we should never abuse that freedom or practice it in such a way that causes others to stumble. On the flip side, those who are legalistic should be careful to not impose their personal convictions upon all other believers.

How do we accomplish this balance, and for what purpose? The answer comes from Paul in chapter 9. "For though I am free from all, I have made myself a servant to all, that I might win more of them... I have become all things to all people, that by all means I might save some. I do it all for the sake of the gospel, that I may share with them in its blessings," (1 Cor. 9:19, 22-23). Who among us wants the guilt of causing another believer to stumble, or preventing a nonbeliever from coming to Christ? We should, like Paul, consider our personal freedom of lesser importance than sharing the gospel and all of its blessings.

Jenny

Prayer: Lord, help us to lay down our rights and our pride for the sake of making you known. Give us the discernment we need to know when we are laying a stumbling block for a brother or sister. Amen.

Psalm of the Day: 114.1-8

Thin Red Line

Daily Reading: 1 Corinthians 10

Do all to the glory of God. (1 Corinthians 10.31)

Devotional Thought: Recently, I saw an American flag with white and black stripes and a black field of white stars. Dissecting the center of the stripes was a thin red line. I was incensed! What have they done to "Old Glory?"

It wasn't until I got home that I looked up on the internet, "Black and white flag with a red line." My attitude immediately changed. I discovered that "Thin Red Line" is a thing. It is a symbol used by fire departments to show respect for firefighters injured or killed in the line of duty - whose sacrifice has glorified "Old Glory." How do they do that? They place their lives second to those they protect. The Thin Red Line depicts the last ounce of courage it takes to overcome fear in order to save lives. As I said, my attitude changed immediately.

The Apostle Paul challenged us to live with a "Thin Red Line" mentality: "So, whether you eat or drink, or whatever you do, do all to the glory of God... just as I try to please everyone in everything I do, not seeking my own advantage, but that of many, that they may be saved" (1 Corinthians 10.31, 33). As Christians, we are to place our lives second to those who are lost. That takes courage and confidence. That takes sacrifice and strength.

Is your life a "Thin Red Line"?

Prayer: Father, help me to have the mind of Christ who did "nothing from selfish ambition or conceit, but in humility counted others more significant than [himself]." Amen.

Psalm of the Day: 115.1-8

Convicted, not Condemned

Daily Reading: 1 Corinthians 11

> *When we are judged by the Lord, we are disciplined so that we may not be condemned.* (1 Corinthians 11.32)

Devotional Thought: I was taken aback recently when I heard two sports commentators talking about a particular quarterback's *campaign* for the Heisman. At first, I thought I had misunderstood, but as they spoke on, I realized that they were serious. There are actually campaigns to get people selected for Heisman voting! This quarterback and his coach welcomed people to enter into judgment on his performance, on his credibility as a Heisman candidate. They were begging for him to be judged!

That's a far cry from the direction in which our culture is moving. Instead of inviting judgment, the cry today is, "Don't judge me!" It has gotten to the place where we cannot deem one culture superior to another, or one lifestyle better than another. We are moving steadily in the direction of "anything goes."

But, is that a healthy mindset? Does such an attitude foster improvement, or does it contribute to indulgence? Does it lead to discipline and strength, or to decadence and stagnation?

Are judgment and discipline good only for the athlete? I think not, for Paul challenged the Corinthians to be more like the Heisman candidate *in their spiritual lives!* He asserted that being judged by the Lord was good for us, bringing us to a place of improvement and readiness. Further, Paul stated that when we lack judgment and discipline in our spiritual lives, we run the risk of being condemned! The word is actually a composite word meaning judged *against,* in other words condemned. The discipline of judgment prevents the condemnation of judgment.

Praise God for his soul-freeing discipline and judgment!

Prayer: Thank you, Lord, that you give me the Word and the Spirit to help me judge my attitudes and actions. May I willingly be disciplined by this judgment, so that I may escape condemnation. Amen.

Psalm of the Day: 115.9-13

Body and Soul
Daily Reading: 1 Corinthians 12-13

> *Now you are the body of Christ and individually members of it.*
> (1 Corinthians 12.27)

Devotional Thought: A few weeks ago, I found myself in a great place - Mackinac Island, MI. While there, I saw firsthand the truth of Paul's words: "Now you are the body of Christ and individually members of it." Each one of us enjoyed the trip as individuals, but we also enjoyed it as a family. Over the few days we were together, family members "took turns" being sick with a 24-hour bug. When one of us was sick, however, the others immediately did what was needed to make up the difference. Emily couldn't care for Ellis... We took up the slack. Amy couldn't oversee the schedule... We teamed up to make sure we kept moving through all the activities. The family and the family members had a great time!

Paul said that the Church is like that - both the team and the individual are important. The "you" who are "the body of Christ" is plural. That is the team, the family. The members are individuals. For the body to function, the plural and the singular have to be working together. The team needs all the members. The members need the team. And, sometimes compromise by individuals is necessary, so that the whole family can get the job done.

Christ said he would build his Church and the gates of Hades would not prevail against it. The Church will accomplish its mission - rescuing lost souls - together! But, how is he building this mission-accomplishing Church? What are the building blocks? Individual Christians! Without the individuals, the Church isn't being built. So, let's function as the body of Christ - many individuals working together for one mission.

Prayer: Thank you, Lord, that I am a member of the body, the Church of Jesus Christ! Help me to do my part, so that the Church may grow strong and accomplish her mission. All for the glory of God. Amen.

Psalm of the Day: 115.14-18

Clarion Call
Daily Reading: 1 Corinthians 14

> *And if the bugle gives an indistinct sound, who will get ready for battle?*
> (1 Corinthians 14.8)

Devotional Thought: One Christmas my daughter Jenny received the (dubious?) honor of playing the horse whinny in "Sleigh Ride." It was a very distinct and obvious sound - unmistakable. I was always so proud of her playing not only the whinny, but all the rest of her trumpet solos.

The trumpet is designed to give a clear and distinct sound. When blown correctly, it is unmistakable. Before the advent of radios, it was indispensable in military operations. A "clarion call" was used to rally the troops, to initiate action, to sound a cease-fire, and even to call for strategic retreat. A battle could be lost before it ever began, if the trumpet sounded an indistinct signal.

God - though a God of mystery - speaks clearly and decisively. And, when he speaks, things happen. We, like him, should be distinct. That was a concern that Paul had for the church in Corinth. Somehow or another, the church there had co-mingled the Spirit-inspired Pentecostal gift of 'earthly' languages, with a pagan practice of the day - speaking in unknown, ecstatic outbursts of 'heavenly' languages. Paul warned against the practice, equating it with "indistinct sounds", which were totally useless to "get ready for battle."

What the Church needed then and needs now is a "clarion call" - a brilliantly clear call to action. Selfishness and wickedness have multiplied in society and have infiltrated the Church, causing sickness and weakness that must be routed. But, if the preaching is unclear, if the message is indistinct, the battle will not even be engaged.

Let us be clear and distinct, sounding the trumpet of God's love!

Prayer: Lord, through your Word and through your prophets, may the trumpet sound! And, may my life be a clear and vibrant witness to the holiness and grace of God. Amen.

Psalm of the Day: 116.1-4

As a Matter of Fact...

Daily Reading: 1 Corinthians 15

But in fact Christ has been raised from the dead. (1 Corinthians 15.20a)

Devotional Thought: I love the 15th chapter of 1 Corinthians, where Paul establishes the fact of the resurrection along with other items of "first importance" - Christ died for our sins; Christ was buried; Christ appeared to many; Christ appeared to me; Christ changed me! All of this was predicated on the fact of the resurrection - Christ was raised on the third day. Without the resurrection, as a matter of fact, our faith is futile and we are to be pitied. But, in fact, Christ has been raised! Hallelujah!

As Paul wrote about the resurrection, he did not feel the need to offer verifiable historical proof because the resurrection was historically recent. Instead, Paul relied upon the reality of his own experience of the resurrected Christ, and upon the veracity of other witness who also experienced Christ. Is establishing the resurrection today any different? Two thousand years have passed since the resurrection, and historical facts can be blurred and skewed with the passage of time. But, what cannot be disputed is the experience of innumerable believers alive today who know the fact of the resurrection, because they have experienced the resurrected One. He has changed them.

The greatest proof of the resurrection today is the fact that those who believe in Christ have been changed. Lives wrecked and bound by sin, are healed and set free by grace. Live with confidence in that grace today. "Therefore, my beloved brothers, be steadfast, immovable, always abounding in the work of the Lord, knowing that in the Lord your labor is not in vain" (1 Corinthians 15.58).

Amen!

Prayer: Thank you, Lord, for the fact of the resurrection. May the same power that raised Jesus from death to life, enable me to live - fully live! - this new life of promise. And, may I be a living proof of the resurrection to others. Amen.

Psalm of the Day: 116.5-9

Open Door

Daily Reading: 1 Corinthians 16

A wide door for effective work has opened to me. (1 Corinthians 16.9)

Devotional Thought: Having built four houses in my life, I have discovered that I like wide doors. I designed the first one - in Concord, NC - with a double door in the walkout basement. I wanted to make sure that I could get my lawnmower and other equipment in and out. I needed a wide door for effective work. Wide doors make work more effective.

The Apostle Paul knew that. He explained his delay to the Corinthians, by pointing out a wide open door for effective work in Ephesus. Consider...

- *The door.* Jesus Christ, of course, is the Door! As we seek to do effective work, we must remember that all work done for him must be done through him! If we try to work without him, we will be like the seven sons of Sceva in Acts 19, who failed terribly.
- *The work.* What was Paul's work in Ephesus? Acts 19, reveals that people were coming to faith and learning to live their faith. In short, Paul was making disciples!
- *The opener.* Paul was always busy, always seeking what to do next, but his work was not aimless. The Spirit guided him. In our work, we must walk by the Spirit, or we will only be fulfilling our interests.
- *The worker.* While Paul knew he must do the work of Jesus by the power of the Spirit, he also knew that he himself had to do the work. The wide door was opened for him.
- *The adversaries.* Paul did not let opposition turn him away. Instead, he found that adversaries could spur him forward in his work. We must adopt the same mindset, or we will grow weary in doing good.

Prayer: Lord, help me to go through the door, by the power of the Spirit, to do the work that you have given me. Guide me and grow my effectiveness, O Lord, as I trust in you. Amen.

Psalm of the Day: 116.10-14

Are You Comfortable?

Daily Reading: 2 Corinthians 1

> Blessed be the God and Father of our Lord Jesus Christ, the Father of mercies and God of all comfort, who comforts us in all our affliction, so that we may be able to comfort those who are in any affliction...
> (2 Corinthians 1.3-4)

Devotional Thought: In Paul's second letter to the church in Corinth, he reminds the believers of the comfort given to them by God the Father, the Father of mercies and God of all comfort. This word "comfort" in the original Greek, was written as "paraklēsis." Since Paul uses the word so much in the opening of this letter, it is good for us to consider its original meaning.

We sometimes have a negative connotation with the word "comfort" in our Christian walk, as it implies that we are not leaving our "comfort zone" to do the necessary work of spreading the gospel. Used in this context, that is certainly right. We should be bold for Christ, and at times (often), that is uncomfortable. However, Paul is using a Greek word with a broader meaning than what we normally associate with comfort. Paraklēsis is a calling alongside, for exhortation, strong appeal, and consolation.

The early church was not comfortable by any definition! They faced persecution, dissent, and false teaching. They needed each other for mutual encouragement and consolation, because they were facing suffering and afflictions on a daily basis. They needed reminders of who their Comforter was, and his ability to comfort those in any affliction. During our times of suffering, we are called alongside other believers, to receive consolation, but also exhortation. This has a grander purpose, "so that we may be able to comfort those who are in any affliction, with the comfort with which we ourselves are comforted by God," (v.4). Even though life is sometimes uncomfortable, we can rest in full assurance that "it is God who establishes us with you in Christ... and who has also put his seal on us and given us his Spirit in our hearts as a guarantee" (vv. 21-22).

Jenny

Prayer: Lord, give us hope and joy as we face suffering. In our own times of comfort, give us the strength of character to reach out and be a comfort to others who are suffering. Thank you for your Spirit, whom you have put in our hearts as a guarantee! Amen.

Psalm of the Day: 116.15-19

The Best Kind of Boldness

Daily Reading: 2 Corinthians 2-3

Since we have such a hope, we are very bold. (2 Corinthians 3.12)

Devotional Thought: In hospitals, I am somewhat cautious about closed doors. I pay attention to signs and respect the wishes of the hospital staff. Some pastors I know are bolder than I am, thinking they have special privileges as ministers. In one hospital I was visiting, I decided to be bold and take the stairs, ignoring the signs that said emergency exit only. I found myself stuck in the stairwell! I went up and down the stairs to various floors. All the doors were locked - even the floor from which I had entered! My only option was the emergency exit. So, I pushed open the door, set off the alarm, and found myself outside in the rain! I didn't hang around long, though, knowing that soon someone would be coming to see who had boldly ignored the signs!

I learned a lesson that day. Boldness can be good, but it must be grounded upon good facts! I was mistakenly bold!

As Christians, we can be very bold because in Jesus "we have such a hope." On what good facts do we ground this hope and boldness? Paul reveals the source of his boldness and ours, too: "Such is the confidence that we have through Christ toward God. Not that we are sufficient in ourselves to claim anything as coming from us, but our sufficiency is from God, who has made us sufficient..." (2 Corinthians 3.4-6a).

Boldness that is based upon Jesus - not upon our own sufficiency - is the right kind of boldness to have. It may not push open all the doors of the world, but it will push open the doors of heaven, bringing us into the presence of God!

Prayer: Thank you, Lord Jesus, for giving me boldness to come into the presence of the Father. Help me always to base my boldness, my confidence, and my hope upon you. Amen.

Psalm of the Day: 117.1-2

The Worst Kind of Blindness

Daily Reading: 2 Corinthians 4-5

The god of this world has blinded the minds of the unbelievers.
(2 Corinthians 4.4)

Devotional Thought: Have you ever been in a situation, when you couldn't see because of what you saw? My friend, Dale, had that experience recently. While driving, he was suddenly 'blinded' by a downpour. He could 'see' well enough, but all he could see was the rain on his windshield! Blinded, he cautiously moved to the shoulder, only to get a little too close to the guardrail! He told me the other day, how he misses that car!

Satan works that way in our lives. Paul wrote, that the god of this world blinds the minds of unbelievers. Satan pours it on heavier than a summer downpour!

What are some of the things that Satan uses to blind unbelievers, and sometimes even believers?
- Power: We all operate under the delusion of self-sovereignty. We want to be in control, and Satan frightens us with a distorted view of God as an oppressor.
- Passion: There are some things that are dear to us, but we know are inconsistent with the Christian lifestyle. Satan reminds us of those things.
- Pride: It has become acceptable to denigrate Christians as intolerant and ignorant. Satan tells us that if we follow Christ, we will be labeled as such.
- Popularity: "I'll lose my drinking buddies!" Satan tells us that if we follow Christ, we won't have any friends.
- Parody: The world has a distorted view of what being a Christian is. Sadly, that view is promulgated by some believers - even ministers! Satan tells us we will turn into mean-spirited bigots if we follow Jesus.

In Jesus, however, we have the ability to see through the lies of Satan. Better than wipers and Rainex(R), Jesus clears our vision when we look to him.

Prayer: Lord, I know that Satan is the father of all lies. Help me to see through all the lies he tells me, and help my friends and family, who don't know you yet, to see clearly your great love and grace. Amen.

Psalm of the Day: 118.1-4

Two Forms of ID
Daily Reading: 2 Corinthians 6-7

> *As servants of God we commend ourselves in every way.*
> (2 Corinthians 6.4)

Devotional Thought: Recently, I opened an account for Momentum Ministries. The instructions were to bring "two forms of ID" - a government-issued ID and a credit card. The bank wanted to make sure I was who I said I was. I didn't mind. It would be terrible to have somebody doing business in my name without my permission!

When I make prison or jail visits, I have to be able to verify my ID - and to demonstrate that I am a minister. I am not offended by that; it's just a part of modern ministry.

The Apostle Paul had no such ID. His life was his ID. His work and faithfulness, his love and holy living, his sacrifice and suffering for Christ - these were what validated his ministry: "As servants of God we commend ourselves in every way: by great endurance, in afflictions, hardships, calamities, beatings, imprisonments, riots, labors, sleepless nights, hunger; by purity, knowledge, patience, kindness, the Holy Spirit, genuine love; by truthful speech, and the power of God; with the weapons of righteousness for the right hand and for the left; through honor and dishonor, through slander and praise. We are treated as impostors, and yet are true; as unknown, and yet well known; as dying, and behold, we live; as punished, and yet not killed; as sorrowful, yet always rejoicing; as poor, yet making many rich; as having nothing, yet possessing everything" (2 Corinthians 6.4-10).

How are you commending yourself? To do the business of living for Christ, we need to commend ourselves in the way that Paul did. Better yet, we must do so in the way that Jesus did - emptying himself and becoming a servant (Philippians 2).

Prayer: Lord, help this mind be in me which was also in you - to empty myself of privilege and pride and to take on the nature of a servant. In that way, may I commend myself to you and those around me. Amen.

Psalm of the Day: 118.5-9

The King's Gone Wild!

Daily Reading: 2 Corinthians 8-9

So now finish doing it as well, so that your readiness in desiring it may be matched by your completing it out of what you have.
(2 Corinthians 8.11)

Devotional Thought: My family and I have recently taken up a game called 5 Crowns. As you work through the 5 suited cards, each number becomes wild, until finally the kings - the highest cards in the game - are wild. The catch phrase for the game is, "It's not over until the kings go wild!"

Paul told that to the Corinthians. He was concerned that the Corinthians were talking a good game, but not following through with the requisite action. He had already told them in his first letter that "The kingdom of God does not consist in talk but in power" (1 Corinthians 4.20). Paul, once again, needed to remind them that talk was cheap, but faithfulness was costly. Intentions were nice, but completion was necessary.

The Corinthians had made a big promise to help out the saints in Jerusalem, as they weathered a famine coupled with persecution. In all likelihood, the promise was made with much fanfare. That's the way the Corinthians liked to operate. The time for helping had come and gone, however, and Paul had to remind them of their former pledge: "It's not over until you actually do it. It's not over until King Jesus has gone 'wild' in your life."

Are there things in your life that you were ready - at one time - to do, but that have now been put on the back burner? Are there promises you have made to Jesus? Is there service you have meant to perform for the church? Are there character traits you have pledged to change for the better? Frankly, until Jesus fully reigns in your life, you will probably not get past the talking stage.

Has the King gone wild in your life?

Prayer: King Jesus, forgive me for having big intentions with small follow-through. I now surrender my life to you completely. "Go wild" in my life, Lord, taking control of every action, as well as every intention. Amen.

Psalm of the Day: 118.10-13

No Need to Get Pushy!

Daily Reading: 2 Corinthians 10

I, Paul, myself entreat you, by the meekness and gentleness of Christ.
(2 Corinthians 10.1a)

Devotional Thought: Have you seen the videos of Tokyo commuters boarding a train? They are literally stuffed in by conductors along the boarding platform! Those conductors certainly can't be meek, can they? They just have to put their hands on the boarding passengers - wherever and however they can - and push! My Western notion of personal space, wouldn't last through one train ride!

Paul was not a Japanese conductor, as he helped the Corinthians board the "gospel train." Instead of pushing and shoving, he used meekness and gentleness. Where did he learn that? Jesus!

Paul had already told the Corinthians, that the Kingdom of God did not consist in talk, but in power. But, the kind of power that works in the Kingdom is not forceful, vengeful, or manipulative. Jesus came, he said, not to force others to serve him, but rather he came to serve them. He laid down his life, in apparent weakness that brought about the power of the Kingdom. His sacrificial death made possible his powerful resurrection. Assured of this, Jesus did not feel compelled to force his will upon anybody. He presented the love of God and allowed people to choose for themselves. It is true that he reprimanded the Pharisees and expelled the profiteers, but even in those instances, Jesus showed great restraint. After all, he could have called twelve legions of angels to come to his aid! (See Matthew 26.53)

So much of what is passed off as discourse today - even Christian discourse - is really mean-spirited attempts at shaming and control. But, like Jesus, Paul entreated with gentleness and meekness. How about you?

Prayer: Thank you, Lord, that as a father has compassion on his children, so you have compassion on those who fear you. Help me to have that same compassion, showing gentleness and meekness to others. Amen.

Psalm of the Day: 118.14-18

Counterfeit Light

Daily Reading: 2 Corinthians 11

Even Satan disguises himself as an angel of light. (2 Corinthians 11.14)

Devotional Thought: And, it's only the midterms... I keep hearing myself say that. There is so much noise in the political arena these days. If you believed everything you heard or read, your head would be spinning. Each politician and each pundit, however, avers that they are telling the truth - not just the truth, but the truth that could save America, the light that could change the course of history! Credulity is stretched to the limit. Do you ever get tired of it?

It's nothing new. As Paul reminds us, Satan has been doing that very thing for as long as he's been in business. Satan is the proper name derived from the word meaning adversary, or accuser. Satan is our adversary, but he knows that we would resist him if he presented himself as an enemy. So, he cloaks his lies in light.

Disguising himself as an angel and his message as light, Satan spreads lies and fear and false confidence. Sometimes he works with impressions / suggestions to deter us. Sometimes he uses memories - true ones and false ones - to deceive us. At other times he uses people - some very well-intentioned - to discourage us. At all times he is working to "lead astray, if possible, even the elect" (Matthew 24.24). I am getting tired of it.

But, thanks be to God - we have "the word of faith" (Romans 10.8), for God "has shone in our hearts to give the light of the knowledge of the glory of God in the face of Jesus Christ" (2 Corinthians 4.6). When you grow weary and suspicious of all you see on the news, look for "the light [that] shines in the darkness" for "the darkness has not overcome it" (John 1.5).

Prayer: Thank you, Lord Jesus, that you are the true Light for all. Help me to recognize and reject the counterfeit light that Satan casts to shadow the real truth. Amen.

Psalm of the Day: 118.19-24

Enough Is Enough
Daily Reading: 2 Corinthians 12-13

> But he said to me, "My grace is sufficient for you, for my power is made perfect in weakness." Therefore I will boast all the more gladly of my weaknesses, so that the power of Christ may rest upon me.
> (2 Corinthians 12.9)

Devotional Thought: Paul had a "thorn in the flesh." While we do not know what this was specifically, most scholars agree that it is likely either Paul's struggle with temptation and the flesh, or a physical, chronic infirmity that pained him. The exact nature of his thorn in the flesh is unimportant, but of utmost importance is the contentedness with which Paul lives with his struggle. He pleads with the Lord to remove the thorn, but accepts and even embraces God's response, even when it is not that for which he had prayed.

When we think about this, it is truly amazing. How many of us are content with weaknesses, insults, hardships, persecutions, and calamities? Paul sees past the here-and-now to the bigger picture: it is through our weaknesses that God's power is made perfect in us. Paul had a better goal than his own comfort, satisfaction, good-standing, and agenda. His ultimate goal was to showcase God's glory! He is not the first man of God to desire this above all else. Moses was a man of self-admitted weakness, and God chose him to lead the Israelites out of Egyptian slavery to freedom. He had his own thorns, but he consistently pursued God above all else. "Please show me your glory" (Exodus 33.18).

We, too, have thorns. As Christians we are called to share in Christ's sufferings (1 Peter 4.13). We can do so with a constant attitude of self-pity, bringing no glory to God, or we can do so with an expectation that in our weaknesses the power, majesty and glory of God will shine forth.

Jenny

Prayer: Lord, help us to be content when we face suffering, persecution, and difficulties. Use us to showcase your glory and win others to your Kingdom! Amen.

Psalm of the Day: 118.25-29

Anointed with the Spirit

Daily Reading: 1 Kings 1

> *There Zadok the priest took the horn of oil from the tent and anointed Solomon.* (1 Kings 1.39)

Devotional Thought: The Books of First and Second Kings tell the history of Israel from the time of King Solomon to the beginning of the Babylonian captivity. At times the story is glorious, and at other times the rulers and the people commit shameful idolatry and immorality.

The story begins on a hopeful note. Even though somewhat turbulent, Solomon's ascension to the throne avoided the violence that often accompanied such "contested" transitions. King Solomon, the son of David, was anointed as king in his father's place, before David's death. That anointing by the priest put to rest all questions about who was to be the king. When David died, "Solomon sat on the throne of David his father, and his kingdom was firmly established" (1 Kings 2.12).

In the New Testament, we read that "It is God who establishes us with you in Christ, and has anointed us, and who has also put his seal on us and given us his Spirit in our hearts as a guarantee" (2 Corinthians 1.21-22). Jesus, our great High Priest (Hebrews 4.14), has anointed us with the Spirit. We have been anointed as sons and daughters of the King! That had been prophesied in Joel, and first happened in the book of Acts at Pentecost when God poured out the Spirit on the Church.

The Bible says that we are a *royal* priesthood, that we shall *reign* with Jesus, and that it is God's pleasure to give us the *Kingdom*. All questions about that promise have been put to rest by God anointing us with his Spirit!

Prayer: Thank you, Jesus, our great High Priest, for anointing us with the Spirit! Amen.

Psalm of the Day: 119.1-8

Show Yourself a Man
Daily Reading: 1 Kings 2

I am about to go the way of all the earth. Be strong, and show yourself a man. (1 Kings 2.2)

Devotional Thought: Did your mother or father give their final message to you, expressing their desires for you and your future before their passing? If so, are those words still clear in your memory? More than 40 years ago, I was with my father who was in the hospital waiting to go to heart bypass surgery. That surgery was not as common then as it is now. I was alone with him in his room and he said, "If I don't make it, I'll see you in heaven." I have never forgotten those words after all these years. You can find many heartwarming stories of a father's final words for their son or daughter, giving their advice for doing the right things and avoiding the mistakes they may have made.

David said to his son, "Be thou strong, therefore, and show thyself a man" (v. 2, *KJV*). David knew that Solomon could not be strong or courageous without obedient fellowship with God. A second mark of manhood that David taught Solomon is wisdom. The fear of God is the beginning of knowledge and wisdom (Proverbs 1.7). David taught Solomon to seek wisdom as if it were silver (Proverbs 2.1-9). A third mark of manhood is saintliness. A saint is one who lives unto God, and in whom God's will is law. "Observe the requirements of the Lord your God, and follow all his ways" (v. 3).

If you have or had an earthly father who offers spiritual guidance, thank God. But, if not, remember that you have a Heavenly Father – a Father to the fatherless (Psalm 68.5).

Pastor Dale

Prayer: Thank you, Father, that you are a Father to the fatherless. Help me to live according to your wisdom and show myself to be a man or woman of God. In the name of your Son Jesus I pray. Amen.

Psalm of the Day: 119.9-16

Pray for an Understanding Mind
Daily Reading: 1 Kings 3

Give your servant therefore an understanding mind to govern your people, that I may discern between good and evil, for who is able to govern this your great people? (1 Kings 3.9)

Devotional Thought: Isn't it amazing that the God of the universe saw Solomon's faithfulness, and asked him specifically about his heart's desires? This testifies to the fact that God cares about your every desire! What is shocking is that Solomon didn't ask to be rich or healthy, but he asked for wisdom. As a young ruler, he needed discernment to help him rule effectively.

When I was younger, my consistent prayer was to have a heart like David's, a man after God's own heart. "God, give me wisdom," is my go-to prayer these days, because life is uncertain. I would rather have a peaceful heart full of wisdom than one full of anxiety.

Let's examine Solomon's life:
- He was young – He understood his life's limitations. Solomon needed help because he was guiding people that came from different backgrounds.
- He recognized God's majesty – He saw himself as God's servant. He knew that God was all-knowing, so that God could help him with the uncertainties of life.
- He realized the importance of his job – Solomon took his job seriously! Since Solomon was leading God's people, he had a great responsibility.

Solomon needed supernatural wisdom to govern the people correctly. Just like Solomon, we all need God to give us wisdom, even with the small things. I challenge you to be like Solomon and pray, "God, give me wisdom!" You will be amazed how he answers your prayer!

Pastor Amber

Prayer: Lord, grant that I would have an understanding mind that I may discern between good and evil and live pleasing to you. Amen.

Psalm of the Day: 119.17-24

Surpassing Wisdom
Daily Reading: 1 Kings 4

> And God gave Solomon wisdom and understanding beyond measure, and breadth of mind like the sand on the seashore, so that Solomon's wisdom surpassed the wisdom of all the people of the east and all the wisdom of Egypt. (1 Kings 4.29-30)

Devotional Thought: "How did Solomon get so rich? Was he just a "lucky guy"? Did he follow some get rich quick plan? The answer to this is that Solomon was wise. He knew how to deal with people. He knew how to make sound financial decisions. "God gave Solomon wisdom and very great insight, and a breadth of understanding as measureless as the sand on the seashore" (1 Kings 4.29).

The reason God gave Solomon wisdom, is because he asked for it. Earlier in the life of Solomon, we know that Solomon was given a choice. God offered him whatever he needed to be the best king he could be. He could have asked for riches, he could have asked for peace from war, but instead he asked God for wisdom to rule the people he had been given (2 Chronicles 1.11-12).

God values wisdom. He wants us to make wise choices. He wants us to ask for wisdom as well. We need God's wisdom if we are to navigate the waters of this life. If you are facing a decision today, ask God for wisdom, he promises to give it to you. This is one subject that the Bible is very clear about. "If any of you lacks wisdom, you should ask God, who gives generously to all without finding fault, and it will be given to you" (James 1.5). So, the next time you are in a quandary about what to do, go to the Lord in prayer, read your Bible, talk to a trusted friend or pastor, but most of all trust that God will give you the wisdom you need for all the problems and decisions you face.

Pastor Cheryl

Prayer: Lord, I do not ask that my wisdom surpass the wisdom of all the people of the east, but I do ask that you would give me all the wisdom I need to follow and serve you. And, in the process, may I bring you glory! Amen.

Psalm of the Day: 119.25-32

You Can't Always Get What You Want

Daily Reading: 1 Kings 5

> David my father could not build a house for the name of the Lord his God because of the warfare with which his enemies surrounded him. (1 Kings 5.3)

Devotional Thought: I love my grandchildren! They are so fun and expressive. One of the youngest ones is learning a hard lesson: he can't always get what he wants. Believe me when I say, this is not a pleasant lesson for him to learn. He has unique and loud ways to show he doesn't approve of that concept! It's not pleasant for me, either, because I want to give him what he wants! Mommy is watching me pretty closely, though!

King David found out that he couldn't always get what he wanted, either. When he told God he wanted to build a house of worship, God told him, "No." God had other things for him to do. David had to strengthen national security and to bring peace, so that Solomon could build the house.

What are some reasons we shouldn't get what we want?
- We may not know it, but what we want may be bad for us. Would David have been more susceptible to pride and arrogance? Would he have focused on the wrong thing in regards to worship?
- What we want may belong to someone else. God had given Solomon the privilege of building a house of worship.
- Getting what we want could prevent us from getting what we need. Had David gotten what he wanted, resources and oversight may have been stretched too thin to turn away an enemy attack.
- The timing isn't right. The nation was not ready for a project such as David wanted to do. They needed the unity that would come with Solomon's reign.

The next time you don't get what you want, thank God!

Prayer: Thank you, Lord of Creation, that you see all things, and you know what I really need. When I don't get what I want, help me to trust you to give me what I need. Amen.

Psalm of the Day: 119.33-40

304

Finally

Daily Reading: 1 Kings 6

In the four hundred and eightieth year after the people of Israel came out of the land of Egypt ... he began to build the house of the Lord. (1 Kings 6.1)

Devotional Thought: The house was purchased. Another house was sold. The move was completed. The "higher priority projects" (Remember, when momma ain't happy, ain't nobody happy!) were done. The materials were acquired. Finally, I could start the work on my study. Finally, I could unpack my books. I was so excited!

I imagine King Solomon felt a similar excitement. Four hundred seventy-nine years had passed since Israel had left Egypt. Funds had been raised. His reign had been established. Materials had been purchased, delivered, paid for, and prepped. Finally, "he began to build the house of the Lord."

Waiting is never easy, is it? It's especially difficult when we are waiting on God, who, we figure, could do things instantly if he wanted to. Frustration is just beneath the surface. If we're not careful, our impatience can bubble over in bad decisions or even in giving up. It takes faith and discipline to wait on God's solution in God's timing.

But, that's not the end of it. Solomon found out that when God brings the wait to an end, it is often just the beginning of the next phase. The temple took seven years to build!

What are you waiting on? Trust in God. See the wonder of how he brings all things together. Seek answers to deeper questions. Share your confidence with others who wait with you. And *finally*, he will bring it to pass.

"They who wait for the Lord shall renew their strength; they shall mount up with wings like eagles; they shall run and not be weary; they shall walk and not faint" (Isaiah 40.31).

Prayer: Lord, I confess that my patience has often worn thin. Forgive me. I admit that waiting is hard. Help me. I turn to you now to renew my strength in the midst of this present delay. Amen.

Psalm of the Day: 119.41-48

Build It Right!

Daily Reading: 1 Kings 7

> *The foundation was of costly stones, huge stones...* (1 Kings 7.10)

Devotional Thought: At the start of our first assignment on the mission field, our supervisor gave us a challenge I will never forget. He challenged us, whatever we built in ministry, to lay a strong foundation, and to build it right the first time. When you are a new missionary, these two goals seem elusive. Some things you learn as you go. Other times you have false starts. Some things you wish you could build over again. But, I think there is wisdom in his challenge. Whenever we do the Lord's work or any work, we must take adequate time to pray, study, and prepare, so that what we build is healthy, strong, and can stand the test of time and challenges of life.

Solomon did not skimp on his building materials. The foundation laid for the temple was built using "costly stones, huge stones." Maybe to us, it seems excessive or exorbitant to use such pricey and robust building materials. To Solomon, it did not. He built the temple to last, to stand the ravages of weather and time. The foundation was strong, and the temple was built right the first time.

What kind of foundations are we laying in our lives? On what kind of values are we building our families and churches? Are we building it right the first time, as best we know how, by the wisdom and direction of God's Spirit, God's Word and godly counsel? Will the foundations we are laying, the work we are doing for the Lord, stand the test of time and challenges of life? Or, are we cutting corners, tossing in hollow, empty values, and other "filler" that won't last?

Costly Stones. Huge Stones. Christ Jesus. Kingdom Values. Let's build with these and build it right.

Pastor Joe Young

Prayer: Lord, help me to build on the foundation of Jesus Christ, using gold, silver, and precious stones - so that my work will survive. In Jesus' name I do pray. Amen.

Psalm of the Day: 119.49-56

You Are That Temple

Daily Reading: 1 Kings 8

That all the peoples of the earth may know that the Lord is God; there is no other. (1 Kings 8.60)

Devotional Thought: In 1 Kings 8, Solomon dedicates the temple he built for the Lord. It is a grand proceeding of a vast assembly celebrating the majestic temple, with sacrifices beyond number.

Look at Solomon's blessing in verses 56-61. He praises God for keeping all his promises, and he entreats God to help keep the people's hearts turned towards God. This is a natural, valid, and vital request. In verses 22-53, Solomon runs through a laundry list of sins the people will commit. And sure enough, they do. But, Solomon, being wise, asks God's forgiveness, "if" the people will turn their hearts back to God. In fact, Solomon's prayer doesn't ask God to forgive, but makes several statements that God will forgive, if we honor the "if" clause.

But, my biggest take away from chapter 8, is reverence for the temple. The temple is so important to God that he calls it his own. In fact, he fills the temple with his glory (vv. 10-11). The filling is so visible that the priests are not able to complete their service within it. How awesome!

It's elementary, but sometimes I need to remind myself of what the temple really is. In the words of the Apostle Paul, "You are that temple" (1 Corinthians 3.17).

John Wade

Prayer: Thank you, Lord Jesus, for building me - a living stone - into the temple of God, which is the Church. Help me to honor you and your body in my words and actions. Amen.

Psalm of the Day: 119.57-64

Finish the House

Daily Reading: 1 Kings 9

Three times a year Solomon used to offer up burnt offerings and peace offerings on the altar that he built to the Lord, making offerings with it before the Lord. So he finished the house. (1 Kings 9.25)

Devotional Thought: "So he finished the house." Solomon's work on the house of God was not completed with the construction. Finishing the temple meant using it according to the divine plan. He had to use the house of God for proper worship. The Law prescribed that the men of Israel were to appear before the Lord in Jerusalem three times a year, bringing their sacrifices. That included the King, too. Solomon was careful to observe that.

Lana and I have been blessed to have built several houses in our lifetime. Each time we have finished the construction, there was one more thing to be done. We needed to move in – to live, to love, and to laugh within those walls. Would those houses ever have been truly finished if we had failed to do that?

Consider for a moment how you and I are to "finish the house." Being saved is but the beginning of the story. We are to faithfully worship the Lord and serve him. There is a life to live, a life of obedience to God. How many Christians I have seen that do not go on and "finish the house." They ask God to forgive them and receive them into his family, but they never faithfully serve him. They never move in. The house isn't occupied! And so, it isn't finished!

Sadly, the historian wrote that "Solomon *used to* offer up..." The manner of his writing indicated that at some point Solomon stopped using the house of God for proper worship. You see, the "finishing" of our spiritual houses is a lifetime event. We must never stop living, loving and laughing in the house of God!

Prayer: Lord, I'm so glad that you are building the Church, and that you have included me. Help me to "finish the house" by "moving in" completely - and living there day by day. Amen.

Psalm of the Day: 119.65-72

Concerning the Name of the Lord
Daily Reading: 1 Kings 10

> *Now when the queen of Sheba heard of the fame of Solomon concerning the name of the Lord, she came to test him with hard questions.*
> (1 Kings 10.1)

Devotional Thought: My granddaughter, Annabelle, is a very, very persistent questioner. If I don't answer a particular question to her liking, she will ask it again in a different form. I've never been able to "take her breath away" - to cause her to stop asking questions. She is the Queen of Questions.

King Solomon's wisdom was known far and wide. People came to him for answers. The Queen of Sheba tested Solomon with questions. Put on the spot, how did he do? The Bible says that "Solomon answered all her questions, there was nothing hidden from the king that he could not explain to her ... There was no more breath in her" (1 Kings 10.3, 5).

The Queen of Sheba was a very wealthy, powerful, and intelligent woman. It would take a lot to take her breath away. But, that's what happened. How was Solomon able to do that?

The answer lies in the line of questioning: "the fame of Solomon concerning the name of the Lord." Though the Bible paints a very flattering picture of Solomon's knowledge and wisdom, I'm sure that he didn't literally know the answer to every question she could have asked. What he did know the answer to, however, were all her questions "concerning the name of the Lord." In other words, Solomon knew all about God, because Solomon knew God.

People have hard questions for the believer. This is true in times of large scale crises (such as the COVID19 pandemic of 2020), but it is also true in times of personal crises (such as death, illness, unemployment). We may not have the answers to all their questions, but we can be ready to answer their questions "concerning the name of the Lord."

Prayer: Lord, help me to be ready to answer questions concerning your name. As you admonish me in 1 Peter 3.15, may I be ready to give "the reason for the hope" I have within me. Amen.

Psalm of the Day: 119.73-80

Adversaries

Daily Reading: 1 Kings 11

And the Lord raised up an adversary against Solomon. (1 Kings 11.14)

Devotional Thought: God had given Solomon wisdom and success. Yet at the end of his life, his ambition outpaced his humility. He turned away from God. God raised up three adversaries against him:

- Hadad the Edomite (v. 14): a defeated foe who escaped the control of Solomon and fled to Egypt. His name means "mighty." After laying low for several years, Hadad rose up to give Solomon problems. There are times that our adversaries are things from our past that we have not properly dealt with. Those things come up to vex us.
- Rezon of Damascus (v. 23): a foreigner who was a source of constant irritation to Israel. His name means "prince" and indicates one who has a commanding presence. Perhaps we could call this a "besetting sin." Our chief adversary, Satan, exploits our weaknesses. We must be constantly vigilant, in order to defeat those unique temptations which constantly assail us.
- Jeroboam the Ephraimite (v. 26): a brother Israelite and gifted leader, who had once been a favored officer in Solomon's administration. Solomon, however, did not know how to share leadership with him. It's interesting that Jeroboam's name means, "the people will contend." For later, when Rehoboam, son of Solomon, refused to seek the partnership of his fellow countrymen, they contended against him. Does that happen in the church? Yes! We need to work together and learn to share leadership.

It's instructive that the Bible says that "God raised up" these adversaries against Solomon. As such, these adversaries were meant to turn Solomon back to God. When we face "adversity," God intends it to turn us back to him. Do you have adversaries? Allow them to turn your heart to God.

Prayer: Lord, too often I am impatient with adversaries. I want to move them out of the way. Help me to step back in adversity and ask, "God, how can I turn toward you in this time?" Amen.

Psalm of the Day: 119.81-88

Get Your Facts Straight

Daily Reading: 1 Timothy 1-2

Without understanding either what they are saying or the things about which they make confident assertions. (1 Timothy 1.7)

Devotional Thought: You've seen them. You've heard them. Sometimes, you've even been them! You know... the people who talk like they know what they are saying and who really have no clue! I remember many years ago, before Lana and I were married, that we attended a hockey game together. Lana's a football girl, so when they announced an offside penalty, she didn't really get it. She asked me what it meant. Trying my best to impress her, I explained in detail - with great confidence and gusto - just what it meant to be offsides. The trouble is, I gave her the definition of a soccer offside penalty. I was mortified when the gentlemen in front of us turned around and corrected me... in front of my girlfriend!

Paul warned Pastor Timothy about people who would talk a big game, but have no idea what they were saying. They do so because they...

- Have false confidence. Some people place their confidence in their own forcefulness or persuasiveness. Instead of placing their confidence in God, their pride drives them to be right - even if they're wrong. And usually, the more they are wrong, the more they assert their position.
- Don't know the facts. If we are going to speak about God (that's theology - God talk), shouldn't we get our facts from him? Today, many people are saying things that simply are not biblically sound. We need to be like the Old Testament scribe Ezra, who "set his heart to study the Law of the Lord, and to do it and to teach his statutes and rules in Israel" (Ezra 7.10).

So, when you talk about God, make sure you understand what you are saying! There's no substitute for studying the Word of God!

Prayer: Lord, may my wisdom and my confidence be based upon your Word. Help me to "Do [my] best to present [my]self to God as one approved, a worker who has no need to be ashamed, rightly handling the word of truth." Amen. (2 Timothy 2.15)

Psalm of the Day: 119.89-96

Manage Your Mess
Daily Reading: 1 Timothy 3-4

If someone does not know how to manage his own household, how will he care for God's church? (1 Timothy 3.5)

Devotional Thought: A Christian must not only master the Word of God, he or she must master themselves. I have known many ministers who have torpedoed their effectiveness because they or their families were poorly managed. Minister's families are not perfect - there are many biblical examples of that - but a leader of God's people must manage their own household - even if their family is not Christian. Yes, it often looks a lot like "damage control," but the child of the Lord, must consistently do his/her best.

So, how does one manage his/her household well? The following verses tell us...

- Our relationships must be under the Lordship of Christ. While you cannot choose your family, you can choose your friends. Our friendships - and that of our minor children - have a great impact on our spiritual lives.
- Our finances are to bring glory to God. Do you honor God with your tithe and offerings? Are you generous toward others in need? Are you over-worked in order to get rich? Are you in debt and unable to pay your bills? A man/woman of God must be in control of their finances.
- Stability - as evinced by reputation, maturity, sobriety, self-control and even punctuality - is important. People won't trust you to show them the way to God if your life is a volatile mess. It's not that things won't go wrong - they will! - but what is important is how you react when they do.
- Gentleness should mark our attitude toward others. We are not to be violent or quarrelsome. That would dishonor God and turn people away from the true faith.

Have you mastered your life for the sake of the Master?

Prayer: Lord, help me to manage my own life and my own household. I want to bring you glory, and to bring others hope when they see me managing my life, even when things go wrong. Amen.

Psalm of the Day: 119.97-104

Family First

Daily Reading: 1 Timothy 5

> *But if a widow has children or grandchildren, let them first learn to show godliness to their own household and to make some return to their parents, for this is pleasing in the sight of God.* (1 Timothy 5.4)

Devotional Thought: Ancient Biblical culture is foreign to us and often misunderstood and taken out of context. In our age of insurance, government assistance, and exceeding wealth (relative to ancient times), the importance that Jesus and the early church places on caring for widows and orphans can be puzzling to us. In Biblical times, responsibility for family was of utmost importance. In the early church, the meaning of family was extended even further, to include brothers and sisters in Christ.

In his letter to Timothy, Paul instructs him to "honor widows who are truly widows. But, if a widow has children or grandchildren, let them first learn to show godliness to their own household... for this is pleasing in the sight of God" (1 Timothy 5.3-4). This is meant to be instructive to the entire family, including the widow herself. Each has God-honoring responsibility to the family. The children/grandchildren are to support the widow, who would have no resources with the loss of her husband. Paul sees this as an opportunity for them to show godliness and to please God. The widow herself is to set her hope on God, and continue in prayer night and day, and not be self-indulgent (self-pitying).

Although we live in a very different culture, there is a lesson here for us as well. Our family is our responsibility first and foremost. While we may not financially abandon our older family members in their need, we may physically or emotionally abandon them. In our culture of increasing busyness, it is tempting to forget or push aside those who have already "lived full lives." To do so is to our own detriment, as well as theirs. Providing comfort, support, and encouragement to those in need is beneficial to us as well – it helps us learn to show godliness and is pleasing to the Lord.

Jenny

Prayer: Lord, give us hearts of compassion for those who need us, especially our own family members. Give us the strength and the character that we need to love and care for those whom you love. Amen.

Psalm of the Day: 119.105-112

That's a Different Doctrine

Daily Reading: 1 Timothy 6

If anyone teaches a different doctrine... (1 Timothy 6.3a)

Devotional Thought: Paul begins his first letter to Timothy concerned about those who "have wandered away", and do not "understand what they are saying" (1.7). Unintentional ignorance? At the end of the letter, however, Paul's concern is about one who "teaches a different doctrine." This seems to indicate that the wrong teaching is definitely deliberate.

From where does deliberate error arise? Against what do I need to be on guard to insure that I do not bend to the way of these teachings? Some warning signs and attitudes to avoid:

- Disagreeing with the words of our Lord Jesus Christ (v. 3). Jesus, the Son of God, has given us the words of life in the Bible. We reject his teaching to our own peril.
- Ignoring the claims of godliness (v. 3). Paul knew of people who thought that grace meant you can sin more and more. That kind of grace, however, leads to recklessness and decadence.
- Being puffed up with conceit (v. 4). Peter thought he knew better than Jesus, when he drew the Lord aside and told him he would never have to die on the cross. If we want to understand the will of the Lord, we need to check our egos at the door!
- Refusing to understand (v. 4). When the truth is at odds against our desires, the temptation is to reject the truth.
- Craving controversy (v. 4). It's hard to get the facts straight when you are constantly stirring up people's anger and emotion. My, how we see that in today's cultural climate!
- Possessing poor motives for godliness (v. 5). Selfish motives lead to selfish conclusions. We must not bend the truth to our own gain!

Guard against different doctrines!

Prayer: Lord, thank you that your Word is truth. Help me to follow your Word, even when it goes against my thoughts and prejudices. Grant me courage to stand against the tide of political correctness. Amen.

Psalm of the Day: 119.113-120

The Promise of Life

Daily Reading: 2 Timothy 1

Paul, an apostle of Christ Jesus by the will of God according to the promise of the life that is in Christ Jesus. (2 Timothy 1.1)

Devotional Thought: On what do you base your Christian confidence? Paul's confidence was not in his superior education, his significant family, or his stellar service, but rather in the promise of Christ Jesus. What type of life is promised in Jesus?

- **New** life. "If anyone is in Christ he is a new creation" (2 Corinthians 5.17). In Christ Jesus, we no longer live in sin. In him, we no longer live in fear. In him, we no longer live in slavery. Instead, we now live in his righteousness, his love, and his freedom.
- **Abundant** life. "I came that they may have life, and have it abundantly" (John 10.10). Jesus doesn't mean for us to barely get by. Our God can do "exceeding abundantly" more than we ask or imagine!
- **Genuine** life. "For now we really live, if you are standing firm in the Lord" (1 Thessalonians 3.8, EHV). When we and those we love are standing firm in the Lord, we are really living, for he is the way, the truth and the life. In Jesus is life!
- **Shared** life. "You are in our hearts... to live together" (2 Corinthians 7.3). We are not alone. With Jesus we have the family of God as our partners in life.
- **Eternal** life. "For God so loved the world, that he gave his only Son, that whoever believes in him should not perish but have eternal life" (John 3.16).

Aren't you glad for this promise of life that is in Christ Jesus?

Prayer: Thank you, Lord Jesus, for the promise that you have made me, the promise of life. Help me so live that I might reflect your life, so that others may live in you, too. Amen.

Psalm of the Day: 119.121-128

Remember Jesus Christ
Daily Reading: 2 Timothy 2

Remember Jesus Christ, risen from the dead, the offspring of David, as preached in my gospel, for which I am suffering. (2 Timothy 2.8-9a)

Devotional Thought: Sometimes, the simplest advice is the best. Paul's words in 2 Timothy 2.8, are like that: "Remember ... Jesus."

Jesus is...
- The conqueror of **death**. Jesus Christ is eternal. Death, therefore, could not hold him. Death is the product of sin. After he died on the cross, he arose from the dead, defeating sin and death and the grave! Whatever problems you face, whatever burdens you bear, remember Jesus is greater; he's our Crusader. Jesus is stronger, and he lasts longer!
- The offspring of **David**. David was the quintessential King of the Old Testament, and the scriptures foretold of One who would come from David's line to restore the Kingdom of God. Jesus is enthroned above all rulers and authorities and powers. "Fear not, little flock, for it is your Father's good pleasure to give you the kingdom" (Luke 12.32).
- The greatest **declaration**. Jesus is "the Alpha and Omega, the first and the last, the beginning and the end" (Revelation 22.13). He predates and outlives every other word of history. There is no greater name than the name of Jesus!
- Our partner in **distress**. While in this world, we will have trouble, but Jesus has overcome the world (John 16.33). Take heart, for the Victor has promised to never leave us or forsake us!

This "saying is trustworthy, for: If we have died with him, we will also live with him; if we endure, we will also reign with him; if we deny him, he also will deny us; if we are faithless, he remains faithful—for he cannot deny himself" (2 Timothy 2.11-13).

Prayer: "There is a name I love to hear; I love to sing its worth. It sounds like music in my ear, the sweetest name on earth." Oh, how I love you, Jesus - because you first loved me! Amen. (Frederick Whitfield)

Psalm of the Day: 119.129-136

Pretense or Power

Daily Reading: 2 Timothy 3

> *Having the appearance of godliness, but denying its power...*
> (2 Timothy 3.5)

Devotional Thought: Halloween was last week. There were many little princesses, superheroes, witches and ghouls running around our neighborhoods! Were you frightened? Of course not! We know it's all pretend. We also know - or at least psychologists tell us - that it is healthy for children to engage in pretend play.

Not all pretending is healthy, though. The Apostle Paul warned Pastor Timothy of those who pretended to be godly but were not. They had the pretense but not the power.

How do we have the pretense of godliness? There are many ways, but consider these three:
- Some people think that by attending church they are godly. But, experience tells us that isn't the case. It takes more than going to a worship service occasionally to make one into a godly person.
- Some act as though saying they are godly makes them godly. Yet, we all know people who talk a big game but do not have real power in their lives.
- Others depend on legalistic behavior to prove their godliness. That doesn't work either. Legalism usually degenerates into judgmentalism and spiritual snobbery.

Well then, how are we to move from pretense to power? In the above examples...
- While church attendance doesn't make one godly, we cannot neglect church. The important thing is not to go as a spectator, but as a participant!
- While talk is cheap, neither can we refuse to testify! As we bear witness to God's grace, we grow in power.
- While legalism turns people off and turns God's power away, living an unholy life does so as well. If you want to have the power of God in your life, move in step with the Spirit!

Prayer: Lord, I do not want to have simply the pretense of power. I want the power. You told your disciples to wait until they be endued with power from on high, so fill me with your Spirit, the Spirit of power, and help me to be your willing partner in power! Amen.

Psalm of the Day: 119.137-144

The Lord Stood by Me
Daily Reading: 2 Timothy 4

The Lord stood by me and strengthened me, so that ... I was rescued from the lion's mouth. (2 Timothy 4.17)

Devotional Thought: As the Apostle Paul neared the end of his life, he found himself - often alone - in a Roman prison, facing the death penalty. The days and nights stretched into unbearable sameness and loneliness. He felt the sting of desertion and the hurt of being forgotten. But, he wasn't alone! Jesus was there to stand with him, to strengthen him, and to save him.

- The Lord stands. When Stephen, the first Christian martyr, was about to be condemned to death "he, full of the Holy Spirit, gazed into heaven and saw the glory of God, and Jesus standing at the right hand of God" (Acts 7.55). Paul remembered that moment, for he was there as one of the executioners. Now, the tables were turned and he knew first hand that Jesus was standing next to him, standing up for him, and standing to receive him.
- The Lord strengthens. Paul found out in Stephen's story that God does not always deliver *out of* the trial. Sometimes, he delivers *through* the trial. To pray, "Do not hold this sin against them" (Acts 7.60), Paul knew that Stephen had accessed a strength beyond himself. Now, again, it was Paul's turn to access that strength, from the one who laid down his life.
- The Lord saves. There are things worse than death. There are things better than life. Paul heard it in Stephen's confident words, "Lord Jesus, receive my spirit" (Acts 7.59). So, now Paul knew that the lion would not devour him. Death would be a doorway into the glorious presence of God. The Lord rescued him!

In the dark night of trial, look to Jesus. He stands with you - to strengthen you and to save you.

Prayer: Lord, in the words of the old hymn, "I need thee every hour!" Thank you that you are faithful. I turn to you in hope and trust. Amen.

Psalm of the Day: 119.145-152

Left on Crete

Daily Reading: Titus 1

> *This is why I left you in Crete, so that you might put what remained into order, and appoint elders in every town as I directed you.* (Titus 1.5)

Devotional Thought: I have a lingering memory from my childhood. With six of us kids in the family, it was quite an ordeal to get everyone out of the house and in the car. Once, I found myself all alone after everyone else had gone. I can see myself just as plain as if it happened this morning, sitting on the stoop with my arm around our dog, Brownie, whimpering, "They forgot me, boy. They left me behind!" Pitiful, right? It was to a 5 year old!

I wonder if sometimes Pastor Titus felt that way. He was on Crete, left there by the Apostle Paul. Crete was a hard place to pastor. The culture was debased and the church was struggling. Paul wanted Titus to know, however, that he wasn't forgotten. Titus wasn't left behind by accident. The same is true for us. Paul's strategy with Titus is an indication of God's strategy for leaving us on our "Cretes." It is...

- Purposeful: "That is why..." God has you here for a reason. Whether it is life in general or a location in particular, God has a plan for you where you are. Stay sensitive, and watch him open the doors to share his hope and peace and love.
- Perfecting: "Put in order..." As part of our delayed departure from "Crete," we are given the opportunity to grow. God is preparing us for our heavenly dwelling. Our sanctification here is preparation for there!
- Pervasive: "In every town..." While we are on "Crete," all areas of our lives are subject to the perfecting grace of God. Let God change you in the most secret places of your heart!

What are you doing on Crete?

Prayer: Lord, as long as I am in "Crete," help me to make use of my time - to discover my purpose, to grow to completion, and to allow you to change every area of my life. Amen.

Psalm of the Day: 119.153-160

But... But... But...
Daily Reading: Titus 2-3

> *But when the goodness and loving kindness of God our Savior appeared, he saved us...* (Titus 3.4-5a)

Devotional Thought: I love the "buts" of the Bible... whenever we encounter this word, we ought to pay particular attention to what was written before and after. In the case of Paul's letter to Titus, this word marks a definite transition. "For we ourselves were once foolish, disobedient, led astray, slaves to various passions and pleasures, passing our days in malice and envy, hated by others and hating one another" (v. 3). This does not paint a lovely picture of us in our sinful state. Sadly, it is an accurate portrayal of the world around us. With all of the rhetoric and pursuit of so-called "personal freedoms," the irony is that our bonds tighten with each progressive victory, as we sink deeper and deeper into slavery to self and to sin.

But... "when the goodness and loving kindness of God our Savior appeared, he saved us, not because of works done by us in righteousness, but according to his own mercy..." (vv. 4-5). Praise God that he does not leave us in this hopeless state! And, it only gets better! He pours out his Spirit "richly through Jesus Christ our Savior, so that being justified by his grace we might become heirs according to the hope of eternal life" (v. 6-7). It is not poured out on us because we deserve it – review verse 3, if you need convincing – but because of God's great mercy towards us. When we are tempted to judge the world around us for their bondage to sin, their relentless pursuit of pleasure, their rebellion against God, their hatred for those with whom they disagree, remember that we were once slaves to the same sin. But for God's goodness and loving kindness, we would be still. Instead of judging unbelievers, we pray for an outpouring of God's mercy in their lives.

Jenny

Prayer: But for your grace, I would be lost. Lord, thank you for not leaving me in my bondage to sin and death, but for saving me from it, from myself! Amen.

Psalm of the Day: 119.161-168

Don't Make Floors into Ceilings

Daily Reading: Philemon 1

Do even more than I say. (Philemon 1.21)

Devotional Thought: Last Saturday, Lana and I were getting ready to be gone for a few days. Lana was busy doing some last minute chores, but I was engrossed in a football game on TV. When she finished ironing - *my* shirts! - she put the ironing board away and then teasingly said, "I thought you would help me with that!" I said something like, "I would have if you had asked me," knowing that it was lame. Why should she have to tell me the obvious?

Do we sometimes wait to be told the obvious? Do we try to get by with just the minimum in our service to Christ and his church? When the Apostle Paul wrote to his friend Philemon, he expected something more.

Paul had written Philemon to request a huge 'favor' - that he take back his fugitive slave, Onesimus, who had become a Christian under Paul's ministry. Paul asked that Philemon forgive Onesimus and do even more - to receive him as a brother! In that culture, that was a big ask. But, Paul was confident that Philemon would "do even more."

I believe that Jesus desires more for and from us than just barely getting by. Too often, we wait to be told what to do, even when it is right there in front of us. We make the floor our ceiling. When we get past the ceiling, however, when we go on the upper floor, we discover that we can see so much more! And, we can do so much more, more than the minimum, even more than what we're told.

That's how I want to live. How about you?

Prayer: Jesus, thank you that you did not hold back on doing the Father's will. Forgive me when I try to get by with the minimum, when I make the floor my ceiling. Help me instead, O Lord, to do even more than you say. Amen.

Psalm of the Day: 119.169-176

Plenty of Blame to Go Around

Daily Reading: 1 Kings 12

"Thus says the Lord, You shall not go up or fight against your relatives the people of Israel. Every man return to his home, for this thing is from me." So they listened to the word of the Lord and went home again, according to the word of the Lord. (1 Kings 12.24)

Devotional Thought: "There's plenty of blame to go around..." That could be the title of today's chapter, 1 Kings 12.

This chapter records the division of Israel into two nations:
- Judah, the southern kingdom, following the line of King David, worshiping in the Jerusalem temple, led by Solomon's son Rehoboam
- Israel, the northern kingdom, breaking away from the Davidic reign, worshiping in Bethel and Dan, led by Solomon's adversary Jeroboam.

It was a sad day in the history of Israel. Who was to blame for this division? As is typically the case when there are problems between God's people, there was plenty of blame to go around:
- Solomon was partially to blame. He did not adjust his policies when he saw what was coming.
- Rehoboam shared in the blame. He could have lightened the load of taxation upon the Israelites.
- Rehoboam's young advisors were quick to exert their influence and show their power.
- The people of Israel were not innocent in the matter, as they were eager to rebel against the heavy hand of Rehoboam.
- Jeroboam bore some of the blame - with his unbridled ambition.

In the midst of all this blame, there is a bright spot. When Rehoboam mustered his army to reclaim the northern tribes, God said, "You shall not go up or fight against your relatives" (v. 24). Finally, wisdom (and obedience) prevailed, and Rehoboam did not intensify the conflict. Even when we have irreconcilable differences, we must not become hateful and hurtful toward our brothers and sisters with whom we disagree.

There are times when we may be technically right, but we can choose to set aside our pride and our "rightness" and come together for the sake of God's Kingdom.

Prayer: Forgive me, Lord, when I have grieved your heart by insisting on being right, when I could have been loving. Help me to be more like you! Amen.

Psalm of the Day: 120.1-7

Compromise

Daily Reading: 1 Kings 13

> *And the man of God said to the king, "If you give me half your house, I will not go in with you. And I will not eat bread or drink water in this place, for so was it commanded me by the word of the Lord..."*
> (1 Kings 13.8-9)

Devotional Thought: "Yesterday, we saw the danger of refusing to compromise with one another. In today's chapter, we see the danger of compromising with "the word of the Lord."

When the man of God's compromised, he did so at the cost of his life for he compromised with the word of the Lord, which is...

- *Unchanging.* The man of God was clear about God's will in this situation. He had very specific instructions on how to conduct himself while in Bethel, which he obeyed at first. He knew better than to listen to the old prophet, but disobedience was looking more and more attractive as he grew hungrier and thirstier.
- *True.* Jesus said, "I am the way and the truth and the life" (John 14.6). What is true of the Son is also true of the Father. His word is absolute – it is the measuring stick by which we can determine the rightness of any other thing. If any principle, morality, philosophy, action, or idea is contrary to the Word of God, then it is false.
- *Authoritative.* While we may pity the prophet who lost his life because of his disobedience, we can also be comforted that there is an absolute authority; right and wrong are not relative to human perspective, as some would have us believe. There is no guessing when the Lord has spoken. We can stand firmly on the promises of the Father, with whom there is no variation or shadow due to change (James 1:17).

Let us look for ways to compromise with one another, but never compromise with the word of the Lord.

Jenny

Prayer: Lord, grant me a discerning spirit that I may see the difference between my opinions about the Word of God, and what the Word of God actually says. Help me to never compromise with the truth. Amen.

Psalm of the Day: 121.1-4

Bronze for Gold?

Daily Reading: 1 Kings 14

King Rehoboam made in their place shields of bronze... (1 Kings 14.27)

Devotional Thought: The King of Egypt – Shishak – "took away the treasure of the house of the Lord... all the shields of gold that Solomon had made." Solomon's reign had been one of unparalleled wealth and wisdom. But, that wealth and wisdom were fleeting. In just one generation, Egypt came and "took away everything."

King Shishak is a picture of Satan. When Satan finds people divided, when he finds people separated from the family of God and the house of worship, he is able to steal their wealth and wisdom and victory. Jesus said that Satan is a thief who comes to "steal and kill and destroy." When a sheep is separated from the sheepfold, the thief has an easy time of doing that very thing. How important it is to stay vitally connected to the church, to a small group. There is strength in Christian relationships that we cannot find elsewhere.

Rehoboam tried to take corrective measures, but he did not get to the root of the problem. The people were living a divided life, appearing to serve God, but not really following him with their whole heart. The Bible speaks of having an "appearance of godliness, but denying its power" (2 Timothy 3.5). The shields that Solomon had placed in the temple were pure gold, valuable beyond compare. Yet, when they were lost, Rehoboam did not attempt to get them back, nor did he call upon God. Instead, Rehoboam made cheap substitutes that looked like the real thing, but were only bronze. They were shiny. They were beautiful. They were impressive. But, they were not pure gold.

Are you missing the pure gold of a relationship with God? Don't substitute a cheap alloy. God has gold for you!

Prayer: Lord, I refuse to substitute bronze for gold. I want the pure gold of a soul on fire for God, a soul totally surrendered to you. Purify my heart so that it is set upon you completely. In Jesus' name, amen.

Psalm of the Day: 121.5-8

I Choose Peace

Daily Reading: 1 Kings 15

> *Now there was war between Rehoboam and Jeroboam all the days of his life.* (1 Kings 15.6)

Devotional Thought: Democrats and Republicans, Browns and Bengals, Buckeyes and Wolverines. Black Lives Matter, Occupy Wall Street, Make America Great, Sharia Law and Western Culture, Threat of Terror and The Right of Privacy. The world seems to be driven by division, doesn't it?

It has been this way from the beginning – or at least from the fall of humanity and the entrance of sin into our world. God created us to be in perfect fellowship with him and with each other, but sin destroyed that. Immediately upon the entrance of sin, humankind has been hiding from God and from one another. It has been necessary to take great pains to protect ourselves from each other, building walls and raising armies. It is tragic.

Division and strife are even more tragic when they exist among the people of God. The House of Rehoboam (Judah) and the House of Jeroboam (Israel) were brothers! They both were of the seed of Abraham. They both had been delivered by God from Egyptian slavery, through the Red Sea and across the Jordan River. Together they had conquered kings and liberated great areas of oppression. If for no other reason than their common history and deliverance, they should have been allies. They should have been working to bring about the blessings of God on earth. Instead, they were at war with one another.

By our words, we divide or unite; we bring strife or peace. By love and compassion and inclusion, we tear down barriers and bring people together. Through forgiveness, generosity, and turning the other cheek, we establish an environment of peace. Even when we must take measures to protect ourselves and our nation, we should keep in mind that after war there must be peace.

Today, do you choose division or peace?

Prayer: Lord, you prayed that your disciples may be one even as you are perfectly one with the Father, so that the world may know that you are from God. Along with you, I pray for unity and peace in your Church. Amen.

Psalm of the Day: 122.1-5

Hell-Bent
Daily Reading: 1 Kings 16

In his days Hiel of Bethel built Jericho. He laid its foundation at the cost of Abiram his firstborn, and set up its gates at the cost of his youngest son Segub, according to the word of the Lord, which he spoke by Joshua the son of Nun. (1 Kings 16.34)

Devotional Thought: The prophetic curse, long forgotten, was about to be fulfilled. Hiel was hell-bent on rebuilding Jericho.

Merriam-Webster defines hell-bent as "very determined to do something especially when the results might be bad; stubbornly and often recklessly determined or intent." You've known people like this, haven't you?
- Someone who doesn't care who he steps on, or what she compromises, in order to get that promotion at work
- Another who is determined to get the next "fix", no matter what it may cost their family
- Or perhaps one who sacrifices health and relationships to get that next dollar

In today's international scene we see examples of nations hell-bent on...
- Gaining nuclear weapons
- Wiping out Israel
- Becoming world powers

Whether an individual or a government, when people are hell-bent on doing something, innocent people suffer.

When Hiel laid the foundation of Jericho, his son Abiram died. Did no one think about the ancient prophecy? Did no one warn him? After Abiram died, did Hiel slow down to find out why? And, I wonder if Segub, Hiel's youngest son, thought: "Dad, you're not really going through with this are you?" How many family members have stood aghast at how their own fathers or mothers sacrificed them for their ambitions or addictions?

Hiel's name means "Brother of God." Even in the family of God, people can become hell-bent on their own ambitions and agendas. Let us listen to the voice of God who always calls us back to himself!

Prayer: Lord, forgive me for being so stubborn that I push ahead with my own agenda. Soften my heart so that I heed your warnings. Prevent my rashness from causing pain to myself and others. By your mercy and grace I pray. Amen.

Psalm of the Day: 122.6-9

327

Never Give Up

Daily Reading: 1 Kings 17

> *Then he stretched himself upon the child three times and cried to the Lord, "O Lord my God, let this child's life come into him again."*
> (1 Kings 17.21)

Devotional Thought: The widow had provided Elijah lodging and food. Then her son became ill and died. Elijah was mortified that that should happen when he was there in the household. Perhaps he had been given the boy's room. So he prayed. He prayed with desperation. He prayed with perseverance.

Elijah "stretched himself upon the child... and cried to the Lord." Nothing happened. I can imagine that the mother was looking anxiously upon the scene. So, Elijah did it again. Still nothing. Finally, after the third cry of desperation, "O Lord my God, let this child's life come into him again," the child's life returned to him. Elijah's prayer was answered.

I wonder how many prayers go unanswered because we give up too soon. I wonder how many blessings we miss because we stop praying in discouragement. Jesus thought that it was important to keep on praying, even when our prayers seemingly go unanswered. He even told his disciples "a parable to the effect that they ought always to pray and not lose heart" (Luke 18.1).

And, there is no "magic number" as to how many times or how long we should persevere in prayer. Elijah prayed three times for the boy who died. But, three times is not always enough. There is a story later in 2 Kings 13, when the prophet Elisha was upset with the king of Israel because he did not strike the floor 5 or 6 times. Instead, the king struck the floor *only* three times. We too, must not think we can stop with just three times of our knees striking the floor when we kneel to pray.

Never give up praying.

Prayer: O God - the God who hears and answers prayer - give me a spirit of desperation and perseverance so that I never give up praying. You are faithful. Help me to be faithful as well - to the glory of your name. Amen.

Psalm of the Day: 123.1-4

Then the Fire of the Lord Fell

Daily Reading: 1 Kings 18

> *Answer me, O Lord, answer me, that this people may know that you, O Lord, are God, and that you have turned their hearts back."* Then the *fire of the Lord fell.* (1 Kings 18.37-38)

Devotional Thought: "Pick on somebody your own size." Sometimes, this is said to shame a bully - to prevent them from harassing someone smaller. It can also be a warning - to make sure that a friend doesn't take on a foe who is bigger than them.

Elijah didn't care. He picked on somebody way bigger than him. On Mount Carmel, he confronted King Ahab and his retinue of "the 450 prophets of Baal and the 400 prophets of Asherah, who eat at Jezebel's table" (1 Kings 18.19). The odds were not in his favor. After he proposed a contest - the God who answers by fire, he is God - Elijah further handicapped himself by drenching his sacrifice with water.

I've always marveled at Elijah's simple prayer in contrast to the prayer of the false prophets, who went on all morning and much of the afternoon crying out and cutting themselves, trying to get Baal's attention. But, today I noticed something for the first time. The initial part of Elijah's prayer was focused on Elijah's vindication - "that I am your servant and that I have done all these things in your name." I don't have a quarrel with the prophet; I simply point out that nothing happened until after Elijah shifted the focus - "that this people may know that you, O Lord, are God, and that you have turned their hearts back." After Elijah prayed for the glory of God and the salvation of people, "Then the fire of the Lord fell."

Do you want the fire of God to fall on you? Do you want the power of God on your testimony and prayers? Perhaps, it is time to change the focus of your prayers.

Prayer: "Answer me, O Lord, answer me, that this people may know that you, O Lord, are God, and that you have turned their hearts back." Amen.

Psalm of the Day: 124.1-5

God Always Calls a Busy Person

Daily Reading: 1 Kings 19

> *So he departed from there and found Elisha the son of Shaphat, who was plowing with twelve yoke of oxen in front of him, and he was with the twelfth. Elijah passed by him and cast his cloak upon him.*
> (1 Kings 19.19)

Devotional Thought: "God always calls a busy person." I remember an old preacher telling me that once. I thought he was crazy! If I want something done, shouldn't I find someone who has the time to do it?

Elijah was nearing the end of his life. So, God revealed to Elijah a prophet to continue Elijah's ministry. The prophet was Elisha, son of Shaphat. Elisha, it was said, was "plowing with twelve yoke of oxen in front of him, and he was with the twelfth." That means that he not only was driving a plow, he was also supervising 11 others. He was a man of industry and responsibility. Some would say, he was too busy to answer God's call. God saw it differently.

Elijah "cast his cloak upon him." By doing so, Elijah was saying that the mantle of prophetic responsibility would now fall on Elisha's shoulders. This was God's call. Elijah didn't explain, didn't apologize, didn't try to ease the responsibility. As a matter of fact, if he did anything at all, he *discouraged* Elisha: "Go back again, for what have I done to you?" He was saying in effect, "This isn't from me. If God isn't calling you, then just go on back home."

Well, God was calling Elisha, and Elisha knew it. He busted up the yokes and built a fire, he slaughtered the twenty-four oxen, and he had a religious feast, commemorating the call of God and his resolute response. "Then he arose and went after Elijah and assisted him." So much for being too busy or having too much responsibility!

Do you want to be used of God in significant ways? Then get busy, for "God always calls a busy person..."

Prayer: Lord, I am embarrassed to think about the number of times I have said, "I'm too busy" when you have called. Forgive me. Lord, right now, right here, I say "Here am I. Send me." Amen.

Psalm of the Day: 124.6-8

Muster and Provision
Daily Reading: 1 Kings 20

> *And the people of Israel were mustered and were provisioned and went against them. The people of Israel encamped before them like two little flocks of goats, but the Syrians filled the country.* (1 Kings 20.27)

Devotional Thought: Do you ever feel overwhelmed? I do! The people of Israel did when they were encamped before their enemy, "like two little flocks of goats", while their enemy "filled the country." But, there was a difference that the Syrians couldn't see. God had said, "I will give all this great multitude into your hands" (v. 28). The king of Israel believed this, and because he believed it, he took the next step. He mustered and provisioned the army.

Are you waiting on God to take the next step? Instead of waiting, perhaps you should muster and provision yourself.
- To muster means assemble troops in preparation. Get your team ready. Get your prayer warriors lined up. Bring them together and pray and plan.
- To provision means to give the troops what they need. Share the vision, invest in the project, and put the tools that they need in their hands.

Then wait. The battle will be joined at the right time. God is waiting for you to make yourself ready.

Several years ago, Lana and I were in a time of transition. We weren't pastoring a church. We didn't have jobs. It had been that way 5 months. We didn't know where we were going next. One day, when I was at the hardware store – I remember it clearly – God spoke to me. He told me, "It's time." I went home and told Lana. We believed God and put the house on the market to get ready for what God was going to do. Within twelve days, we had a signed offer on our house, and an interview scheduled for the church where we eventually were called to serve!

What is God calling you to do? Have you "mustered and provisioned"?

Prayer: Lord, when you show me the way forward, help me to believe you, to take the next step, to "muster and provision." I want to be used by you. Amen.

Psalm of the Day: 125.1-5

Hate the Sin; Love the Sinner

Daily Reading: 1 Kings 21

Ahab said to Elijah, "Have you found me, O my enemy?" He answered, "I have found you, because you have sold yourself to do what is evil in the sight of the Lord." (1 Kings 21.20)

Devotional Thought: With the encouragement of his godless wife Jezebel, King Ahab had fallen back into sin, unable to resist the temptation of idolatry. But, the Lord was merciful. He instructed Elijah to find Ahab, to call him to repentance. This, in spite of the fact that "there was none who sold himself to do what was evil in the sight of the Lord like Ahab" (v. 25). The old maxim is true: "God hates the sin, but loves the sinner."

As believers, we are foreigners and exiles in this world (1 Peter 2:11). We are not of the world (John 17:16). Sin and evil are the natural enemies of those who are made righteous by faith in Christ. It is right for believers to be repulsed and saddened by the terrible evil that surrounds us. But, when we see the sinners as our enemies, we are missing our calling and commission from our Savior. Though the world may be against us, we must love people as Jesus does, desiring that all of his created children would come to know him.

Just as the Lord continued to pursue Ahab's heart through Elijah, let us allow the Spirit to pursue others through us as well, so that they too may no longer be slaves to sin, but sons and heirs through God.

Jenny

Prayer: "Lord, lay some soul upon my heart and love that soul through me. And may I humbly do my part to win that soul for thee." Amen. (Leon Tucker)

Psalm of the Day: 126.1-6

The Lone Voice

Daily Reading: 1 Kings 22

> *Micaiah said, "As the Lord lives, what the Lord says to me, that I will speak."* (1 Kings 22.14)

Devotional Thought: On January 28, 1986, the space shuttle *Challenger* exploded 73 seconds after launch. Seven people lost their lives in the disaster. It was determined that a faulty O-ring was the cause of the explosion. But, as the investigation dug into the details leading up to the launch, it was discovered that a faulty process was the cause of the cause. The engineers and managers responsible for the program, had concerns and fears about the O-ring, but no one was willing to go against the 'groupspeak' that had overtaken the shuttle program. No one wanted to be the lone voice. Seven innocent people died as a result.

Have you ever been the lone voice of reason in a cacophony of insanity? That was the position that the prophet Micaiah found himself in. Micaiah had been called before the kings of Israel and Judah to prophesy about the proposed battle with the Syrians. To a man, all the other prophets had said that the battle should be joined, that Israel and Judah would prevail. Micaiah at first sarcastically said, "Yeah, go ahead..." But, the kings saw through his sarcasm and called him on it. So, he told them the truth: "This is going to hurt."

Sometimes the truth hurts, doesn't it? We don't want to offend people that we love. Sometimes, it's just easier to go along with the crowd. But, when we refuse to speak the truth, the danger is even greater to ourselves and to those we love.

What needs to be said in your situation? Is there something that you have not said because you were afraid of hurting someone, or of looking foolish? Be the lone voice. "Speak the truth in love" (Ephesians 4.15).

Prayer: Father in heaven, give me eyes to see the truth, wisdom to understand the truth, and courage to proclaim the truth. In the name of the One who is the Truth. Amen.

Psalm of the Day: 127.1-5

Good Raisin'

Daily Reading: 1 John 1-2

> *My little children, I am writing these things to you so that you may not sin. But if anyone does sin, we have an advocate with the Father, Jesus Christ the righteous.* (1 John 2.1)

Devotional Thought: "Who raised you?" I was asked that by a 9 or 10 year old boy once. I was visiting with his grandmother, and he was there, sitting at the table while we talked over a cup of coffee. I didn't know what to say, so I waited for him to explain himself. As young boys do, he very quickly obliged: "You sure got some good raisin'. I can tell by how you're behavin' now."

That little boy taught me something that day. People can tell a lot about us by the way we behave. And, our behavior speaks clearly about who raised us!

I think the Apostle John would have liked my little friend, for he said basically the same thing in today's verse. Consider the simplicity of what John is saying in this verse:

- We are God's children. "But to all who did receive him, who believed in his name, he gave the right to become children of God, who were born, not of blood nor of the will of the flesh nor of the will of man, but of God" (John 1.12-13).
- God wants us to behave as his children. What parent wouldn't? And, God has given us his written Word to instruct us. That's "good raisin'."
- Sometimes, we fail to behave as God's children. It's not that we mean to or plan to. Anathema! But sometimes, in our weakness, we are surprised and unprepared, and end up doing what we do not want to do.
- Jesus, the righteous One, is our Advocate with the Father. "If we confess our sins, he is faithful and just to forgive us our sins and to cleanse us from all unrighteousness" (1 John 1.9).

Who raised you? How are you behavin'?

Prayer: Thank you, Jesus, that you are my Advocate with the Father. I do not wish to sin. God forbid! But if I do, show me and help me to confess and be cleansed. You alone are my righteousness! Amen.

Psalm of the Day: 128.1-6

334

Evidence

Daily Reading: 1 John 3

> *By this it is evident who are the children of God, and who are the children of the devil: whoever does not practice righteousness is not of God, nor is the one who does not love his brother.* (1 John 3.10)

Devotional Thought: John, in this letter, has made much of the distinction between true and counterfeit believers. This distinction is a matter of life and death, for as Jesus warns us in Matthew 7, some will hear, "Depart, I never knew you" (v. 23). This is a sobering thought for any believer, and we should inspect our own hearts and motives.

John gives us practical ways to do this, but not a fail-proof methodology. There will be counterfeits who look like they are practicing righteousness, but their hearts are far from God. However, from this text, here are some questions that may help us with our self-examination:

Do we *see* the Father's love for us? (vv. 1-3). The world does not understand this love because it does not know him. It is the unique privilege of the believer to receive spiritual understanding, through the work of the Spirit in their hearts.

Do we make a *practice* of sinning? (vv. 4-10). The question is not "do we ever sin," but rather "do we make a practice of sinning?" Do we make the sin in our life comfortable and settle into it? Or, do we acknowledge our sin with repentance, striving towards righteousness?

Do we *love* one another? (vv. 11-24). We must believe in Jesus and love one another, as he has commanded us. Whoever practices genuine, Christ-like, self-sacrificing love abides in God, and God in him (v. 24). This love is supernatural and can only occur through the Holy Spirit, whom he has given to all who believe.

The Lord knows our hearts... may we ask him to reveal any grievous way in us and lead us in the way everlasting!

Jenny

Prayer: Lord, save us from relying on our own good works to obtain righteousness. We know that we can never be close to you without the saving blood of Jesus. Give us the faith to trust in you alone for salvation. Amen.

Psalm of the Day: 129.1-4

Hidden in Plain View

Daily Reading: 1 John 4

No one has ever seen God; if we love one another, God abides in us and his love is perfected in us. (1 John 4.12)

Devotional Thought: One of my favorite children's books is, "Where's Waldo?" I used to love to find Waldo with my kids - and still do with my grandkids. Have you ever looked for Waldo? He's hard to find, isn't he? Why is that? Usually, it's because he's in a crowd of people that share his characteristics. Waldo is 'hidden in plain view.'

God is like that. I know he's 'hidden' in the pages of the Bible and we can find him there, as we find Waldo in the pages of those fun books. But also, I believe God is hidden in plain view in the Church. Just like Waldo, he's in a crowd, and we can miss him. But, it was in a crowd when I first 'saw' God. The saints at Pioneer, Ohio Church of the Nazarene, showed him to me. The Lord was in that group. I saw him in their love, in their characteristics.

The Apostle John had that experience. He wrote, "No one has ever seen God." But, God was hidden in plain view, for when "we love one another, God abides in us." Like Waldo, God loves to hang out in a crowd of people that share his characteristics. But, unlike Waldo, he doesn't do it to hide. He lives among the people who love him, so that we can see him! When God's love is perfected in you, I see God in you.

One of the most convincing evidences of God is the love we have for one another. That's one reason why we are told we must not forsake meeting together and are commanded to love one another. Our love draws others into his love, so that they can find the One who is hidden in plain view

Prayer: Thank you, Lord, that you are hidden in plain view. Help me to display your characteristics so that others will see you in me. Amen.

Psalm of the Day: 129.5-8

Knowing, Loving, Obeying
Daily Reading: 1 John 5

> *By this we know that we love the children of God, when we love God and obey his commandments.* (1 John 5.2)

Devotional Thought: "The most wonderful time of the year" is just a month away. I love to celebrate Christmas - the irrefutable and irresistible Love of God, shining forth from a manger. But, I also love the opportunity to come together as a family. My love for Christ and my love for my family gets all mixed together, and indeed it is a most wonderful time. I think God is ok with that, with mixing up all that love. After all, as John wrote earlier, "God is love!" Paul said that the love we have in our hearts is put there by the Holy Spirit (Romans 5.5).

John mixed up three different kinds of love in today's verse...
- Love for God. Jesus told us that we are to love God with all our heart and soul and mind and strength. We have to get that right before all the other loves are right.
- Love for the children of God. After we get that first love right, then we are to love our neighbor. This love must be based upon God's love because otherwise it will become idolatrous. We love with true love when we love with God's love.
- Love for the commandments of God. We show our love for the commandments of God by obeying them. Obedience to God's commands keeps our love pure and healthy. True love doesn't do just anything. Sometimes, it has to say no. If love cannot say no, if it leaves out God's commandments, it is mere sentimentality.

Do you have a healthy love? A love that is rooted in God, overflowing to others and grounded upon God's Word? Only such a love will last into eternity.

Prayer: Lord, I want my life to be filled with love. So, help me to love you, to love your children, and to love your commandments. Amen.

Psalm of the Day: 130.1-4

That Is So Exciting!

Daily Reading: 2 John & 3 John

I have no greater joy than to hear that my children are walking in the truth. (3 John 1.4)

Devotional Thought: I remember when my girls took their first steps. Before they did, we did everything we could to help them along. We coaxed, encouraged, even "let go" in order to get them to do it. And, when they did, we were so excited that we called their grandparents, of course! We knew that Grandma and Grandpa would be just as excited as we were. And, they were!

The Apostle John had heard that his children were "walking in the truth." And, he was excited!

He was excited because they "got it." Like any parent, John invested a lot in his spiritual children. But, how could he be sure that it paid off? When he saw them taking those steps, he knew that his labor was not in vain.

He was excited because it would protect them. John knew that, standing still, people were an easy target. He also knew that Diotrophes was sowing discord and doubt among the people. As long as his children were walking in the truth, they would be able to stay ahead of their antagonist.

He was excited because they could now share it. John wanted his children to be "fellow workers for the truth." Truth is not something we keep to ourselves, but it's hard to help someone else walk in the truth, if we are stumbling and staggering around! John couldn't help everyone himself, so when his children shared in the work, he was overjoyed.

He was excited because God would receive the glory. Others see us when we walk. How we live our lives is a testimony to what God is like. John rejoiced that his children were walking in and helping others walk in "a manner worthy of the Lord."

Prayer: Help me, O Lord, to walk in a manner worthy of your name. I want you to be excited when you see me take first steps. Help me, also, to help others take exciting first steps. Amen.

Psalm of the Day: 130.5-8

Spirit-Based Confidence
Daily Reading: Philippians 1

I want you to know, brothers, that what has happened to me has really served to advance the gospel... (Philippians 1.12)

Devotional Thought: Paul sits in a prison cell as he writes this letter to the church in Philippi. Yet, rather than bemoan his circumstances or call for help, his heart and quill overflow with blessing for the church. "And it is my prayer that your love may abound more and more, with knowledge and all discernment, so that you may approve what is excellent, and so be pure and blameless for the day of Christ, filled with the fruit of righteousness that comes through Jesus Christ, to the glory and praise of God" (vv. 9-11).

Speaking of the glory and praise of God, Paul is also quick to point out to these new believers that his circumstances, far from ideal in the world's view, are actually serving to advance the gospel. These were terrifying times for Christians, as they were physically persecuted, even unto death by the Romans. Paul sees only the good that God is working through his imprisonment – the gospel is advanced, and brothers are confident and much bolder to speak the word without fear.

As we keep reading through this chapter, we see that Paul is fully expecting deliverance. Not necessarily a physical deliverance, but rather that Christ would be honored in his body, whether by life or by death. Paul's primary motive, which he doggedly pursues throughout his ministry, is bringing glory to God.

What are our attitudes regarding our less-than-ideal circumstances? Do we seek deliverance from discomfort, or do we seek discovery of God's will? Are we consumed with thoughts and pity for ourselves, or do we look for ways to bless and intercede for others even through our suffering? If Paul can do so from a prison cell, all the while rejoicing, then the Spirit will empower us to as well!

Jenny

Prayer: Lord, we can only accomplish this type of rejoicing, regardless of circumstances, in you. Make known to us the full joy of your salvation, that we would not be defeated by the trials of this world! Amen.

Psalm of the Day: 131.1-3

Making Jesus Happy

Daily Reading: Philippians 2

> *Complete my joy by being of the same mind, having the same love, being in full accord and of one mind. Do nothing from selfish ambition or conceit, but in humility count others more significant than yourselves.* (Philippians 2.2-3)

Devotional Thought: I think that Paul - though he wouldn't say it like this - had a favorite church, and it was the church in Philippi. They were so good to him, unwavering in their support of and confidence in him. Though he was full of joy because of them, he asked them to do something to make his joy complete.

What can we do to make *Jesus'* joy complete?
- Be of the same mind. That doesn't mean that we think exactly alike, but it does mean that we approach life from the same perspective, a Kingdom perspective.
- Have the same love. This is love in action. It goes out of its way to meet the needs of the other.
- Be in full accord. We are to have the same identity. We are first and foremost Christians.
- Be of one mind. This goes beyond being of the same mind. It means that we intentionally focus on the same thing: Jesus Christ!
- Do nothing selfishly. Focused on Jesus, we become like him. Jesus didn't come to be served, but to serve and to give his life as a ransom. What motivates us? Is it the same thing that motivates Jesus?
- Count others ahead of yourself. It's not that I am insignificant. Sometimes, I must care for myself so that I can care for others. But, again it is the motive that's important.

This is a tall order. How can we hope to make Jesus' joy complete? We can't, but Jesus can! Verse 5 says, "Have this mind among yourselves, which is yours in Christ Jesus." Jesus will do it in us! But, we have to stay in the Word and in prayer for that to happen.

Prayer: Lord, help me to be transformed by the renewing of my mind. Help me to have the mind of Christ more and more so that I can please you more and more. Amen.

Psalm of the Day: 132.1-5

340

Let Go!

Daily Reading: Philippians 3

I count everything as loss because of the surpassing worth of knowing Christ Jesus my Lord. (Philippians 3.8)

Devotional Thought: I remember the first time I zip-lined. It was in Guatemala, and one of the zips stretched over 1/4 mile above the canyon floor 450 feet below! But, the highest one wasn't the hardest one. Can you guess the hardest one? It was the first one! It was only 52 feet long and about 25 feet above the ground. But, it was on that first one that I had to learn how to let go! I'm so glad I did! If I hadn't, I would have missed out on the best one.

There are times in life that we are helped as much by what we let go of as by what we hold on to. We can't make any progress at all until we let go of the wrong things and take hold of the right things. Paul wrote to the Philippians that he had to let go of everything so that he could know Jesus Christ. Everything else was counted as loss to him: status, accomplishments, race, privilege, and yes - sin. Paul released all of that in order to know Christ fully. The Bible urges us to "lay aside every weight, and sin which clings so closely, and let us run with endurance the race that is set before us" (Hebrews 12.1). Jesus told a story about a man who let go of everything else: Finding a field with hidden treasure, "in his joy he goes and sells all that he has and buys that field" (Matthew 13.44).

Have you found that treasure and sold everything? Have you laid aside every weight and sin that entangles? Have you counted all other things as loss so that you might know Christ?

Prayer: Thank you, Lord Jesus, that you laid aside everything else, so that you could come and rescue me from sin and separation from God. For your sake - to know you, Lord - I let go of everything else. Amen.

Psalm of the Day: 132.6-10

Is There Peace in Your World?
Daily Reading: Philippians 4

> *Do not be anxious about anything, but in everything by prayer and supplication with thanksgiving let your requests be made known to God.* (Philippians 4.6)

Devotional Thought: The Christmas season is upon us! It is a season of hustle and bustle, of parties and shopping, of cards and visits. In this busy season, it is hard to remember the words of the angel choir outside Bethlehem: "Peace on earth, good will to men!" How can we know the way of peace? In today's verse, the Apostle Paul gave us two keys to finding peace. We turn the first key by what we don't do, and the second by what we do.

1. Do not...
   - Be anxious. The word literally means to be pulled in opposite directions, divided into parts, or go to pieces. We prevent anxiety when we fix our loyalties on one Kingdom. Jesus told us not to be anxious, rather to, "seek first the kingdom of God and his righteousness, and all these things will be added to you" (Matthew 6.33).

2. Do...
   - Pray - talk to God about the things that bother you. We often go to every other source before we go to God!
   - Ask - indicating a heart-felt request arising out of personal need. "You have not because you ask not" (James 4.2).
   - Thank - be grateful and confident that God's grace is working out what is good. "In all things God is working for the good of those who love him" (Romans 8.28).
   - Request - If we make demands, we in essence make ourselves God. Then, our source of peace is in us alone. That won't work!

If we will turn those keys, we will know: "The peace of God, which surpasses all understanding, [and it] will guard your hearts and your minds in Christ Jesus" (Philippians 4.7).

Prayer: "Guide our feet into the way of peace," O Lord. When life's troubles mount, help me to seek your Kingdom alone, and to pray and leave it in your hands. Amen.

Psalm of the Day: 132.11-12

Walk with God

Daily Reading: Luke 1

> *Now while he was serving as priest before God when his division was on duty, according to the custom of the priesthood, he was chosen by lot to enter the temple of the Lord and burn incense.* (Luke 1.8-9)

Devotional Thought: Zechariah and Elizabeth were both old and considered beyond the age of bearing children. But, God had a different plan. Zechariah, who was a priest, was serving in the temple one day, and God sent the angel Gabriel to him with the good news that he and his wife were going to have a baby! What struck me in the story was the fact that God came and blessed this man as he performed the regular – some would say mundane – duties of his ministry. Zechariah was not doing anything extraordinary when he received the visit from Gabriel. His division was on duty. He was fulfilling the custom of the priesthood. He was chosen by lot. None of those things sound terribly exciting or super-spiritual. But, the important fact was that when he did what he knew to do, God appeared on the scene!

Do you need God to appear in your life? Would you benefit from a vision and message from God? I would recommend that you consider Zechariah, and do the things you know to do. Read your Bible. Pray. Serve in the church. Witness. Tithe. Live a holy and compassionate life.

Consider the words of Paul as he quoted Moses: "Do not say in your heart, 'Who will ascend into heaven?' (that is, to bring Christ down), or 'Who will descend into the abyss?' (that is, to bring Christ up from the dead). But what does it say? 'The word is near you, in your mouth and in your heart'" (Romans 10.6-8).

Walk with God! He will come.

Prayer: Lord, in this season I am reminded that after 400 years of silence, you first spoke through an angel to a man doing the "mundane things" of life and service. Come to me this season, Lord, as I walk with you in service, in duty, in custom, and in the "temple." Amen.

Psalm of the Day: 132.13-18

A Light for Revelation

Daily Reading: Luke 2

> For my eyes have seen your salvation, which you have prepared in the sight of all nations: a light for revelation to the Gentiles, and the glory of your people Israel. (Luke 2.30-32)

Devotional Thought: His name was Simeon. Not a priest nor a prophet, he was, however, "righteous and devout, waiting for the consolation of Israel." Moved by the Holy Spirit, he went into the temple courts. Mary and Joseph brought Jesus into the courts, and Simeon "took him in his arms and praised God" (v. 28). With the insight of the Spirit, Simeon recognized Jesus right away as the promised Messiah. He said, "… my eyes have seen your salvation, which you have prepared in the sight of all nations: a light of revelation to the Gentiles, and the glory of your people Israel" (vv. 30-32).

Mary and Joseph, recipients of divine visions at Jesus' conception, marveled at Simeon's words. While even Jesus' own mother and earthly father did not fully comprehend God's plan, Simeon was given understanding through the Holy Spirit's revelation.

This same Spirit is alive today and is given to all believers at the point of salvation. Do we understand the power and insight that is meant for us when we receive this gift? As Paul declares in 1 Corinthians 2:12, "Now we have received not the spirit of the world, but the Spirit who is from God, that we might understand the things freely given us by God." We have an amazing Helper, without whom the Word of God would not be understood: "The person without the Spirit does not accept the things that come from the Spirit of God but considers them foolishness, and cannot understand them because they are discerned only through the Spirit" (1 Corinthians 2.14).

Have your eyes "seen" the salvation of God? Let God's light illuminate this season so that Jesus can reveal his glory in you and through you to a world in darkness.

Jenny

Prayer: Lord, just as you revealed yourself to an old man in the temple 2000 years ago, I pray that you would reveal yourself to me, that I might reveal your glory in this day. Amen.

Psalm of the Day: 133.1-3

Fruits in Keeping with Repentance
Daily Reading: Luke 3

Bear fruits in keeping with repentance. (Luke 3.8)

Devotional Thought: John the Baptist was a rather brusque figure, refusing to curry the favor of the crowds. But, crowds he had. People were flocking to him to hear his message. Even the religious authorities could not resist going to the wilderness to hear this fiery preacher. To everyone – commoner, ruler, saint, sinner – John had the same message: "Repent!" It was exactly the message they needed to hear. The crowds responded, but the elites from Washington, Hollywood, and New York – I mean Jerusalem! – did not.

John's repentance, however, was not a simple apology or feeling bad about getting caught. John insisted on bearing "fruits in keeping with repentance." Today, too much of what passes for being "born-again" is simply a catharsis for guilt and a desire to get away with sinful behavior. John would have nothing to do with that kind of religion. Neither would Jesus. Without life change – fruits in keeping with repentance – there was no real conversion. When asked what these fruits were, John responded quite clearly: generosity, honesty, integrity, and fairness. Jesus explained "fruits in keeping with repentance" even more succinctly: "Go and sin no more" (John 8.11).

Followers of Christ are to be the most compassionate and morally upright people in the community. Any attempt to follow Jesus, without real life-change, is doomed to failure. The Apostle Paul later wrote, "Do not be deceived: neither the sexually immoral, nor idolaters, nor adulterers, nor men who practice homosexuality, nor thieves, nor the greedy, nor drunkards, nor revilers, nor swindlers will inherit the kingdom of God. And such were some of you. But you were washed, you were sanctified, you were justified in the name of the Lord Jesus Christ and by the Spirit of our God" (1 Corinthians 6.9-11).

Hallelujah!

Prayer: Thank you, Lord, for washing me, sanctifying me, and justifying me. Now, help me to live clean, holy, and righteous. Amen.

Psalm of the Day: 134.1-3

Is the Spirit of the Lord upon You?

Daily Reading: Luke 4

The Spirit of the Lord is upon me, because he has anointed me to...
(Luke 4.18)

Devotional Thought: "After surviving the spiritual onslaught of Satan in the wilderness, Jesus went to the synagogue in his hometown. There, his physical life was threatened. Nothing like going to church to get beat up!

In "church" that day, Jesus read from the scroll of Isaiah, and indicated that the ancient prophecy pointed to what he had come to do:

- *Proclaim good news to the poor.* Just as in our day, there was a vast population of poor who could not break out of the cycle of poverty. Held in generational poverty, they needed good news. Jesus offered them "redemption and lift." Most importantly, the poor in spirit would receive the good news of the Kingdom of God!
- *Proclaim liberty to the captives.* History is filled with the unjust treatment of people, enslaving them and devaluing their human worth. Jesus' Kingdom is one of freedom from tyranny. Those held in bondage to sin, addiction and fear are set free by the grace of God!
- *Proclaim recovering of sight to the blind.* Jesus healed blinded eyes, but he also opened spiritual eyes.
- *Set at liberty those who are oppressed.* Oppression takes many forms. Marriage partners can oppress their spouses. Employers can oppress their employees. Parents can oppress their children. Society can oppress the marginal. Governments can oppress the citizens. In the midst of oppression, Jesus brings freedom!
- *Proclaim the year of the Lord's favor.* When does all this start? Now! "Behold, now is the favorable time; behold, now is the day of salvation" (2 Corinthians 6.2). We don't have to wait. We can tap into God's grace right now!

How about you? Is the Spirit of the Lord upon you? Let Jesus live out his justice through you. Now is the day!

Prayer: Lord, our world is filled with suffering and injustice. Help me to be a vessel of peace and love, bringing your justice to those in bondage, your peace to those in turmoil. Amen.

Psalm of the Day: 135.1-7

Jesus, Me, Action

Daily Reading: Luke 5

> *And Simon answered, "Master, we toiled all night and took nothing! But at your word I will let down the nets." (Luke 5.5)*

Devotional Thought: Do you know what's better than having a boat? Having a friend with a boat! Jesus' friend, Peter, had a boat, and Jesus borrowed it for a pulpit. After he preached, Jesus said to Peter, "Let's do a little fishing!" Peter had his objections, but responded in a telling way. Consider...

- *Master...* Peter decided something about **Jesus**. Jesus was the Master; Peter was the disciple. Jesus was the Teacher; Peter was the student. Jesus was the Leader; Peter was the follower. How about you? Have you made Jesus your Master?
- *We toiled all night and took nothing...* Peter knew something about **himself**. Pride is a hard foe to defeat. But, the facts spoke for themselves. Peter – a great fisherman in his own eyes, I'm sure – had worked all night long and come home empty. What a blow to his ego. And, then have a carpenter tell him what to do? Peter recognized that his own ability had been inadequate for the job. Have you ever been there? Have you ever worked all night – or all day, or all month, or all year – and come away empty-handed? Rejoice! You are a candidate for a miracle. When we confess our need and our weakness, Jesus will step in. He says, "My power is made perfect in weakness."
- *But at your word I will let down the nets...* Peter committed to a new course of **action**. Recognizing who Jesus is, and who we are, is just the beginning. We have to let down the nets. Life isn't easy, and success isn't automatic. We have to do what Jesus says! Have you committed to a new course of action, a new way of living?

Prayer: Lord, you are *my* Master. I don't want to do this thing called life on my own, for I will fail. But, with you, I can do all things. At your word, O Lord, I will take action and "let down my nets" today. Amen.

Psalm of the Day: 135.8-14

Top Off Your Tank

Daily Reading: Luke 6

Judge not, and you will not be judged; condemn not, and you will not be condemned; forgive, and you will be forgiven; give, and it will be given to you. Good measure, pressed down, shaken together, running over, will be put into your lap. For with the measure you use it will be measured back to you. (Luke 6.37-38)

Devotional Thought: My father-in-law, Nick, was very generous. I remember that he used to ride with me to the gas station to fill my car with gas when we would visit them. Do you remember the days when we would *top off* the gas tank after we filled it? (The EPA – along with the car manufacturers – tells us not to do that anymore.) Nick always made sure that I topped off the tank. As long as he was buying, he wanted to make sure it was full! One time, he even made sure that the car was pointed down the slight grade at the gas station so that the tank would hold more! Nick believed in a good measure, pressed down, shaken together, running over!

That's how our heavenly Father is with us, too. When we give, he gives to us in return. He gives even more than we give. Often, I refer to this truth to encourage people to tithe and to give to good causes. But, as we look at the context, it is even more basic than that. We are encouraged to give mercy and forgiveness to others. When we do that, we receive even more mercy and forgiveness from God! Matthew remembered Jesus saying this in conjunction with the Lord's Prayer: "For if you forgive others their trespasses, your heavenly Father will also forgive you, but if you do not forgive others their trespasses, neither will your Father forgive your trespasses" (Matthew 6.14-15).

Do you want to live with the overflowing abundance of God's mercy and forgiveness – a good measure, pressed down, shaken together? Then give mercy and forgiveness freely. You will find God's grace piled high upon your lap. He will top off your tank!

Prayer: Thank you, Lord, for giving me mercy and forgiveness. As I have received these gifts from you, so I will give them to others. And, Jesus, thank you for topping off my tank with grace upon grace. I love you, Lord! Amen.

Psalm of the Day: 135.15-21

348

Do Not Weep

Daily Reading: Luke 7

Do not weep. (Luke 7.13)

Devotional Thought: As he entered a town called Nain, a funeral procession was coming out. A widow was now twice aggrieved. Having already lost her husband, she was now burying her only son. Jesus was moved with compassion for her and said, "Do not weep."

"What? Do not weep? You're kidding, right?" No. Jesus meant what he said. You see, he had plans for this woman and her dead son:

- The *immediate* plans were to raise her son from the dead. Jesus saw her circumstances and her broken heart. Jesus did not do this for everybody, but for a reason known only to him, he decided that he would do it for her: "Young man, I say to you, arise." Those words changed everything. Do not weep!
- There was also an *intermediate* plan, not explicitly stated in the story. When her husband had died, God had given her grace and resources through family and friends. She had survived that ordeal. She would survive this ordeal, too. God, who had helped her in the past, was with her to help her now. The support of family and friends was a testament to that. Do not weep!
- And finally there was the *ultimate* plan. Later, Jesus would say, "I am the resurrection and the life. Whoever believes in me, though he die, yet shall he live, and everyone who lives and believes in me shall never die" (John 11.25-26). For the countless broken hearts from that time to this, there is hope. Do not weep!

You may feel that your sun is setting, but remember there is a dawn awaiting all those who trust in God. "Weeping may endure for the night, but joy comes in the morning!" (Psalm 30.5)

Prayer: Thank you, Father in heaven, for your grace to help us in our time of need. Help me to trust your immediate, intermediate, and ultimate plan. In Jesus' name, amen.

Psalm of the Day: 136.1-9

What Is Your Name?

Daily Reading: Luke 8

> *Jesus then asked him, "What is your name?" And he said, "Legion."*
> (Luke 8.30)

Devotional Thought: The people in 'Legion's' town did not see the man as Jesus did. They saw a crazy man, who lived in the cemetery, howling like an animal. They saw a man who cut himself – perhaps to try to 'bleed' the fever of demons from his body. He refused to wear clothes, and when arrested he easily escaped, continuing to terrify them.

Jesus saw something different. He didn't see a maniac. He saw a man. A man with a name, a name he wanted to know: "What is your name?" The question in Greek indicates that Jesus used the singular pronoun to address the man. He was talking to the man, not the demons. He was interested in him. The demons couldn't tolerate being ignored, and they desired to assert their control over the man. So, they interrupted the conversation and told Jesus their name. Jesus dealt with them so that he could help the man he saw.

I wonder how many people had bothered to ask the man his name. I wonder how many people had shown any interest in the man himself. We tend to see people by the inconvenience that they cause us: "That's the guy who cut me off in traffic." Or, "She's the one who took the last eggroll." We write them off, and don't even bother to ask their names, much less try to discover the pain that lies just beneath the surface - the demons that haunt their lives.

Jesus isn't like that. He wants to know people, and in knowing them to help them reach their full potential. You may feel that everybody judges you, or thinks you an inconvenience, or simply wants to use you to their advantage. But, Jesus is asking your name. He sees you as a friend.

Prayer: Thank you, Jesus, for caring about us, for asking our names, for casting out our "demons" of fear, doubt, and self-loathing. What a Friend we have in you, Jesus! Amen.

Psalm of the Day: 136.10-16

The Way of the Cross
Daily Reading: Luke 9

And he said to all, "If anyone would come after me, let him deny himself and take up his cross daily and follow me. For whoever would save his life will lose it, but whoever loses his life for my sake will save it. For what does it profit a man if he gains the whole world and loses or forfeits himself?" (Luke 9.23-25)

Devotional Thought: What sane person of the world would willingly trade comfort, wealth, and status for the hardships of following a Nazarene nobody? Or, even more unbelievable, who would willingly face persecution and even death, if they were not utterly convinced of the truth of the gospel?

Though his disciples did not yet fully understand what it would mean to take up their crosses daily and follow him, they certainly understood after Jesus' resurrection. These men were so convinced of the truth of the gospel that they were martyred for their faith in many cases, refusing to abandon their beliefs. They clung to Jesus' words as they died; "whoever would save his life will lose it, but whoever loses his life for my sake will save it" (v.24).

"What does it profit a man if he gains the whole world and loses or forfeits himself?" In our world, self-sacrifice is drowned out: each man for himself; carpe diem; YOLO (you only live once); you deserve some pampering; if it feels right, do it. For those who want to be like Jesus, the attitude should be just the opposite. "For even the Son of Man came not to be served but to serve, and to give his life as a ransom for many" (Mark 10:45). Those who chase after the things of this world will not be able to chase after the things of heaven as well. They're in opposite directions! Let us pursue the way of selfless love, and proclaim the gospel with complete confidence to those around us.

Jenny

Prayer: Lord, the way of the cross is so antithetical to the way of the world. Help me to deny myself, take up my cross, and follow you. In doing this, I will save my life. Amen.

Psalm of the Day: 136.17-26

What Kind of Friend
Daily Reading: Luke 10

And he said to them, "I saw Satan fall like lightning from heaven. Behold, I have given you authority to tread on serpents and scorpions, and over all the power of the enemy, and nothing shall hurt you. Nevertheless, do not rejoice in this, that the spirits are subject to you, but rejoice that your names are written in heaven." (Luke 10.18-20)

Devotional Thought: Jesus sent out seventy-two of his disciples to preach and heal – to bring hope! When they returned, they were so excited that they had the power to change lives. But, Jesus corrected their misguided enthusiasm, telling them not to get too excited about what they could do in the spiritual realm, but rather to rejoice that their names were written in heaven!

Jesus had spiritual power, too. He, himself, was there when Satan was cast out of heaven. But, he didn't rejoice in that. Instead, he rejoiced that he and the Father were one. Jesus didn't care about power. Jesus didn't care about accolades. He cared about pleasing his Father. For Jesus, it really was "all about relationships."

You know what I mean. You have 'friends' and then you have friends. There are some friends who are close to you as long as you have something to offer them. Then there are other friends, friends who stick closer than a brother (Proverbs 18.24).

What about you? Are you 'into Christ' for what you can get out of it? Or, are you just thrilled to be in love with Jesus? In short, what kind of friend are you to God?

Prayer: Jesus, in this age of "transactional" religion, help me to love you for who you are, not for what you can do for me. You are the King of kings and the Lord of lords! You are the Creator of all things, and I worship you. Amen.

Psalm of the Day: 137.1-9

The Door That Stays Open
Daily Reading: Luke 11

> *Do not bother me; the door is now shut, and my children are with me in bed. I cannot get up and give you anything.* (Luke 11.7)

Devotional Thought: Have you ever gotten a phone call in the middle of the night? Or more startling, a knock on your door? You did not want to get up out of bed, did you? The homes in Jesus' day were quite small. Often, just one room. The living room and the bedroom were the same. And, everybody had the same bed. When the parents finally got all the kids to bed, they didn't want anything disturbing them. Especially some pesky neighbor who just needed a loaf of bread! "Go away! Can't you see I'm in bed?"

God is a different kind of neighbor. We can cry out to him anytime, day or night. He is always awake. The Bible says, "He who keeps you will not slumber. Behold, he who keeps Israel will neither slumber nor sleep. The Lord is your keeper; the Lord is your shade on your right hand. The sun shall not strike you by day, nor the moon by night" (Psalm 121.3-6).

When I am counseling couples, I can get a sense of the health of their relationship by observing what they do for one another. Do they do small things to serve each other? In premarital counseling, I like to ask soon-to-be husbands something like this: "You say you would take a bullet for your wife, but would you do the dishes for her?" If a marriage is to be happy and healthy, then couples need to be watching for ways to serve one another.

God enjoys helping us with the small things of life as well as the big things. So, don't hesitate to call upon your heavenly Father. Day or night. Major or mundane. He is ready to help you.

Prayer: Father, I am so glad that I have never heard you say, "Don't bother me." Thank you that your door is never shut. In the name of your Child, who invites us to become his child. Amen.

Psalm of the Day: 138.1-8

Vulnerability and Dependence
Daily Reading: Luke 12

> *Are not five sparrows sold for two pennies? And not one of them is forgotten before God. Why, even the hairs of your head are all numbered. Fear not; you are of more value than many sparrows.* (Luke 12.6-7)

Devotional Thought: In Luke 11, we learned that in Jesus' day two sparrows were sold for a penny. Today, we read about quantity discounts: Five sparrows were sold for two pennies! But, the message was the same. God sees the sparrow, and God sees you.

Jesus warned his disciples that there would be people who did not appreciate their testimony for him. They would be ridiculed and rejected. That is true in today's world, too, isn't it? But, Jesus' message to us is the same as it was to them: Fear not! It was a message that he could share from experience.

This time of year, our minds often go to Christmas, remembering how Jesus was born a helpless Babe. Jesus, the King of kings and Lord of lords, became vulnerable: to King Herod's jealous intent, to disease and sickness, to politics and power, to religious elites and demon-possessed. But through it all, he had God's eye and ear: "Father, I thank you that you have heard me. I knew that you always hear me" (John 11.41-42).

Jesus was not only vulnerable, he was dependent. He depended upon his mother's body to feed and nourish him for 9 months. He depended upon wise men to finance his family's trip to safety in Egypt. He depended upon a step-father to clothe and shelter him as he grew. He depended upon a band of well-to-do women to support his ministry. More than that, however, he depended upon his heavenly Father to guide him. He wouldn't do anything apart from the will of God.

We avoid vulnerability and dependence, don't we? But, Jesus left the security and comfort of heaven to do the Father's will. He trusted God, and so can we. Fear not!

Prayer: Lord, to you I am worth more than many sparrows. This world judges my worth by my beauty, my profitability, my skill, but you see me as your precious child. I thank you in Jesus' name. Amen.

Psalm of the Day: 139.1-6

Five Keys to Freedom
Daily Reading: Luke 13

Woman, you are freed from your disability. (Luke 13.13)

Devotional Thought: She suffered for eighteen years, finding no freedom. When she met Jesus, however, she was set free! Neil Lozano, in his book *Unbound*, offers Five Keys for Freedom:
- *Repentance and Faith.* The first thing we need to be free is peace with God. We do that by repenting from our sins and trusting in Jesus for salvation. We don't do anything to earn his love. He loves us because he loves us. We simply have to turn to him in faith.
- *Forgiveness in the Name of Jesus.* When we are given the freedom of God's forgiveness, we need to forgive others. We are unable - humanly - to do that. We must do it in the name of Jesus. Forgiveness is not something you feel. It is something you give.
- *Renunciation in the Name of Jesus.* What are those things that bind you? Fear? Jealousy? Lust? Pride? Take time to search deep within your heart. When those things are revealed, renounce them: "In the name of Jesus, I renounce the spirit of _____."
- *Taking Authority in the Name of Jesus.* Verbalize your authority. "In the name of Jesus, I command the spirit of _____ to leave me and never to return." This is not the same as casting out a demon. It is simply refusing to let things like fear, anger, self-condemnation and so on have a place in your life.
- *Receiving the Father's Blessing.* Remember: God loves you. He wants to bless you and make you a blessing. When you offer yourself to him, he works his good will in your life.

Jesus wants to set you free. Use these Five Keys to Freedom!

Prayer: Father, I thank you for setting me free. I turn to you in faith and receive that freedom. I forgive those who have wronged me. I renounce and cast out those things that have controlled me in the past, and I receive your blessing. In Jesus' name, amen.

Psalm of the Day: 139.7-16

Move Up Higher

Daily Reading: Luke 14

Friend, move up higher. (Luke 14.10)

Devotional Thought: Lana and I attended a beautiful wedding and reception last weekend. When we arrived at the reception hall, we missed the seating chart. After we seated ourselves (near the cake!), we were informed that we were in someone else's seat and needed to move. Not a big deal, but it made us feel a little sheepish.

Jesus told a story about a guest being seated in the wrong place. When that happens, how much better to be told to "Move up higher." God is telling us to move up higher:

- We can **move up closer in friendship with Jesus**. Jesus wants us to 'do life' at his side. He desires to have a close relationship with us. We are his friends! I saw on the news yesterday, that a company in China is offering a facial recognition app that you can use on social media to identify someone. Snap a picture, upload it and voila – this is who they are. Aren't you glad that we don't need that with Jesus? We're close enough to hear him speak, to follow his lead, to receive his help. Open up your heart every day to his companionship!
- One way to do that is respond to his invitation to **move up higher in prayer**. I would venture a guess that most of us would say we could pray more – more time, more focus, more urgency. The greatest way to move up higher in prayer, though, might just be to *say less and listen more*.

There are other ways to move up higher: in service and in love, in holiness and Christ-likeness, in faith and obedience.

God is saying to you today, "Friend, move up higher!"

Prayer: Lord, forgive me when I am content to live on a low level. Help me to hear your invitation to move up higher. By your grace, I will do just that! Amen.

Psalm of the Day: 139.17-24

He Receives Sinners

Daily Reading: Luke 15

This man receives sinners and eats with them. (Luke 15.2)

Devotional Thought: When the religious elites made the accusation, "this man receives sinners and eats with them," Jesus did not deny it. As a matter of fact, he told three stories that *confirmed* the charge: the lost sheep, the lost coin, and the lost son.

In today's politically correct climate, leaders and celebrities are often called upon to disavow this person or that person who hold questionable or objectionable positions on a variety of issues. If they refuse to do so, then they are charged with holding the same views and attitudes. Recently, Chip and Joanna Gaines - hosts on HGTV's "Fixer Upper"- were the targets of such an inquisition. "How dare they attend a church that does not support gay marriage!" Pressure mounts against networks and advertisers to distance themselves from such people.

Jesus, however, used the charges of consorting with "the enemy" to show that they were in fact not enemies, certainly not his enemies. Jesus is a friend of sinners! Aren't you glad? Too many people, however, have the junior high attitude: "If you're friends with that person, then you can't be friends with me!" Jesus will not be bullied into rejecting anybody.

That doesn't mean, of course, that Jesus condones sinful attitudes and behaviors. He died to give us victory over those very things. But, that doesn't change the fact that he loves the sinner. He sees him or her as worth finding, worth receiving, worth saving.

I am so glad that Jesus searched the hills, swept the house and scanned the horizon for me!

Prayer: "Out of my bondage, sorrow, and night, Jesus, I come! Jesus, I come! Into Thy freedom, gladness, and light, Jesus, I come to Thee! Out of my sickness into Thy health, Out of my want and into Thy wealth, Out of my sin and into Thyself, Jesus, I come to Thee!" Amen. (William Sleeper)

Psalm of the Day: 140.1-6

In the Sight of God

Daily Reading: Luke 16

What is exalted among men is an abomination in the sight of God.
(Luke 16.15)

Devotional Thought: They loved money, position, and power. They weren't impressed with Jesus. But, Jesus had some sobering words for them: "You are those who justify yourselves before men, but God knows your hearts. For what is exalted among men is an abomination in the sight of God."

What is exalted among men today? Much like the powerful Roman culture of Jesus' day, wealth, independence, power, control, success, progressive thinking, and tolerance are now considered the highest virtues.

But, God did not design us to be proudly independent, rather to be humbly dependent on him. He did not design us to be in control, but to surrender control to him. We are not to put our hope in the treasures of this world, but to store up treasures in heaven. We are not to conform to the patterns of the world in regards to personal wealth and success, but rather be transformed by the renewing of our minds through the Spirit.

If we are living to justify ourselves before men, we cannot also be living as "slaves to righteousness" (Rom. 6:18) – the two goals could not be more different. As Jesus declares in this chapter, "No servant can serve two masters, for either he will hate the one and love the other, or he will be devoted to the one and despise the other" (v.13). If we (our actions or our ideals) are not coming against any worldly opposition, then the question must be asked: Whom are we living to please?

Jenny

Prayer: Father, help me to love what you love and to hate what you hate. I do not want to be justified in my own sight, O Lord, but to be justified in your sight. Amen.

Psalm of the Day: 140.7-13

A Lot to Remember

Daily Reading: Luke 17

Remember Lot's wife. (Luke 17.32)

Devotional Thought: In speaking of his return, Jesus told his disciple to "Remember Lot's wife!" Why do we need to remember her?

Lot's story is told in Genesis 19. He and his daughters escaped the destruction of Sodom and Gomorrah by fleeing to the hills. Lot's wife, however, did not make it all the way. She had been warned not to look back, but she did - and became a pillar of salt. We need to remember her so that we don't make the same mistake. What do we need to remember about Lot's wife?

- *She lingered behind.* Lot's wife was behind Lot. In our spiritual journeys, we do not want to fall behind Jesus. As he leads us to safety, the attractions of the world and the distractions of life can cause us to fall behind and lose sight of him. What pulls you away from Christ?
- *She looked back.* Hers was not a fearful glance over her shoulder to see how close danger was. Instead, she looked longingly for the ease, for the comforts, for the pleasures of Sodom. In her heart, she didn't really believe the warning and didn't really want to leave. Jesus tells us that when we once begin to follow him, putting our hands 'to the plow' we are not to look back. We must be all in... all the time!
- *She lost her way.* Lot's wife became a 'pillar of salt.' The destruction was not intended for her, but she got swept away with the unrighteous residents of Sodom and Gomorrah. Her husband was bereft and her daughters were orphaned. Sin's attraction leads to sin's destruction, not only for us, but for those we love.

Remember Lot's wife!

Prayer: Father in heaven, you have made a way of escape for me through Jesus Christ, your Son. Help me to keep up with Jesus, to keep my eyes on Jesus, and to keep on the way of safety. There's too much at stake to miss it. In Jesus' name, amen.

Psalm of the Day: 141.1-10

What Do You Want for Christmas?

Daily Reading: Luke 18

What do you want me to do for you? (Luke 18.41)

Devotional Thought: My wife asked, "How many meatballs do you want?" Our daughter's boyfriend answered, "Six." I started to laugh on the inside because I knew what was coming. "How about three?" I later explained to him, "That's one of 'those' questions."

On his way to Jerusalem, Jesus took time to heal a blind man. Even in the approaching shadow of the cross, Jesus respected others' dignity and freedom. He asked the man, "What do you want me to do for you?" He didn't tell him what he wanted, He asked him. Our Great Savior!

Jesus wasn't like that with the blind man outside Jericho. He took the time to ask the man what he wanted and then to listen. Now, I don't believe Jesus is like the perfect Santa – giving us whatever we ask for – but I do believe he is concerned about what we want. In asking, Jesus showed the man – and us – that he respects our dignity and desire. When he truly knows better, he will try to convince us to go a different way. But, he will not force his will upon us.

This Christmas, one of the best gifts you have is the gift of God's listening ear. He cares about you and wants to hear from you. In the midst of your busyness, loneliness, and even disappointment this season, pause and listen. Jesus is asking you, "What do you want?"

Prayer: Lord, I know that every good gift comes down from above. Help me to not get distracted by earthly lights, but to see the heavenly lights this season - and to tell you from a surrendered heart what I really want. Amen.

Psalm of the Day: 142.1-7

Go Climb a Tree
Daily Reading: Luke 19

> *He was seeking to see who Jesus was, but on account of the crowd he could not, because he was small in stature.* (Luke 19.3)

Devotional Thought: Can you hear those transcendent words: "Zacchaeus was a wee little man, and a wee little man was he"? Zacchaeus was a tax collector. Nobody liked tax collectors, no matter whether they were wee little men or great big men! The good news about Zacchaeus was that he wanted to see Jesus. The bad news, however, was that he could not.

Two reasons are given:
- *Zacchaeus could not see through the crowd.* Zacchaeus was insulated from Jesus by everybody and everything around him. Truth be told, most of the people were probably not friendly toward Zacchaeus. I like the fact that Zacchaeus did not let them remain barriers. He pressed through them until he came to Jesus. He swallowed his pride, endured the rejection, and found a way to victory! What crowds out Jesus in your life? What will you face today that will be an obstacle? Our troubles, temptations, and treasures may act as insulators, but we can rise above the 'crowd' and see Jesus!
- *Zacchaeus was small in stature.* When he saw the crowd – the enormity of the challenge – Zacchaeus could have let his small stature defeat him. And, not only was he small physically, but he was small in character as well, having cheated and stolen and lied his way to the top. But, the prospect of seeing Jesus, changed all that for him. While he couldn't do anything about his physical stature, he was determined to do something about his spiritual stature! Instead of giving up, we need to have enough faith to run ahead and climb a tree.

This Christmas season find a tree to climb so that you can see Jesus!

Prayer: Thank you, Lord, for the story of the man Zacchaeus, who was small in stature and small in character. You helped him that day to find a tree that he could climb to see you. When he saw you and responded to you, you changed him into a great man. I want to see you this season. Help me to find and climb the right tree! Amen.

Psalm of the Day: 143.1-6

361

God and Government

Daily Reading: Luke 20

Render to Caesar the things that are Caesar's, and to God the things that are God's. (Luke 20.25)

Devotional Thought: Oh, how they wanted to argue with Jesus! Instead of being drawn into their political argument, however, Jesus made a simple, yet powerful declaration: "Render to Caesar the things that are Caesar's, and to God the things that are God's." If you are a citizen who benefits from being in a city, a state, or a nation, then part of your responsibility is to pay taxes. Everyone – from the richest to the poorest – should bear part of the burden required to keep the government operating.

But there are some things that belong to God and to God alone. To God you give such things as:
- Unflinching trust
- Unbending obedience
- Unequaled loyalty
- Unparalleled love
- Unleashed worship

So, government is not bad, and supporting the government is expected. It is a problem when we give to the government those things that belong to God alone, and we expect from the government those things which God alone can provide.

I think that Jesus knew the temptation to conflate government and God, and so he encouraged keeping them separate. But, they do not exist side by side with equal status. Instead, our loyalty to government exists within our larger fealty to God. So, pay your taxes, but place your ultimate trust in God alone.

Prayer: Lord Jesus, it was said of you, "The government shall be upon his shoulders." You alone are faithful to fulfill all God's purposes. I trust in you. Help me, within my Christian faith, to give what is right to the government. Amen.

Psalm of the Day: 143.7-12

Led Astray
Daily Reading: Luke 21

See that you are not led astray. (Luke 21.8)

Devotional Thought: "Let's stand as we go to the Lord in prayer..." I said it confidently. I said it commandingly. I said it clearly. I said it... wrong. Somehow, I had gotten the wrong service order tucked in my Bible. The worship team sat there frozen. On the screen, a video in honor of our veterans was beginning to play. Oops... I was leading everybody astray!

That's funny - even though it is embarrassing. But, Jesus spoke of a time when to be led astray would be anything but humorous, and embarrassment would be the least of our concerns. He is returning, and we need to be ready.

In Luke 21, we read about some things that could lead us astray:
- Nations (v. 9): History teaches us that nations are always at war and that civilizations rise and fall. To follow a particular party or leader could lead to disaster!
- Earthquakes, famines, pestilences, terrors, and signs in heaven (v. 11): Focus on these things will cause us to fear. Fear leads to bad decisions.
- Persecution (v. 12): Satan brings this pressure to bear upon us to cause us to deny our faith.
- Dissipation and drunkenness and cares of this life (v. 34): When we get too attached to "things" they may drag us over a cliff.

It is up to us to "see that we are not led astray." We can do that by:
- Knowing the Bible.
- Holding loosely to the things of this world.
- Staying connected to the people of God.
- Praying for wisdom and strength.
- Counting the cost.

Keep your eyes on Jesus! He will never lead you astray.

Prayer: Grant me wisdom, O Lord, to know the truth and courage to follow it. Amen.

Psalm of the Day: 144.1-8

Jesus and Prayer

Daily Reading: Luke 22

> *And he withdrew from them about a stone's throw, and knelt down and prayed.* (Luke 22.41)

Devotional Thought: Before Jesus was arrested, he made his way to Gethsemane and prayed. What do we learn about prayer in Gethsemane?

- *Jesus came out to pray.* When I am working in my office, and someone comes in to talk with me, I usually get up and move away from my desk. Why? Because if I don't get away from my work, it will be a constant distraction. In the same way, prayer demands our attention.
- *Jesus had a custom of praying.* Jesus didn't just pray when he felt like it. He prayed on a schedule, with regularity.
- *There were some things that Jesus had to pray for by himself.* When it came time to talk to his Father about his deepest requests, Jesus withdrew even from his disciples. There are some things you can only say to God!
- *Jesus' disciples followed him in prayer.* Jesus did not always pray alone. Prayer is often a group activity. We gain strength, wisdom and direction from one another as we pray together.
- *Jesus encouraged prayer as a means of overcoming temptation.* At the beginning of his ministry, it was forty days of prayer that helped Jesus overcome the temptations of the devil. He knew that his disciples would need that kind of strength, too.
- *Jesus knelt down to pray.* Though he was God's Son, Jesus showed humility and respect to his Father.
- *As he prayed, Jesus placed his will beneath the Father's will.* Not only did Jesus respect his Father, he obeyed him. The two are inextricably connected.
- *Jesus' prayer brought the presence of comforting angels.* I've never seen an angel. I doubt that you have either. But, that doesn't mean they aren't there.

Take time to pray today!

Prayer: What a gift is prayer, O Lord! Thank you for the amazing opportunity to come to you, and for the assurance that you hear us and answer our prayers, according to your wisdom and will. In Jesus' name, amen.

Psalm of the Day: 144.9-15

The End?

Daily Reading: Luke 23

> Then Jesus, calling out with a loud voice, said, "Father, into your hands I commit my spirit!" And having said this he breathed his last. (Luke 23.46)

Devotional Thought: What if the story of Jesus ended here? Certainly none of his friends, family, or followers expected anything different. This was a day of grief, the day that Jesus – miracle-worker, teacher, healer, and friend – was finished. His life ended, his story was sure to be told for some generations, but ultimately equated with the other prophets in Jewish history. His followers, who had hoped that Jesus was the long-awaited Messiah sent to rescue Israel from political oppression, were confused, scattered, ashamed, and terrified for their own lives.

But, the story doesn't end with Luke 23. Praise God for Luke 24! Jesus' proclamation that it was finished had nothing to do with his own death, but rather the end of the dominion of sin and death over all of humanity! His disciples, finally discerning the meaning of Jesus' words after his resurrection, were no longer afraid, but rejoicing!

If the story ended with Luke 23, we would be without hope. Imagine the only begotten Son of God forever defeated by human wickedness, the plans of the Creator foiled by those he created, surprised by the depth of our depravity. No, God was neither surprised nor defeated; rather he used the most wretched deed of mankind to bring about salvation.

As you anticipate Christmas, reflect on the grace and love of our Father, who sent His only Son as a helpless baby to dwell among us, ultimately becoming the sacrificial Lamb who "takes away the sin of the world" (John 1:29).

Jenny

Prayer: Thank you, Lord, that the story doesn't end in Luke 23. Another chapter was written - the chapter of your victory over death! And, there is yet another chapter. In this Advent season, we anticipate that final Advent when Jesus shall come to take us home. Amen!

Psalm of the Day: 145.1-9

The Reason for the Season

Daily Reading: Luke 24

Why do you seek the living among the dead? (Luke 24.5b)

Devotional Thought: On this Christmas Eve, let us consider that question ourselves. Jesus is the ever-living One who came to give us life. But, are we seeking life in things that pass away?

- Don't look for life in the lights and sounds of Christmas. These are wonderful reminders of the meaning of Christmas, but in themselves they do not bring life. Having celebrated Christmas with our kids last week, and knowing that we will be headed to SC at any time for the birth of our granddaughter Ellis, Lana and I busied ourselves yesterday with taking down our Christmas tree and packing away our decorations. I know! You will say, "Scrooge! Christmas isn't even here yet!" It was hard to take the tree down before Christmas, but it reminded me that Christmas is not in a tree, but in our hearts. And, you will have to take your tree down sometime, too!

- Don't look for life wrapped up in pretty paper underneath the tree. Like anybody else, I like to receive gifts at Christmas time. I also like to give gifts. I'm sure you do, too. But, Christmas doesn't come with those presents under the tree. "The Best Christmas Ever" isn't about having more presents than any other year. It's almost embarrassing how commercial Christmas has become, isn't it? How many people are hoping to fill the void in their lives with gifts that will be tucked away in the closet and forgotten?

As you celebrate Christmas, remember that old cliché which is still true today: "Jesus is the reason for the season." Find life and meaning in Jesus!

Prayer: Lord, there is life in you alone. I turn to you this season for that life. Help me, having found life, to share life with others - to share hope and peace and joy and love in Jesus' name. Amen.

Psalm of the Day: 145.10-21

Merry Christmas!

Daily Reading: Luke 2.1-20

¹ In those days a decree went out from Caesar Augustus that all the world should be registered. ² This was the first registration when Quirinius was governor of Syria. ³ And all went to be registered, each to his own town.

⁴ And Joseph also went up from Galilee, from the town of Nazareth, to Judea, to the city of David, which is called Bethlehem, because he was of the house and lineage of David, ⁵ to be registered with Mary, his betrothed, who was with child.⁶ And while they were there, the time came for her to give birth. ⁷ And she gave birth to her firstborn son and wrapped him in swaddling cloths and laid him in a manger, because there was no place for them in the inn.

⁸ And in the same region there were shepherds out in the field, keeping watch over their flock by night. ⁹ And an angel of the Lord appeared to them, and the glory of the Lord shone around them, and they were filled with great fear.¹⁰ And the angel said to them, "Fear not, for behold, I bring you good news of great joy that will be for all the people.¹¹ For unto you is born this day in the city of David a Savior, who is Christ the Lord. ¹² And this will be a sign for you: you will find a baby wrapped in swaddling cloths and lying in a manger."

¹³ And suddenly there was with the angel a multitude of the heavenly host praising God and saying, ¹⁴ "Glory to God in the highest, and on earth peace among those with whom he is pleased!"

¹⁵ When the angels went away from them into heaven, the shepherds said to one another, "Let us go over to Bethlehem and see this thing that has happened, which the Lord has made known to us." ¹⁶ And they went with haste and found Mary and Joseph, and the baby lying in a manger. ¹⁷ And when they saw it, they made known the saying that had been told them concerning this child. ¹⁸ And all who heard it wondered at what the shepherds told them. ¹⁹ But Mary treasured up all these things, pondering them in her heart.²⁰ And the shepherds returned, glorifying and praising God for all they had heard and seen, as it had been told them.

Prayer: With your love, may our hearts glow brighter than all our Christmas lights. In your hope, may we share the gift of hope. With your peace, may we fill our home with peace. In our joy, may we ring glad tidings of great joy to the world. Amen.

Psalm of the Day: 146.1-10

Whose Kid Are You?

Daily Reading: Ephesians 1

In love he predestined us for adoption. (Ephesians 1.5)

Devotional Thought: I have friends who have pre-arranged three adoptions of babies yet to be born. In each situation, all the details were arranged, expenses paid, and the soon-to-be parents excitedly awaited the news that the baby had arrived. In all three cases, the babies were destined to become a part of their family, in the eyes of the law and in the depths of their hearts. In the first two instances, however, their hearts were broken with the news that the birth mother had had a change of heart. The third one was carried out as planned, and they brought their little baby girl home with great joy and love.

In love, each of the babies were destined to be theirs. But, only one became so. In love, each of them were chosen for adoption. But, only one was adopted. Why? There was another party involved in the decision. And, that party said, "No."

In love, God the Father "predestined us for adoption through Jesus Christ... according to the purpose of his will." But, just as it was with my friends, there is another party involved in the adoption. It is not until we have "believed in him" that we are "sealed with the promised Holy Spirit" (v. 13). It is not God's will "that any should perish, but that all should reach repentance" (2 Peter 3.9). Why is not everyone saved if that is God's will? The price has been paid and the offer has been made, but there is another party involved. And, as Paul wrote, "not everyone has faith" (2 Thessalonians 3.2).

Christmas is over. We have celebrated that God gave his Son, that "whosoever believeth in him should not perish, but have everlasting life" (John 3.16 *KJV*). Now, "whosoever will, let him take the water of life freely" (Revelation 22.17, *KJV*).

Prayer: Thank you, Lord, that you have chosen me to be holy and blameless before you. In love, you predestined me for adoption. I say yes to your offer of new life with a new family - the family of God. Amen!

Psalm of the Day: 147.1-11

At This Time
Daily Reading: Ephesians 2

Remember that you were at that time... (Ephesians 2.12a)

Devotional Thought: There is an old hymn that I grew up singing. It goes like this:

"Once I was bound by sin's galling fetters, Chained like a slave, I struggled in vain; But I received a glorious freedom, When Jesus broke my fetters in twain. Glorious freedom, wonderful freedom, No more in chains of sin I repine! Jesus the glorious Emancipator, Now and forever He shall be mine." (Haldor Lillenas, Glorious Freedom.)

I like it because it says that what I was, I am no longer!

I think the Apostle Paul would have enjoyed that hymn. He reminded the Ephesians that they were at one time...
- Separated from Christ. The great gulf between the holiness of God and the sinfulness of humanity is deeper than the Grand Canyon and wider than the Pacific Ocean. How could they ever cross it?
- Alienated from God's people. Not only were they spiritually dead, but they were also far removed from people who could help them find their way to God.
- Strangers to the covenant. God has been reaching out to humanity from the beginning, desiring to bless them. The Ephesians didn't have a clue about any of that.
- Hopeless. No life. No friends. No blessings. No hope.
- Without God. This was the crux of the problem. They had lived their lives apart from God, not giving a thought to his requirements.

Yes, they were thoroughly lost, and so were we. The good news? God crossed the divide when Jesus came to earth 2000 years ago. "Now in Christ Jesus you who once were far off have been brought near by the blood of Christ" (v. 13). Hallelujah! I am no longer bound by sin, but am now washed by the blood!

Prayer: Thanks be to you, O God, for giving me hope, for giving me new life in Christ. The old has passed away. Behold! All things have become new! Amen.

Psalm of the Day: 147.12-20

That's a Lot!

Daily Reading: Ephesians 3

Now to him who is able to do far more abundantly than all that we ask or think, according to the power at work within us, to him be glory... (Ephesians 3.20-21)

Devotional Thought: In this section of Paul's letter to the Ephesians, he speaks of the mystery of the gospel, and how through the Spirit this mystery can be known. The Jewish Messiah came to save not just the Jews, but the Gentiles as well. The mystery that has been clearly perceived through God's creation (Romans 1.20) has been finally revealed to all believers through the Holy Spirit.

Paul then goes on to pray for spiritual strength for the church. In this prayer, he asks that they be strengthened with power through his Spirit, that they be able to comprehend the breadth and length and height and depth of the love of Christ that surpasses knowledge. How are we to comprehend this if it surpasses knowledge? God "is able to do far more abundantly than all that we ask or think, according to the power at work within us" (v. 20). It is only through the Spirit that we are able to understand spiritual things.

When we really consider the meaning of verse 20, it is astounding. When we pray; when we lay our most desperate, heart-felt requests before the Lord, he not only hears us, but he is able to accomplish more for us than we could have ever imagined! God is not limited by our lack of imagination, or even our lack of faith. When we are paralyzed by fear or sorrow in our lives, this does not limit the work of God. "For we do not know what to pray for as we ought, but the Spirit himself intercedes for us with groanings too deep for words... according to the will of God" (Romans 8.26-27). We continue to cry out to the Lord, laying our requests before him, trusting that he knows exactly what we need most.

Jenny

Prayer: Lord, we ask for spiritual strength for ourselves and for our loved ones. Through your Spirit, may we comprehend the breadth and length and height and depth of your great love for us. Amen.

Psalm of the Day: 148.1-6

Make Your New Year Happy
Daily Reading: Ephesians 4

Put off your old self ... Put on the new self. (Ephesians 4.22, 24)

Devotional Thought: Are there things you need to lose from the current year - excess pounds, negative attitudes, bad habits - to name just a few? Are there some things you want to gain - more friends, new experiences, better habits? Paul wrote to the Ephesians that there were some things that they needed to lose and other things they needed to gain, things they were to put off and to put on. This is good counsel for us as we enter the new year:

Put off:
- Futility. "There is a way that seems right to a man, but its end is the way to death" (Proverbs 14.12). Alienation, sensuality, and greed are empty ways of living.
- Focusing on self. "A person wrapped up in himself makes a pretty small package." Look beyond yourself, and see others. "Submit to one another in Christ," means to recognize the inherent value of others.
- Falsehood. When we tell lies, we believe lies. When we believe lies, we live lies. Jesus is the Truth that sets us free!

Put on:
- Renewal of your mind. Watch less TV and read some good books this year. Spend time in the Bible and prayer. Make new friends who are not 'like you.' Question your prejudices and welcome the mind of Christ.
- Righteousness of Christ. Christ died to set you free from sin and make you into a truly righteous person. Let him change the things that make you angry, the way you work, and your words to others.
- Responding to the Spirit. The Holy Spirit is our Comforter and Friend, but he is also a gracious Guest. He will respond to us as we respond to him. Do not grieve the Spirit by ignoring him.

Prayer: Lord, there are old things that I need to let go of. Help me to do so in the coming year. There are new things I need to embrace. Clothe me in your righteousness, O Lord! Amen.

Psalm of the Day: 148.7-14

Are You Happy (and Do You Know It)?

Daily Reading: Ephesians 5

Do not get drunk with wine, for that is debauchery, but be filled with the Spirit. (Ephesians 5.18)

Devotional Thought: I remember one time being asked, "Are you always like this?" It was a good thing! The question had to do with my happy-go-lucky ways. I was honored. Another time a co-worker said of me, "Just think what he would be like if he drank!" I think I was getting on their nerves, but that was OK. I'm a happy guy, and I tend to show it. I'm glad I don't need to get drunk to be happy. I feel sorry for those who do.

Paul contrasted the joy of drunkenness with the joy of the Lord, being filled with wine versus being filled with the Spirit. Drunkenness, Paul said, is "debauchery." What is that? The word is *asotia* and means "that which can't be saved, that which is wasted." We all know that drunkenness wastes our lives. Time, energy, opportunity, money, relationships, reputation, self-respect, hope... these things waste away for the drunk. It describes the prodigal son in Luke 15.

Does that tell me anything about Spirit-filled living? I think of the woman who broke open the alabaster jar of oil and poured it on Jesus' head (Mark 14). Those nearby said, "Why was the ointment wasted like that?" But, the woman saw it differently. Jesus saw it differently. He said it was "a beautiful thing." Spirit-filled living pours out everything for Jesus' sake. It does not care who is watching or what they might think.

What is that phrase... "Dance like no one is watching"? Although I'm a terrible dancer, I think that is good advice for how we should live. Drink deeply of the goodness of the Lord! Be filled with the Spirit and dance!

Prayer: I thank you, O Lord, for the happiness that is mine because Jesus is my Friend and Savior. Fill me with your Spirit, that I might dance with joy! Amen.

Psalm of the Day: 149.1-9

Finally!

Daily Reading: Ephesians 6

> *Peace be to the brothers, and love with faith, from God the Father and the Lord Jesus Christ. Grace be with all who love our Lord Jesus Christ with love incorruptible.* (Ephesians 6.23-24)

Devotional Thought: You know what it means when the preacher says, "And finally..." don't you? Absolutely nothing! Actually, it means you start listening for the benediction.

When Paul came to the end of his letter to the Ephesians, he gave them a final benediction, a 'blessing.' We can ask for similar blessings on us and our loved ones:

- Peace. The peace of God guards our hearts and minds in Christ Jesus. There may be some regrets from the past year. Leave them to the mercy of God, and enter the new year intent on a fresh start through Jesus.
- Love. Paul wrote elsewhere, "The greatest of these is love" (1 Corinthians 13.13). At the end of the year, thank God for those whom you have loved and those who have loved you. Commit to loving them better and to loving someone new this year - perhaps even an 'enemy'!
- Faith. Not everything was rosy this past year, was it? There were times when faith was all you had to sustain you. Thank God for that faith - though it was as small as a mustard seed - and ask him, "Help my unbelief" (Mark 9.24).
- Grace. While mercy is not getting what you do deserve (punishment), grace is getting what you don't deserve. Receive the gifts of God with gratitude and generosity.
- Immortality. To be incorruptible means not subject to decay. Death no longer has dominion over us, for nothing can separate us from the love of God!

The year has ended. Thank God we conclude it with a benediction of God's grace. Amen!

Jenny Wade

Prayer: Thank you, Lord, for your bountiful goodness in the past year. You have been with me in my success and in my failure, in my joy and in my sorrow. I enter the new year with the benediction of your grace. Amen.

Psalm of the Day: 150.1-6

Acknowledgments...

In addition to author Scott Wade, others have contributed devotional articles to The Climb: Stay Focused. Jenny Wade, Scott's oldest daughter, has co-written with her father for over six years, contributing a weekly article to their daily email devotionals, "A-Chapter-A-Day."

Besides Jenny, there are other guest authors whose articles appear from time to time. Their names appear with the articles they have contributed. These articles are used with permission.

I want to also thank...

- My wife, Lana, for editing and proof-reading the final manuscript. Also for her partnership in ministry!

- My kids - Jenny, Emily, Aaron, Amy, and Evan - for pushing me to "get out of the boat" and focus on my writing.

- My brother John who not only wrote several articles but also did a thorough review of the final manuscript. He caught many things I missed!

- Dale Stoops and the staff at One Stop Publications who were so helpful in getting this devotional book published. I especially want to thank Mark Baker for his heroic efforts to get this work typeset when it became necessary to include many textual corrections!

- Al, John Keith, and Steve - the board at Momentum Ministries - who encouraged me and helped me maintain momentum without overdoing it.

- My district superintendents - Dr. Bob Mahaffey, SWO District Church of the Nazarene; and Dr. Samuel Flores, SC District Church of the Nazarene - for their encouragement and help in promoting these books.

NOTES:

NOTES:

NOTES:

NOTES:

THE CLIMB
Series Information

Book 1: Start Here
New Testament, Psalms, and Genesis - Numbers

Book 2: Stay Focused
New Testament, Psalms, and Deuteronomy - 1 Kings

Book 3: Stick With It
New Testament, Psalms, and 2 Kings - Job

Book 4: Stretch Yourself
New Testament, Psalms, Proverbs, Isaiah, and Jeremiah

Book 5: Stand Tall
New Testament, Psalms, Ecclesiastes, Song of Sol, and Lamentations - Malachi

How to Order...

Visit Momentum Ministries website at https://www.momentumministries.org to order copies of this and other books that will help you attain, maintain, and regain spiritual momentum!

About the Author...

Scott Wade has been walking with Christ for nearly five decades, having been saved as a teenager in a small, evangelistic, and exciting church. Scott and his wife, Lana, have three daughters, their husbands, and best of all - seven grandchildren! Scott and Lana served together in pastoral ministry for twenty-nine years before being led by God to "get out of the boat" and begin **Momentum Ministries**. With an emphasis on writing and preaching, Pastor Scott seeks to help individuals and churches attain, maintain, and regain spiritual momentum.

Made in United States
Orlando, FL
25 April 2025

60761213R00216